T0337686

# Honda 125/150 Scooters
# Service and Repair Manual
## by Matthew Coombs

*(4873 - 272 - 9AQ1)*

### Models covered

| | |
|---|---|
| SH125/150 | 2001 to 2004 |
| SH125/150i | 2005-on |
| Dylan 125/150 | 2002 to 2008 |
| @125/150 | 2000 to 2006 |
| PS125/150i | 2006-on |
| Pantheon 125/150 | 2003 to 2006 |
| S-wing 125/150 | 2007-on |

© J H Haynes & Co. Ltd. 2017

A book in the **Haynes Service and Repair Manual Series**

ISBN **978 1 84425 873 4**

**British Library Cataloguing in Publication Data**
A catalogue record for this book is available from the British Library.

**J H Haynes & Co. Ltd.**
**Haynes North America, Inc**

www.haynes.com

# Contents

## LIVING WITH YOUR SCOOTER

### Pre-ride checks

## MAINTENANCE

### Routine maintenance and servicing

# Contents

## REPAIRS AND OVERHAUL

## REFERENCE

The 2009 SH125i

The PS125i

Honda's success with the step-thru lightweight motorcycle can be traced right back to the Cub models which first appeared in the late fifties. The Cub range, and in particular the C90, is a legend in two-wheeled circles and even today still provides many people around the world with an economic form of transport. In April 2008 Honda celebrated 50 years of Cub production and announced that a staggering 60 million units had been produced since the first C100 model in 1958!

So many of the current scooter designs have their routes in the Cub range, and of the models covered in this manual the SH125 best emulates the qualities of the original design with its large diameter 13 inch wheels and open style step-thru bodywork. The SH prefix was first used on the 50cc two-stroke City Express produced from the mid 1980s to 2002. As a 125, fitted with the 124.7cc four-stroke engine developed for the @125 the previous year, the UK SH125 (or SH150 as it was in other European countries) proved to be

an ideal commuter vehicle, cheap to run and capable of keeping up with mainstream traffic speed.

The SH125 continued without change until 2005 when stricter emission laws forced the fitting of fuel injection for many motorcycles and scooters over 50cc. The PGM-FI injection system was the same as already fitted to the 125/150cc Pantheon models. Cosmetically, redesigned bodywork and clear lens turn signals gave the scooter a fresh look. After another four years, a further round of improvements resulted in new bodywork and lighting, a new front brake caliper, and a rear disc brake option (together with linked braking); the lesser priced rear drum brake model remained in the range and was dubbed the SH125/150-D.

The NES @ and SES Dylan models were produced alongside the SH. They used the same engine and transmission unit, but were styled in typical scooter mould, with fuller bodywork and smaller diameter 13 inch

wheels. Both remained in the range, without change, until discontinued in 2006 and 2008 respectively.

The PES125/150 models, or simply PS as their bodywork decals show, were introduced in 2006 and superseded the @ and Dylan models. All PS models were fitted with Honda's PGM-FI fuel injected engine and used the cable-operated linked braking system employed on other rear drum brake models. Apart from colour and graphic updates they remained unchanged during their production range.

Large-bodied scooters are now common in most manufacturers' ranges and provide the serious commuter with good storage capacity, comfort and weather protection. The Pantheon and the S-wing which superseded it, use the same fuel injected engine and variable transmission fitted to the SH and PS models, but are physically much bigger, and heavier, scooters. Linked disc brakes are fitted front and rear, and there is an option of ABS on the S-wing.

# Acknowledgements

Our thanks are due to Bransons Motorcycles of Yeovil, V & J Motorcycles of Yeovil, Fowlers of Bristol and Gina Deacon who supplied the scooters featured in the photographs throughout this manual. We would also like to thank NGK Spark Plugs (UK) Ltd for supplying the colour spark plug condition photos, Avon Tyres for supplying the tyre sidewall illustration and Draper Tools Ltd for some of the workshop tools shown.

# About this Manual

The aim of this manual is to help you get the best value from your scooter. It can do so in several ways. It can help you decide what work must be done, even if you choose to have it done by a dealer; it provides information and procedures for routine maintenance and servicing; and it offers diagnostic and repair procedures to follow when trouble occurs.

We hope you use the manual to tackle the work yourself. For many simpler jobs, doing it yourself may be quicker than arranging an

appointment to get the scooter into a dealer and making the trips to leave it and pick it up. More importantly, a lot of money can be saved by avoiding the expense the shop must pass on to you to cover its labour and overhead costs. An added benefit is the sense of satisfaction and accomplishment that you feel after doing the job yourself.

References to the left or right side of the scooter assume you are sitting on the seat, facing forward.

**We take great pride in the accuracy of information given in this manual, but manufacturers make alterations and design changes during the production run of machines about which they do not inform us. No liability can be accepted by the authors or publishers for loss, damage or injury caused by any errors in, or omissions from, the information given.**

| Model name | Model code | Production year |
|---|---|---|
| SH125 | SH125-1 | 2001/2002 |
| SH125 | SH125-3 | 2003 |
| SH125 | SH125-4 | 2004 |
| SH125i | SH125-5 | 2005 |
| SH125i | SH125-6 | 2006 |
| SH125i | SH125-7 | 2007 |
| SH125i | SH125-8 | 2008 |
| SH125i | SH125-9 | 2009 |
| SH125i | SH125-D9 | 2009 |
| SH150 | SH150-1 | 2001/2002 |
| SH150 | SH150-3 | 2003 |
| SH150 | SH150-4 | 2004 |
| SH150i | SH150-5 | 2005 |
| SH150i | SH150-6 | 2006 |
| SH150i | SH150-7 | 2007 |
| SH150i | SH150-8 | 2008 |
| SH150i | SH150-9 | 2009 |
| SH150i | SH150-D9 | 2009 |
| Dylan 125 | SES125-2 | 2002 |
| Dylan 125 | SES125-3 | 2003 |
| Dylan 125 | SES125-4 | 2004 to 2008 |
| Dylan 150 | SES150-2 | 2002 |
| Dylan 150 | SES150-3 | 2003 |
| Dylan 150 | SES150-4 | 2004 to 2008 |
| @ 125 | NES125-Y | 2000 |
| @ 125 | NES125-1 | 2001 |
| @ 125 | NES125-2 | 2002 |
| @ 125 | NES125-3 | 2003 |
| @ 125 | NES125-4 | 2004 |
| @ 125 | NES125-5 | 2005 |
| @ 125 | NES125-6 | 2006 |
| @ 150 | NES150-Y | 2000 |
| @ 150 | NES150-1 | 2001 |
| @ 150 | NES150-2 | 2002 |
| @ 150 | NES150-3 | 2003 |
| @ 150 | NES150-4 | 2004 |
| @ 150 | NES150-5 | 2005 |
| @ 150 | NES150-6 | 2006 |
| PS125i | PES125-6 | 2006 |
| PS125i | PES125-7 | 2007 |
| PS125i | PES125-8 | 2008 |
| PS125i | PES125-9 | 2009 |
| PS150i | PES150-6 | 2006 |
| PS150i | PES150-7 | 2007 |
| PS150i | PES150-8 | 2008 |
| PS150i | PES150-9 | 2009 |
| Pantheon 125 | FES125-3 | 2003 |
| Pantheon 125 | FES125-4 | 2004 |
| Pantheon 125 | FES125-5 | 2005/2006 |
| Pantheon 150 | FES150-3 | 2003 |
| Pantheon 150 | FES150-4 | 2004 |
| Pantheon 150 | FES150-5 | 2005/2006 |
| S-wing 125 | FES125-7 | 2007/2008 |
| S-wing 125 | FES125-A7 | 2007/2008 |
| S-wing 125 | FES125-9 | 2009 |
| S-wing 125 | FES125-A9 | 2009 |
| S-wing 150 | FES150-7 | 2007/2008 |
| S-wing 150 | FES150-A7 | 2007/2008 |
| S-wing 150 | FES150-9 | 2009 |
| S-wing 150 | FES150-A9 | 2009 |

## Frame and engine numbers

The frame serial number, or VIN (Vehicle Identification Number) as it is often known, is stamped into the frame, and also appears on the identification (VIN) plate. The engine number is stamped into either the rear of the transmission casing or the left-hand side of the crankcase, depending on model. Both of these numbers should be recorded and kept in a safe place so they can be furnished to law enforcement officials in the event of a theft.

The frame and engine numbers should also be kept in a handy place (such as with your driving licence) so they are always available when purchasing or ordering parts for your scooter.

A colour code label is stuck to the inside of the storage compartment under the seat – this will be needed if ordering colour matched parts.

The procedures in this manual identify models by their model name and production year (e.g. 2003 Pantheon), or by whether they have a carburettor or fuel injection system, or by the engine size and/or model code (e.g. FES125-3) – refer to the list below for details. The model code and production year are on the VIN plate.

## Buying spare parts

When ordering replacement parts, it is essential to identify exactly the model for which the parts are required. While in some cases it is sufficient to identify the machine by its title e.g. 'Dylan 125', any modifications made to components mean that it is usually essential to identify the scooter by its year of production, or better still by its frame or engine number prefix.

To be absolutely certain of receiving the correct part, not only is it essential to have the scooter engine or frame number prefix to hand, but it is also useful to take the old part for comparison (where possible). Note that where a modified component has superseded the original, a careful check must be made that there are no related parts which have also been modified and must be used to enable the replacement to be correctly refitted; where such a situation is found, purchase all the necessary parts and fit them, even if this means replacing apparently unworn items.

Purchase replacement parts from an authorised Honda dealer or someone who specialises in scooter parts; they are more likely to have the parts in stock or can order them quickly from the importer. Pattern parts may be available for certain components; if used, ensure these are of recognised quality brands which will perform as well as the original.

Expendable items such as lubricants, spark plugs, bearings, bulbs and tyres can usually be obtained at lower prices from accessory shops, motor factors or from specialists advertising in the national motorcycle press.

The frame number is stamped into the frame on the right-hand side . . .

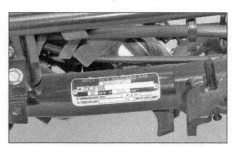

. . . and also appears on the VIN plate

The engine number is stamped into either the rear of the transmission casing . . .

. . . or the left-hand side of the crankcase

A colour code label (arrowed) is stuck on the helmet storage compartment under the seat

Professional mechanics are trained in safe working procedures. However enthusiastic you may be about getting on with the job at hand, take the time to ensure that your safety is not put at risk. A moment's lack of attention can result in an accident, as can failure to observe simple precautions.

There will always be new ways of having accidents, and the following is not a comprehensive list of all dangers; it is intended rather to make you aware of the risks and to encourage a safe approach to all work you carry out on your bike.

## Asbestos

● Certain friction, insulating, sealing and other products - such as brake pads, clutch linings, gaskets, etc. - contain asbestos. Extreme care must be taken to avoid inhalation of dust from such products since it is hazardous to health. If in doubt, assume that they do contain asbestos.

## Fire

● Remember at all times that petrol is highly flammable. Never smoke or have any kind of naked flame around, when working on the vehicle. But the risk does not end there - a spark caused by an electrical short-circuit, by two metal surfaces contacting each other, by careless use of tools, or even by static electricity built up in your body under certain conditions, can ignite petrol vapour, which in a confined space is highly explosive. Never use petrol as a cleaning solvent. Use an approved safety solvent.

● Always disconnect the battery earth terminal before working on any part of the fuel or electrical system, and never risk spilling fuel on to a hot engine or exhaust.

● It is recommended that a fire extinguisher of a type suitable for fuel and electrical fires is kept handy in the garage or workplace at all times. Never try to extinguish a fuel or electrical fire with water.

## Fumes

● Certain fumes are highly toxic and can quickly cause unconsciousness and even death if inhaled to any extent. Petrol vapour comes into this category, as do the vapours from certain solvents such as trichloro-ethylene. Any draining or pouring of such volatile fluids should be done in a well ventilated area.

● When using cleaning fluids and solvents, read the instructions carefully. Never use materials from unmarked containers - they may give off poisonous vapours.

● Never run the engine of a motor vehicle in an enclosed space such as a garage. Exhaust fumes contain carbon monoxide which is extremely poisonous; if you need to run the engine, always do so in the open air or at least have the rear of the vehicle outside the workplace.

## The battery

● Never cause a spark, or allow a naked light near the vehicle's battery. It will normally be giving off a certain amount of hydrogen gas, which is highly explosive.

● Always disconnect the battery ground (earth) terminal before working on the fuel or electrical systems (except where noted).

● If possible, loosen the filler plugs or cover when charging the battery from an external source. Do not charge at an excessive rate or the battery may burst.

● Take care when topping up, cleaning or carrying the battery. The acid electrolyte, evenwhen diluted, is very corrosive and should not be allowed to contact the eyes or skin. Always wear rubber gloves and goggles or a face shield. If you ever need to prepare electrolyte yourself, always add the acid slowly to the water; never add the water to the acid.

## Electricity

● When using an electric power tool, inspection light etc., always ensure that the appliance is correctly connected to its plug and that, where necessary, it is properly grounded (earthed). Do not use such appliances in damp conditions and, again, beware of creating a spark or applying excessive heat in the vicinity of fuel or fuel vapour. Also ensure that the appliances meet national safety standards.

● A severe electric shock can result from touching certain parts of the electrical system, such as the spark plug wires (HT leads), when the engine is running or being cranked, particularly if components are damp or the insulation is defective. Where an electronic ignition system is used, the secondary (HT) voltage is much higher and could prove fatal.

# Remember...

✗ **Don't** start the engine without first ascertaining that the transmission is in neutral.

✗ **Don't** suddenly remove the pressure cap from a hot cooling system - cover it with a cloth and release the pressure gradually first, or you may get scalded by escaping coolant.

✗ **Don't** attempt to drain oil until you are sure it has cooled sufficiently to avoid scalding you.

✗ **Don't** grasp any part of the engine or exhaust system without first ascertaining that it is cool enough not to burn you.

✗ **Don't** allow brake fluid or antifreeze to contact the machine's paintwork or plastic components.

✗ **Don't** siphon toxic liquids such as fuel, hydraulic fluid or antifreeze by mouth, or allow them to remain on your skin.

✗ **Don't** inhale dust - it may be injurious to health (see Asbestos heading).

✗ **Don't** allow any spilled oil or grease to remain on the floor - wipe it up right away, before someone slips on it.

✗ **Don't** use ill-fitting spanners or other tools which may slip and cause injury.

✗ **Don't** lift a heavy component which may be beyond your capability - get assistance.

✗ **Don't** rush to finish a job or take unverified short cuts.

✗ **Don't** allow children or animals in or around an unattended vehicle.

✗ **Don't** inflate a tyre above the recommended pressure. Apart from overstressing the carcass, in extreme cases the tyre may blow off forcibly.

✔ **Do** ensure that the machine is supported securely at all times. This is especially important when the machine is blocked up to aid wheel or fork removal.

✔ **Do** take care when attempting to loosen a stubborn nut or bolt. It is generally better to pull on a spanner, rather than push, so that if you slip, you fall away from the machine rather than onto it.

✔ **Do** wear eye protection when using power tools such as drill, sander, bench grinder etc.

✔ **Do** use a barrier cream on your hands prior to undertaking dirty jobs - it will protect your skin from infection as well as making the dirt easier to remove afterwards; but make sure your hands aren't left slippery. Note that long-term contact with used engine oil can be a health hazard.

✔ **Do** keep loose clothing (cuffs, ties etc.

and long hair) well out of the way of moving mechanical parts.

✔ **Do** remove rings, wristwatch etc., before working on the vehicle - especially the electrical system.

✔ **Do** keep your work area tidy - it is only too easy to fall over articles left lying around.

✔ **Do** exercise caution when compressing springs for removal or installation. Ensure that the tension is applied and released in a controlled manner, using suitable tools which preclude the possibility of the spring escaping violently.

✔ **Do** ensure that any lifting tackle used has a safe working load rating adequate for the job.

✔ **Do** get someone to check periodically that all is well, when working alone on the vehicle.

✔ **Do** carry out work in a logical sequence and check that everything is correctly assembled and tightened afterwards.

✔ **Do** remember that your vehicle's safety affects that of yourself and others. If in doubt on any point, get professional advice.

● If in spite of following these precautions, you are unfortunate enough to injure yourself, seek medical attention as soon as possible.

**Note:** *The Pre-ride checks outlined in your Owner's Handbook cover those items which should be inspected before riding the scooter.*

# Engine oil level check

### The correct oil
● Modern, high-revving engines place great demands on their oil. It is very important that the correct oil for your bike is used.
● Always top up with a good quality motorcycle/scooter oil of the specified type and viscosity and do not overfill the engine. Do not use engine oil designed for car use.

| Oil type | API grade SG or higher, JASO grade MA or MB |
|---|---|
| Oil viscosity | SAE 10W30 or 10W40 |

*Caution: Do not use chemical additives or oils labelled 'ENERGY CONSERVING'.*
*\*If you are using the scooter constantly in extreme conditions of heat or cold, other more suitable viscosity ranges may be used – refer to the viscosity table to select the oil best suited to your conditions.*

### Before you start
✔ Support the scooter upright on level ground.
✔ Start the engine and let it idle for 3 to 5 minutes.

*Caution: Do not run the engine in an enclosed space such as a garage or workshop.*
✔ Stop the engine and leave it for a few minutes for the oil level to stabilise.

### Scooter care
● If you have to add oil frequently, check the engine joints, oil seals and gaskets for oil leakage. If not, the engine could be burning oil, in which case there will be white smoke coming out of the exhaust (see *Fault Finding*).

**1** Unscrew the oil filler cap/level dipstick from the right-hand side of the engine.

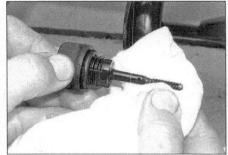

**2** Wipe the dipstick clean.

**3** Insert the dipstick so that the cap contacts the engine, but **do not** screw it in.

**4** Remove the dipstick and check the oil mark – it should lie between the upper and lower level lines (arrowed).

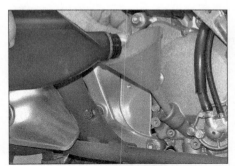

**5** If the level is on or below the lower line, top up the engine with the recommended grade and type of oil to bring the level almost up to the upper line. Do not overfill.

**6** On completion, make sure the O-ring (arrowed) on the underside of the cap is in good condition and properly seated. Fit a new one if necessary. Wipe it clean and smear new oil onto it. Fit the cap and tighten it by hand.

# Coolant level check

⚠ **Warning: DO NOT remove the radiator pressure cap to add coolant. Topping up is done via the coolant reservoir tank filler. DO NOT leave open containers of coolant about, as it is poisonous.**

## Before you start

✔ On SH and PS models the coolant reservoir is located behind the upper front panel, and is visible through the grille, or by removing the upper front cover for an improved view (see Chapter 9). If top-up is needed, remove the upper front panel.

✔ On Dylan and @ models the coolant reservoir is located behind the upper front panel, and is visible via an aperture in the inner front cover. If top-up is needed remove the upper front panel (see Chapter 9).

✔ On Pantheon and S-wing models the coolant reservoir is located under the floor panel on the left-hand side and is visible via an aperture in the lower cover. If top-up is

needed remove the rubber mat from the floor panel and lift the access panel.

✔ Make sure you have a supply of coolant available (a mixture of 50% distilled water and 50% corrosion inhibited ethylene glycol anti-freeze is needed).

✔ Support the scooter upright on level ground.

✔ Start the engine and let it warm up. Check the coolant level with the engine running at normal operating temperature.

*Caution: Do not run the engine in an enclosed space such as a garage or workshop.*

## Bike care

● Use only the specified coolant mixture. It is important that anti-freeze is used in the system all year round, and not just in the winter. Do not top-up the system with water only, as the coolant will become too diluted.

● Do not overfill the reservoir tank. The coolant level should be just below the MAX mark. Any

surplus should be siphoned or drained off to prevent the possibility of it being expelled.

● If the coolant level falls steadily, check the system for leaks (see Chapter 1). If no leaks are found and the level continues to fall, it is recommended that the machine is taken to a Honda dealer for a pressure test.

**1** Coolant level UPPER and LOWER level lines on SH and PS models, with upper front panel removed.

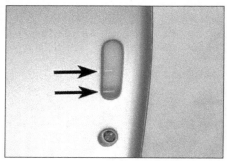

**2** Coolant level UPPER and LOWER level lines on Dylan and @ models . . .

**3** . . . if top-up is needed remove the upper front panel to access the reservoir cap (arrowed).

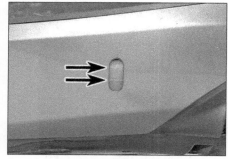

**4** Coolant level UPPER and LOWER level lines on Pantheon and S-wing models . . .

**5** . . . if top-up is needed peel back the rubber mat and remove the access panel.

**6** Remove the reservoir cap.

**7** Top-up with the specified coolant mixture to bring the level almost up to the UPPER line. Do not overfill.

# Brake fluid level check

⚠️ *Warning: Brake fluid can harm your eyes and damage painted surfaces, so use extreme caution when handling and pouring it and cover surrounding surfaces with rag. Do not use fluid that has been standing open for some time, as it absorbs moisture from the air which can cause a dangerous loss of braking effectiveness.*

## Before you start

✔ Support the scooter in an upright position on level ground and turn the handlebars until the brake reservoir is as level as possible – remember to check both reservoirs if your scooter is equipped with a rear disc brake.

✔ Make sure you have a supply of DOT 4 brake fluid.

✔ Access to the reservoir cover is restricted on some models by the handlebar cover. If necessary, remove the cover to top up the fluid level (see Chapter 9).

✔ Wrap a rag around the reservoir to ensure that any spillage does not come into contact with painted or plastic surfaces. If any fluid is spilt, wash it off immediately with cold water.

## Bike care

● The fluid in the brake master cylinder reservoir(s) will drop as the brake pads wear. If the fluid level is low check the brake pads for wear (see Chapter 1), and replace them with new ones if necessary (see Chapter 8). Do not

top the reservoir(s) up until the new pads have been fitted, and then check to see if topping up is still necessary – when the caliper pistons are pushed back to accommodate the extra thickness of the pads some fluid will be displaced back into the reservoir.

● If the reservoir requires repeated topping-up this is an indication of a fluid leak somewhere in the system, which should be investigated immediately.

● Check for signs of fluid leakage from the brake hoses and components – if found, rectify immediately.

● Check the operation of the brakes before riding the machine. If there is evidence of air in the system (a spongy feel to the lever), bleed the brake as described in Chapter 8.

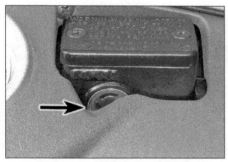

**1** Set the handlebars so the reservoir is level and check the fluid level through the window in the reservoir body, via the aperture in the handlebar cover where appropriate – the level must be above the LOWER level line (arrowed).

**2** Where necessary, remove the handlebar cover (see Chapter 9). Undo the reservoir cover screws and remove the cover, diaphragm plate and diaphragm.

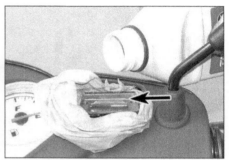

**3** Top up with new clean DOT 4 hydraulic fluid, until the level is up to the UPPER line (arrowed) on the inside of the reservoir. Do not overfill and take care to avoid spills (see **Warning** above).

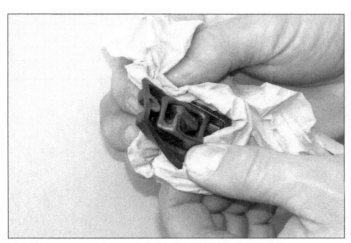

**4** Wipe any moisture out of the diaphragm with a tissue.

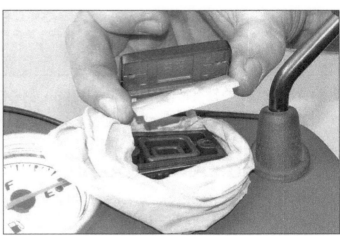

**5** Ensure that the diaphragm is correctly seated before fitting the plate and cover. Secure the cover with its screws.

# Tyre checks

### The correct pressures

● The tyres must be checked when **cold**, not immediately after riding. Note that low tyre pressures may cause the tyre to slip on the rim or come off. High tyre pressures will cause abnormal tread wear and unsafe handling.

● Use an accurate pressure gauge. Many forecourt gauges are wildly inaccurate. If you buy your own, spend as much as you can justify on a quality gauge.

● Proper air pressure will increase tyre life and provide maximum stability and ride comfort.

● Refer to the tables below for the correct tyre pressures for your model.

**Pantheon and S-wing**

|            | Front                  | Rear                   |
|------------|------------------------|------------------------|
| **Rider only** | 25 psi<br>(1.75 Bar) | 29 psi<br>(2.00 Bar) |
| **Rider and passenger** | 25 psi<br>(1.75 Bar) | 36 psi<br>(2.50 Bar) |

**All other models**

| ı          | Front                  | Rear                   |
|------------|------------------------|------------------------|
| **Rider only** | 25 psi<br>(1.75 Bar) | 29 psi<br>(2.00 Bar) |
| **Rider and passenger** | 25 psi<br>(1.75 Bar) | 33 psi<br>(2.25 Bar) |

### Tyre care

● Check the tyres carefully for cuts, tears, embedded nails or other sharp objects and excessive wear. Operation of the scooter with excessively worn tyres is extremely hazardous, as traction and handling are directly affected.

● Check the condition of the tyre valve and ensure the dust cap is in place.

● Pick out any stones or nails which may have become embedded in the tyre tread. If left, they will eventually penetrate through the casing and cause a puncture.

● If tyre damage is apparent, or unexplained loss of pressure is experienced, seek the advice of a tyre fitting specialist without delay.

### Tyre tread depth

● At the time of writing UK law requires that tread depth must be at least 1 mm over 3/4 of the tread breadth all the way around the tyre,

with no bald patches. Many riders, however, consider 2 mm tread depth minimum to be a safer limit. Honda recommend a minimum of 1.5 mm on the front and 2 mm on the rear. Refer to the tyre tread legislation in your country.

● Many tyres now incorporate wear indicators in the tread. Identify the location marking on the tyre sidewall to locate the indicator bar and replace the tyre if the tread has worn down to the bar.

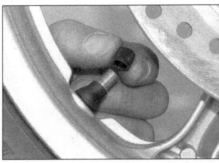

**1** Remove the dust cap from the valve and do not forget to fit it after checking the pressure.

**2** Check the tyre pressures when the tyres are **cold**.

**3** Measure tread depth at the centre of the tyre using a tread depth gauge.

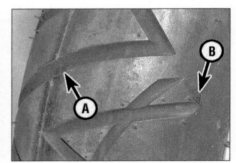

**4** Tyre tread wear indicator bar (A) and its location marking (B) (usually an arrow, a triangle or the letters TWI) on the sidewall.

# Suspension and steering checks

● Check that the front and rear suspension operates smoothly without binding.

● Check that the steering moves smoothly from lock-to-lock.

# Legal and safety checks

### Lighting and signalling

● Take a minute to check that the headlight, tail light, brake light, instrument lights and turn signals all work correctly.

● Check that the horn sounds when the switch is operated.

● A working speedometer graduated in mph is a statutory requirement in the UK.

### Safety

● Check that the throttle grip rotates smoothly and snaps shut when released, in all steering positions.

● Check that stand return springs hold the stand(s) securely up when retracted.

● Check that both brakes work correctly when applied and free off when released.

### Fuel

● This may seem obvious, but check that you have enough fuel to complete your journey. Do not wait until the fuel gauge or warning light tells you that the level in the tank is low before filling up.

● If you notice signs of leakage you must rectify the cause immediately.

● Ensure you use the correct grade unleaded petrol, minimum 91 octane (RON).

# Chapter 1
# Routine maintenance and servicing

## Contents

## Degrees of difficulty

| **Easy,** suitable for novice with little experience | **Fairly easy,** suitable for beginner with some experience | **Fairly difficult,** suitable for competent DIY mechanic | **Difficult,** suitable for experienced DIY mechanic | **Very difficult,** suitable for expert DIY or professional |
|---|---|---|---|---|

## Introduction

**1** This Chapter is designed to help the home mechanic maintain his/her scooter for safety, economy, long life and peak performance.

**2** Deciding where to start or plug into a service schedule depends on several factors. If the warranty period on your scooter has just expired, and if it has been maintained according to the warranty standards, you will want to pick up routine maintenance as it coincides with the next mileage or calendar interval. If you have owned the machine for some time but have never performed any maintenance on it, then you may want to start at the nearest interval and include some additional procedures to ensure that nothing important is overlooked. If you have just had a major engine overhaul, then you will want to start the maintenance routine from the beginning as with a new machine. If you have a used scooter and have no knowledge of its history or maintenance record, you may desire to combine all the checks into one large service initially and then settle into the maintenance schedule prescribed.

**3** Before beginning any maintenance or repair, clean your scooter thoroughly, especially around the suspension, brakes, engine and gearbox covers. Cleaning will help ensure that dirt does not contaminate the working parts and will allow you to detect wear and damage that could otherwise easily go unnoticed.

**4** Certain maintenance information is sometimes printed on decals attached to the scooter. If the information on the decals differs from that included here, use the information on the decal.

**Note 1:** *Pre-ride checks are listed at the beginning of this manual. Always perform the pre-ride inspection at every maintenance interval (in addition to the procedures listed).*

**Note 2:** *The intervals listed below are the intervals recommended by the manufacturer for each particular operation during the model years covered in this manual.*

**Note 3:** *An initial (one-off) service will be performed by a Honda dealer after the first 600 miles (1000 km) from new. Thereafter, the scooter should be serviced according to the intervals specified in the service schedules which follow.*

# SH125 and 150, 2001 to 2004

## Model identification

| | |
|---|---|
| Engine | 125 or 150 cc single cylinder, liquid-cooled four-stroke |
| Gearbox | Variable speed automatic, belt driven |
| Ignition | Capacitor discharge ignition (CDI) |
| Fuel system | CV carburettor |
| Front suspension | Telescopic fork |
| Rear suspension | Swingarm and twin shock |
| Front brake | Hydraulic disc |
| Rear brake | Drum |
| Front tyre size | 100/80-16 |
| Rear tyre size | 120/80-16 |
| Overall length | 2020 mm |
| Overall width | 705 mm |
| Overall height | 1145 mm |
| Wheelbase | 1335 mm |
| Seat height | 790 mm |
| Ground clearance | 148 mm |
| Dry weight | 122 kg |
| Curb weight | 131 kg |
| Fuel tank capacity | 8.3 litres |

## Servicing specifications and lubricants

| | |
|---|---|
| Spark plug type | |
|    Standard | NGK CR8EH-9 or Denso U24FER9 |
|    Extended high speed riding | NGK CR9EH-9 or Denso U27FER9 |
| Spark plug electrode gap | 0.8 to 0.9 mm |
| Idle speed | 1400 to 1600 rpm |
| Disc brake pad and drum brake shoe wear limits | see Text |
| Rear brake lever freeplay | 15 to 25 mm |
| Drum brake lining maximum diameter | 131 mm |
| Drive belt wear limit (see text) | 21.5 mm |
| Throttle twistgrip freeplay | 2 to 6 mm |
| Valve clearances (engine COLD) | |
|    Intake valve | 0.14 to 0.18 mm |
|    Exhaust valve | 0.23 to 0.27 mm |
| Fuel | Petrol (unleaded) min 91 octane |
| Engine oil type | SAE 10W30 or 10W40, API SG min, JASO MA or MB |
| Engine oil capacity | |
|    After draining | 0.9 litre |
|    After engine disassembly | 1.0 litre |
| Coolant type | see Pre-ride checks |
| Cooling system capacity | 1.15 litres |
| Gearbox oil | SAE 90W Hypoid gear oil or engine oil (see above) |
| Gearbox oil capacity | |
|    After draining | 210 ml |
|    After engine disassembly | 220 ml |
| Brake fluid | DOT 4 |
| Torque settings | |
|    Engine oil drain plug | 20 Nm |
|    Spark plug | 12 Nm |
|    Gearbox oil drain plug | 27 Nm |
|    Gearbox oil level plug | 13 Nm |

## Service schedule

**Note:** *Always perform the Pre-ride checks before every service interval – see the beginning of this Manual.*

| | Text section in this Chapter | Every 2500 miles (4000 km) | Every 5000 miles (8000 km) | Every 7500 miles (12,000 km) | Every 15,000 miles (24,000 km) |
|---|---|---|---|---|---|
| Air filter – replace* | 1 | | | ✔ | |
| Battery – check | 2 | ✔ | | | |
| Brake pad and shoe – wear check | 3 | ✔ | | | |
| Brake system – check** | 4 | ✔ | | | |
| Clutch – check | 5 | | ✔ | | |
| Cooling system – check*** | 6 | | ✔ | | |
| Crankcase breather – clean | 7 | ✔ | | | |
| Drive belt – check | 8 | | ✔ | | |
| Drive belt – replace | 8 | | | | ✔ |
| Engine oil – change | 9 | ✔ | | | |
| Fuel system – check | 10 | ✔ | | | |
| Gearbox oil change | 11 | | | | Every 2 years |
| Headlight aim – check | 12 | ✔ | | | |
| Idle speed – check and adjust | 13 | ✔ | | | |
| Nuts and bolts – tightness check | 14 | | ✔ | | |
| PAIR system – check | 15 | | | ✔ | |
| Spark plug – replace | 16 | | ✔ | | |
| Stand(s) – check and lubricate | 17 | ✔ | | | |
| Steering head bearings – check | 18 | | | ✔ | |
| Suspension – check | 19 | ✔ | | | |
| Throttle – check and adjust | 20 | ✔ | | | |
| Transmission case filter – clean | 21 | ✔ | | | |
| Valve clearances – check | 22 | ✔ | | | |
| Wheels and tyres – check | 23 | ✔ | | | |

*\* Replace the air filter more often if the scooter is ridden in constantly wet or dusty conditions.*
*\*\* The brake fluid must be changed every 2 years, irrespective of mileage.*
*\*\*\*Drain and refill with fresh coolant every 2 years, irrespective of mileage*

# SH125i and 150i, 2005 to 2008

## Model identification

| | |
|---|---|
| Engine | 125 or 150 cc single cylinder, liquid-cooled four-stroke |
| Gearbox | Variable speed automatic, belt driven |
| Ignition | Fully transistorised |
| Fuel system | PGM-FI fuel injection |
| Front suspension | Telescopic fork |
| Rear suspension | Swingarm and twin shock |
| Front brake | Hydraulic disc |
| Rear brake | Drum |
| Front tyre size | 100/80-16 |
| Rear tyre size | 120/80-16 |
| Overall length | 2020 mm |
| Overall width | 705 mm |
| Overall height | 1140 mm |
| Wheelbase | 1335 mm |
| Seat height | 790 mm |
| Ground clearance | 140 mm |
| Curb weight | 134 kg |
| Fuel tank capacity | 7.5 litres |

## Servicing specifications and lubricants

| | |
|---|---|
| **Spark plug type** | |
|   Standard | NGK CR8EH-9 or Denso U24FER9 |
|   Extended high speed riding | NGK CR9EH-9 or Denso U27FER9 |
| Spark plug electrode gap | 0.8 to 0.9 mm |
| Idle speed | 1400 to 1600 rpm |
| Disc brake pad and drum brake shoe wear limits | see Text |
| Rear brake lever freeplay | 10 to 20 mm |
| Drum brake lining maximum diameter | 131 mm |
| Drive belt wear limit (see text) | 21.5 mm |
| Throttle twistgrip freeplay | 2 to 6 mm |
| **Valve clearances (engine COLD)** | |
|   Intake valve | 0.14 to 0.18 mm |
|   Exhaust valve | 0.23 to 0.27 mm |
| Fuel | Petrol (unleaded) min 91 octane |
| Engine oil type | SAE 10W30 or 10W40, API SG min, JASO MA or MB |
| **Engine oil capacity** | |
|   After draining | 0.9 litre |
|   After engine disassembly | 1.0 litre |
| Coolant type | see *Pre-ride checks* |
| **Cooling system capacity** | |
|   Radiator and engine | 0.95 litre |
|   Reservoir | 0.4 litre |
| Gearbox oil | SAE 90W Hypoid gear oil or engine oil (see above) |
| **Gearbox oil capacity** | |
|   After draining | 190 ml |
|   After engine disassembly | 220 ml |
| Brake fluid | DOT 4 |
| **Torque settings** | |
|   Engine oil drain plug | 20 Nm |
|   Spark plug | 12 Nm |
|   Gearbox oil drain plug | 27 Nm |
|   Gearbox oil level plug | 13 Nm |

## Service schedule

**Note:** *Always perform the Pre-ride checks before every service interval – see the beginning of this Manual.*

| | Text section in this Chapter | Every 2500 miles (4000 km) | Every 5000 miles (8000 km) | Every 7500 miles (12,000 km) | Every 15,000 miles (24,000 km) |
|---|---|---|---|---|---|
| Air filter – replace* | 1 | | | ✔ | |
| Battery – check | 2 | ✔ | | | |
| Brake pad and shoe – wear check | 3 | ✔ | | | |
| Brake system – check** | 4 | ✔ | | | |
| Clutch – check | 5 | | ✔ | | |
| Cooling system – check*** | 6 | | ✔ | | |
| Crankcase breather – clean | 7 | ✔ | | | |
| Drive belt – check | 8 | | ✔ | | |
| Drive belt – replace | 8 | | | | ✔ |
| Engine oil – change | 9 | ✔ | | | |
| Fuel system – check | 10 | ✔ | | | |
| Gearbox oil change | 11 | | | | Every 2 years |
| Headlight aim – check | 12 | ✔ | | | |
| Nuts and bolts – tightness check | 14 | | ✔ | | |
| PAIR system – check | 15 | | | ✔ | |
| Spark plug – replace | 16 | | ✔ | | |
| Stand(s) – check and lubricate | 17 | ✔ | | | |
| Steering head bearings – check | 18 | | | ✔ | |
| Suspension – check | 19 | ✔ | | | |
| Throttle – check and adjust | 20 | ✔ | | | |
| Transmission case filter – clean | 21 | ✔ | | | |
| Valve clearances – check | 22 | ✔ | | | |
| Wheels and tyres – check | 23 | ✔ | | | |

*\* Replace the air filter more often if the scooter is ridden in constantly wet or dusty conditions.*
*\*\* The brake fluid must be changed every 2 years, irrespective of mileage.*
*\*\*\*Drain and refill with fresh coolant every 2 years, irrespective of mileage*

# SH125i and 150i, 2009-on

## Model identification

| | |
|---|---|
| Engine | 125 or 150 cc single cylinder, liquid-cooled four-stroke |
| Gearbox | Variable speed automatic, belt driven |
| Ignition | Fully transistorised |
| Fuel system | PGM-FI fuel injection |
| Front suspension | Telescopic fork |
| Rear suspension | Swingarm and twin shock |
| Front brake | Hydraulic disc |
| Rear brake | |
| SH-9 models | Hydraulic disc |
| SH-D9 models | Drum |
| Front tyre size | 100/80-16 |
| Rear tyre size | 120/80-16 |
| Overall length | 2025 mm |
| Overall width | 700 mm |
| Overall height | 1230 mm |
| Wheelbase | 1335 mm |
| Seat height | 785 mm |
| Ground clearance | 156 mm |
| Curb weight | |
| SH-9 models | 136 kg |
| SH-D9 models | 134 kg |
| Fuel tank capacity | 7.5 litres |

## Servicing specifications and lubricants

| | |
|---|---|
| Spark plug type | |
| Standard | NGK CR8EH-9 or Denso U24FER9 |
| Extended high speed riding | NGK CR9EH-9 or Denso U27FER9 |
| Spark plug electrode gap | 0.8 to 0.9 mm |
| Idle speed | 1400 to 1600 rpm |
| Disc brake pad and drum brake shoe wear limits | see Text |
| Rear brake lever freeplay (D9 models) | 10 to 20 mm |
| Drum brake lining maximum diameter (D9 models) | 131 mm |
| Drive belt wear limit (see text) | 21.5 mm |
| Throttle twistgrip freeplay | 2 to 6 mm |
| Valve clearances (engine COLD) | |
| Intake valve | 0.14 to 0.18 mm |
| Exhaust valve | 0.23 to 0.27 mm |
| Fuel | Petrol (unleaded) min 91 octane |
| Engine oil type | SAE 10W30 or 10W40, API SG min, JASO MA or MB |
| Engine oil capacity | |
| After draining | 0.9 litre |
| After engine disassembly | 1.0 litre |
| Coolant type | see Pre-ride checks |
| Cooling system capacity | |
| Radiator and engine | 0.95 litre |
| Reservoir | 0.4 litre |
| Gearbox oil | SAE 90W Hypoid gear oil or engine oil (see above) |
| Gearbox oil capacity | |
| After draining | 190 ml |
| After engine disassembly | 220 ml |
| Brake fluid | DOT 4 |
| Torque settings | |
| Engine oil drain plug | 20 Nm |
| Spark plug | 12 Nm |
| Gearbox oil drain plug | 27 Nm |
| Gearbox oil level plug | 13 Nm |

## Service schedule

*Note: Always perform the Pre-ride checks before every service interval – see the beginning of this Manual.*

|  | Text section in this Chapter | Every 2500 miles (4000 km) | Every 5000 miles (8000 km) | Every 7500 miles (12,000 km) | Every 15,000 miles (24,000 km) |
|---|---|---|---|---|---|
| Air filter – replace* | 1 |  |  | ✔ |  |
| Battery – check | 2 | ✔ |  |  |  |
| Brake pad and shoe – wear check | 3 | ✔ |  |  |  |
| Brake system – check** | 4 | ✔ |  |  |  |
| Clutch – check | 5 |  | ✔ |  |  |
| Cooling system – check*** | 6 |  | ✔ |  |  |
| Crankcase breather – clean | 7 | ✔ |  |  |  |
| Drive belt – check | 8 |  | ✔ |  |  |
| Drive belt – replace | 8 |  |  |  | ✔ |
| Engine oil – change | 9 | ✔ |  |  |  |
| Fuel system – check | 10 | ✔ |  |  |  |
| Gearbox oil change | 11 |  |  |  | Every 2 years |
| Headlight aim – check | 12 | ✔ |  |  |  |
| Nuts and bolts – tightness check | 14 |  | ✔ |  |  |
| PAIR system – check | 15 |  |  | ✔ |  |
| Spark plug – replace | 16 |  | ✔ |  |  |
| Stand(s) – check and lubricate | 17 | ✔ |  |  |  |
| Steering head bearings – check | 18 |  |  | ✔ |  |
| Suspension – check | 19 | ✔ |  |  |  |
| Throttle – check and adjust | 20 | ✔ |  |  |  |
| Transmission case filter – clean | 21 | ✔ |  |  |  |
| Valve clearances – check | 22 | ✔ |  |  |  |
| Wheels and tyres – check | 23 | ✔ |  |  |  |

*\* Replace the air filter more often if the scooter is ridden in constantly wet or dusty conditions.*
*\*\* The brake fluid must be changed every 2 years, irrespective of mileage.*
*\*\*\*Drain and refill with fresh coolant every 2 years, irrespective of mileage*

# Dylan 125 and 150

## Model identification

| | |
|---|---|
| Engine | 125 or 150 cc single cylinder, liquid-cooled four-stroke |
| Gearbox | Variable speed automatic, belt driven |
| Ignition | Capacitor discharge ignition (CDI) |
| Fuel system | CV carburettor |
| Front suspension | Telescopic fork |
| Rear suspension | Swingarm and twin shock |
| Front brake | Hydraulic disc |
| Rear brake | Drum |
| Front tyre size | 110/90-13 |
| Rear tyre size | 130/70-13 |
| Overall length | 1949 mm |
| Overall width | 698 mm |
| Overall height | 1142 mm |
| Wheelbase | 1328 mm |
| Seat height | 795 mm |
| Ground clearance | 137 mm |
| Dry weight | 122 kg |
| Curb weight | 131 kg |
| Fuel tank capacity | 9.0 litres |

## Servicing specifications and lubricants

| | |
|---|---|
| Spark plug type | |
|     Standard | NGK CR8EH-9 or Denso U24FER9 |
|     Extended high speed riding | NGK CR9EH-9 or Denso U27FER9 |
| Spark plug electrode gap | 0.8 to 0.9 mm |
| Idle speed | 1500 to 1700 rpm |
| Disc brake pad and drum brake shoe wear limits | see Text |
| Rear brake lever freeplay | 15 to 25 mm |
| Drum brake lining maximum diameter | 131 mm |
| Drive belt wear limit (see text) | 21.5 mm |
| Throttle twistgrip freeplay | 2 to 6 mm |
| Valve clearances (engine COLD) | |
|     Intake valve | 0.14 to 0.18 mm |
|     Exhaust valve | 0.23 to 0.27 mm |
| Fuel | Petrol (unleaded) min 91 octane |
| Engine oil type | SAE 10W30 or 10W40, API SG min, JASO MA or MB |
| Engine oil capacity | |
|     After draining | 0.9 litre |
|     After engine disassembly | 1.0 litre |
| Coolant type | see Pre-ride checks |
| Cooling system capacity | 0.95 litres |
| Gearbox oil | SAE 90W Hypoid gear oil or engine oil (see above) |
| Gearbox oil capacity | |
|     After draining | 210 ml |
|     After engine disassembly | 220 ml |
| Brake fluid | DOT 4 |
| Torque settings | |
|     Engine oil drain plug | 20 Nm |
|     Spark plug | 12 Nm |
|     Gearbox oil drain plug | 27 Nm |
|     Gearbox oil level plug | 13 Nm |

## Service schedule

**Note:** *Always perform the Pre-ride checks before every service interval – see the beginning of this Manual.*

|  | Text section in this Chapter | Every 2500 miles (4000 km) | Every 5000 miles (8000 km) | Every 7500 miles (12,000 km) | Every 15,000 miles (24,000 km) |
|---|---|---|---|---|---|
| Air filter – replace* | 1 | | | ✔ | |
| Battery – check | 2 | ✔ | | | |
| Brake pad and shoe – wear check | 3 | ✔ | | | |
| Brake system – check** | 4 | ✔ | | | |
| Clutch – check | 5 | | ✔ | | |
| Cooling system – check*** | 6 | | ✔ | | |
| Crankcase breather – clean | 7 | ✔ | | | |
| Drive belt – check | 8 | | ✔ | | |
| Drive belt – replace | 8 | | | | ✔ |
| Engine oil – change | 9 | ✔ | | | |
| Fuel system – check | 10 | ✔ | | | |
| Gearbox oil change | 11 | | | | Every 2 years |
| Headlight aim – check | 12 | ✔ | | | |
| Idle speed – check and adjust | 13 | ✔ | | | |
| Nuts and bolts – tightness check | 14 | | ✔ | | |
| PAIR system – check | 15 | | | ✔ | |
| Spark plug – replace | 16 | | ✔ | | |
| Stand(s) – check and lubricate | 17 | ✔ | | | |
| Steering head bearings – check | 18 | | | ✔ | |
| Suspension – check | 19 | ✔ | | | |
| Throttle – check and adjust | 20 | ✔ | | | |
| Transmission case filter – clean | 21 | ✔ | | | |
| Valve clearances – check | 22 | ✔ | | | |
| Wheels and tyres – check | 23 | ✔ | | | |

* Replace the air filter more often if the scooter is ridden in constantly wet or dusty conditions.
** The brake fluid must be changed every 2 years, irrespective of mileage.
***Drain and refill with fresh coolant every 2 years, irrespective of mileage

## @ 125 and 150

## Model identification

| | |
|---|---|
| Engine | 125 or 150 cc single cylinder, liquid-cooled four-stroke |
| Gearbox | Variable speed automatic, belt driven |
| Ignition | Capacitor discharge ignition (CDI) |
| Fuel system | CV carburettor |
| Front suspension | Telescopic fork |
| Rear suspension | Swingarm and twin shock |
| Front brake | Hydraulic disc |
| Rear brake | Drum |
| Front tyre size | 110/90-13 |
| Rear tyre size | 130/70-13 |
| Overall length | 1937 mm |
| Overall width | 698 mm |
| Overall height | 1174 mm |
| Wheelbase | 1328 mm |
| Seat height | 805 mm |
| Ground clearance | 141 mm |
| Dry weight | 122 kg |
| Curb weight | 131 kg |
| Fuel tank capacity | 9.0 litres |

## Servicing specifications and lubricants

| | |
|---|---|
| Spark plug type | |
|     Standard | NGK CR8EH-9 or Denso U24FER9 |
|     Extended high speed riding | NGK CR9EH-9 or Denso U27FER9 |
| Spark plug electrode gap | 0.8 to 0.9 mm |
| Idle speed | 1400 to 1600 rpm |
| Disc brake pad and drum brake shoe wear limits | see Text |
| Rear brake lever freeplay | 15 to 25 mm |
| Drum brake lining maximum diameter | 131 mm |
| Drive belt wear limit (see text) | 21.5 mm |
| Throttle twistgrip freeplay | 2 to 6 mm |
| Valve clearances (engine COLD) | |
|     Intake valve | 0.14 to 0.18 mm |
|     Exhaust valve | 0.23 to 0.27 mm |
| Fuel | Petrol (unleaded) min 91 octane |
| Engine oil type | SAE 10W30 or 10W40, API SG min, JASO MA or MB |
| Engine oil capacity | |
|     After draining | 0.9 litre |
|     After engine disassembly | 1.0 litre |
| Coolant type | see *Pre-ride checks* |
| Cooling system capacity | 0.95 litres |
| Gearbox oil | SAE 90W Hypoid gear oil or engine oil (see above) |
| Gearbox oil capacity | |
|     After draining | 210 ml |
|     After engine disassembly | 220 ml |
| Brake fluid | DOT 4 |
| Torque settings | |
|     Engine oil drain plug | 20 Nm |
|     Spark plug | 12 Nm |
|     Gearbox oil drain plug | 27 Nm |
|     Gearbox oil level plug | 13 Nm |

## Service schedule

*Note: Always perform the Pre-ride checks before every service interval – see the beginning of this Manual.*

| | Text section in this Chapter | Every 2500 miles (4000 km) | Every 5000 miles (8000 km) | Every 7500 miles (12,000 km) | Every 15,000 miles (24,000 km) |
|---|---|---|---|---|---|
| Air filter – replace* | 1 | | | ✔ | |
| Battery – check | 2 | ✔ | | | |
| Brake pad and shoe – wear check | 3 | ✔ | | | |
| Brake system – check** | 4 | ✔ | | | |
| Clutch – check | 5 | | ✔ | | |
| Cooling system – check*** | 6 | | ✔ | | |
| Crankcase breather – clean | 7 | ✔ | | | |
| Drive belt – check | 8 | | ✔ | | |
| Drive belt – replace | 8 | | | | ✔ |
| Engine oil – change | 9 | ✔ | | | |
| Fuel system – check | 10 | ✔ | | | |
| Gearbox oil change | 11 | | | | Every 2 years |
| Headlight aim – check | 12 | ✔ | | | |
| Idle speed – check and adjust | 13 | ✔ | | | |
| Nuts and bolts – tightness check | 14 | | ✔ | | |
| PAIR system – check | 15 | | | ✔ | |
| Spark plug – replace | 16 | | ✔ | | |
| Stand(s) – check and lubricate | 17 | ✔ | | | |
| Steering head bearings – check | 18 | | | ✔ | |
| Suspension – check | 19 | ✔ | | | |
| Throttle – check and adjust | 20 | ✔ | | | |
| Transmission case filter – clean | 21 | ✔ | | | |
| Valve clearances – check | 22 | ✔ | | | |
| Wheels and tyres – check | 23 | ✔ | | | |

* Replace the air filter more often if the scooter is ridden in constantly wet or dusty conditions.
** The brake fluid must be changed every 2 years, irrespective of mileage.
***Drain and refill with fresh coolant every 2 years, irrespective of mileage

# PS125i and 150i

## Model identification

| | |
|---|---|
| Engine | 125 or 150 cc single cylinder, liquid-cooled four-stroke |
| Gearbox | Variable speed automatic, belt driven |
| Ignition | Fully transistorised |
| Fuel system | PGM-FI fuel injection |
| Front suspension | Telescopic fork |
| Rear suspension | Swingarm and twin shock |
| Front brake | Hydraulic disc |
| Rear brake | Drum |
| Front tyre size | 110/90-13 |
| Rear tyre size | 130/70-13 |
| Overall length | 1990 mm |
| Overall width | 700 mm |
| Overall height | 1150 mm |
| Wheelbase | 1340 mm |
| Seat height | 800 mm |
| Ground clearance | 125 mm |
| Curb weight | 135 kg |
| Fuel tank capacity | 8.3 litres |

## Servicing specifications and lubricants

| | |
|---|---|
| Spark plug type | |
|     Standard | NGK CR8EH-9 or Denso U24FER9 |
|     Extended high speed riding | NGK CR9EH-9 or Denso U27FER9 |
| Spark plug electrode gap | 0.8 to 0.9 mm |
| Idle speed | 1400 to 1600 rpm |
| Disc brake pad and drum brake shoe wear limits | see Text |
| Rear brake lever freeplay | 10 to 20 mm |
| Drum brake lining maximum diameter | 131 mm |
| Drive belt wear limit (see text) | 21.5 mm |
| Throttle twistgrip freeplay | 2 to 6 mm |
| Valve clearances (engine COLD) | |
|     Intake valve | 0.14 to 0.18 mm |
|     Exhaust valve | 0.23 to 0.27 mm |
| Fuel | Petrol (unleaded) min 91 octane |
| Engine oil type | SAE 10W30 or 10W40, API SG min, JASO MA or MB |
| Engine oil capacity | |
|     After draining | 0.9 litre |
|     After engine disassembly | 1.0 litre |
| Coolant type | see Pre-ride checks |
| Cooling system capacity | |
|     Radiator and engine | 0.9 litre |
|     Reservoir | 0.4 litre |
| Gearbox oil | SAE 90W Hypoid gear oil or engine oil (see above) |
| Gearbox oil capacity | |
|     After draining | 190 ml |
|     After engine disassembly | 220 ml |
| Brake fluid | DOT 4 |
| Torque settings | |
|     Engine oil drain plug | 20 Nm |
|     Spark plug | 12 Nm |
|     Gearbox oil drain plug | 27 Nm |
|     Gearbox oil level plug | 13 Nm |

## Service schedule

**Note:** Always perform the Pre-ride checks before every service interval – see the beginning of this Manual.

| | Text section in this Chapter | Every 2500 miles (4000 km) | Every 5000 miles (8000 km) | Every 7500 miles (12,000 km) | Every 15,000 miles (24,000 km) |
|---|---|---|---|---|---|
| Air filter – replace* | 1 | | | ✔ | |
| Battery – check | 2 | ✔ | | | |
| Brake pad and shoe – wear check | 3 | ✔ | | | |
| Brake system – check** | 4 | ✔ | | | |
| Clutch – check | 5 | | ✔ | | |
| Cooling system – check*** | 6 | | ✔ | | |
| Crankcase breather – clean | 7 | ✔ | | | |
| Drive belt – check | 8 | | ✔ | | |
| Drive belt – replace | 8 | | | | ✔ |
| Engine oil – change | 9 | ✔ | | | |
| Fuel system – check | 10 | ✔ | | | |
| Gearbox oil change | 11 | | | | Every 2 years |
| Headlight aim – check | 12 | ✔ | | | |
| Nuts and bolts – tightness check | 14 | | ✔ | | |
| PAIR system – check | 15 | | | ✔ | |
| Spark plug – replace | 16 | | ✔ | | |
| Stand(s) – check and lubricate | 17 | ✔ | | | |
| Steering head bearings – check | 18 | | | ✔ | |
| Suspension – check | 19 | ✔ | | | |
| Throttle – check and adjust | 20 | ✔ | | | |
| Transmission case filter – clean | 21 | ✔ | | | |
| Valve clearances – check | 22 | ✔ | | | |
| Wheels and tyres – check | 23 | ✔ | | | |

* Replace the air filter more often if the scooter is ridden in constantly wet or dusty conditions.
** The brake fluid must be changed every 2 years, irrespective of mileage.
***Drain and refill with fresh coolant every 2 years, irrespective of mileage

# Pantheon 125 and 150

## Model identification

| | |
|---|---|
| Engine | 125 or 150 cc single cylinder, liquid-cooled four-stroke |
| Gearbox | Variable speed automatic, belt driven |
| Ignition | Fully transistorised |
| Fuel system | PGM-FI fuel injection |
| Front suspension | Telescopic fork |
| Rear suspension | Swingarm and twin shock |
| Front brake | Hydraulic disc |
| Rear brake | Hydraulic disc |
| Front tyre size | 110/90-13 |
| Rear tyre size | 130/70-12 |
| Overall length | 2090 mm |
| Overall width | 735 mm |
| Overall height | 1460 mm |
| Wheelbase | 1490 mm |
| Seat height | 770 mm |
| Ground clearance | 130 mm |
| Dry weight | 142 kg |
| Curb weight | 149 kg |
| Fuel tank capacity | 9.4 litres |

## Servicing specifications and lubricants

| | |
|---|---|
| Spark plug type | |
|     Standard | NGK CR8EH-9 or Denso U24FER9 |
|     Extended high speed riding | NGK CR9EH-9 or Denso U27FER9 |
| Spark plug electrode gap | 0.8 to 0.9 mm |
| Idle speed | 1400 to 1600 rpm |
| Disc brake pad wear limits | see Text |
| Drive belt wear limit (see text) | 21.5 mm |
| Throttle twistgrip freeplay | 2 to 6 mm |
| Valve clearances (engine COLD) | |
|     Intake valve | 0.13 to 0.19 mm |
|     Exhaust valve | 0.22 to 0.28 mm |
| Fuel | Petrol (unleaded) min 91 octane |
| Engine oil type | SAE 10W30 or 10W40, API SG min, JASO MA or MB |
| Engine oil capacity | |
|     After draining | 0.9 litre |
|     After engine disassembly | 1.0 litre |
| Coolant type | see Pre-ride checks |
| Cooling system capacity | |
|     Radiator and engine | 0.95 litre |
|     Reservoir | 0.26 litre |
| Gearbox oil | SAE 90W Hypoid gear oil or engine oil (see above) |
| Gearbox oil capacity | |
|     After draining | 190 ml |
|     After engine disassembly | 220 ml |
| Brake fluid | DOT 4 |
| Torque settings | |
|     Engine oil drain plug | 20 Nm |
|     Spark plug | 12 Nm |
|     Gearbox oil drain plug | 31 Nm |
|     Gearbox oil level plug | 13 Nm |

## Service schedule

*Note:* Always perform the Pre-ride checks before every service interval – see the beginning of this Manual.

| | Text section in this Chapter | Every 2500 miles (4000 km) | Every 5000 miles (8000 km) | Every 7500 miles (12,000 km) | Every 15,000 miles (24,000 km) |
|---|---|---|---|---|---|
| Air filter – replace* | 1 | | | ✔ | |
| Battery – check | 2 | ✔ | | | |
| Brake pad and shoe – wear check | 3 | ✔ | | | |
| Brake system – check** | 4 | ✔ | | | |
| Clutch – check | 5 | | ✔ | | |
| Cooling system – check*** | 6 | | ✔ | | |
| Crankcase breather – clean | 7 | ✔ | | | |
| Drive belt – check | 8 | | ✔ | | |
| Drive belt – replace | 8 | | | | ✔ |
| Engine oil – change | 9 | ✔ | | | |
| Fuel system – check | 10 | ✔ | | | |
| Gearbox oil change | 11 | | | | Every 2 years |
| Headlight aim – check | 12 | ✔ | | | |
| Nuts and bolts – tightness check | 14 | | ✔ | | |
| Spark plug – replace | 16 | | ✔ | | |
| Stand(s) – check and lubricate | 17 | ✔ | | | |
| Steering head bearings – check | 18 | | | ✔ | |
| Suspension – check | 19 | ✔ | | | |
| Throttle – check and adjust | 20 | ✔ | | | |
| Transmission case filter – clean | 21 | ✔ | | | |
| Valve clearances – check | 22 | ✔ | | | |
| Wheels and tyres – check | 23 | ✔ | | | |

* Replace the air filter more often if the scooter is ridden in constantly wet or dusty conditions.
** The brake fluid must be changed every 2 years, irrespective of mileage.
***Drain and refill with fresh coolant every 2 years, irrespective of mileage

# S-wing 125 and 150

## Model identification

| | |
|---|---|
| Engine | 125 or 150 cc single cylinder, liquid-cooled four-stroke |
| Gearbox | Variable speed automatic, belt driven |
| Ignition | Fully transistorised |
| Fuel system | PGM-FI fuel injection |
| Front suspension | Telescopic fork |
| Rear suspension | Swingarm and twin shock |
| Front brake | Hydraulic disc, ABS on A models |
| Rear brake | Hydraulic disc, ABS on A models |
| Front tyre size | 110/90-13 |
| Rear tyre size | 130/70-12 |
| Overall length | 2090 mm |
| Overall width | 745 mm |
| Overall height | 1435 mm |
| Wheelbase | 1490 mm |
| Seat height | 772 mm |
| Ground clearance | 132 mm |
| Curb weight | |
|     S-wing 125 | 156 kg |
|     S-wing 125A | 158 kg |
|     S-wing 150 | 158 kg |
|     S-wing 150A | 160 kg |
| Fuel tank capacity | 9.4 litres |

## Servicing specifications and lubricants

| | |
|---|---|
| Spark plug type | |
|     Standard | NGK CR8EH-9 or Denso U24FER9 |
|     Extended high speed riding | NGK CR9EH-9 or Denso U27FER9 |
| Spark plug electrode gap | 0.8 to 0.9 mm |
| Idle speed | 1400 to 1600 rpm |
| Disc brake pad wear limits | see Text |
| Drive belt wear limit (see text) | 21.5 mm |
| Throttle twistgrip freeplay | 2 to 6 mm |
| Valve clearances (engine COLD) | |
|     Intake valve | 0.14 to 0.18 mm |
|     Exhaust valve | 0.23 to 0.27 mm |
| Fuel | Petrol (unleaded) min 91 octane |
| Engine oil type | SAE 10W30 or 10W40, API SG min, JASO MA or MB |
| Engine oil capacity | |
|     After draining | 0.9 litre |
|     After engine disassembly | 1.0 litre |
| Coolant type | see Pre-ride checks |
| Cooling system capacity | |
|     Radiator and engine | 0.95 litre |
|     Reservoir | 0.26 litre |
| Gearbox oil | SAE 90W Hypoid gear oil or engine oil (see above) |
| Gearbox oil capacity | |
|     After draining | 190 ml |
|     After engine disassembly | 220 ml |
| Brake fluid | DOT 4 |
| Torque settings | |
|     Engine oil drain plug | 20 Nm |
|     Spark plug | 12 Nm |
|     Gearbox oil drain plug | 25 Nm |
|     Gearbox oil level plug | 13 Nm |

## Service schedule

*Note:* Always perform the Pre-ride checks before every service interval – see the beginning of this Manual.

| | Text section in this Chapter | Every 2500 miles (4000 km) | Every 5000 miles (8000 km) | Every 7500 miles (12,000 km) | Every 15,000 miles (24,000 km) |
|---|---|---|---|---|---|
| Air filter – replace* | 1 | | | ✔ | |
| Battery – check | 2 | ✔ | | | |
| Brake pad and shoe – wear check | 3 | ✔ | | | |
| Brake system – check** | 4 | ✔ | | | |
| Clutch – check | 5 | | ✔ | | |
| Cooling system – check*** | 6 | | ✔ | | |
| Crankcase breather – clean | 7 | ✔ | | | |
| Drive belt – check | 8 | | ✔ | | |
| Drive belt – replace | 8 | | | | ✔ |
| Engine oil – change | 9 | ✔ | | | |
| Fuel system – check | 10 | ✔ | | | |
| Gearbox oil change | 11 | | | | Every 2 years |
| Headlight aim – check | 12 | ✔ | | | |
| Nuts and bolts – tightness check | 14 | | ✔ | | |
| PAIR system – check | 15 | | | ✔ | |
| Spark plug – replace | 16 | | ✔ | | |
| Stand(s) – check and lubricate | 17 | ✔ | | | |
| Steering head bearings – check | 18 | | | ✔ | |
| Suspension – check | 19 | ✔ | | | |
| Throttle – check and adjust | 20 | ✔ | | | |
| Transmission case filter – clean | 21 | ✔ | | | |
| Valve clearances – check | 22 | ✔ | | | |
| Wheels and tyres – check | 23 | ✔ | | | |

* Replace the air filter more often if the scooter is ridden in constantly wet or dusty conditions.
** The brake fluid must be changed every 2 years, irrespective of mileage.
***Drain and refill with fresh coolant every 2 years, irrespective of mileage

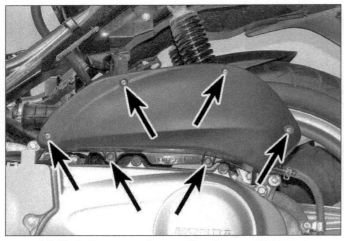

1.1 Undo the screws (arrowed) and remove the cover

1.2 Remove the filter

**Note:** *Refer to the model specifications at the beginning of this Chapter for service intervals*

## 1  Air filter

*Caution: If the machine is ridden in continuously wet or dusty conditions, the filter should be checked more frequently – if it is still serviceable you can clean it as in Step 3, rather than replacing it with a new one.*

**1** Undo the air filter cover screws and remove the cover **(see illustration)**. On Pantheon and S-wing models undo the two screws securing the filter element.
**2** Remove the filter from the housing, noting how it fits **(see illustration)**. Honda specify that it is replaced with a new one at every service interval.
**3** Clean the inside of the filter housing and the cover. Make sure the rubber sealing rings fitted in the grooves in the housing and cover rims are in good condition and properly seated – replace them with new ones if damaged, deformed or deteriorated **(see illustration)**.
**4** To clean the filter in between service intervals, tap it on a hard surface, with the

outer side facing down, to dislodge any dirt, then blow through it with compressed air, directing the air in the opposite way to normal flow, i.e. from the inner side. Do not use any solvents or cleaning agents on the element.
**5** Fit the filter into the housing, making sure it is properly seated **(see illustration 1.2)**. On Pantheon and S-wing models secure it with the two screws.
**6** Fit the filter cover and secure it with its screws **(see illustration)**.

## 2  Battery

*Caution: Be extremely careful when handling or working around the battery. The electrolyte is very caustic and an explosive gas (hydrogen) is given off when the battery is charging.*

**1** All models covered in this manual are fitted with a sealed MF (maintenance free) battery. **Note:** *Do not attempt to remove the battery caps to check the electrolyte level or battery specific gravity. Removal will damage the caps, resulting in electrolyte leakage and battery damage.*
**2** All that should be done is to check that

the terminals are clean and tight and that the casing is not damaged or leaking. See Chapter 10 for further details.
**3** If the machine is not in regular use, disconnect the battery, and give it a refresher charge every month to six weeks (see Chapter 10).
**4** See Chapter 10 for battery voltage test.

## 3  Brake pads and shoes

### *Disc brake pad wear check*

**1** Each brake pad has wear indicators, either in the form of cut-outs in the face of the friction material, or in the form of a groove in the side of the friction material. The wear indicators should be plainly visible by looking at the edges of the friction material from the best vantage point, but note that an accumulation of road dirt and brake dust could make them difficult to see **(see illustration)**.
**2** If the indicators aren't visible, then the amount of friction material remaining should be, and it will be obvious when the pads need replacing. Honda do not specify a minimum thickness for the friction material, but anything less than 1 mm should be considered worn.

1.3 Make sure each sealing ring (arrowed) is in good condition and seated correctly

1.6 Fit the cover

3.1 Front brake pad wear indicator cut-out (arrowed)

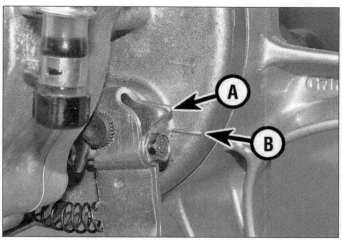

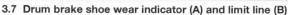

**3.7 Drum brake shoe wear indicator (A) and limit line (B)**

**3.8 Check and measure the drum lining**

**Note:** *Some after-market pads may use different indicators to those on the original equipment.*

3 If the pads are worn to or beyond the wear indicator (i.e. the bottom of the cut-out or the beginning of the groove) or there is little friction material remaining, they must be replaced with new ones, though it is advisable to fit new pads before they become this worn.

4 If the pads are dirty or if you are in doubt as to the amount of friction material remaining, remove them for inspection (see Chapter 8). If the pads are excessively worn, check the brake discs (see Chapter 8).

5 Refer to Chapter 8 for details of pad removal and installation.

### Drum brake shoe and drum wear check

6 Make sure the amount of rear brake pedal freeplay is correct (see Section 4). As the brake shoes wear and the freeplay is adjusted to compensate, the wear indicator moves closer to the wear limit line on the casing.

7 Apply the brake and check the position of the wear indicator on the top of the brake arm in relation to the limit line on the casing **(see illustration)**. If the indicator has reached the line replace the brake shoes with new ones (see Chapter 8).

8 With the wheel removed check the condition of the drum lining, and measure its internal diameter **(see illustration)**. If it has worn to or beyond the service limit specified replace the wheel with a new one.

### 4 Brake system

**Note:** *All models are fitted with a linked braking system, whereby operation of the left-hand brake lever actuates not only the rear brake but also the front brake. Operation*

of the right-hand brake lever actuates only the front brake.

1 A routine check of the brake system will ensure that any problems are discovered and remedied before the rider's safety is jeopardised.

2 Make sure all brake fasteners, including the reservoir cover screws, brake hose banjo bolts and caliper mounting bolts, are tight.

3 Make sure the brake light operates when each brake lever is pulled in. The brake light switches are not adjustable. If they fail to operate properly, check them (see Chapter 10).

### Brake levers

4 Check the brake levers for looseness, rough action, excessive play and other damage. Replace any worn or damaged parts with new ones (see Chapter 7).

5 The lever pivots should be lubricated periodically to reduce wear and ensure safe and trouble-free operation.

6 In order for the lubricant to be applied where it will do the most good, the lever should be removed (see Chapter 7). However, if an aerosol lubricant is being used, it can be applied to the pivot joint gaps and will usually work its way into the areas where friction occurs. If motor oil or light grease is being

used, apply it sparingly as it may attract dirt (which could cause the controls to bind or wear at an accelerated rate). **Note:** *One of the best lubricants for the control lever pivots is a dry-film lubricant.*

7 Where disc brakes are fitted, if the lever action is spongy (i.e. the lever does not come up hard and can travel all the way to the handlebar, first check the fluid level (see *Pre-ride checks*), then bleed the brakes (see Chapter 8).

8 Where a rear drum brake is fitted check the amount of freeplay in the left-hand brake lever (measured in terms of the amount of travel in the end of the lever) before the brake comes on **(see illustration)** – it should be as specified at the beginning of the Chapter. If not adjust it by turning the adjuster nut on the brake drum end of the brake cable as required until the freeplay is correct – to reduce freeplay in the lever, turn the nut clockwise; to increase freeplay, turn the nut anti-clockwise **(see illustration)**. Make sure the nut is set so its cut-out seats around the pivot piece in the arm. After adjustment turn the rear wheel and check that there is no brake drag. Following adjustment of the drum brake the cable for the linked braking system connected to the front brake must also be checked and if necessary adjusted. Remove the front handlebar cover

**4.8a Check the amount of freeplay at the lever end . . .**

**4.8b . . . and adjust if necessary using the nut on the end of the cable**

4.8c Check for the correct amount of freeplay at the end of the cable (arrowed) . . .

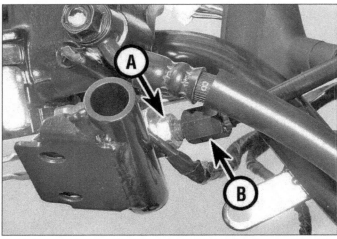

4.8d . . . and adjust if necessary by slackening the nut (A) and turning the adjuster (B)

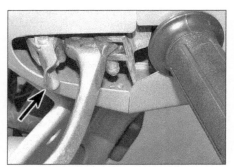

4.8e Check the brake lock lever (arrowed – metal type shown) as described

(see Chapter 9). Check that there is 0.5 to 1.0 mm of freeplay between the cable end and the cable joint piece (see illustration). If adjustment is required slacken the locknut on the adjuster, then turn the adjuster in or out as required until the amount of freeplay is correct, then tighten the locknut (see illustration).

Now check the operation of the brake lock – pull the brake lever in, then pull the lock lever in so that it sets (see illustration). Release the brake lever – the lock lever should stay in. Now pull the brake lever in again and check that the lock lever releases itself.

9 Where a rear disc brake is fitted place the scooter on its centrestand and raise the front wheel off the ground. Operate the left-hand brake lever and check that it actuates not only the rear brake, but also the front brake, by trying to spin the front wheel.

### Brake hoses and pipes

**Note:** *For a complete check of all brake hose and pipe connections, especially on models with a rear disc brake and on S-wing A models with ABS, remove the body covers and panels as required according to model for access (see Chapter 9).*

10 Where disc brakes are fitted, look for leaks at the hose connections. Twist and flex the hose while looking for cracks, bulges and

seeping fluid. Check extra carefully where the hose connects to the banjo fittings as this is a common area for hose failure. On 2009-on SH models with a rear disc brake, and on all Pantheon and S-wing models also check the hoses and pipes linking the front and rear brake systems via the delay valve, and on S-wing models with ABS via the modulator, removing the body panels as required for access – refer to Chapters 8 and 9.

11 Inspect the banjo fittings, and where applicable the pipe fittings; if they are rusted, cracked or damaged, fit new hoses.

12 Inspect the banjo union connections, and where applicable the pipe gland nuts, for leaking fluid (see illustrations). If they leak when tightened securely, unscrew the banjo bolt and fit new washers, or fit a new pipe and gland nuts (see Chapter 8).

13 Flexible hydraulic hoses will deteriorate with age and should be replaced with new ones every three years regardless of their apparent condition (see Chapter 8).

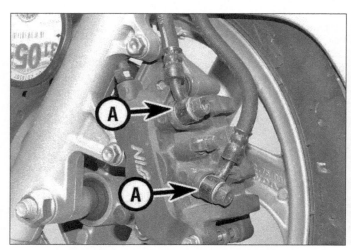

4.12a Check all hoses and banjo unions (A) . . .

4.12b . . . and any hose to pipe joints and pipe gland nuts (B)

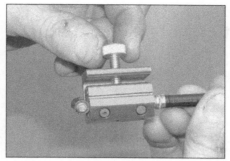
4.23a Fit the cable into the adapter . . .

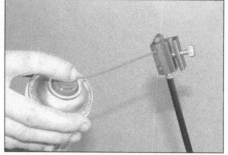
4.23b . . . and tighten the screw to seal it in . . .

4.23c . . . then apply the lubricant using the nozzle provided inserted in the hole in the adapter

### Brake fluid

**14** The fluid level in the master cylinder reservoir(s) should be checked before riding the machine (see *Pre-ride checks*).

**15** Brake fluid will degrade over a period of time. Honda recommends that it should be changed every 2 years, or whenever a new master cylinder or caliper is fitted. Refer to the brake bleeding and fluid change section in Chapter 8.

### Brake caliper and master cylinder seals

**16** Check the brake master cylinder(s) and caliper(s) for signs of leaking fluid.

**17** Brake system seals will deteriorate over a period of time and lose their effectiveness. Old master cylinder seals will cause sticky operation of the brake lever; old caliper seals will cause the pistons to stick or fluid to leak out. The seals should be renewed if defects are evident.

**18** Replace all the seals in the caliper(s) as a set – a rebuild kit for each caliper is available. Master cylinder seals are supplied as a kit along with a new piston and spring assembly (see Chapter 8).

### Drum brake cable

**19** The rear wheel should spin freely when the brake lever is not activated. If the brake is binding without the handlebar lever being pulled, first check that the lever is moving freely, and that there is the correct amount of freeplay (see Steps 4 to 6, and 8).

**20** Disconnect the cable from the left-hand brake lever, the actuating arm on the back of the brake drum, and the arm under the front brake lever (see Chapter 8). Check that the inner cable slides smoothly in the outer cable. If the action is stiff, inspect along the length of the outer cable for splits and kinks, and the ends of the inner cable for frays, and replace it with a new one if necessary (see Chapter 8).

**21** If there are no signs of damage, lubricate the cable (see Step 23). If the cable is still stiff after lubrication, replace it with a new one (see Chapter 8).

**22** The cable should be lubricated periodically to ensure safe and trouble-free operation.

**23** To lubricate the cable, disconnect it at its upper end and use a pressure adapter and aerosol cable lubricant **(see illustrations)**.

**24** Reconnect the cable and adjust the freeplay (see Step 8).

**25** If the handlebar lever and cable are in good condition, check the operation of the brake cam (see below).

### Drum brake cam

**26** To check the operation of the brake cam, first disconnect the end of the cable from the brake actuating arm. Note the fitting of the bush in the arm and the location of the cable return spring, and make sure that it is not damaged **(see illustrations)**.

**27** Apply the brake using hand pressure on the arm and ensure that the arm returns to the rest position when it is released. If the brake arm is binding in the backplate, follow the procedure in Chapter 8 to remove the brake shoes and inspect the brake cam and the springs on the brake shoes.

**28** Apply some copper grease to the bearing surfaces of the cam and its shaft before reassembly. Adjust the freeplay on completion (see Step 8).

*Caution: Do not apply too much grease otherwise there is a risk of it contaminating the brake drum and shoe linings.*

### 5 Clutch

**1** Refer to Chapter 3, remove the clutch drum, and check the condition and thickness of the friction material on the clutch shoes. If the friction material has worn down to or

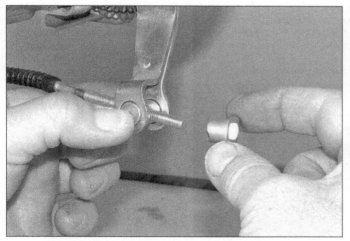
4.26a Fully unscrew the nut and draw the cable out . . .

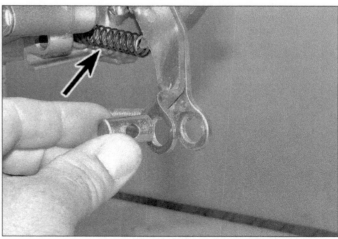
4.26b . . . retrieving the bush and noting the fitting of the return spring (arrowed)

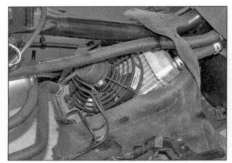

6.3a  Check the radiator and all cooling system hoses . . .

6.3b  . . . between it and the engine as described – Dylan shown

6.6  Straighten any fins that are bent

beyond the minimum thickness specified at the beginning of Chapter 3, or is otherwise damaged or contaminated, replace the shoes with a new set.

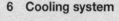
## 6  Cooling system

> **Warning: The engine must be cool before beginning this procedure.**

**1** Check the coolant level (see *Pre-ride checks*).
**2** Remove upper front panel on SH, Dylan, @ and PS models, and the floor panel(s) on all models (see Chapter 9). Check the entire cooling system for evidence of leaks. Examine each coolant hose along its entire length. Look for cracks, abrasions and other damage. Squeeze the hoses at various points. They should feel firm, yet pliable, and return to their original shape when released. If they are hard or perished, replace them with new ones (see Chapter 4).
**3** Check for evidence of leaks at each cooling system joint. Ensure that the hoses are pushed fully onto their unions and that the hose clips are tight **(see illustrations)**. Check the tension of any hose spring clips and replace them with new ones if they are loose.
**4** Check the hole in the underside of the water pump in right-hand crankcase cover for evidence of leakage – the hole drains any coolant should the internal pump seal fail **(see illustration 6.3b)**. If there is evidence of leakage remove the pump and replace the seals with new ones (see Chapter 4).

**5** Check the radiator for leaks and other damage. Leaks in the radiator leave tell-tale scale deposits or coolant stains on the outside of the core below the leak. If leaks are noted, remove the radiator (see Chapter 4) and have it repaired or replace it with a new one.
*Caution: Do not use a liquid leak stopping compound to try to repair leaks.*
**6** Inspect the radiator fins for mud, dirt and insects which will impede the flow of air through the radiator. If the fins are dirty, remove the radiator (see Chapter 4) and clean it using water or low pressure compressed air directed through the fins from the back. If the fins are bent or distorted, straighten them carefully with a screwdriver **(see illustration)**. If the air flow is restricted by bent or damaged fins over more than 30% of the radiator's surface area, fit a new radiator.
**7** Check the condition of the coolant in the reservoir. If it is rust-coloured or if accumulations of scale are visible, drain, flush and refill the system with new coolant (see Chapter 4). **Note:** *Honda recommend draining and refilling the cooling system with fresh coolant every 2 years.*
**8** Check the antifreeze content of the coolant with an antifreeze hydrometer. Sometimes coolant looks like it's in good condition, but is too weak to offer adequate protection. If the hydrometer indicates a weak mixture, drain, flush and refill the system (see Chapter 4).
**9** Start the engine and let it reach normal operating temperature, then check for leaks again.
**10** If the coolant level is consistently low, and no

evidence of leaks can be found, have the entire system pressure checked by a Honda dealer.

## 7  Crankcase breather

*Caution: If the machine is continually ridden in wet conditions or at full throttle, the crankcase breather should be drained more frequently. It should also be checked after washing the scooter, and if it has fallen over.*
**1** Locate the crankcase breather drain tube on the rear of the transmission casing, and place a suitable container or a wad of rag under it **(see illustration)**.
**2** Remove the plug and allow any deposits to drain into the container or onto the rag. Refit the plug when all deposits have drained.

## 8  Drive belt

**1** Referring to Chapter 3, remove the drive belt cover. Check along the entire length of the belt for cracks, splits, frays and damaged teeth and replace the belt with a new one if any damage is found **(see illustration)**.
**2** The edges of the belt will gradually wear away – black dust inside the casing is evidence of belt wear. Measure the width of the outer face of the belt and compare the result with the Specifications at the beginning of the Chapter **(see illustration)**.

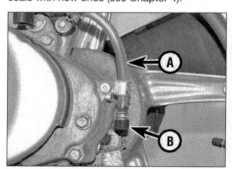

7.1  Crankcase breather drain tube (A) and its plug (B)

8.1  Check the condition of the belt . . .

8.2  . . . and measure its width as shown

**9.4 Unscrew the oil filler cap to act as a vent**

**9.5a Unscrew the oil drain plug (arrowed) . . .**

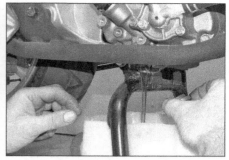

**9.5b . . . and allow the oil to completely drain**

**3** If the drive belt has worn below the limit, or if the belt shows signs of fraying or cracking, or if it is contaminated with oil or grease, or at the specified interval regardless of condition, it must be replaced with a new one (see Chapter 3). **Note:** *If there is any doubt about the condition of the drive belt, replace it with a new one just in case – a broken belt could cause severe damage to engine or gearbox components.*

**4** In the event of premature belt wear, the cause should be investigated (see Chapter 3).

**5** Oil or grease inside the casing is evidence that a crankshaft, gearbox shaft or clutch assembly seal has failed. Trace the source of the leak and fit a new seal.

**6** Clean any dust from inside the casing before installing the drive belt cover.

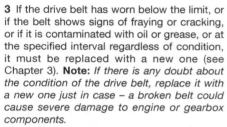

## 9 Engine oil and strainer

> *Warning: Be careful when draining the oil, as the exhaust pipe, the engine, and the oil itself can cause severe burns. To avoid getting oil over your hands it is best to wear some disposable latex or nitrile gloves, cheaply available from most chemists and hardware stores.*

**1** Consistent routine oil changes are the single most important maintenance procedure you can perform. The oil not only lubricates the internal parts of the engine, but it also acts as a coolant, a cleaner, a sealant, and a protector. Because of these demands, the oil takes a terrific amount of abuse and should be replaced often with new oil of the recommended grade and type. Saving a little money on the difference in cost between a good oil and a cheap oil won't pay off if the engine is damaged.

**2** The instrument cluster features an oil change indicator light that comes on or flashes (depending on model) after the specified mileage has been covered since the last oil change. After changing the oil be sure to reset the indicator light so that it will come on again

after the next specified mileage has been covered – see Step 11. If the oil is changed before the indicator light comes on, make sure you reset it in the same way.

*Caution: Do not run the engine in an enclosed space such as a garage or workshop.*

**3** Before changing the oil, warm up the engine so the oil will drain easily. Stop the engine and turn the ignition OFF, and wait for a few minutes to allow the oil to drain to the bottom of the engine. Support the scooter on its centre stand, and position a clean drain tray under the engine.

**4** Unscrew the oil filler cap to vent the crankcase and to act as a reminder that there is no oil in the engine **(see illustration)**.

**5** Unscrew the oil drain plug and remove the spring and the strainer, and allow the oil to flow into the drain tray **(see illustrations)**.

Discard the O-ring on the drain plug as a new one must be used on reassembly.

**6** Clean the strainer in solvent and remove any debris caught in the mesh **(see illustration)**. Check the mesh for splits or holes and replace it with a new one if necessary.

**7** When the oil has completely drained, fit a new O-ring smeared with clean oil onto the drain plug **(see illustration)**. Fit the spring onto the drain plug and the strainer with its rounded end facing down into the spring as shown, then insert them into the crankcase and tighten the drain plug to the torque setting specified at the beginning of the Chapter **(see illustrations)**. Do not overtighten the plug as damage to the threads will result.

**8** Refill the engine to the correct level using the recommended type and amount of oil (see *Pre-ride checks*). Make sure the O-ring on the underside of the filler cap is in good

**9.6 Clean the strainer and check the mesh**

**9.7a Fit a new O-ring onto the drain plug . . .**

**9.7b . . . then assemble the plug, spring and strainer as shown . . .**

**9.7c . . . and fit them into the engine**

**9.11a Reset button (arrowed) – @ model shown**

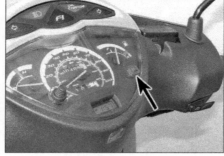

**9.11b Clock reset button (arrowed) – SH shown, PS similar**

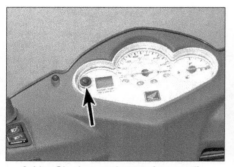

**9.11c Clock reset button (arrowed) – Dylan**

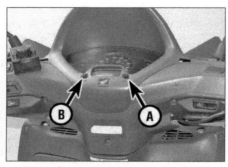

**9.11d Clock reset button (A) and trip reset (B) – Pantheon**

condition and properly seated. Fit a new one if necessary. Wipe it clean and smear new oil onto it. Fit the cap and tighten it by hand.

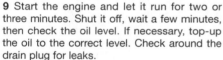

**HAYNES HINT** *Saving a little money on the difference between good and cheap oils won't pay off if the engine is damaged as a result.*

**9** Start the engine and let it run for two or three minutes. Shut it off, wait a few minutes, then check the oil level. If necessary, top-up the oil to the correct level. Check around the drain plug for leaks.
**10** The old oil drained from the engine cannot be re-used and should be disposed of properly. Check with your local refuse disposal company, disposal facility or environmental agency to see whether they will accept the

used oil for recycling. Don't pour used oil into drains or onto the ground.

**HAYNES HINT** *Check the old oil carefully – if it is very metallic coloured, then the engine is experiencing wear from break-in (new engine) or from insufficient lubrication. If there are flakes or chips of metal in the oil, then something is drastically wrong internally and the engine will have to be disassembled for inspection and repair.*

**11** Now reset the oil change indicator light as described for you model:
● On 2001 to 2004 SH models and all @ models, turn the ignition switch on – the light will come on and stay on; if the oil was changed before the light was on, it will

come on and then go off. Push the reset button *(see illustration)* and hold it down for more than one second, until the light either goes off (if it was on), or until the light blinks twice (if it was off). Release the reset button and turn the ignition switch off.
● On 2005-on SH models and all PS models, make sure the ignition switch is off. Hold the clock reset button *(see illustration)* down and turn the ignition switch on, and keep the button held down until the indicator light goes off (if the oil was changed because the indicator light was on), or comes on for two seconds (if the oil was changed before the light was on). Release the reset button and turn the ignition switch off.
● On Dylan models, make sure the ignition switch is off. Hold the clock reset button *(see illustration)* down and turn the ignition switch on, then release the reset button. Turn the ignition switch off, then turn it on again and check that the indicator light does not come on.
● On Pantheon models, turn the ignition switch on. Hold the clock reset and trip reset buttons *(see illustration)* down simultaneously, and keep the buttons held down until the indicator light goes off (if the oil was changed because the indicator light was on), or comes on for two seconds (if the oil was changed before the light was on). Release the reset buttons and turn the ignition switch off.
● On S-wing models, make sure the ignition switch is off. Hold the reset button (the right-hand of the two reset buttons in the centre of the instrument cluster) down and turn the ignition switch on, and keep the button held down until the indicator light goes off (if the oil was changed because the indicator light was on), or comes on for two seconds (if the oil was changed before the light was on). Release the reset button and turn the ignition switch off.

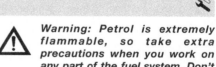

**10 Fuel system**

**⚠ Warning:** *Petrol is extremely flammable, so take extra precautions when you work on any part of the fuel system. Don't smoke or allow open flames or bare light bulbs near the work area, and don't work in a garage where a natural gas-type appliance is present. If you spill any fuel on your skin, rinse it off immediately with soap and water. When you perform any kind of work on the fuel system, wear safety glasses and have a fire extinguisher suitable for a Class B type fire (flammable liquids) on hand.*

**1** Remove the storage compartment (see Chapter 9).

**10.2a Fuel tap (arrowed) and hoses on carburettor models**

**10.2b Fuel hose connection with the fuel pump on fuel injection models**

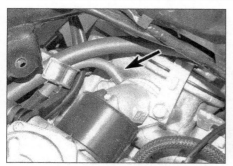

10.4 Fuel tap vacuum hose connection (arrowed) at the carburettor end

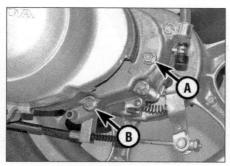

11.1 Gearbox oil filler/level plug (A), and oil drain plug (B)

11.3 Unscrew the filler/level plug . . .

**2** Check the fuel tank and the fuel hose between it and the carburettor or throttle body for signs of leakage, deterioration or damage **(see illustrations)**. In particular check that there is no leakage from the fuel hose. Replace the fuel hose with a new one if it is cracked or deteriorated. Make sure that the hose is secure on its union at each end.

**3** If there is evidence of leakage from around the tap or the fuel pump, remove the tap or pump and replace the sealing O-ring with a new one (see Chapter 5A or B).

**4** The fuel tap on carburettor models is vacuum operated and should be closed when the engine is not running. Disconnect the fuel hose (the upper hose) from the tap to check that the valve inside is not leaking **(see illustration 10.2a)**. If the valve is leaking, fit a new tap (see Chapter 5A). Make sure the vacuum hose is secure on its union at each end, and check for cracks and deterioration **(see illustration)**. Replace it with a new one if necessary.

**5** On carburettor models cleaning or replacement of the fuel filter is advised after a particularly high mileage has been covered or if fuel starvation is suspected (see Chapter 5A). The filter is fitted to the tap inside the tank, and is available separately from the tap. On Fuel injection models the filter is an integral component of the fuel pump and is not available separately.

**6** If the carburettor gaskets are leaking, the carburettor should be disassembled and

rebuilt using new gaskets and seals (see Chapter 5A).

**7** If fuel starvation is suspected, and if there is a suction on the fuel filler cap caused by a vacuum inside the tank as fuel is used, the vent in the fuel cap is blocked. You could try to clear the vent, but it is best to fit a new cap.

**8** If the fuel gauge is believed to be faulty, check the operation of the gauge and sensor (see Chapter 5A or B).

## 11 Gearbox oil

### Level check

**1** The oil level is checked via the filler plug which also acts as a level plug; the filler/level plug is on the rear of the gearbox casing **(see illustration)**.

**2** Place the scooter on its centrestand on level ground, making sure the rear wheel is off the ground, then start the engine and run it fast enough to get the rear wheel turning. Stop the engine and leave it for a couple of minutes. Check for leaks around the filler/level plug, and the drain plug.

**3** Clean around the filler/level plug then unscrew the plug from the gearbox casing **(see illustration)**.

**4** The oil level should come up to the lower

threads so that it is visible on the threads, and may just dribble out over them **(see illustration)**.

**5** If there is no oil visible top the gearbox up with the grade and type of oil specified at the beginning of the chapter using a pump-type oil can or oil bottle with a pipe fitting that can be inserted in the hole **(see illustration)**. Do not overfill. If necessary allow any excess oil to dribble out until the level is correct as described in Step 4.

**6** Fit the plug and tighten it to the torque setting specified at the beginning of the Chapter **(see illustration 11.3)**.

⚠ *Warning: If the oil level is very low, or oil is leaking from the gearbox, refer to Chapter 3 and inspect the condition of the seals and gaskets and replace them with new ones as necessary.*

### Oil change

**7** Position a clean drain tray below the gearbox **(see illustration 11.1)**. Unscrew the filler/level plug to vent the case and to act as a reminder that there is no oil in it **(see illustration 11.3)**.

**8** Unscrew the oil drain plug and allow the oil to drain into the tray **(see illustration)**. Discard the sealing washer on the plug as a new one should be used.

**9** When the oil has completely drained, fit the drain plug using a new sealing washer, and tighten it to the torque setting specified at the

11.4 . . . the oil should be visible and just dribble over the threads

11.5 Using an oil can to top the gearbox up

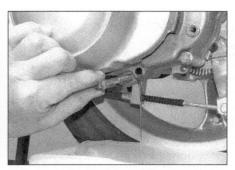

11.8 Unscrew the drain plug and allow the oil to drain

**11.9 Fit the drain plug using a new sealing washer**

**12.3a Headlight adjuster screw (arrowed) – SH models**

**12.3b Headlight adjuster screw (arrowed) – PS models**

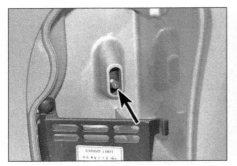

**12.4 Headlight adjuster screw (arrowed) – Dylan and @ models**

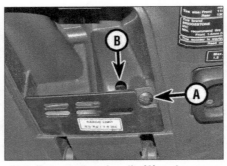

**12.5 Release the trim clip (A) and remove the guard to access the adjuster screw (B)**

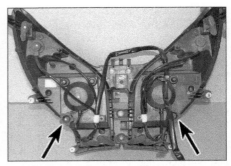

**12.6 Headlight adjuster knobs (arrowed)**

beginning of the Chapter **(see illustration)**. Avoid over-tightening, as damage to the casing will result.

**10** Refill the gearbox using the grade and type of oil specified at the beginning of the chapter until it is at the level of the filler/level plug hole threads (see Steps 5 and 4). Fit the filler/level plug and tighten it to the specified torque setting.

**11** Refer to Steps 2 to 5 and check the oil level again after riding the scooter for a few minutes and, if necessary, add more oil. Check around the drain plug for leaks.

**12** The old oil drained from the gearbox cannot be re-used and should be disposed of properly. Check with your local refuse disposal company, disposal facility or environmental agency to see whether they will accept the used oil for recycling. Don't pour used oil into drains or onto the ground.

## 12 Headlight aim

**Note:** *An improperly adjusted headlight may cause problems for oncoming traffic or provide poor, unsafe illumination of the road ahead. Before adjusting the headlight aim, be sure to consult with local traffic laws and regulations.*

**1** The headlight beam can be adjusted vertically. Before making any adjustment, check that the tyre pressures are correct and the suspension is adjusted as required. Make any adjustments to the headlight aim with the machine on level

ground, with the fuel tank half full and with an assistant sitting on the seat. If the bike is usually ridden with a passenger on the back, have a second assistant to do this.

**2** Adjustment is made by turning the adjuster screw on the headlight unit as follows.

**3** On SH and PS models the adjuster screw is located at the front centre below the headlight unit **(see illustrations)**. Using a screwdriver turn the screw anti-clockwise to move the beam up, and clockwise to move it down.

**4** On Dylan and @ models, open the glove box. Use a screwdriver to turn the adjuster screw on the back of the headlight unit to move the beam up or down as required **(see illustration)**.

**5** On Pantheon models, open the glove box, then release the trim clip (see Chapter 9, Section 1) and remove the guard **(see illustration)**. The adjuster screw is on the back of the headlight unit. Using a screwdriver turn the screw

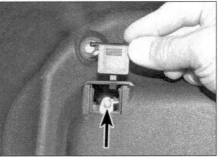
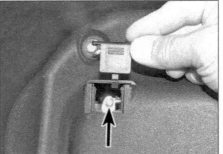

**13.2 Remove the small panel to access the adjuster screw (arrowed)**

clockwise to move the beam down, and anti-clockwise to move it up.

**6** On S-wing models, the adjuster knob for each headlight is located behind the headlight and is accessed by reaching up under it from the front. Turn the knob clockwise to move the beam up, and anti-clockwise to move it down **(see illustration)**.

## 13 Idle speed

### *Carburettor models*

**1** The idle speed (engine running with the throttle twistgrip closed) should be checked and adjusted when it is obviously too high or too low. Before adjusting the idle speed, make sure the throttle cable is correctly adjusted, the spark plug is in good condition with the correct gap, the air filter is clean, and the valve clearances are correct, referring to the relevant Sections in this Chapter).

**2** The engine should be at normal operating temperature, which is usually reached after 10 to 15 minutes of stop-and-go riding. Support the machine on its centre stand and make sure the rear wheel is clear of the ground. Lift the seat and remove the small access panel from the storage compartment to access the idle speed adjuster screw **(see illustration)**.

⚠ *Warning: Do not allow exhaust gases to build up in the work area; either perform the check*

15.1a  PAIR control valve (arrowed) . . .

15.1b  . . . and reed valve (arrowed)

16.3  Pull the cap off the spark plug

*outside or use an exhaust gas extraction system*

**3** With the engine running, turn the screw as required to set the idle speed correctly.

**4** As no tachometer is fitted to enable the idle speed to be compared with that specified, it is sufficient to ensure that at idle the engine speed is steady and does not falter, and that it is not so high that the automatic gearbox engages, or so low that the engine stalls. If you are unsure as to what the correct speed should be take the scooter to a Honda dealer.

**5** Snap the throttle open and shut a few times, then recheck the idle speed. If necessary, repeat the adjustment procedure.

**6** If a smooth, steady idle can't be achieved, and all the items listed in Step 1 have been checked, the fuel/air mixture may be incorrect (see Chapter 5A).

**7** If the idle speed has been adjusted, recheck the throttle cable freeplay.

### Fuel injection models

**8** The idle speed is controlled electronically by the idle air control valve and is not adjustable – if it is incorrect, or the engine is difficult to start and/or does not idle smoothly, refer to Chapter 5B, Section 5.

## 14  Nuts and bolts

**1** Since vibration tends to loosen fasteners, all nuts, bolts, screws, etc. should be periodically checked for proper tightness.

**2** Pay particular attention to the following:

*Spark plug*
*Carburettor/throttle body clamps*
*Engine oil drain plug*
*Gearbox oil filler/level and drain plugs*
*Stand pivot bolts*
*Engine mounting bolts*
*Suspension bolts*
*Wheel bolts*
*Brake caliper mounting bolts (disc brakes)*
*Brake hose banjo bolts (disc brakes)*
*Exhaust system bolts/nuts*

**3** If a torque wrench is available, use it along with the torque specifications given throughout this manual.

## 15  PAIR (pulse secondary air supply) system

**Note:** *Fitted to all models except the Pantheon*

**1** To reduce the amount of unburned hydrocarbons released in the exhaust gases, a pulse secondary air supply (PAIR) system is fitted. The system consists of an air supply hose connected between the air compensation chamber or filter housing (according to model) and a control valve, and another hose between the control valve and a reed valve on the engine, which is linked to the exhaust port via an air passage **(see illustrations)**. The control valve is actuated electronically by the ECU.

**2** Under normal running conditions, the ECU opens up the PAIR control valve which then allows filtered air to be drawn through it and the reed valve and cylinder head passage and into the exhaust port. The air mixes with the exhaust gases, causing any unburned particles of the fuel in the mixture to be burnt in the exhaust port/pipes. This process changes a considerable amount of hydrocarbons and carbon monoxide into relatively harmless carbon dioxide and water. The reed valve in the valve cover is fitted to prevent the flow of exhaust gases back up the cylinder head passage and into the control valve and air filter housing. When the throttle is closed on over-run the ECU closes the control valve to prevent popping in the exhaust.

**3** The system is not adjustable and requires little maintenance. Check that the hoses are

16.5  Unscrew and remove the plug

not kinked or pinched, are in good condition and are securely connected at each end – refer to Chapter 5A or 5B for access. Replace any hoses that are cracked, split or generally deteriorated with new ones.

**4** Refer to Chapter 5A or 5B for further information on the system and for checks if it is believed to be faulty.

## 16  Spark plug

**1** Make sure your spark plug socket is the correct size (16 mm hex) before attempting to remove the plug – a suitable one is supplied in the Scooter's tool kit.

**2** Remove the maintenance access panel to the spark plug on the right-hand side of the engine (see Chapter 9).

**3** Pull the cap off the spark plug **(see illustration)**.

**4** Clean the area around the base of the spark plug to prevent any dirt falling into the engine.

**5** Using either the plug removing tool supplied in the toolkit or a deep spark plug socket, unscrew and remove the plug from the cylinder head **(see illustration)**.

**6** Check the condition of the electrodes, referring to the spark plug reading chart at the end of this manual if signs of contamination are evident.

**7** Clean the plug with a wire brush. Examine the tips of the electrodes; if a tip has rounded off, the plug is worn. Measure the gap between the two electrodes using a feeler gauge or a wire type gauge **(see illustration)**. The gap should be

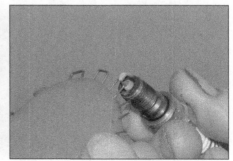

16.7a  Using a wire type gauge to measure the spark plug electrode gap

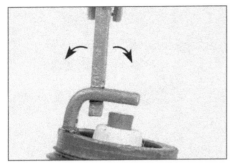

**16.7b  Adjusting the gap using the fitting provided on the tool**

as given in the Specifications at the beginning of this chapter; if necessary adjust the gap by bending the side electrode (see illustration).

8 Check the threads, the washer and the ceramic insulator body for cracks and other damage.

9 If the plug is worn or damaged, or if any deposits cannot be cleaned off, replace the plug with a new one. If in any doubt as to the condition of the plug replace it with a new one – the expense is minimal. At the prescribed interval, whatever the condition of the existing spark plug, remove the plug as described above and install a new one.

10 Thread the plug into the cylinder head until the washer seats **(see illustration)**. Since the cylinder head is made of aluminium, which is soft and easily damaged, thread the plug as far as possible by hand. Once the plug is finger-tight, the job can be finished with the tool supplied or a socket drive **(see illustration 16.5)**. If a new plug is being installed, tighten it by 1/2 a turn after the washer has seated. If the old plug is being reused, tighten it by 1/8 to 1/4 turn after the washer has seated, or if a torque wrench can be applied, tighten the spark plug to the torque setting specified at the beginning of the Chapter. Otherwise tighten it according to the instructions on the box. Do not over-tighten it.

11 Fit the spark plug cap, making sure it locates correctly onto the plug **(see illustration**

  *Stripped plug threads in the cylinder head can be repaired with a Heli-Coil insert – see 'Tools and Workshop Tips' in the Reference section.*

**16.3)**. Install the access panel (see Chapter 9).

## 17 Stand(s)

1 The return spring(s) must be capable of retracting the stand fully and holding it retracted when the machine is in use. If the spring has sagged or broken it must be renewed (see Chapter 7).

2 Since the stand is exposed to the elements, from time to time, depending on the extent of use, the condition of the stand and the conditions the scooter is ridden in, it should be lubricated periodically to ensure safe and trouble-free operation.

3 In order for the lubricant to be applied where it will do the most good, the stand should be removed, and the old grease cleaned off (see Chapter 7). However, if chain and cable lubricant is being used, it can be applied to the pivot joint gaps and will usually work its way into the areas where friction occurs. If motor oil or light grease is being used, apply it sparingly as it may attract dirt (which could cause the controls to bind or wear at an accelerated rate).

## 18 Steering head bearings

### Check

1 The steering head bearings consist of ball bearings which run in races at the top and

bottom of the steering head. The races can become dented or rough during normal use and the balls will gradually wear. In extreme cases, worn or loose steering head bearings can cause steering wobble – a condition that is potentially dangerous.

2 Support the scooter on its centre stand with the front wheel off the ground. **Note:** *Do not rest the weight of the scooter on the belly panel – have an assistant push down on the rear or place a support under the frame once the belly panel has been removed (see Chapter 9).*

3 Point the front wheel straight-ahead and slowly turn the handlebars from side-to-side. Any dents or roughness in the bearing races will be felt and the bars will not move smoothly and freely. If the bearings are damaged they must be replaced with new ones (see Chapter 7).

4 Again point the wheel straight-ahead, and tap the front of the wheel to one side. The wheel should 'fall' under its own weight to the limit of its lock, indicating that the bearings are not too tight (take into account the restriction that cables and wiring may have). Check for similar movement to the other side.

5 Next, grasp the front suspension and try to move it forwards and backwards **(see illustration)**. Any freeplay in the steering head bearings will be felt as front-to-rear movement of the steering stem. If play is felt in the

**HAYNES HiNT** *Make sure you are not mistaking any movement between the bike and stand, or between the stand and the ground, for freeplay in the bearings. Do not pull and push the forks too hard – a gentle movement is all that is needed.*

bearings, follow the procedure described below to adjust them.

6 Over a period of time the grease in the bearings will harden or may be washed

**16.10  Thread the plug into the head by hand to prevent cross-threading**

**18.5  Checking for freeplay in the steering head bearings**

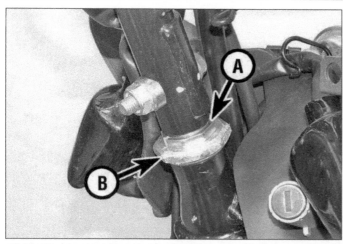

18.8a Steering head bearing locknut (A) and adjuster nut (B) – PS model shown

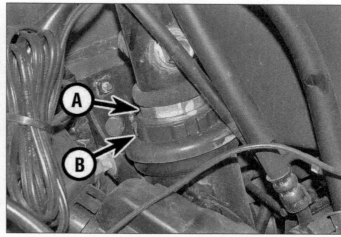

18.8b Steering head bearing locknut (A) and adjuster nut (B) – Pantheon/S-wing type

out. Follow the procedure in Chapter 7 to disassemble the steering head and re-grease the bearings. If the bearings are damaged they must be replaced with new ones (see Chapter 7).

### Adjustment

7 On SH, PS and S-wing models remove the inner front panel (see Chapter 9). On Dylan, @ and Pantheon models remove the upper front panel, and then if required for better access the inner front panel (see Chapter 9).
8 Slacken the locknut **(see illustrations)**.
9 Turn the adjuster nut, on Pantheon and S-wing models using a suitable drift located in one of the notches, either clockwise to tighten the head bearings or anti-clockwise to loosen them, and only moving it a small amount at a time. After each small adjustment recheck the freeplay as described in steps 2 to 5, before making further adjustments. The object is to set the adjuster nut so that the bearings are under a very light loading, just enough to remove any freeplay, but not so much that the steering does not move freely from side-to-side as described in the check procedure above.
*Caution: Take great care not to apply excessive pressure because this will cause*

*premature failure of the bearings.*
10 If the bearings cannot be correctly adjusted, disassemble the steering head and check the bearings and races (see Chapter 7).
11 With the bearings correctly adjusted, tighten the locknut tight – where no lock washer is fitted between the locknut and adjuster nut make sure the adjuster nut does not turn as you tighten the locknut **(see illustration)**.
12 Check the bearing adjustment as described in steps 2 to 5 and re-adjust if necessary.
13 Install the body panel(s) as required according to model (see Chapter 9).

## 19 Suspension

1 The suspension components must be maintained in top operating condition to ensure rider safety. Loose, worn or damaged suspension parts decrease the scooter's stability and control.

### Front suspension

2 While standing alongside the scooter, apply the front brake and push on the handlebars to

compress the suspension several times **(see illustration)**. See if it moves up-and-down smoothly without binding. If binding is felt, the suspension should be disassembled and inspected (see Chapter 7).
3 Inspect the area around the dust seal for signs of oil leaks, then carefully lever up the seal using a flat-bladed screwdriver and inspect the area below it **(see illustration)**. If corrosion due to the ingress of water is evident, the seals must be replaced with new ones (see Chapter 7).
4 If oil is leaking, the oil seal has failed and the fork leg must be dismantled and a new seal fitted (see Chapter 7).
5 The chromed finish on the forks is prone to corrosion and pitting, so it is advisable to keep them as clean as possible and to spray them regularly with a rust inhibitor, otherwise the seals will not last long. If corrosion and pitting is evident, tackle it as early as possible to prevent it getting worse, and if necessary replace the fork inner tubes with new ones.
6 Check the tightness of all suspension nuts and bolts to ensure none have worked loose. Refer to the torque settings specified at the beginning of Chapter 7.

### Rear suspension

7 Inspect the rear shock absorbers for fluid

18.11 Where no washer is fitted between them, counter-hold the adjuster nut while tightening the locknut

19.2 Compress and release the front suspension

19.3 Check the tube for damage and signs of oil leakage

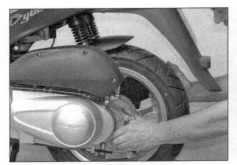

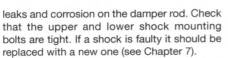

**19.9 Checking for play in the engine mounts**

**19.11 Checking for play in the rear shock mountings**

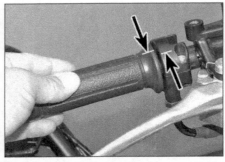

**20.4 Throttle cable freeplay is measured in terms of twistgrip rotation**

leaks and corrosion on the damper rod. Check that the upper and lower shock mounting bolts are tight. If a shock is faulty it should be replaced with a new one (see Chapter 7).

**8** With the aid of an assistant to support the scooter, compress the rear suspension several times. It should move up and down freely without binding. If any binding is felt, the worn or faulty component must be identified and renewed. The problem could be due to either the shock absorber or the front engine mounting/pivot assembly.

**9** Support the scooter on its centre stand so that the rear wheel is off the ground. Grip the engine/gearbox unit at the rear and attempt to rock it from side to side – there should be no discernible freeplay felt between the engine and frame **(see illustration)**. If there is movement, refer to the engine removal section in Chapter 2 and check the tightness of the bolts securing the front engine pivot assembly.

**10** Re-check for movement. If freeplay is felt, disconnect the rear shock absorber lower mountings and displace the shock, then check again – any freeplay in the front engine mountings should be more evident. If there is freeplay, inspect the mounting bushes in the front of the crankcase and the pivot bracket for wear (see Chapter 2).

**11** Reconnect the rear shock absorbers,

then grasp the top of the rear wheel and pull it upwards – there should be no discernible freeplay before the shock begins to compress **(see illustration)**. Any freeplay indicates a worn shock or shock mountings. The worn components must be identified and replaced with new ones (see Chapter 7).

## 20 Throttle

**1** Ensure the throttle twistgrip rotates easily from fully closed to fully open with the handlebars turned at various angles, and that the twistgrip returns automatically to the fully closed position when released.

**2** If the throttle sticks, this is probably due to a cable fault. Follow the procedure in Chapter 5A and disconnect the cable at the twistgrip end, then lubricate it using a pressure adapter and aerosol cable lubricant **(see illustrations 4.23a, b and c)**.

**3** If the throttle action is still stiff, remove the body panels as required to access the cable and check for a trapped or damaged section. If required, follow the procedure in Chapter 5A and install a new cable.

**4** With the throttle operating smoothly, check

for a small amount of freeplay in the cable, measured in terms of the amount of twistgrip rotation before the throttle opens, and compare the amount to the Specifications at the beginning of this Chapter **(see illustration)**.

**5** If there is insufficient or excessive freeplay, pull back the boot on the cable adjuster at the twistgrip end **(see illustration)**. Loosen the locknut on the adjuster, then turn it until the specified amount of freeplay is evident. Tighten the locknut. If the adjuster has reached its limit of adjustment, reset it so that freeplay is at a maximum. Remove the storage compartment (see Chapter 9). Loosen the nuts securing the lower end of the cable in the carburettor or throttle body bracket and thread them up or down the cable as required until the freeplay is correct, and tighten the locknut **(see illustration)**. If the freeplay cannot be set correctly replace the cable with a new one (see Chapter 5A or B).

**6** Start the engine and check the idle speed. If the idle speed is too high, this could be due to incorrect adjustment of the cable. Loosen the locknut and turn the adjuster in – if the idle speed falls as you do, there is insufficient freeplay in the cable. Reset the adjuster (see Step 4). Turn the handlebars from side to side and check that the idle speed does not change as you do. If it does, the throttle cable

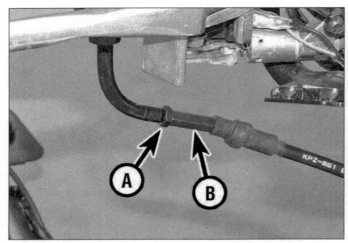

**20.5a Pull back the boot, then slacken the adjuster locknut (A) and turn the adjuster (B) as required – throttle end**

**20.5b Slacken and adjust the nuts (arrowed) as required**

is routed incorrectly. Rectify the problem before riding the scooter.

## 21 Transmission case filter

1 Remove the left-hand lower panel, floor panel or body cover as required according to model for access to the transmission cover on the left-hand side of the engine (see Chapter 9).

2 Unscrew the two bolts and remove the filter housing from the cover (see illustration). Remove the O-ring from its groove and discard it – a new one should be used (see illustration).

3 Release the tabs and remove the inner cover from the housing (see illustration). Remove the filter from the housing (see illustration).

4 Clean the filter in solvent and squeeze it dry. Check the condition of the filter and replace it with a new one if damaged, deformed or deteriorated.

5 Install the new or cleaned filter in a reverse of the removal procedure.

## 22 Valve clearances

1 The engine must be completely cold for this maintenance procedure, so let the machine sit overnight before beginning. On SH models remove the maintenance panel, then if required for better access the body cover (see Chapter 9). On Dylan and @ models remove the floor panel (see Chapter 9). On PS models remove the body cover and belly panel (see Chapter 9). On Pantheon models remove the small maintenance access panel in each floor panel, then if required for better access remove the floor panels (see Chapter 9). On S-wing models remove the centre cover, then if required for better access the body cover (see Chapter 9).

2 Remove the spark plug (see Section 16). Remove the transmission case filter housing (see Section 21). Unscrew the timing inspection cap (see illustration).

3 Remove the valve cover (see Chapter 2).

4 The valve clearances are checked with the piston at top dead centre (TDC) on its compression stroke (both valves are closed and a small clearance can be felt at each rocker arm). Turn the engine anti-clockwise using a socket on the drive pulley nut until the line next to the T mark on the alternator rotor aligns with the static timing mark, which is a notch in the inspection hole rim, and the index line on the camshaft sprocket is parallel and flush with the cylinder head top surface, with the number 1 at the top of the sprocket and the number 2 at the bottom (see

**21.2a  Unscrew the bolts and remove the cover . . .**

**21.2b  . . . and the O-ring**

**21.3a  Remove the inner cover . . .**

**21.3b  . . . and the filter**

illustrations). If everything else aligns but the 1 is at the bottom and the 2 at the top, rotate the engine anti-clockwise one full turn (360°). There should now be some freeplay in each rocker arm (i.e. they are not contacting the valve stem).

5 With the engine in this position, check the clearance of each valve by inserting a feeler

**22.2  Remove the timing inspection cap**

**22.4a  Turn the engine anti-clockwise . . .**

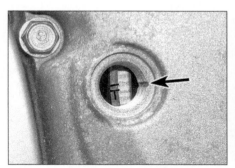

**22.4b  . . . until the line next to the T mark aligns with the notch (arrowed) . . .**

**22.4c  . . . and the camshaft sprocket numbers are as shown**

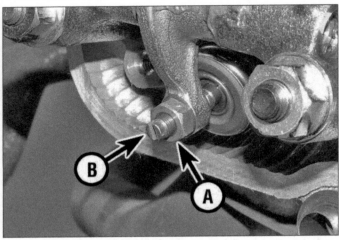

**22.5 Insert the feeler gauge between the base of the adjuster on the arm and the top of the valve stem as shown**

**22.6 Slacken the locknut (A) then turn the adjuster (B) using a screwdriver until the gap is correct**

gauge of the same thickness as the correct valve clearance (see Specifications) in the gap between the rocker arm and the valve stem **(see illustration)**. The intake valve is on the top of the cylinder head and the exhaust valve is on the bottom. The gauge should be a firm sliding fit – you should feel a slight drag when you pull the gauge out.

**6** If the gap (clearance) is either too wide or too narrow, slacken the locknut on the adjuster in the rocker arm and turn the adjuster as required using a screwdriver until the gap is as specified and the feeler gauge is a sliding fit, then hold the adjuster still and tighten the locknut **(see illustration)**. Recheck the clearance after tightening the locknut.

**7** When the clearances are correct install the

**23.2 Checking for play in the front wheel bearings**

valve cover (see Chapter 2) and the spark plug (Section 16).

**8** Install the timing inspection cap using a new O-ring, and smear the O-ring and the cap threads with clean oil and the cap threads with grease **(see illustration 22.2)**. Install the transmission case filter housing (see Section 21).

**9** On completion, check and adjust the idle speed (see Section 13).

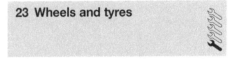

## 23 Wheels and tyres

### Wheels

**1** Cast wheels are virtually maintenance free, but they should be kept clean and checked periodically for cracks and other damage. Also check the wheel runout and alignment (see Chapter 8). Never attempt to repair damaged cast wheels; they must be replaced with new ones.

**2** The front wheel bearings will wear over a period of time and result in handling problems. Support the scooter on its centre stand and check for any play in the bearings by pushing and pulling the wheel against the hub **(see illustration)**. Also rotate the wheel and check that it turns smoothly.

**3** If any play is detected in the hub, or if the wheel does not rotate smoothly (and this is not due to brake drag), the wheel bearings must be inspected for wear or damage (see

Chapter 8).

**4** Follow the same procedure to check for play in the rear wheel. There are no rear wheel bearings as such. The wheel is mounted directly onto the gearbox output shaft which turns on bearings located inside the gearbox. If any play is detected, refer to Chapter 3 to check the gearbox. Also check that play is not due to a fault or wear in the rear suspension (see Section 19).

### Tyres

**5** Check the tyre condition and tread depth thoroughly – see *Pre-ride checks*.

**6** Check that the directional arrow on the tyre sidewall is pointing in the normal direction of wheel rotation.

**7** Check the valve rubber for signs of damage or deterioration and have it replaced if necessary by a tyre specialist.

**8** Make sure the valve stem cap is in place and tight. On some types, the cap doubles as a tool for the valve core. If a tyre looses pressure, and this is not due to damage to the tyre itself, check that the valve core is tight (these caps are available in automotive accessory shops).

**9** A smear of soapy water will indicate if the valve is leaking – the leak will show as bubbles in the water. If required, use the valve cap to unscrew the old valve and install a new one.

**10** If fitted, check that the wheel balance weights are firmly attached to the rim.

# Chapter 2
## Engine

## Contents

## Degrees of difficulty

| **Easy,** suitable for novice with little experience | **Fairly easy,** suitable for beginner with some experience | **Fairly difficult,** suitable for competent DIY mechanic | **Difficult,** suitable for experienced DIY mechanic | **Very difficult,** suitable for expert DIY or professional |
|---|---|---|---|---|

## Specifications

### General

| | |
|---|---|
| Type | Four-stroke single |
| Capacity | |
|   125 models | 124.6 cc |
|   150 models | 152.7 cc |
| Bore | |
|   125 models | 52.4 mm |
|   150 models | 58.0 mm |
| Stroke | 57.8 mm |
| Compression ratio | 11.0 to 1 |
| Cylinder compression | 200 psi (14.0 Bar) @ 600 rpm |
| Cooling system | Liquid-cooled |
| Lubrication | Wet sump, trochoid pump |

### Camshaft and followers

| | |
|---|---|
| Intake lobe height service limit (min) | 29.637 mm |
| Exhaust lobe height service limit (min) | 29.395 mm |
| Rocker arm bore diameter | |
|   Standard | 10.000 to 10.015 mm |
|   Service limit (min) | 10.05 mm |
| Rocker arm shaft diameter | |
|   Standard | 9.972 to 9.987 mm |
|   Service limit (min) | 9.937 mm |
| Rocker arm-to-shaft clearance | |
|   Standard | 0.013 to 0.043 mm |
|   Service limit (min) | 0.63 mm |

## Cylinder head
Warpage (max) . . . . . . . . . . . . . . . . . . . . . . . . . . . . . . . . . . . . . . . . 0.05 mm

## Valves, guides and springs
Valve clearances . . . . . . . . . . . . . . . . . . . . . . . . . . . . . . . . . . . . . . . see Chapter 1
Stem diameter
  Intake valve
    Standard . . . . . . . . . . . . . . . . . . . . . . . . . . . . . . . . . . . . . . . 4.975 to 4.990 mm
    Service limit (min) . . . . . . . . . . . . . . . . . . . . . . . . . . . . . . . . 4.90 mm
  Exhaust valve
    Standard . . . . . . . . . . . . . . . . . . . . . . . . . . . . . . . . . . . . . . . 4.955 to 4.970 mm
    Service limit (min) . . . . . . . . . . . . . . . . . . . . . . . . . . . . . . . . 4.90 mm
Guide bore diameter – intake and exhaust valves
  Standard . . . . . . . . . . . . . . . . . . . . . . . . . . . . . . . . . . . . . . . . . 5.000 to 5.012 mm
  Service limit (max) . . . . . . . . . . . . . . . . . . . . . . . . . . . . . . . . . 5.03 mm
Stem-to-guide clearance
  Intake valve
    Standard . . . . . . . . . . . . . . . . . . . . . . . . . . . . . . . . . . . . . . . 0.010 to 0.037 mm
    Service limit . . . . . . . . . . . . . . . . . . . . . . . . . . . . . . . . . . . . 0.08 mm
  Exhaust valve
    Standard . . . . . . . . . . . . . . . . . . . . . . . . . . . . . . . . . . . . . . . 0.030 to 0.057 mm
    Service limit . . . . . . . . . . . . . . . . . . . . . . . . . . . . . . . . . . . . 0.075 mm
Seat width – intake and exhaust valves
  Standard . . . . . . . . . . . . . . . . . . . . . . . . . . . . . . . . . . . . . . . . . 0.90 to 1.10 mm
  Service limit (max) . . . . . . . . . . . . . . . . . . . . . . . . . . . . . . . . . 1.80 mm
Valve guide height above cylinder head – intake and exhaust valves . . 11.35 to 11.65 mm
Valve spring free length – intake and exhaust valves
  Standard . . . . . . . . . . . . . . . . . . . . . . . . . . . . . . . . . . . . . . . . . 36.2 mm
  Service limit (min) . . . . . . . . . . . . . . . . . . . . . . . . . . . . . . . . . 34.4 mm

## Cylinder
Bore
  125 engines
    Standard . . . . . . . . . . . . . . . . . . . . . . . . . . . . . . . . . . . . . . . 52.400 to 52.410 mm
    Service limit (max) . . . . . . . . . . . . . . . . . . . . . . . . . . . . . . . 52.44 mm
  150 engines
    Standard . . . . . . . . . . . . . . . . . . . . . . . . . . . . . . . . . . . . . . . 58.000 to 58.010 mm
    Service limit (max) . . . . . . . . . . . . . . . . . . . . . . . . . . . . . . . 58.04 mm
Warpage (max) . . . . . . . . . . . . . . . . . . . . . . . . . . . . . . . . . . . . . . . 0.05 mm
Ovality (out-of-round) (max) . . . . . . . . . . . . . . . . . . . . . . . . . . . . 0.05 mm
Taper (max) . . . . . . . . . . . . . . . . . . . . . . . . . . . . . . . . . . . . . . . . . . 0.05 mm

## Piston
Piston diameter (measured 10 mm up from skirt, at 90° to piston pin axis)
  125 engines
    Standard . . . . . . . . . . . . . . . . . . . . . . . . . . . . . . . . . . . . . . . 52.37 to 52.39 mm
    Service limit (min) . . . . . . . . . . . . . . . . . . . . . . . . . . . . . . . . 52.30 mm
  150 engines
    Standard . . . . . . . . . . . . . . . . . . . . . . . . . . . . . . . . . . . . . . . 57.97 to 57.99 mm
    Service limit (min) . . . . . . . . . . . . . . . . . . . . . . . . . . . . . . . . 57.90 mm
Piston-to-bore clearance
  Standard . . . . . . . . . . . . . . . . . . . . . . . . . . . . . . . . . . . . . . . . . 0.01 to 0.04 mm
  Service limit (min) . . . . . . . . . . . . . . . . . . . . . . . . . . . . . . . . . 0.10 mm*
Piston pin diameter
  Standard . . . . . . . . . . . . . . . . . . . . . . . . . . . . . . . . . . . . . . . . . 13.994 to 14.000 mm
  Service limit (min) . . . . . . . . . . . . . . . . . . . . . . . . . . . . . . . . . 13.982 mm
Piston pin bore diameter in piston
  Standard . . . . . . . . . . . . . . . . . . . . . . . . . . . . . . . . . . . . . . . . . 14.002 to 14.008 mm
  Service limit (max) . . . . . . . . . . . . . . . . . . . . . . . . . . . . . . . . . 14.02 mm
Piston pin-to-piston pin bore clearance
  Standard . . . . . . . . . . . . . . . . . . . . . . . . . . . . . . . . . . . . . . . . . 0.002 to 0.014 mm
  Service limit . . . . . . . . . . . . . . . . . . . . . . . . . . . . . . . . . . . . . . 0.02 mm

*If the piston-to-bore clearance exceeds the service limit, the cylinder can be rebored – Honda supply +0.25 and +0.5 oversize piston and ring sets. Following rebore, the piston-to-bore clearance must be as standard for a normal piston.

## Piston rings

Ring end gap (installed)
  125 engines
    Top ring
      Standard . . . . . . . . . . . . . . . . . . . . . . . . . . . . . . . . . . . . . . . . . . . . . . . . . . . . . . . . . 0.15 to 0.30 mm
      Service limit (max) . . . . . . . . . . . . . . . . . . . . . . . . . . . . . . . . . . . . 0.40 mm
    Second ring
      Standard . . . . . . . . . . . . . . . . . . . . . . . . . . . . . . . . . . . . . . . . . . . . . . . . . . . . . . . . . 0.30 to 0.45 mm
      Service limit (max) . . . . . . . . . . . . . . . . . . . . . . . . . . . . . . . . . . . . 0.65 mm
    Oil ring side-rail
      Standard . . . . . . . . . . . . . . . . . . . . . . . . . . . . . . . . . . . . . . . . . . . . . . . . . . . . . . . . . 0.20 to 0.70 mm
      Service limit (max) . . . . . . . . . . . . . . . . . . . . . . . . . . . . . . . . . . . . 0.90 mm
  150 engines
    Top ring
      Standard . . . . . . . . . . . . . . . . . . . . . . . . . . . . . . . . . . . . . . . . . . . . . . . . . . . . . . . . . 0.10 to 0.25 mm
      Service limit (max) . . . . . . . . . . . . . . . . . . . . . . . . . . . . . . . . . . . . 0.45 mm
    Second ring
      Standard . . . . . . . . . . . . . . . . . . . . . . . . . . . . . . . . . . . . . . . . . . . . . . . . . . . . . . . . . 0.35 to 0.50 mm
      Service limit (max) . . . . . . . . . . . . . . . . . . . . . . . . . . . . . . . . . . . . 0.70 mm
    Oil ring side-rails
      Standard . . . . . . . . . . . . . . . . . . . . . . . . . . . . . . . . . . . . . . . . . . . . . . . . . . . . . . . . . 0.20 to 0.70 mm
      Service limit (max) . . . . . . . . . . . . . . . . . . . . . . . . . . . . . . . . . . . . 0.90 mm
Ring-to-groove clearance
  125 engines
    Top ring
      Standard . . . . . . . . . . . . . . . . . . . . . . . . . . . . . . . . . . . . . . . . . . . . . . . . . . . . . . . . . 0.030 to 0.065 mm
      Service limit (max) . . . . . . . . . . . . . . . . . . . . . . . . . . . . . . . . . . . . 0.105 mm
    Second ring
      Standard . . . . . . . . . . . . . . . . . . . . . . . . . . . . . . . . . . . . . . . . . . . . . . . . . . . . . . . . . 0.015 to 0.050 mm
      Service limit (max) . . . . . . . . . . . . . . . . . . . . . . . . . . . . . . . . . . . . 0.095 mm
  150 engines
    Top ring
      Standard . . . . . . . . . . . . . . . . . . . . . . . . . . . . . . . . . . . . . . . . . . . . . . . . . . . . . . . . . 0.030 to 0.065 mm
      Service limit (max) . . . . . . . . . . . . . . . . . . . . . . . . . . . . . . . . . . . . 0.105 mm
    Second ring
      Standard . . . . . . . . . . . . . . . . . . . . . . . . . . . . . . . . . . . . . . . . . . . . . . . . . . . . . . . . . 0.015 to 0.055 mm
      Service limit (max) . . . . . . . . . . . . . . . . . . . . . . . . . . . . . . . . . . . . 0.095 mm

## Starter clutch

Starter driven gear hub OD
  Standard . . . . . . . . . . . . . . . . . . . . . . . . . . . . . . . . . . . . . . . . . . . . . . . . . . . . . . . . . . . 39.622 to 39.635 mm
  Service limit (min) . . . . . . . . . . . . . . . . . . . . . . . . . . . . . . . . . . . . . . . 39.58 mm
Starter driven gear bush ID
  Standard . . . . . . . . . . . . . . . . . . . . . . . . . . . . . . . . . . . . . . . . . . . . . . . . . . . . . . . . . . . 22.026 to 22.045 mm
  Service limit (min) . . . . . . . . . . . . . . . . . . . . . . . . . . . . . . . . . . . . . . . 22.10 mm

## Oil pump

Inner rotor tip-to-outer rotor tip clearance
  Standard . . . . . . . . . . . . . . . . . . . . . . . . . . . . . . . . . . . . . . . . . . . . . . . . . . . . . . . . . . . 0.15 mm
  Service limit (max) . . . . . . . . . . . . . . . . . . . . . . . . . . . . . . . . . . . . . . 0.20 mm
Outer rotor-to-body clearance
  Standard . . . . . . . . . . . . . . . . . . . . . . . . . . . . . . . . . . . . . . . . . . . . . . . . . . . . . . . . . . . 0.15 to 0.20 mm
  Service limit (max) . . . . . . . . . . . . . . . . . . . . . . . . . . . . . . . . . . . . . . 0.25 mm
Rotor end-float
  Standard . . . . . . . . . . . . . . . . . . . . . . . . . . . . . . . . . . . . . . . . . . . . . . . . . . . . . . . . . . . 0.04 to 0.09 mm
  Service limit (max) . . . . . . . . . . . . . . . . . . . . . . . . . . . . . . . . . . . . . . 0.12 mm

## Connecting rod

Big-end side clearance
  Standard . . . . . . . . . . . . . . . . . . . . . . . . . . . . . . . . . . . . . . . . . . . . . . . . . . . . . . . . . . . 0.10 to 0.35 mm
  Service limit (max) . . . . . . . . . . . . . . . . . . . . . . . . . . . . . . . . . . . . . . 0.60 mm
Big-end radial clearance
  Standard . . . . . . . . . . . . . . . . . . . . . . . . . . . . . . . . . . . . . . . . . . . . . . . . . . . . . . . . . . . 0.000 to 0.008 mm
  Service limit (max) . . . . . . . . . . . . . . . . . . . . . . . . . . . . . . . . . . . . . . 0.05 mm
Small-end inside diameter
  Standard . . . . . . . . . . . . . . . . . . . . . . . . . . . . . . . . . . . . . . . . . . . . . . . . . . . . . . . . . . . 14.016 to 14.034 mm
  Service limit . . . . . . . . . . . . . . . . . . . . . . . . . . . . . . . . . . . . . . . . . . . . . . 14.06 mm

## Crankshaft
Runout (max) . . . . . . . . . . . . . . . . . . . . . . . . . . . . . . . . . . . . . . . . 0.10 mm

## Torque settings
Camshaft holder nuts. . . . . . . . . . . . . . . . . . . . . . . . . . . . . . . . 27 Nm
Cam chain sprocket bolts to camshaft . . . . . . . . . . . . . . . . . . 9 Nm
Cam chain tensioner blade pivot bolt . . . . . . . . . . . . . . . . . . 10 Nm
Crankcase bolts. . . . . . . . . . . . . . . . . . . . . . . . . . . . . . . . . . . . 12 Nm
Engine hanger bracket-to-engine bolt/nut. . . . . . . . . . . . . . . 49 Nm
Engine hanger bracket-to-frame bolts nuts . . . . . . . . . . . . . . 49 Nm
Starter clutch bolts. . . . . . . . . . . . . . . . . . . . . . . . . . . . . . . . . 30 Nm
Valve cover bolts . . . . . . . . . . . . . . . . . . . . . . . . . . . . . . . . . . 12 Nm

## 1 General information

The engine is a single cylinder, overhead-camshaft four-stroke, with pumped liquid cooling (see Chapter 4). The camshaft is chain-driven off the crankshaft and operates the valves via rocker arms.

The crankshaft assembly is pressed together, incorporating the connecting rod.

The crankcase divides vertically – the left-hand crankcase is an integral part of the transmission casing and gearbox.

## 2 Operations possible with the engine in the frame

Most components and assemblies, with the exception of the crankshaft assembly and its bearings, can be worked on without having to remove the engine/transmission unit from the frame. If a number of areas require attention at the same time, removal of the engine is recommended, as it is an easy task to undertake.

## 3 Compression test

**Special tool:** *A compression gauge (with a 10 mm threaded adapter to fit the spark plug hole in the cylinder head) and a 16 mm hex size spark plug socket will be needed. Depending* on the outcome of the initial test, a squirt-type oil can may also be needed.

1 Poor engine performance may be caused by leaking valves, incorrect valve clearances, a leaking head gasket, or a worn piston, piston rings or cylinder bore. A cylinder compression check will highlight these conditions and can also indicate the presence of excessive carbon deposits in the cylinder head.
2 Make sure the valve clearances are correctly set (see Chapter 1) and that the camshaft holder nuts are tightened to the correct torque setting (see Section 10).
3 Run the engine until it is at normal operating temperature. Remove the spark plug (see Chapter 1). Fit the plug back into the plug cap and ground the plug against the engine away from the plug hole – if the plug is not grounded the ignition system could be damaged.
4 Fit the adaptor and gauge into the spark plug hole.
5 With the ignition switch ON, the throttle held fully open and the spark plug grounded, turn the engine over on the starter motor until the gauge reading has built up and stabilised.
6 Compare the reading on the gauge to the cylinder compression figure specified at the beginning of the Chapter (under General specifications).
7 If the reading is low, it could be due to a worn cylinder bore, piston or rings, failure of the head gasket, or worn valve seats. To determine which is the cause, pour a small quantity of engine oil into the spark plug hole to seal the rings, then repeat the compression test. If the figures are noticeably higher the cause is worn cylinder, piston or rings. If there is no change the cause is a leaking head gasket or worn valve seats.
8 If the reading is high there could be a build-up of carbon deposits in the combustion chamber. Remove the cylinder head and scrape all deposits off the piston and the cylinder head.

## 4 Engine removal and installation

*Caution: The engine/transmission unit is not heavy, however removal and installation should be carried out with the aid of an assistant; personal injury or damage could occur if the engine falls or is dropped.*

### Removal

#### 2001 to 2004 SH models, all Dylan models, all @ models

1 Support the scooter on its centrestand. Work can be made easier by raising the machine to a suitable height on a hydraulic ramp or a suitable platform. Make sure it is secure and will not topple over.
2 Remove the body cover and floor panel (see Chapter 9).
3 If the engine is dirty, particularly around its mountings, wash it thoroughly before starting any major dismantling work. This will make work much easier and rule out the possibility of dirt falling inside.
4 Drain the engine oil (see Chapter 1) and coolant (see Chapter 4).
5 Disconnect the battery negative terminal (see Chapter 10). Disconnect the engine earth (ground) lead **(see illustration)**.
6 Remove the exhaust system (see Chapter 5A).
7 Disconnect the coolant inlet and outlet hoses from their unions on the engine **(see illustrations)**.

**4.5 Unscrew the bolt (arrowed) and detach the lead**

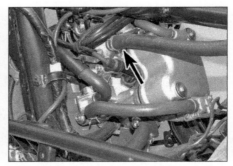
**4.7a Release the clamps and detach the outlet hose (arrowed) . . .**

**4.7b . . . and the inlet hose (arrowed)**

4.11a Disconnect the relevant wiring connectors

4.11b Ignition coil primary wiring connectors – Dylan

4.13 Unscrew the bolt and displace the cable guide

8 Remove the air filter housing and if required the air compensation chamber (see Chapter 5A).

9 If required now either remove the carburettor, or displace it from the cylinder head leaving the throttle cable attached, but note that either can be done after removing the engine, in which case just disconnect the fuel hose and the fuel tap vacuum hose from their unions on the carburettor and inlet manifold respectively, and disconnect the throttle cable, and the automatic choke and throttle position sensor wiring connectors (see Chapter 5A).

10 Either remove the starter motor, or disconnect the lead(s) from it (see Chapter 10).

11 Trace the wiring from the alternator and ignition pulse generator coil from the right-hand side of the engine and disconnect it at the connectors (see illustration). Disconnect the common wiring connector for the PAIR system control valve, coolant temperature sensor and thermostat housing earth wire. Disconnect the primary wiring connectors from the ignition coil (see illustration). Free the wiring from any relevant clips or ties on the engine and frame.

12 If you are going to be removing the rear wheel loosen the rear wheel nut at this point before disconnecting the rear brake. Note: The rear wheel and centrestand provide a convenient support for the unit once it is removed from the scooter.

13 Disconnect the brake cable from the brake arm (see Chapter 8). Detach the cable guide(s)

from the underside of the transmission casing (see illustration).

14 Check that all relevant wiring, cables and hoses are free and clear of the engine/transmission unit.

15 Place a suitable support under the rear of the bottom section of the frame. Remove the rear shock absorbers (see Chapter 7).

16 Unscrew the bolts securing the engine hanger bracket to the frame (see illustration). Either manoeuvre the engine unit back and out of the frame, or alternatively lift the frame up off the engine unit and move it clear, making sure it is properly supported (see illustration).

17 As required and if not already done remove the carburettor and air intake chamber, and the PAIR control valve (see Chapter 5A), and the ignition coil (see Chapter 6). Unscrew the nut and withdraw the bolt securing the hanger bracket and detach it from the engine (see illustration).

18 If required, remove the centre stand (see Chapter 7) and the rear wheel (see Chapter 8), but see the Note in Step 12.

19 Check the condition of the engine mounting bushes and bump pads in the hanger bracket and the bushes in the engine and replace them with new ones if worn or deteriorated.

### 2005-on SH models, all PS models, all Pantheon and S-wing models

20 Support the scooter on its centrestand. Work can be made easier by raising the

machine to a suitable height on a hydraulic ramp or a suitable platform. Make sure it is secure and will not topple over.

21 Remove the body cover and floor panel(s) (see Chapter 9).

22 If the engine is dirty, particularly around its mountings, wash it thoroughly before starting any major dismantling work. This will make work much easier and rule out the possibility of dirt falling inside.

23 Drain the engine oil (see Chapter 1) and coolant (see Chapter 4).

24 Disconnect the battery negative terminal (see Chapter 10). On SH and PS models disconnect the engine earth (ground) lead (see illustration 4.5).

25 Remove the exhaust system (see Chapter 5B).

26 Disconnect the coolant inlet and outlet hoses from their unions on the engine (see illustrations 4.7a and b).

27 Remove the air filter housing and the air intake chamber (SH and PS models) or duct (Pantheon and S-wing models) (see Chapter 5B).

28 Remove the fuel injector/throttle body/ECM assembly (see Chapter 5B).

29 Either remove the starter motor, or disconnect the leads from it (see Chapter 10).

30 Trace the wiring from the alternator and ignition pulse generator coil from the right-hand side of the engine and disconnect it at the connectors. Disconnect the PAIR system control valve wiring connector. Pull the cap off the spark plug. Disconnect the

4.16a Unscrew the bolt (arrowed) on each side . . .

4.16b . . . and manoeuvre the engine unit back

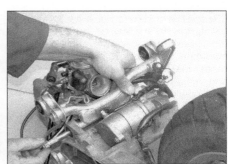

4.17 Unscrew the nut, withdraw the bolt and remove the bracket

**4.30 Coolant temperature sensor wiring connector (arrowed)**

wire from the coolant temperature sensor **(see illustration)**. On Pantheon and S-wing models trace the wiring from the speed sensor next to the left-hand shock absorber and disconnect it at the wiring connector. Free the wiring from any relevant clips or ties on the engine and frame.

**31** If you are going to be removing the rear wheel loosen the rear wheel nut at this point before disconnecting the rear brake. **Note:** *The rear wheel and centrestand provide a convenient support for the unit once it is removed from the scooter.*

**32** On models fitted with a drum rear brake, disconnect the brake cable from the brake arm (see Chapter 8). Detach the cable guide(s) from the underside of the transmission casing **(see illustration 4.13)**.

**33** On models fitted with a disc rear brake, displace the brake caliper and the brake hose guide (see Chapter 8).

**34** Check that all relevant wiring, cables and hoses are free and clear of the engine/ transmission unit.

**35** Place a suitable support under the rear of the bottom section of the frame. Remove the rear shock absorbers (see Chapter 7).

**36** Unscrew the bolts securing the engine hanger bracket to the frame **(see illustration 4.16a)**. Either manoeuvre the engine unit back and out of the frame, or alternatively lift the frame up off the engine unit and move it clear, making sure it is properly supported **(see illustration 4.16b)**.

**37** Unscrew the nut and withdraw the bolt securing the hanger bracket and detach it from the engine **(see illustration 4.17)**.

**38** If required, remove the centre stand (see Chapter 7) and the rear wheel (see Chapter 8), but see the **Note** in Step 31.

**39** Check the condition of the engine mounting bushes and bump pads in the hanger bracket and the bushes in the engine and replace them with new ones if worn or deteriorated.

## Installation

**40** Installation is the reverse of removal, noting the following:
● Make sure no wires, cables or hoses become trapped between the engine and the frame when installing the engine.

● Tighten the engine hanger bracket bolts bolt to the torque settings specified at the beginning of the chapter.
● Make sure all wires, cables and hoses are correctly routed and connected, and secured by any clips or ties.
● Check the operation of the rear brake before riding the machine (see Chapter 8).

---

## 5 Engine disassembly and reassembly general information

**1** Before beginning the engine overhaul, read through the related procedures to familiarise yourself with the scope and requirements of the job. Overhauling an engine is not all that difficult, but it is time consuming. Check on the availability of parts and make sure that any necessary special tools are obtained in advance.

**2** Most work can be done with a decent set of typical workshop hand tools, although a number of precision measuring tools are required for inspecting parts to determine if they are worn.

**3** To ensure maximum life and minimum trouble from a rebuilt engine, everything must be assembled with care and lubricated as directed, in a spotlessly clean environment.

### Disassembly

**4** Before disassembling the engine, thoroughly clean and degrease its external surfaces. This will prevent contamination of the engine internals, and will also make the job a lot easier and cleaner. A high flash-point solvent, such as paraffin (kerosene) can be used, or better still, a proprietary engine degreaser such as Gunk. Use old paintbrushes and toothbrushes to work the solvent into the various recesses of the casings. Take care to exclude solvent or water from the electrical components and intake and exhaust ports.

> ⚠ *Warning: The use of petrol (gasoline) as a cleaning agent should be avoided because of the risk of fire.*

**5** When clean and dry, position the engine on the workbench, leaving suitable clear area for working. Gather a selection of small containers, plastic bags and some labels so that parts can be grouped together in an easily identifiable manner. Also get some paper and a pen so that notes can be taken. You will also need a supply of clean rag, which should be as absorbent as possible.

**6** Before commencing work, read through the appropriate section so that some idea of the necessary procedure can be gained. When removing components note that great force is seldom required, unless specified (checking the specified torque setting of the particular bolt being removed will indicate how tight it is, and therefore how much force should be needed). In many cases, a component's reluctance to be removed is indicative of an

incorrect approach or removal method – if in any doubt, re-check with the text.

**7** A complete engine stripdown should be done in the following general order with reference to the appropriate Sections.
● Remove the valve cover
● Remove the camshaft and rocker arms
● Remove the cylinder head
● Remove the cam chain and blades
● Remove the cylinder block and piston
● Remove the starter motor (see Chapter 10)
● Remove the transmission assembly (see Chapter 3)
● Remove the water pump (see Chapter 4)
● Remove the alternator and starter clutch (see Chapter 10)
● Remove the oil pump
● Separate the crankcase halves
● Remove the crankshaft

### Reassembly

**8** Reassembly is accomplished by reversing the general disassembly sequence.

---

## 6 Valve cover

**Note:** *This procedure can be carried out with the engine in the frame. If the engine has been removed, ignore the steps that do not apply.*

### Removal

**1** On SH models remove the maintenance panel, then if required for better access the body cover (see Chapter 9). On Dylan and @ models remove the floor panel (see Chapter 9). On PS models remove the body cover (see Chapter 9). On Pantheon models remove the small maintenance access panel in each floor panel, then if required for better access remove the floor panels (see Chapter 9). On S-wing models remove the centre cover, then if required for better access the body cover (see Chapter 9).

**2** Release the clips and detach the crankcase breather and PAIR system hoses from the valve cover **(see illustration)**.

**3** Unscrew the bolts securing the valve cover,

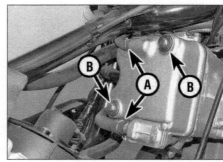

**6.2 Detach the hoses (A), then unscrew the bolts (B) . . .**

then lift the cover off **(see illustration)**. If the cover is stuck, tap around the joint face between the cover and the cylinder head with a soft-faced mallet to free it. Do not try to lever the cover off as this may damage the sealing surfaces.

4 Remove the air passage collar and O-ring **(see illustration)**. Remove the gasket. Discard both as new ones should be used. Check the condition of the bolt sealing washers and replace them with new ones if necessary.

### Installation

5 Clean the mating surfaces of the cylinder head and the valve cover with a suitable solvent to remove any traces of old gasket or sealant.

6 Fit the air passage collar, then fit a new O-ring smeared with oil around it **(see illustration 6.4)**. Fit the sealing washers onto the bolts, making sure the UP mark faces the head of the bolt.

7 Fit the new gasket into the groove in the valve cover using dabs of grease to keep it in place **(see illustration)**.

8 Position the valve cover on the cylinder head, making it locates over the air passage collar and the gasket stays in place **(see illustration 6.3)**. Fit the bolts and tighten them evenly and a bit at a time to the torque setting specified at the beginning of the Chapter **(see illustration)**.

9 Fit the crankcase breather and PAIR system hoses fully onto their unions and secure them with the clamps **(see illustration 6.2)**.

10 Install the body covers and panels as required (see Chapter 9).

| 7 | Cam chain tensioner |
|---|---|

**Note:** *This procedure can be carried out with the engine in the frame. If the engine has been removed, ignore the steps that do not apply.*

### Removal

1 Remove the body cover (see Chapter 9).

2 Undo the tensioner cap screw and remove the O-ring **(see illustration)**. Slacken the tensioner mounting bolts slightly.

6.3 . . . and remove the cover

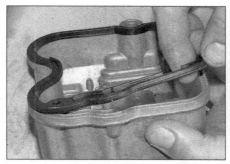
6.7 Fit a new gasket into the groove

3 Insert a small flat-bladed screwdriver in the end of the tensioner so that it engages the slotted plunger **(see illustration)**. Turn the screwdriver clockwise until the plunger is fully retracted and hold it in this position, then unscrew and remove the tensioner mounting bolts and withdraw the tensioner, moving the hose/cable bracket aside **(see illustration)**. Release the screwdriver – the plunger will spring back out, but can be easily reset on installation.

4 Discard the gasket and O-ring as new ones must be used on installation. Do not attempt to dismantle the tensioner.

### Inspection

5 Examine the tensioner components for signs of wear or damage.

6 Check that the plunger moves smoothly when wound into the tensioner and springs back out freely when released. Ensure the

6.4 Remove the collar and its O-ring (arrowed)

6.8 Fit the bolts with their washers, using new ones if necessary and making sure they are the correct way up

tensioner and cylinder block surfaces are clean and dry.

### Installation

7 Ensure the tensioner and cylinder block surfaces are clean and dry.

8 Fit a new gasket onto the tensioner body. Insert a small flat-bladed screwdriver in the end of the tensioner so that it engages the slotted plunger, then turn the screwdriver clockwise until the plunger is fully retracted and hold it in this position, then fit the tensioner and the bracket and tighten the mounting bolts **(see illustration 7.3b)**. Release and remove the screwdriver – you should see the winding mechanism turn as the plunger extends and takes up the slack.

9 Fit a new O-ring smeared with clean oil onto the tensioner, then fit the cap screw and tighten it **(see illustration 7.2)**.

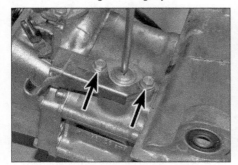
7.2 Undo the cap screw, then slacken the bolts (arrowed)

7.3a Use a small screwdriver to retract the plunger . . .

7.3b . . . then remove the tensioner

**10** It is advisable to remove the valve cover (see Section 6) and check that the cam chain is tensioned – refer to Section 8, Step 4 and turn the engine a few times. If it is slack, the tensioner plunger did not release. Remove the tensioner and check the operation of the plunger again.

**11** Install the body panels (see Chapter 9).

## 8 Camshaft and rocker arms

**Note:** *The camshaft and rockers can be removed with the engine in the frame. Stuff clean rag into the cam chain tunnel to prevent anything dropping into the engine. When setting the position of the crankshaft for the engine timing (Steps 4 and 19), be sure that you have the correct timing mark on the flywheel – do not confuse the T mark that denotes top dead centre (TDC) for engine timing with the F mark that denotes the firing (ignition timing) point.*

### Removal

**1** On SH models remove the body cover (see Chapter 9). On Dylan and @ models remove the body cover and floor panel (see Chapter 9). On PS models remove the body cover and belly panel (see Chapter 9). On Pantheon models remove the body cover and floor panels (see Chapter 9). On S-wing models remove the body cover (see Chapter 9).

**2** Remove the spark plug (see Chapter 1).

**8.2 Remove the timing inspection cap**

Remove the transmission case filter housing (see Chapter 1). Unscrew the timing inspection cap **(see illustration)**.

**3** Remove the valve cover (see Section 6).

**4** The engine must be at top dead centre (TDC) on its compression stroke. Turn the engine anti-clockwise using a socket on the drive pulley nut until the line next to the T mark on the alternator rotor aligns with the static timing mark, which is a notch in the inspection hole rim, and the index line on the camshaft sprocket is parallel and flush with the cylinder head top surface, with the number 1 at the top of the sprocket and the number 2 at the bottom **(see illustrations)**. If everything else aligns but the 1 is at the bottom and the 2 at the top, rotate the engine anti-clockwise one full turn (360°). There should now be some freeplay in each rocker arm (i.e. they are not contacting the valve stem).

**5** Remove the cam chain tensioner (see Section 7).

**6** Counter-hold the engine using a socket on the drive pulley nut to prevent it turning **(see illustration 8.4a)**. and unscrew the bolts securing the cam chain sprocket to the camshaft **(see illustration 8.4c)**. Slip the sprocket off its flange on the end of the camshaft and disengage it from the chain **(see illustration)**. Prevent the chain from dropping down its tunnel by securing it with a piece of wire.

**7** Remove the circlip securing the camshaft in the holder, then draw the camshaft out **(see illustration)**. Discard the circlip if it has deformed and fit a new one on assembly. While the camshaft is out do not rotate the crankshaft – the chain may drop down and bind between the crankshaft and case, which could damage these components.

**8** Working on one rocker shaft at a time, remove the shaft circlip, then thread a 5mm bolt into the end of the shaft and use it as a handle to draw the shaft out – hold the rocker arm and remove it when free **(see illustration)**. Slide the rocker back onto its shaft to prevent related parts getting mixed up – both rocker arms are identical and are therefore interchangeable. If required mark them according to their location so they can be installed in their original position. The shafts are different – the intake side shaft has two grooves in it.

**9** Place a rag over the cylinder head.

### Inspection

**10** Check the bearing on each end of the

**8.4a Turn the engine anti-clockwise . . .**

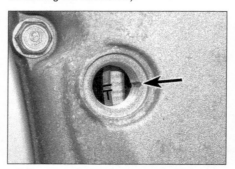

**8.4b . . . until the line next to the T mark aligns with the notch (arrowed) . . .**

**8.4c . . . and the camshaft sprocket numbers are as shown**

**8.6 Slip the sprocket off the camshaft and out of the chain**

**8.7 Release the circlip (arrowed) and withdraw the camshaft**

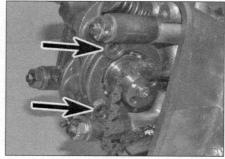

**8.8 Release the circlips (arrowed) then withdraw the shafts and remove the rockers as described**

8.10 Check the camshaft bearings

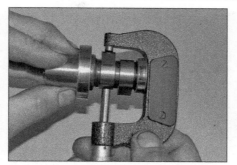

8.11 Measuring the camshaft lobe height with a micrometer

8.12 Inspect the contact surfaces on the rocker arms and cam lobes for wear and pitting

camshaft – they must run smoothly, quietly and freely, and there should be no excessive play between the inner and outer races, or between the inner race and the camshaft, or between the outer race and the holder **(see illustration)**. If not, replace the bearings and/or camshaft and/or holder with new ones as required – on some models the camshaft and bearings are available separately, while on others they are only available as an assembly – check with your dealer. Refer to Section 10 to remove the holder.

**11** Check the camshaft lobes for heat discoloration (blue appearance), score marks, chipped areas, flat spots and spalling **(see illustration 8.12)**. Measure the height of each lobe with a micrometer **(see illustration)** and compare the results to the minimum height listed in this Chapter's Specifications. If damage is noted or wear is excessive, the camshaft must be replaced with a new one.

 **HAYNES HiNT** *Refer to Tools and Workshop Tips in the Reference section for details of how to read a micrometer.*

**12** Check the rocker arms for heat discoloration (blue appearance), score marks, chipped areas, flat spots and spalling where they contact the camshaft lobes **(see illustration)**. Similarly check the bottom of each clearance adjuster and the top of each valve stem. If damage is noted or wear is excessive, the rocker arms, camshaft and

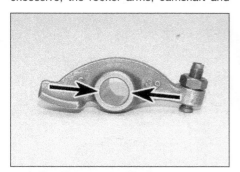

8.13a Measure the ID of the bore . . .

valves must be replaced with new ones as required.

**13** Check for freeplay between each rocker arm and its shaft. The arms should move freely with a light fit but no appreciable freeplay. Measure the internal diameter of the arm bores and the corresponding diameter of the shaft, and calculate the difference to obtain the clearance **(see illustrations)**. Replace the arms and/or shafts according to their measurements if the clearance is greater than the maximum specified at the beginning of the Chapter. Check that the rocker shaft holes in the holder are neither worn nor damaged.

**14** Except in cases of oil starvation, the cam chain should wear very little. If the chain has stretched excessively, which makes it difficult to maintain proper tension, or if it is stiff or the links are binding or kinking, replace it with a new one (see Section 9).

**15** Check the sprocket for wear and damage, and replace it with a new one if necessary. If the sprocket is worn, the cam chain is also worn, and so probably is the sprocket on the crankshaft (see Section 9). If severe wear is apparent, the entire engine should be disassembled for inspection.

**16** Inspect the cam chain guide and tensioner blades (see Section 9).

## Installation

**17** Working on one rocker shaft at a time, and remembering that the grooved shaft goes in the intake side of the holder, lubricate the shaft and arm with molybdenum disulphide oil (a 50/50 mixture of molybdenum disulphide

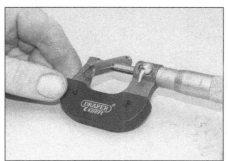

8.13b . . . and the OD of the shaft

grease and engine oil). Position the rocker arm in its location in the holder, making sure the adjuster is on the outside, and slide its shaft through, making sure the threaded end is on the outer end **(see illustration 8.8)**. Fit the shaft circlip, making sure it locates in its groove.

**18** Lubricate the camshaft bearings with clean engine oil and the camshaft lobes with molybdenum disulphide oil. Slide the camshaft into the holder with its lobes pointing towards the cylinder head and away from the contact faces on the rocker arms, and aligning the sprocket bolt holes parallel with the top of the cylinder head, and secure it with the circlip, using a new one if necessary **(see illustration 8.7)**.

**19** Check that the line next to the T mark on the alternator rotor aligns with the notch in the inspection hole rim **(see illustration 8.4b)**. Engage the cam chain sprocket with the chain, making sure the crankshaft does not rotate, that the front run of the chain between the sprockets is tight and that any slack is in the rear run so it will be taken up by the tensioner, that the index line is facing out and is flush with the cylinder head, i.e. below the bolt holes, with the number 1 at the top of the sprocket and the number 2 at the bottom, and that the bolt holes align, and fit the sprocket onto the flange **(see illustration 8.6)**.

**20** Fit the cam chain sprocket bolts and tighten them to the specified torque setting **(see illustration 8.4c)**.

**21** Use a piece of wooden dowel or other suitable tool to press on the back of the cam chain tensioner blade via the tensioner bore in the cylinder block to ensure that any slack in the cam chain is taken up and transferred to the rear run of the chain. At this point check that all the timing marks are still in **exact** alignment as described in Step 4 **(see illustrations 8.4b and c)**. Note that it is easy to be slightly out (one tooth on the sprocket) without the marks appearing drastically out of alignment. If the marks are out unscrew the sprocket's bolts and slide the sprocket off the camshaft, then disengage it from the chain. Move the camshaft and/or crankshaft round as required, then fit the sprocket back into the chain and onto the camshaft, and check the marks again. With everything correctly aligned, tighten the bolts to the specified torque setting.

*Caution: If the marks are not aligned exactly as described, the valve timing will be incorrect and the valves may strike the piston, causing extensive damage to the engine.*

22 Install the cam chain tensioner (see Section 7).

23 Turn the engine anti-clockwise through two full turns and check again that all the timing marks still align (see Step 4) **(see illustrations 8.4a, b and c)**. Check the valve clearances and adjust them if necessary (see Chapter 1).

24 Install the timing inspection cap using a new O-ring, and smear the O-ring and the cap threads with clean oil and the cap threads with grease **(see illustration 8.2)**.

25 Install the valve cover (see Section 6). Install the spark plug and transmission case filter housing (see Chapter 1).

26 Install the body panels (see Chapter 9).

## 9 Cam chain, blades and sprockets

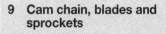

**Note:** *The cam chain and its blades can be removed with the engine in the frame.*

### *Removal*

#### Cam chain

1 Remove the camshaft sprocket (see Section 8, Steps 1 to 6).

2 Remove the transmission drive pulley (see Chapter 3).

3 Unscrew the crankcase oil seal retainer bolts and remove the retainer **(see illustration)**. Prise the oil seal out – discard it as a new one must be used **(see illustration)**.

4 Draw the cam chain off the crankshaft sprocket, noting that it engages with the middle set of teeth, and out of the engine **(see illustration)**.

#### Tensioner blade

5 Remove the cylinder head (see Section 10).

6 Remove the transmission drive pulley (see Chapter 3).

**9.3a Unscrew the bolts and remove the retainer . . .**

7 Unscrew the crankcase oil seal retainer bolts and remove the retainer **(see illustration 9.3a)**.

8 Unscrew the tensioner blade pivot bolt. Draw the blade out of the top of the cylinder block **(see illustration)**. Discard the pivot bolt O-ring – a new one must be used.

#### Guide blade

9 Remove the cylinder head (see Section 10).

10 Draw the guide blade out of the top of the cylinder block, noting how it locates **(see illustration)**.

### *Inspection*

#### Cam chain and sprockets

11 Check the chain for binding, kinks and any obvious damage and replace it with a new one if necessary. Check the camshaft and crankshaft sprocket teeth for wear and damage and replace the cam chain, camshaft sprocket and crankshaft sprocket with a new set if necessary – the drive sprocket on the crankshaft is pressed on, so the crankshaft will have to be taken to a workshop or dealer equipped with an hydraulic press to remove it and to fit a new one. When fitting the new sprocket make sure that the tip of any one tooth aligns with the punch mark on the left-hand end of the crankshaft where present, or if not then with the centre of the crank pin, according to model. Note that for certain later models the sprocket is not listed as being available separately from the crankshaft assembly, but check with a dealer before assuming you have to buy a new crankshaft –

**9.3b . . . then remove the oil seal**

it may be that a sprocket from an earlier model can be used.

#### Tensioner and guide blades

12 Check the sliding surface and edges of the blades for excessive wear, deep grooves, cracking and other obvious damage, and replace them with new ones if necessary.

### *Installation*

13 Installation of the cam chain and blades is the reverse of removal. Make sure the bottom of the guide blade sits in its seat and the lugs near its top locate in the cut-outs in the cylinder block. Use a new O-ring smeared with oil on the tensioner blade pivot bolt and tighten the bolt to the torque setting specified at the beginning of the Chapter. Lubricate the new crankcase seal lips with oil. Do not forget the seal retainer. Refer to Section 8, Step 19-on for installation of the camshaft sprocket.

## 10 Cylinder head removal and installation

**Note:** *The cylinder head can be removed with the engine in the frame.*

*Caution: The engine must be completely cool before beginning this procedure or the cylinder head may become warped.*

### *Removal*

1 Remove the carburettor or fuel injector/ throttle body/ECM assembly, according to model (see Chapter 5A or B).

**9.4 Draw the chain out via the hole for the oil seal**

**9.8 Unscrew the pivot bolt and withdraw the blade**

**9.10 Withdraw the blade, noting how it locates**

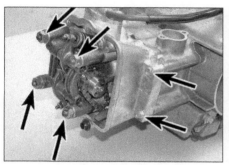

10.5 Undo the smaller bolts on the side first then undo the main nuts (arrowed)

10.8a The dowels (arrowed) could be in the block . . .

10.8b . . . or the head, or one in each

**2** Remove the exhaust system (see Chapter 5A or B).
**3** Drain the cooling system (see Chapter 4). Detach the thermostat housing from the head (see Chapter 4).
**4** Remove the camshaft sprocket (see Section 8, Steps 1 to 6).
**5** Unscrew and remove the two bolts on the side of the head, then unscrew the camshaft holder nuts, slackening them evenly and a little at a time in a criss-cross sequence, and remove them and their washers **(see illustration)**.
**6** Lift off the holder complete with the camshaft and rockers. Remove the two locating dowels from the studs or the underside of the holder if they are loose.
***Caution: Make sure the holder lifts up squarely and evenly and does not stick on a dowel.***
**7** Lift the cylinder head off carefully, feeding the cam chain down through the tunnel in the head. If the head is stuck, tap around the joint face between the head and the cylinder with a soft-faced mallet to free it. Do not try to lever the head off as this may damage the sealing surfaces. **Note:** *Avoid lifting the cylinder off the crankcase when the head is removed, otherwise a new cylinder base gasket will have to be fitted (see Section 12).*
**8** Remove the old cylinder head gasket and discard it as a new one must be fitted on reassembly **(see illustration 10.13)**. Remove the dowels from the cylinder block or the underside of the cylinder head if they are loose **(see illustrations)**.

**9** Secure the cam chain over the front of the block to prevent it dropping into the engine.
**10** Inspect the cylinder head gasket and the mating surfaces on the cylinder head and cylinder for signs of leaks, which could indicate that the head is warped. Refer to Section 11 and check the head mating surface for warpage.
**11** Clean all traces of old gasket material from the cylinder head and cylinder with a suitable solvent. Take care not to scratch or gouge the soft aluminium. Be careful not to let any of the gasket material fall into the crankcase, the cylinder bore or the oil or coolant passages.

### Installation

**12** Lubricate the cylinder bore with engine oil. If removed, fit the dowels into the cylinder block **(see illustration 10.8a)**. Make sure the cam chain guide blade is correctly seated (see Section 9).
**13** Ensure both cylinder head and cylinder block mating surfaces are clean. Lay the new head gasket over the studs, the cam chain and blades and onto the block, locating it over the dowels and making sure all the holes are correctly aligned **(see illustration)**. Never reuse the old gasket.
**14** Carefully fit the cylinder head over the studs and the cam chain guide blade and onto the block, feeding the cam chain up through the tunnel as you do, and making sure it locates correctly onto the dowels. Secure the chain in place with a piece of wire to prevent it from falling in.
**15** If the camshaft and rocker arms have not

been removed from the holder, make sure the camshaft is positioned so its lobes face away from the contact faces on the arms. Make sure the crankshaft is correctly positioned (see Section 8, Step 19). If removed fit the dowels over the studs and into the cylinder head. Fit the camshaft holder assembly over the studs and onto the head, making sure the sprocket end of the camshaft is over the cam chain tunnel, and that the rocker arms locate correctly onto the valve stem ends, and locate it onto the dowels, making sure it is correctly seated on all sides.
**16** Smear clean engine oil onto the seating surfaces of the nuts. Fit the nuts with their washers and tighten them evenly and a little at a time in a criss-cross sequence to the torque setting specified at the beginning of the Chapter **(see illustration)**.
**17** Fit the two bolts into the side of the head and tighten them **(see illustration 10.5)**.
**18** Install the camshaft sprocket (see Section 8, Steps 19-on).
**19** Install the remaining components in the reverse order of removal, referring to the relevant Chapters and Sections as directed.

### 11 Cylinder head and valve overhaul

**1** Because of the complex nature of this job and the special tools and equipment required, most owners leave servicing of the valves, valve seats and valve guides to a professional. However, you can make an initial assessment of whether the valves are seating correctly, and therefore sealing, by pouring a small amount of solvent into each of the valve ports. If the solvent leaks past any valve into the combustion chamber area the valve is not seating correctly and sealing.
**2** With the correct tools (a valve spring compressor is essential – make sure it is suitable for motorcycle work), you can also remove the valves and associated components from the cylinder head, clean them and check them for wear to assess the extent of the work needed, and, unless seat cutting or guide replacement is required, grind in the valves and reassemble them in the head.

10.13 Locate the new gasket over the dowels

10.16 Tighten the nuts as described to the specified torque

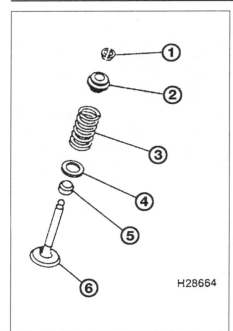

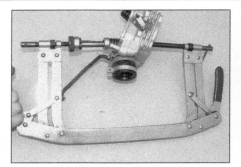

**11.6a Compressing the valve springs using a valve spring compressor**

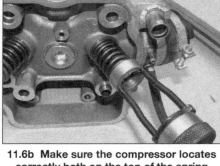

**11.6b Make sure the compressor locates correctly both on the top of the spring retainer . . .**

**11.5 Valve components**

| | |
|---|---|
| 1 Collets | 4 Spring seat |
| 2 Spring retainer | 5 Valve stem seal |
| 3 Valve spring | 6 Valve |

H28664

**11.6c . . . and on the bottom of the valve**

**11.7a Remove the collets . . .**

**3** A dealer service department or specialist can replace the guides and re-cut the valve seats.

**4** After the valve service has been performed, be sure to clean the head very thoroughly before installation to remove any metal particles or abrasive grit that may still be present from the valve service operations. Use compressed air, if available, to blow out all the holes and passages.

### Disassembly

**5** Before proceeding, arrange to label and store the valves along with their related components in such a way that they can be returned to their original locations without getting mixed up **(see illustration)**. Labelled plastic bags or a plastic container with two compartments are ideal.

**6** Compress the valve spring on the first valve with a spring compressor, making sure it is correctly located onto each end of the valve assembly **(see illustration)**. On the top of the valve the adaptor needs to be about the same size as the spring retainer – if it is too small it will be difficult to remove and install the collets **(see illustration)**. On the underside of the head make sure the plate on the compressor only contacts the valve and not the soft aluminium of the head **(see illustration)** – if the plate is too big for the valve, use a

spacer between them. Do not compress the springs any more than is absolutely necessary.

**7** Remove the collets, using a magnet or a screwdriver with a dab of grease on it **(see illustration)**. Carefully release the valve spring compressor and remove the spring retainer, noting which way up it fits, the spring and the valve **(see illustrations)**. If the valve binds in the guide and won't pull through, push it back into the head and deburr the area around the collet groove with a very fine file or whetstone **(see illustration)**.

**11.7b . . . the spring retainer and the spring . . .**

**11.7c . . . and the valve**

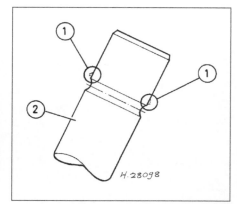

**11.7d If the valve stem (2) won't pull through the guide, deburr the area above the collet groove (1)**

11.8a Pull the seal off the valve guide . . .

11.8b . . . then remove the spring seat

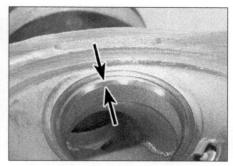

11.15 Measure the valve seat width

**8** Pull the valve stem seal off the top of the valve guide with pliers and discard it (the old seals should never be reused), then remove the spring seat noting which way up it fits **(see illustrations)**.

**9** Repeat the procedure for the other valve. Remember to keep the parts for each valve together so they can be reinstalled in the same location.

**10** Clean the cylinder head with solvent and dry it thoroughly. Compressed air will speed the drying process and ensure that all holes and recessed areas are clean. **Note:** *Do not use a wire brush mounted in a drill motor to clean the combustion chambers as the head material is soft and may be scratched or eroded away by the wire brush.*

**11** Clean the valve springs, collets, retainers and spring seats with solvent and dry them thoroughly. Do the parts from one valve at a time so that no mixing of parts between valves occurs.

**12** Scrape off any deposits that may have formed on the valve, then use a motorised wire brush to remove deposits from the valve heads and stems. Again, make sure the valves do not get mixed up.

### Inspection

**13** Inspect the head very carefully for cracks and other damage. If cracks are found, a new head is required.

**14** Using a precision straight-edge and a feeler gauge set to the warpage limit listed in the specifications at the beginning of the Chapter, check the head gasket mating surface

for warpage. Take six measurements, one along each side and two diagonally across. If the head is warped beyond the limit specified at the beginning of this Chapter, consult a Honda dealer or take it to a specialist repair shop for an opinion, though be prepared to have to buy a new one.

**15** Examine the valve seats in the combustion chamber. If they are pitted, cracked or burned, the head will require work beyond the scope of the home mechanic. Measure the valve seat width and compare it to this Chapter's Specifications **(see illustration)**. If it exceeds the service limit, or if it varies around its circumference, overhaul is required.

**16** Working on one valve and guide at a time, measure the valve stem diameter **(see illustration)**. Clean the valve's guide using a guide reamer to remove any carbon build-up – insert the reamer from the underside of the head and turn it clockwise only. Now measure the inside diameter of the guide (at both ends and in the centre of the guide) with a small bore gauge, then measure the gauge with a micrometer **(see illustration)**. Measure the guide at the ends and at the centre to determine if they are worn in a bell-mouth pattern (more wear at the ends). Subtract the stem diameter from the valve guide diameter to obtain the valve stem-to-guide clearance. If the stem-to-guide clearance is greater than listed in this Chapter's Specifications, replace whichever component is beyond its specification limits with a new one – take the head to a specialist for valve guide

replacement. If the valve guide is within specifications, but is worn unevenly, it should be replaced with a new one. Repeat for the other valve.

**17** Carefully inspect each valve face, stem and collet groove area for cracks, pits and burned spots.

**18** Rotate the valve and check for any obvious indication that it is bent, in which case it must be replaced with a new one. Check the end of the stem for pitting and excessive wear. The presence of any of the above conditions indicates the need for valve servicing.

**19** Check the end of each valve spring for wear and pitting. Measure the spring free lengths and compare them to the specifications **(see illustration)**. If any spring is shorter than specified it has sagged and must be replaced with a new one. Also place the spring upright on a flat surface and check it for bend by placing a ruler against it, or alternatively lay it against a set square. If the bend in any spring is excessive, it must be replaced with a new one.

**20** Check the spring seats, retainers and collets for obvious wear and cracks. Any questionable parts should not be reused, as extensive damage will occur in the event of failure during engine operation.

**21** If the inspection indicates that no overhaul work is required, the valve components can be reinstalled in the head.

### Reassembly

**22** Unless a valve service has been performed, before installing the valves in the

11.16a Measure the valve stem diameter with a micrometer

11.16b Measure the valve guide with a small bore gauge, then measure the bore gauge with a micrometer

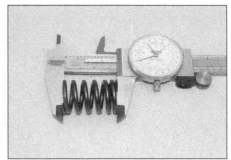

11.19 Measure the free length of the valve springs and check them for bend

11.24 Make sure the contact areas are as described

11.28 Fit the spring seat using a rod to guide it if necessary

11.29a Fit a new valve stem seal . . .

head they should be ground in (lapped) to ensure a positive seal between the valves and seats. This procedure requires coarse and fine valve grinding compound and a valve grinding tool (either hand-held or drill driven – note that some drill-driven tools specify using only a fine grinding compound). If a grinding tool is not available, a piece of rubber or plastic hose can be slipped over the valve stem (after the valve has been installed in the guide) and used to turn the valve.

23 Apply a small amount of coarse grinding compound to the valve face. Smear some molybdenum disulphide oil (a 50/50 mixture of molybdenum disulphide grease and engine oil) to the valve stem, then slip the valve into the guide (see illustration 11.7c). Note: *Make sure each valve is installed in its correct guide and be careful not to get any grinding compound on the valve stem.*

24 Attach the grinding tool to the valve and rotate the tool between the palms of your hands. Use a back-and-forth motion (as though rubbing your hands together) rather than a circular motion (i.e. so that the valve rotates alternately clockwise and anti-clockwise rather than in one direction only). If a motorised tool is being used, take note of the correct drive speed for it – if your drill runs too fast and is not variable, use a hand tool instead. Lift the valve off the seat and turn it at regular intervals to distribute the grinding compound properly. Continue the grinding procedure until the valve face and seat contact area is of uniform width,

and unbroken around the entire circumference (see illustration and 11.15).

25 Carefully remove the valve and wipe off all traces of grinding compound, making sure none gets in the guide. Use solvent to clean the valve and wipe the seat area thoroughly with a solvent soaked cloth.

26 Repeat the procedure with fine valve grinding compound, then use solvent to clean the valve and flush the guide, and wipe the seat area thoroughly with a solvent soaked cloth. Repeat the entire procedure for the other valve. On completion thoroughly clean the entire head again, then blow through all passages with compressed air. Make sure all traces of the grinding compound have been removed before assembling the head.

27 Coat the valve stem with molybdenum disulphide oil (a 50/50 mixture of molybdenum disulphide grease and engine oil), then fit it into its guide (see illustration 11.7c). Check that the valve moves up-and-down freely.

28 Working on one valve at a time, lay the spring seat in place in the cylinder head with its shouldered side facing up (see illustration).

29 Fit a new valve stem seal over the valve stem and onto the guide, using finger pressure, a stem seal fitting tool or an appropriate size deep socket, to push the seal squarely onto the end of the valve guide until it is felt to clip into place (see illustrations).

30 Next fit the spring, with its closer-wound coils facing down into the cylinder head, then fit the spring retainer, with its shouldered side

facing down so that it fits into the top of the springs (see illustration 11.7b).

31 Apply a small amount of grease to the inside of the collets to help hold them in place. Compress the valve springs with a spring compressor, making sure it is correctly located onto each end of the valve assembly (see Step 6) (see illustrations 11.6a, 11.6b and 11.6c). Do not compress the springs any more than is necessary to slip the collets into place. Locate each collet in turn into the groove in the valve stem using a screwdriver with a dab of grease on it (see illustration). Carefully release the compressor, making sure the collets seat and lock in the retaining groove.

32 Repeat the procedure for the other valve.

33 Support the cylinder head on blocks so the valves can't contact the work surface, then tap the end of each valve stem lightly using a copper or plastic hammer to seat the collets in their grooves (see illustration).

 *Check for proper sealing of the valves by pouring a small amount of solvent into each of the valve ports. If the solvent leaks past any valve into the combustion chamber the valve grinding operation on that valve should be repeated.*

34 After the cylinder head and camshaft holder have been installed, check the valve clearances and adjust as required (see Chapter 1).

11.29b . . . and press it squarely into place

11.31 Locate each collet in its groove in the top of the valve stem

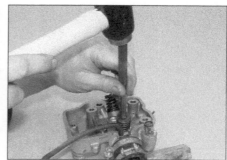

11.33 Seat the collets as described

## 12 Cylinder block

**Note:** *The cylinder block can be removed with the engine in the frame.*

### Removal

**1** Remove the cylinder head (see Section 10).
**2** Draw the cam chain guide blade out of the top of the block, noting how it locates **(see illustration 9.10)**.
**3** Slacken the clamp securing the coolant hose to the block and detach it, being prepared with a rag to catch any residual coolant **(see illustration)**.
**4** Hold the cam chain up and pull the cylinder block up off the crankcase, supporting the piston so the connecting rod does not knock against the engine, then pass the cam chain down through the tunnel **(see illustration)**. Do not let the chain fall into the engine – lay it over the front and secure it with a piece of wire. If the block is stuck, tap around the joint faces with a soft-faced mallet. Do not attempt to free it by inserting a screwdriver between the block and crankcase mating surfaces – you'll damage them.
**5** Remove the base gasket and discard it as a new one must be used. If they are loose, remove the dowels from the crankcase or the underside of the cylinder block.
**6** Stuff some clean rag into the cam chain tunnel and around the connecting rod to protect and support it and the piston and to prevent anything falling into the engine.
**7** Clean all traces of old gasket material from the cylinder block and crankcase. If a scraper is used, take care not to scratch or gouge the soft aluminium. Be careful not to let any of the gasket material fall into the engine.

### Inspection

**Note:** *Do not attempt to separate the cylinder liner from the cylinder block.*
**8** Check the cylinder walls carefully for scratches and score marks.
**9** Using a precision straight-edge and a feeler gauge set to the warpage limit listed in the specifications at the beginning of the Chapter, check the block top surface for warpage. Take six measurements, one along each side and two diagonally across. If the block is warped beyond the limit specified at the beginning of this Chapter, consult a Honda dealer or take it to a specialist repair shop for an opinion, though be prepared to have to buy a new one.
**10** Using a telescoping bore gauge and a micrometer, check the dimensions of the cylinder to assess the amount of wear, taper and ovality. Measure near the top (but below the level of the top piston ring at TDC), centre and bottom (but above the level of the oil ring at BDC) of the bore, both parallel to and across the crankshaft axis **(see illustrations)**. Compare the results to the specifications at

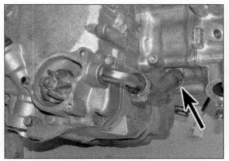

**12.3 Slacken the clamp (arrowed) and detach the hose**

the beginning of the Chapter. If the cylinder is worn, oval or tapered beyond the service limit it can be re-bored – oversize (+0.25 and +0.5) piston and ring sets are available. Note that the person carrying out the re-bore must be aware of the piston-to-bore clearance (see Specifications).
**11** If the precision measuring tools are not available, take the cylinder block to a Honda dealer or specialist motorcycle repair shop for assessment and advice.

### Installation

**12** Check that the mating surfaces of the cylinder block and crankcase are free from oil or pieces of old gasket.
**13** Check that all the studs are tight in the crankcase. If any are loose, or need to be replaced with new ones, remove them, noting that those on the left-hand side of the crankcase are longer than those on the right. Clean their threads and smear them with clean engine oil. Fit them into the crankcase and tighten them using a stud tool, or by threading two of the camshaft holder nuts onto the top of the stud and tightening them together so they are locked on the stud, then tighten the stud by turning the upper of the two nuts. The distance between the top of each stud and the crankcase surface should be 175.5 mm on the right-hand side and 181.5 mm on the left.
**14** If removed, fit the dowels over the studs and into the crankcase and push them firmly home.

**12.4 Carefully lift the block up off the crankcase**

**15** Remove the rags from around the piston and the cam chain tunnel, taking care not to let the connecting rod fall against the rim of the crankcase, and lay the new base gasket in place, locating it over the dowels. The gasket can only fit one way, so if all the holes do not line up properly it is the wrong way round. Never re-use the old gasket.
**16** Ensure the piston ring end gaps are positioned correctly before fitting the cylinder block (see Section 14) **(see illustration 14.11)**. If possible, have an assistant to support the cylinder block while the piston rings are fed into the bore.
**17** Rotate the crankshaft so that the piston is at its highest point (top dead centre). It is useful to place a support under the piston so that it remains at TDC while the block is fitted, otherwise the downward pressure will turn the crankshaft and the piston will drop. Lubricate the cylinder bore, piston and piston rings with clean engine oil.
**18** Carefully lower the block over the studs and onto the piston until the crown fits into the bore, holding the underside of the piston if you are not using a support to prevent it dropping, and making sure it enters the bore squarely and does not get cocked sideways **(see illustration 12.4)**. Feed the cam chain up the tunnel and slip a piece of wire through it to prevent it falling back into the engine. Keep the chain taut to prevent it becoming disengaged from the crankshaft sprocket.
**19** Carefully compress and feed each ring into the bore as the cylinder is lowered **(see**

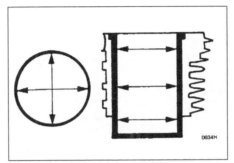

**12.10a Measure the cylinder bore in the directions shown . . .**

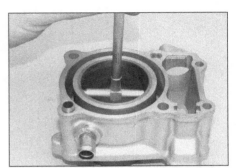

**12.10b . . . using a telescoping gauge, then measure the gauge with a micrometer**

**12.19 Carefully feed each ring into the bore as you lower the block**

**13.3a Prise out the circlip using a suitable tool in the notch . . .**

**13.3b . . . then push out the pin and separate the piston from the rod**

**illustration)**. If necessary, use a soft mallet to gently tap the cylinder down, but do not use force if it appears to be stuck as the piston and/or rings will be damaged.

**20** When the piston and rings are correctly located in the bore, remove the support if used then press the cylinder block down onto the base gasket, making sure the dowels locate.

**21** Hold the block down and turn the crankshaft to check that everything moves as it should.

**22** Connect the coolant hose to its union and secure it with its clamp.

**23** Install the cam chain guide blade, making sure the bottom of the blade sits in its seat and the lugs near its top locate in the cut-outs in the cylinder block **(see illustration 9.10)**.

**24** Install the cylinder head (see Section 10).

## 13 Piston

### Removal

**1** Remove the cylinder block (see Section 12). Check that the holes into the crankcase and the cam chain tunnel are completely blocked with rag.

**2** Note that the piston crown is marked IN (though the mark is likely to be invisible until the piston is cleaned) and this mark faces the intake side of the cylinder **(see illustration 13.15)**.

**3** Carefully prise out the circlip on one side of

**13.10 Measure the piston ring-to-groove clearance with a feeler gauge**

the piston using needle-nose pliers or a small flat-bladed screwdriver inserted into the notch **(see illustration)**. Push the piston pin out from the other side to free the piston from the connecting rod **(see illustration)**. Remove the other circlip and discard them as new ones must be used.

**HAYNES HiNT** *If the piston pin is a tight fit in the piston bosses, heat the piston using a heat gun – this will expand the alloy piston sufficiently to release its grip on the pin. If the piston pin is particularly stubborn, extract it using a drawbolt tool, but be careful to protect the piston's working surfaces.*

**4** Using your thumbs or a piston ring removal and installation tool, carefully remove the rings from the piston **(see illustrations 14.10, 14.9, 14.8 and 14.6c, b and a)**. Do not nick or gouge the piston in the process. Carefully note which way up each ring fits and in which groove as they must be installed in their original positions if being re-used. The upper surface of the top ring should be marked with the letter R at one end (according to Honda's manual, though on the engine we stripped it wasn't), and the second (middle) ring is marked RN **(see illustration 14.8)**. The rings can also be identified by their differing profiles if necessary – the top ring has a chamfered top inner edge.

**5** Scrape all traces of carbon from the top of the piston. A hand-held wire brush or a piece

**13.11 Measure the piston diameter with a micrometer at the specified distance from the bottom of the skirt**

of fine emery cloth can be used once most of the deposits have been scraped away. Do not, under any circumstances, use a wire brush mounted in a drill motor to remove deposits from the piston; the piston material is soft and will be eroded away by the wire brush.

**6** Use a piston ring groove cleaning tool to remove any carbon deposits from the ring grooves. If a tool is not available, a piece broken off an old ring will do the job. Be very careful to remove only the carbon deposits. Do not remove any metal and do not nick or gouge the sides of the ring grooves.

**7** Once the deposits have been removed, clean the piston with solvent and dry them thoroughly. Make sure the oil return holes below the oil ring groove are clear.

### Inspection

**8** Carefully inspect the piston for cracks around the skirt, at the pin bosses and at the ring lands. Normal piston wear appears as even, vertical wear on the thrust surfaces. If the skirt is scored or scuffed, the engine may have been suffering from overheating and/or abnormal combustion, which caused excessively high operating temperatures. Also check that the circlip grooves are not damaged.

**9** A hole in the top of the piston, in one extreme, or burned areas around the edge of the piston crown, indicate that pre-ignition or knocking under load have occurred. If you find evidence of any problems the cause must be corrected or the damage will occur again (see *Fault Finding* in the *Reference* section).

**10** Measure the piston ring-to-groove clearance by laying each piston ring in its groove and slipping a feeler gauge in beside it **(see illustration)**. Make sure you have the correct ring for the groove (see Step 4). Check the clearance at three or four locations around the groove. If the clearance is greater than specified, replace both the piston and rings as a set. If new rings are being used, measure the clearance using the new rings. If the clearance is greater than that specified, the piston is worn and must be replaced with a new one.

**11** Check the piston-to-bore clearance by measuring the bore (see Section 12), then measure the piston 10 mm up from the bottom of the skirt and at 90° to the piston pin axis **(see illustration)**. Refer to the Specifications

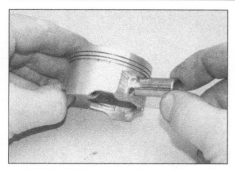

13.12a Fit the pin into the piston and check for any freeplay

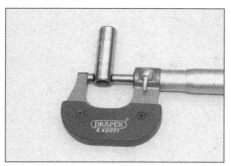

13.12b Measure the external diameter of each end of the pin . . .

13.12c . . . and the internal diameter of the bore in the piston on each side

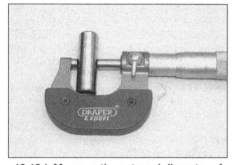

13.12d Measure the external diameter of the middle of the pin . . .

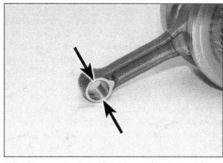

13.12e . . . and the internal diameter of the small-end of the connecting rod

13.15 Make sure the IN mark faces the intake side

at the beginning of the Chapter and Subtract the piston diameter from the bore diameter to obtain the clearance. If it is greater than the specified figure, the piston must be replaced with a new one (assuming the bore itself is within limits).

12 Apply clean engine oil to the piston pin, insert it into the piston and check for any freeplay between the two (see illustration). Measure the pin external diameter at each end (see illustration), and the pin bore in the piston (see illustration). Calculate the difference to obtain the piston pin-to-piston pin bore clearance. Compare the result to the specifications at the beginning of the Chapter. If the clearance is greater than specified, replace the components that are worn beyond their specified limits. Repeat the check between the middle of the pin and the connecting rod small-end (see illustrations).

## Installation

13 Inspect and install the piston rings (see Section 14).
14 Lubricate the piston pin, the piston pin bore and the connecting rod small-end bore with molybdenum disulphide oil (a 50/50 mixture of molybdenum disulphide grease and clean engine oil).
15 When fitting the piston onto the connecting rod make sure the IN mark on the piston crown faces the intake side (back) of the engine (see illustration).
16 Fit a *new* circlip into one side of the piston (do not reuse old circlips). Line up the piston on the connecting rod and insert the piston pin from the other side (see illustration 13.3b). Secure the pin with the other *new* circlip (see illustration). When fitting the circlips, compress them only just enough to fit them in the piston, and make sure they are

properly seated in their grooves with the open end away from the removal notch.
17 Install the cylinder block (see Section 12).

## 14 Piston rings

## Inspection

1 It is good practice to replace the piston rings with new ones when an engine is being overhauled. Before installing the rings, check the end gaps with the rings fitted in the bore, as follows.
2 Fit the top ring into the bottom of the bore and square it up with the bore walls by pushing it in with the top of the piston (see illustrations). The ring should be roughly

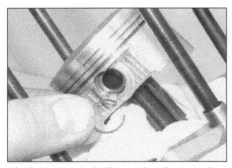

13.16 Use new circlips and make sure they locate correctly

14.2a Fit the ring in its bore . . .

14.2b . . . and set it square using the piston . . .

14.2c . . . then measure the end gap using a feeler gauge

14.6a Fit the oil ring expander in its groove . . .

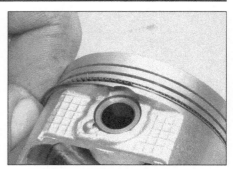

14.6b . . . then fit the lower side rail . . .

half way up the bore. Slip a feeler gauge between the ends of the ring and compare the measurement to the specifications at the beginning of the Chapter (see illustration).

3 If the gap is larger or smaller than specified, double check to make sure that you have the correct ring before proceeding; excess end gap is not critical unless it exceeds the service limit.

4 If the service limit is exceeded with new rings, check the bore for wear (see Section 12). If the gap is too small, the ring ends may come in contact with each other during engine operation, which can cause serious damage.

5 Repeat the procedure for the middle ring and the oil control ring side-rails, but not the expander ring.

### Installation

6 Install the oil control ring (lowest on the piston) first. It is composed of three separate components, namely the expander and the upper and lower side-rails. Slip the expander into the groove, making sure the ends don't overlap, then fit the lower side-rail (see illustrations). Do not use a piston ring installation tool on the side-rails as they may be damaged. Instead, place one end of the side-rail into the groove between the expander and the ring land. Hold it firmly in place and slide a finger around the piston while pushing the rail into the groove. Next, fit the upper side-rail in the same manner (see illustration). Check that the ends of the expander have not overlapped.

7 After the three oil ring components have been installed, check to make sure that both the upper and lower side-rails can be turned smoothly in the ring groove.

8 Identify which of the top and middle rings is which – the upper surface of the top ring should be marked with the letter R at one end (according to Honda's manual, though on the engine we stripped it wasn't), and the second (middle) ring is marked RN (see illustration). The rings can also be identified by their differing profiles if necessary – the top ring has a chamfered top inner edge.

9 Install the second (middle) ring next. Make sure that the identification letter near the end gap is facing up. Fit the ring into the middle groove in the piston (see illustration). Do not expand the ring any more than is necessary to slide it into place. To avoid breaking the ring, use a piston ring installation tool.

10 Finally, fit the top ring in the same manner into the top groove in the piston (see illustration). Make sure the identification letter (where present) near the end gap is facing up, or that the chamfered section of the inner edge is at the top.

11 Once the rings are correctly installed, check they move freely without snagging, and stagger their end gaps as shown (see illustration).

14.6c . . . and the upper side rail on each side of it

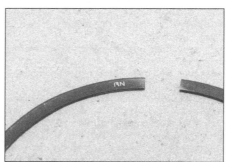

14.8 Note the marking on the ring and make sure it faces up

14.9 Install the middle ring . . .

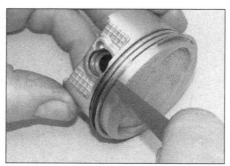

14.10 . . . and the top ring as described

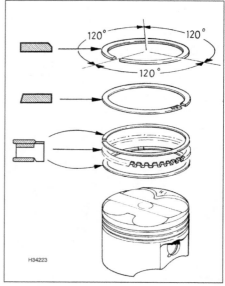

14.11 Piston ring installation details – stagger the ring end gaps as shown

**15.3 Check the operation of the clutch as described**

**15.4 Withdraw the driven gear**

**15.5a Check the sprags (A) and the driven gear hub (B)**

## 15 Starter clutch and gears

**Note:** *The starter clutch can be removed with the engine in the frame. If the engine has been removed, ignore the steps which do not apply.*

### Check

1 The operation of the starter clutch can be checked while it is in situ. Remove the starter motor (see Chapter 10). Check that the idle/reduction gear is able to rotate freely anti-clockwise as you look at it via the starter motor aperture, but locks when rotated clockwise. If not, the starter clutch is faulty and should be removed for inspection.

### Removal

2 Remove the alternator rotor (see Chapter 10) – the starter clutch is bolted to the back of it. If the starter driven gear does not come away with the rotor slide it off the crankshaft.

### Inspection

3 With the alternator face down on a workbench, check that the starter driven gear rotates freely clockwise and locks against the rotor anti-clockwise **(see illustration)**. If it doesn't, the starter clutch should be dismantled for further investigation.

4 Withdraw the starter driven gear from the

starter clutch, rotating it clockwise as you do **(see illustration)**.

5 Check the condition of the sprags inside the clutch body and the corresponding surface on the driven gear hub **(see illustration)**. If they are damaged, marked or flattened at any point, they should be replaced with new ones. Measure the outside diameter of the hub and check that it has not worn beyond the service limit specified **(see illustration)**. To remove the starter clutch assembly, hold the alternator rotor using a holding strap and unscrew the three bolts inside the rotor **(see illustration)**. The clutch outer and sprag piece come as an assembly on some models, while on others the sprag assembly is listed as being available separately – check with your dealer. Lift the sprag assembly out of the housing, noting which way round it fits. Install the new assembly in a reverse sequence – the sprag assembly fits into the lipped side of the housing, and the lipped side faces the alternator rotor. Apply a suitable non-permanent thread locking compound to the bolts and tighten them to the torque setting specified at the beginning of the Chapter.

6 Check the bush in the starter driven gear hub and its bearing surface on the crankshaft **(see illustration)**. If the bush shows signs of excessive wear (the holes or groove in the surface of the bush for holding the oil will be barely visible) replace the driven gear with a new one. You can also measure the internal

diameter of the bush and check that it has not worn beyond the service limit specified.

7 Check the teeth of the reduction and idle gears and the corresponding teeth of the starter driven gear and starter motor drive shaft. Replace the gears and/or starter motor if worn or chipped teeth are discovered on related gears. Also check the idle gear shaft for damage, and check that the gear is not a loose fit on it. Check the reduction gear shaft ends and the bores they run in for wear.

### Installation

8 Lubricate the outside of the starter driven gear hub, the bush in its centre, and the clutch sprags with clean engine oil, then fit the gear into the clutch, rotating it clockwise as you do so to spread the sprags and allow the hub to enter **(see illustration 15.4)**.

9 Install the alternator rotor (see Chapter 10).

## 16 Oil pump

**Note:** *This procedure can be carried out with the engine in the frame.*

### Removal

1 Remove the alternator rotor (see Chapter 10).

**15.5b Measure the diameter of the hub**

**15.5c The starter clutch is secured by the bolts (arrowed)**

**15.6 Check the bush (arrowed) for wear**

16.2 Unscrew the bolt (arrowed) and remove the cover

16.4a Release the circlip . . .

16.4b . . . and remove the sprocket and chain

2 Unscrew the driven sprocket cover bolt and remove the cover (see illustration).
3 Mark the chain and sprocket so they can be fitted the same way round.
4 Remove the circlip securing the sprocket, then draw the sprocket off the shaft and remove it along with the chain (see illustrations). It is best to use a new circlip on installation, and essential if the original one distorts when removed.
5 Unscrew the pump retaining bolts, then remove the oil conveyor and withdraw the pump from the engine (see illustration). If a gasket is fitted behind the pump, discard it as a new one must be fitted.

### Inspection

6 Check the pump body for obvious signs of damage. Turn the pump shaft by hand and check that the pump rotates smoothly.
7 Withdraw the shaft from the pump.

8 Undo the screw securing the inner cover to the pump body and remove cover (see illustrations). Remove the locating pin if it is loose.
9 Note any reference marks on the pump rotors, and make your own if none are visible – they must be reassembled the same way round. Lift the inner and outer rotors out of the pump body.
10 Clean the pump components with a suitable solvent and dry them with compressed air, if available. Inspect the pump body, rotors and shaft for scoring and wear. If any damage, scoring, uneven or excessive wear is evident, either replace the pump with a new one, or fit new rotors, according to what is necessary.
11 Fit the inner and outer rotors the correct way round into the pump body (see illustration 16.8b). Fit the shaft through the body and into the inner rotor, aligning the flats. Align an inner rotor tip with an outer rotor tip then measure the clearance with a feeler

gauge and compare it to the service limit listed in the specifications at the beginning of the Chapter (see illustration). Rotate the shaft and repeat the measurement at several points. If any one clearance measured is greater than the maximum specified at the beginning of the Chapter, replace the rotors with new ones.
12 Measure the clearance between the outer rotor and the pump body with a feeler gauge and compare it to the maximum clearance listed in the specifications at the beginning of the Chapter (see illustration). Repeat the measurement at several points. If any one clearance measured is greater than the maximum specified at the beginning of the Chapter, fit a new pump.
13 Lay a straight-edge across the rotors and the pump body and, using a feeler gauge, measure the rotor end-float (the gap between the rotors and the straight-edge (see

16.5 Unscrew the bolts and remove the conveyor and the pump

16.8a Undo the screw and remove the cover

16.8b Oil pump components

16.11 Measure the inner rotor tip-to-outer rotor clearance as shown

16.12 Measure the outer rotor-to-body clearance as shown

16.13 Measure rotor end-float as shown

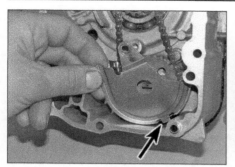

16.19 Fit the conveyor, locating the tab in the slot (arrow)

17.5 Undo the crankcase bolts (arrowed) evenly

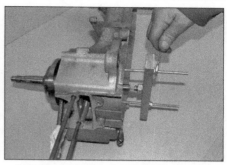

17.7 Pressing the crankshaft out of the left-hand crankcase half

illustration). If the clearance measured is greater than the maximum listed, replace the pump with a new one.

14 If the pump is good, reassemble all the components in reverse order, lubricating them with new oil and making sure the rotors are fitted the same way round and the flats on the shaft and inner rotor are aligned and correctly engaged.

15 Fit the locating pin if removed, then fit the cover and tighten the screw (see illustration 16.8a). Rotate the pump shaft by hand to check that the rotors turn smoothly and freely.

16 Inspect the pump drive chain and sprockets for wear or damage, and renew them as a set if necessary – the drive sprocket on the crankshaft is pressed on, so the crankshaft will have to be taken to a workshop or dealer equipped with an hydraulic press to remove it and to fit a new one. Note that for certain later models the sprocket is not listed as being available separately from the crankshaft assembly, but check with a dealer before assuming you have to buy a new crankshaft – it may be that a sprocket from an earlier model can be used.

### Installation

17 Fit the pump into the crankcase with the M mark at the top, and aligning the bolt holes. Fit the oil conveyor, aligning the holes, then fit the bolts and tighten them (see illustration 16.5).

18 Fit the sprocket into the chain, then loop the chain around the drive sprocket on the crankshaft and fit the driven sprocket onto the pump shaft, aligning the flats (see illustration 16.4b). Fit a new circlip with its chamfered side facing in, and making sure it locates correctly in the groove (see illustration 16.4a).

19 Fit the sprocket cover, fitting its tab into the slot in the conveyor, and tighten its bolt (see illustration).

20 Install the alternator rotor (see Chapter 10).

### 17 Crankcases, crankshaft assembly and bearings

Note: To separate the crankcase halves, the engine must be removed from the frame.
1 The crankshaft assembly should give many

thousands of miles of service. The most likely problems to occur will be worn bearings. A worn big-end bearing produces a pronounced knocking noise, most audible when the engine is under load, and increasing as engine speed rises. A worn small-end bearing produces a lighter, metallic rattle. Worn main bearings produce rumbling noise and vibration. The bearings should all be replaced with new ones as part of a complete engine overhaul, or required due to wear or failure.

2 To access the crankshaft and the big-end bearing, the crankcase must be split into two parts.

### Crankcase separation and crankshaft removal

3 Refer to Section 4 and remove the engine from the frame.

4 Before the crankcase halves can be separated the following components must be removed:
● Cylinder head (Section 10)
● Camchain, blades and sprockets (Section 9)
● Cylinder block (Section 12)
● Alternator rotor (Chapter 10)
● Transmission drive pulley (Chapter 3)
● Starter motor (Chapter 10)
● Oil pump (Section 16)

5 Tape some rag around the connecting rod to prevent it knocking against the cases. Unscrew the three crankcase bolts on the right-hand side evenly, a little at a time until they are all finger-tight, then remove them (see illustration). Note: Ensure that all the crankcase bolts have been removed before attempting to separate the cases.

 Make a cardboard template of the crankcase and punch a hole for each bolt location. This will ensure all bolts are installed correctly on reassembly – this is important as some bolts may be of different lengths.

6 Support the engine with the left-hand side facing down and with the crankcase resting on wooden blocks so the crankshaft is clear of the surface. Using either the Honda service

tool (part No. 07SMC-0010001, or a suitable equivalent two or three-legged puller, bolted into the right-hand crankcase half and with the central bolt bearing onto right-hand end of the crankshaft, or using a home-made set-up using a metal bar and threaded rod and nuts, carefully draw the right-hand crankcase half off the left-hand half, making sure it comes away evenly on all sides. In all cases thread an old nut onto the end of the crankshaft, or use a piece of brass or aluminium plate between the puller bolt or plate, to protect the end of the shaft.

7 Now press the crankshaft assembly out of the left-hand crankcase half, using either a hydraulic press or the set-up shown (see illustration). Again thread an old nut onto the end of the crankshaft or use a piece of brass or aluminium plate to protect the end of the shaft, and make sure you have an assistant ready to prevent the crankshaft dropping when it comes free. Note: If the crankcase halves do not separate easily, first ensure all fasteners have been removed. Apply steady pressure with the tools described and heat the bearing housings with a hot air gun. Do not try and separate the halves by levering against the mating surfaces as they are easily scored and will not seal correctly afterwards. Do not strike the ends of the crankshaft with a hammer as damage to the end threads or the shaft itself will result.

8 The main bearings should remain in place in the crankcase halves during disassembly but could come out with the crankshaft assembly.

9 Remove the two dowels from either crankcase half for safekeeping if they are loose.

### Crankcase inspection

10 Remove all traces of old gasket sealant from the mating surfaces.

11 Clean the crankcases thoroughly with new solvent and dry them with compressed air. Blow out all oil passages with compressed air. Caution: Be very careful not to nick or gouge the crankcase mating surfaces or oil leaks will result. Check both crankcase halves very carefully for cracks and other damage.

12 Clean up minor damage to mating surfaces

**17.17 Measuring connecting rod side clearance**

**17.18 Checking for up-and-down play in the big-end bearing**

with a fine sharpening stone or grindstone. Small cracks or holes in aluminium castings can be repaired with an epoxy resin adhesive as a temporary measure or with one of the low temperature welding kits. Permanent repairs can only be done by TIG (tungsten inert gas or heli-arc) welding, and only a specialist in this process is in a position to advise on the economy or practical aspect of such a repair. If any damage is found that can't be repaired, replace the crankcase halves as a set.

**13** Damaged threads can be economically reclaimed using a diamond section wire insert, for example of the Heli-Coil type (though there are other makes), which are easily fitted after drilling and re-tapping the affected thread.

**14** Studs or bolts that have sheared below their bore in the case can usually be removed with extractors, which consist of a tapered, left-hand thread screw of very hard steel. These are tightened into a hole that must be drilled into the stud or screw, and usually succeed in dislodging the most stubborn stud or screw. If a stud or bolt has sheared above its bore line, it can be removed using a conventional stud extractor which avoids the need for drilling.

***Haynes Hint: Refer to Tools and Workshop Tips for details of installing a thread insert and using screw extractors.***

## Crankshaft and connecting rod inspection

**15** Clean the crankshaft and connecting rod with solvent. If available, blow them dry with compressed air.

**16** Place the crankshaft on V-blocks and check for runout using a dial gauge – on the left-hand side set the gauge 100 mm along the shaft from the outside of the web, and the right set it 50 mm from the web. Compare the reading to the maximum specified at the beginning of the Chapter. If the runout exceeds the limit, the crankshaft must be replaced with a new one.

**17** Measure the connecting rod side clearance (the gap between the connecting rod big-end and the crankshaft web) with a feeler gauge **(see illustration)**. If the clearance is greater than the service limit listed in this Chapter's Specifications, replace the crankshaft with a new one.

**18** Hold the crankshaft still and check for any radial (up and down) play in the big-end bearing by pushing and pulling the rod against the crank **(see illustration)**. If a dial gauge is available measure the amount of radial play and compare the reading to the maximum specified at the beginning of the Chapter. If the play exceeds the limit, the crankshaft must be replaced with a new one.

**19** Have the rod checked for twist and bend by a Honda dealer if you are in doubt about its straightness.

**20** Refer to Section 13 and check the connecting rod small end and piston pin for wear.

**21** Refer to Sections 9 and 16 and inspect the camshaft and oil pump drive sprocket teeth on the crankshaft for damage or wear.

**22** The connecting rod and its bearing are an integral part of the crankshaft assembly which comes as a pressed-up unit – individual components are not available.

### Main bearings

**23** Check the condition of the bearings (see *Tools and Workshop Tips* in the *Reference* section) and only remove them if they are unserviceable. Always renew both main bearings at the same time, never individually. When driving the bearings out and in make sure the crankcase is squarely and adequately supported under the bearing housing on a block or blocks of wood or on a flat surface such as an MDF or ply board on a workbench, the idea being not to have the crankcase resting on anything that can damage a mating surface

**24** To remove the bearings from the crankshaft use a bearing puller **(see illustration)**. If the crankshaft is worn or damaged where the bearings seat a new assembly will have to be fitted.

**25** To remove the bearings from the cases, heat the bearing housings with a hot air gun and tap them out from the outside of the case using a bearing driver or suitable socket.

**26** New bearings should be fitted into the crankcases, not onto the crankshaft. Place the bearings in the freezer for a while and heat the crankcases in an oven or using a hot air gun around the bearing housings just before you fit the cold bearings – while the temperature differences sometimes allow the bearings to drop nicely into their housings, it is likely you will still need to drive them in using a bearing driver or a socket that bears only on the outer race. Lubricate the bearing housings with a smear of clean oil and drive the bearings in from the inside of the casing with the marked side of the bearing facing up, until they seat. Once they have seated check that the distance from the crankcase mating surface to the bearing inner race surface is 24.54 to 24.62 mm for the right-hand bearing and 21.55 to 21.63 mm for the left-hand bearing – this can be done quite easily by laying a straight edge across the crankcase mating surface and using a Vernier gauge.

### Reassembly

**27** Draw the crankshaft assembly into the left-hand crankcase half first, ensuring that the connecting rod is aligned with the crankcase mouth, and that the crankshaft enters the bearing squarely. Lubricate the shaft and bearing with clean engine oil and tape some rag around the connecting rod to prevent it knocking against the cases. Pull the assembly into place either with the service tools (part Nos. 07965-VM00100 and 07965-VM00200) or using the set-up shown **(see illustration)**. Pull the crankshaft fully into the bearing until it seats. Heating the bearing and cooling the crankshaft will ease installation.

**28** Wipe the mating surfaces of both crankcase halves with a rag soaked in a suitable solvent.

**17.24 Using a puller to draw a bearing off the crankshaft**

**17.27 Drawing the crankshaft into the left-hand crankcase**

**17.29 Pressing the right-hand crankcase onto the crankshaft**

Fit the dowels. Apply a small amount of suitable sealant to the mating surface of the right-hand case. Lubricate around the connecting rod big-end and bearing with clean oil.

**29** Now fit the right-hand crankcase half. Lubricate the shaft and bearing with clean engine oil. Press the crankcase half onto the crankshaft, either with the service tools (part Nos. 07YMF-KFG0300, 07965-VM00100 and 07965-VM00200) or using the set-up shown **(see illustration)**. Press the crankcase on until it seats. Heating the bearing and cooling the crankshaft will ease installation.

**30** Check that the crankcase halves are seated all the way round. If the casings are not correctly seated, heat the bearing housings

while applying firm pressure with the assembly tools used previously. **Note:** *Do not attempt to pull the crankcase halves together using the crankcase bolts as the casing will crack and be ruined.*

**31** Clean the threads of the crankcase bolts and install them finger-tight, then tighten them evenly a little at a time to the torque setting specified at the beginning of the Chapter **(see illustration 17.5)**. Support the connecting rod and rotate the crankshaft by hand – if there are any signs of undue stiffness, tight or rough spots, or of any other problem, the fault must be rectified before proceeding further.

**32** Install the remaining components in the reverse order of removal.

## 18 Initial start-up and running-in

**1** Make sure the engine oil and coolant levels are correct (see *Pre-ride checks*). Make sure there is fuel in the tank.

**2** Start the engine and allow it to run at a moderately fast idle until it reaches operating temperature.

 *Warning: If the oil pressure warning light doesn't go off, or it comes on while the engine is running, stop the engine immediately.*

**3** If a lubrication failure is suspected, stop the engine immediately and try to find the cause. If an engine is run without oil, even for a short period of time, severe damage will occur.

**4** Check carefully that there are no oil or coolant leaks and make sure the transmission and controls, especially the brakes, function properly before road testing the machine.

**5** Treat the machine gently for the first few miles to make sure oil has circulated throughout the engine and any new parts installed have started to seat.

**6** Even greater care is necessary if a new piston and rings or a new cylinder have been fitted, and the bike will have to be run in as when new. This means a restraining hand on the throttle until at least 300 miles (500 km) have been covered. There's no point in keeping to any set speed limit – the main idea is to keep from labouring the engine and to gradually increase performance up to the 300 miles (500 km) mark. Experience is the best guide, since it's easy to tell when an engine is running freely.

**7** Upon completion of the road test, and after the engine has cooled down completely, recheck the valve clearances (see Chapter 1) and check the engine oil and coolant levels (see *Pre-ride checks*).

**Notes**

# Chapter 3
# Transmission

## Contents

## Degrees of difficulty

| | | | | |
|---|---|---|---|---|
| **Easy,** suitable for novice with little experience  | **Fairly easy,** suitable for beginner with some experience | **Fairly difficult,** suitable for competent DIY mechanic | **Difficult,** suitable for experienced DIY mechanic | **Very difficult,** suitable for expert DIY or professional  |

## Specifications

### Variator

Roller diameter
  Standard ................................................... 19.92 to 20.08 mm
  Service limit .............................................. 19.5 mm
Sleeve diameter
  125 cc engines
    Standard ................................................. 23.960 to 23.974 mm
    Service limit ............................................ 23.93 mm
  150 cc engines
    Standard ................................................. 23.986 to 24.000 mm
    Service limit ............................................ 23.956 mm
Bush diameter
  125 cc engines
    Standard ................................................. 23.989 to 24.052 mm
    Service limit ............................................ 24.09 mm
  150 cc engines
    Standard ................................................. 24.015 to 24.026 mm
    Service limit ............................................ 24.064 mm

### Clutch and driven pulley

Clutch drum inside diameter
  Standard ................................................... 125.0 to 125.2 mm
  Service limit .............................................. 125.5 mm
Pulley inner face shaft OD
  Standard ................................................... 33.965 to 33.985 mm
  Service limit .............................................. 33.94 mm
Pulley outer face bore ID
  Standard ................................................... 34.000 to 34.025 mm
  Service limit .............................................. 34.06 mm
Spring free length
  Standard ................................................... 143.3 mm
  Service limit .............................................. 123.0 mm
Clutch shoe lining thickness
  Standard ................................................... 4.0 mm
  Service limit .............................................. 2.0 mm

## Drive belt

Width

| | |
|---|---|
| Standard | 22.5 mm |
| Service limit | 21.5 mm |

## Torque settings

| | |
|---|---|
| Drive belt cover bolts | 10 Nm |
| Drive pulley nut | 59 Nm |
| Clutch drum nut | 49 Nm |
| Clutch assembly nut | 54 Nm |

### 1 General information

The transmission is fully automatic. Power is transmitted from the engine to the rear wheel by belt, via a variable size drive pulley (the variator), an automatic clutch and a variable driven pulley and finally a reduction gearbox. Both the variator and the automatic clutch work on the principal of centrifugal force. As the speed of the drive pulley increases the variator squeezes the two sides of the pulley together which makes the belt climb up the walls, its effective diameter increasing as it does. As this happens the effective diameter of the belt around the driven pulley at the rear decreases. The result of the increasing front/decreasing rear pulley as speed builds, and vice versa as speed reduces, gives a variable gear ratio.

The transmission can be worked on with the engine in the frame.

### 2 Drive belt cover

#### Removal

1 Remove the left-hand lower panel, floor panel or body cover as required according to model for access to the transmission cover on the left-hand side of the engine (see Chapter 9).

2 If required remove the air filter housing (see Chapter 5A or B). Unscrew the two bolts and remove the transmission filter housing from the cover **(see illustration)**. Remove the O-ring and discard it – a new one should be used **(see illustration)**.

3 On all except Pantheon and S-wing models unscrew the rear brake cable guide bolt and displace the cable **(see illustration)**.

4 Undo the transmission cover bolts and remove the cover **(see illustration)** – if it will not lift away easily, tap it gently around the edge with a soft-faced hammer. Remove the gasket – if it is damaged, discard it and fit a new one on reassembly. Note the location of the dowels and remove them for safekeeping if they are loose **(see illustration)**.

5 Clean any dust or dirt from the inside of the

2.2a Unscrew the bolts and remove the cover . . .

2.2b . . . and the O-ring

2.3 Unscrew the bolt and displace the cable guide

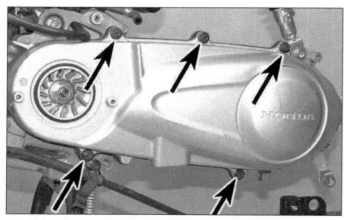

2.4a Unscrew the bolts (arrowed) and remove the cover

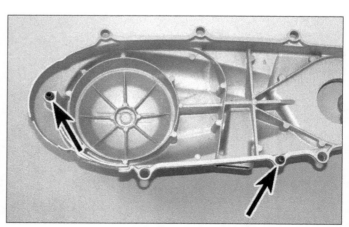

2.4b Remove the dowels (arrowed) if loose

**2.6a  Fit a new seal (arrowed) onto each bolt if necessary**

casing with a suitable solvent, taking care to avoid contact with the belt and the drive faces of the pulleys. Any evidence of oil inside the casing suggests a worn seal either on the crankshaft or the gearbox input shaft which must be rectified. Evidence of grease inside the casing suggests worn seals in the clutch centre which should also be rectified.

### Installation

6  Installation is the reverse of removal, noting the following:
- Check the condition of the rubber seals on the bolts and fit new ones if they are damaged or deformed or have deteriorated **(see illustration)**
- If removed, fit the dowels in the case **(see illustration 2.4b)**
- Fit the gasket, using a new one if necessary, over the dowels **(see illustration)**

**3.2  Using a holding tool while unscrewing the drive pulley nut**

**3.3b  Slide off the outer face of the pulley . . .**

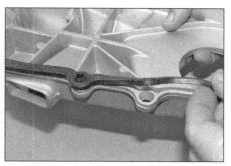

**2.6b  Lay the gasket over the dowels**

### 3  Drive pulley and variator

### Removal

**Note:** *It is not necessary to remove the drive belt from the machine during this procedure. If the belt is removed, note any directional*

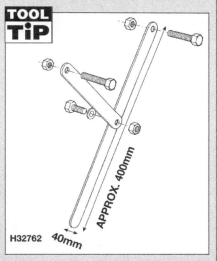

*A holding tool can be made using two strips of steel bolted together in the middle, and with a nut and bolt through each end which locate into the holes, or between the fins, on the pulley.*

**3.3c  . . . then move the belt aside . . .**

arrows or mark the belt so that it can be installed the same way round.

1  Remove the drive belt cover (see Section 2).
2  To slacken the drive pulley nut, the pulley must be held to prevent it turning. Honda produce a holding tool (Part No. 07725-0030000) that locates in the holes in the outer face of the pulley, and similar holding tools are commercially available from good suppliers. Alternatively a tool that can be made from two strips of steel will hold the pulley in a similar way (see **Tool Tip**). In all cases make sure the tool is securely located **(see illustration)**.
3  With the pulley held, unscrew the nut and remove the washer **(see illustration)**. Slide the outer half of the drive pulley off the shaft **(see illustration)**. Move the drive belt aside, or of required slip it out of the driven pulley and remove it **(see illustration)**. Grip the variator assembly so that the ramp plate at the back is held into the housing, then draw the assembly, including the centre sleeve, off the crankshaft **(see illustration)**.
4  Withdraw the centre sleeve, then lift out the ramp plate, noting how it fits **(see illustration 3.12b)**.
5  Lift out the rollers, noting which way round they fit **(see illustration 3.12a)**.
6  Clean all the components using a suitable solvent.

### Inspection

7  Inspect the surface of each roller for wear and flat spots. Measure the diameter of the rollers and compare the result to the

**3.3a  Unscrew the nut and remove the washer**

**3.3d  . . . and slide off the inner face and variator assembly as described**

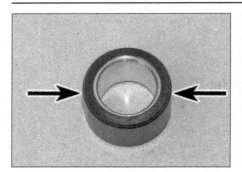

**3.7 Measure the diameter of each roller**

**3.12a Fit the rollers onto the ramps**

**3.9 Check the sleeve and bush (arrowed) for wear and damage**

**3.12b Fit the guides (arrowed) onto the ramp plate, then fit the plate**

specifications at the beginning of this Chapter **(see illustration)**. Replace the rollers with a new set if any are worn below the minimum diameter.

**8** Inspect the surface of the ramps in the variator body and the ramp plate for wear or damage **(see illustrations 3.12a and b)**. Also check the splines in the centre of the ramp plate and renew the plate if they are worn. Check the slots in the ramp plate guides where they fit in the variator body and fit new guides if necessary.

**9** Inspect the surfaces of the sleeve and the bush in the housing for wear – the sleeve should be a good sliding fit in the bush with no excessive freeplay between them **(see illustration)**. Measure the external diameter of the sleeve and the internal diameter of the bush – if either component is worn beyond the specified service limit replace it with a new one.

**10** Check the condition of the splines in the centre of the outer half of the drive pulley. Inspect the inner faces of the pulley halves for signs of overheating or blueing, caused by the pulley running out of alignment. Fit a new pulley assembly if it is damaged.

## Installation

**11** Ensure the inner surfaces of both pulley halves, the sleeve, the rollers and the ramps are clean and oil-free.

**12** Fit the rollers onto the ramps, making sure they are fitted in their original positions (unless new ones are used) **(see illustration)**. Check that the ramp guides are correctly fitted on the ramp plate, then fit the plate **(see illustration)**. Insert the centre sleeve.

**13** Grip the variator so that the ramp plate is held into the housing, then slide the assembly all the way onto the crankshaft **(see illustration 3.3d)**. **Note:** *If the ramp plate moves and the*

*rollers are dislodged, disassemble the variator and reposition the rollers correctly.*

**14** Position the drive belt around the driven pulley if removed from it, and around the end of the shaft **(see illustration 3.3c)**. If fitting a new belt, make sure any directional arrows point in the direction of normal rotation. Ensure there is sufficient slack in the belt to avoid it being trapped when the outer half of the pulley is installed – if necessary, grasp the driven pulley and pull it towards the clutch to compress the spring and press the drive belt into the pulley to create slack at the front to ease fitting of the drive pulley.

**15** Slide the outer half of the drive pulley onto the crankshaft **(see illustration 3.3b)**.

**16** Lubricate the nut threads and inner seating face with clean oil. Fit the washer and tighten the nut finger-tight **(see illustration 3.3a)**. Make sure the outer pulley half butts against the centre sleeve and is not skewed by the drive belt.

**17** Use the method employed on removal to prevent the pulley turning and tighten the nut to the torque setting specified at the beginning of this Chapter **(see illustration 3.2)**.

**18** Ease the drive belt out of the driven pulley to reduce the slack in the belt.

**19** Install the drive belt cover (see Section 2).

## 4 Clutch and driven pulley

## Removal

**1** Remove the drive belt cover (see Section 2).

**2** To slacken the clutch nut it is necessary to hold the clutch drum and stop it from turning. Honda produce a holding tool (Part No. 07725-0040000) that locates around and grips the outer rim of the drum, and similar strap-type rotor holding tools are commercially available from good suppliers.

**3** With the drum securely held, unscrew the nut, then remove the washer **(see illustration)**. Remove the clutch drum **(see illustration)**.

**4** Draw the clutch and driven pulley assembly off the gearbox input shaft **(see illustration)**. Disengage the drive belt from the pulley. **Note:** *If the belt is removed from the machine, note*

**4.3a Counter-hold the clutch drum and unscrew the nut**

**4.3b remove the drum**

**4.4 Draw the assembly off the shaft**

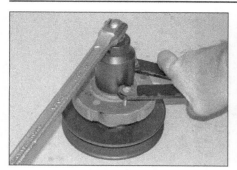

**4.5a  Loosen the clutch assembly nut . . .**

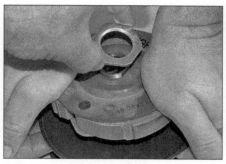

**4.5b  . . . then press down to compress the clutch spring and unscrew the nut fully**

**4.6  Relax the spring and remove the clutch . . .**

*any directional arrows or mark the belt so that it can be installed the same way round.*

**5** To disassemble the clutch and pulley assembly, it is necessary first to hold it using a holding tool to initially slacken the nut, then to compress and hold the clutch spring while the nut is undone and removed. Lay the clutch on a flat surface, fit a holding tool (see Section 3, Step 2) in the holes in the backplate and loosen the nut **(see illustration)**. Now have an assistant press down on the clutch to compress the clutch spring while the nut is finally unscrewed by hand and removed **(see illustration)**.

⚠ *Warning: The clutch assembly is under pressure from the centre spring – take care to maintain downwards pressure on the backplate to avoid damage or injury.*

**6** Carefully release the downward pressure on the clutch, allowing the spring to relax, and remove the clutch **(see illustration)**.

**7** Remove the spring collar, the spring, the spring seat and the washer **(see illustrations)**.
**8** Lift the centre sleeve off the boss, then pull out the guide pins, noting how they fit, and separate the pulley halves **(see illustrations)**. Note the location of the seals and the O-rings in the boss **(see illustration 4.17)** – new

O-rings should be fitted on reassembly, and new seals must be fitted if there is any evidence of grease having worked its way past them and onto the shaft on the inner half of the pulley **(see illustrations)**.
**9** Clean all the components with a suitable solvent.

**4.7a  . . . then remove the spring collar . . .**

**4.7b  . . . the spring . . .**

**4.7c  . . . and the spring seat and washer**

**4.8a  Remove the sleeve . . .**

**4.8b  . . . and the guide pins . . .**

**4.8c  . . . then separate the pulley halves**

**4.8d  Remove the old O-rings and discard them . . .**

**4.8e  . . . and if necessary lever the seals out**

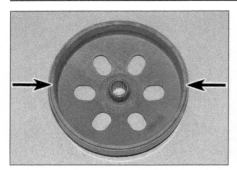

4.10 Measure the diameter of the clutch drum

4.11a Measure the thickness of the friction material

4.11b Remove the E-clips . . .

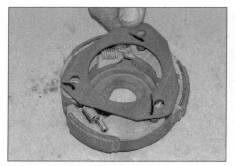

4.11c . . . then lift off the back plate . . .

4.11d . . . and remove the shoes and springs as described

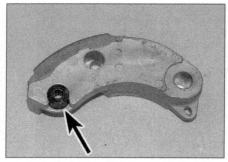

4.11e Rubber damper located in shoe cut-out (arrow)

## Inspection

**10** Check the inner surface of the clutch drum for damage and scoring and inspect the splines in the centre – the clutch drum should be a firm fit on the gearbox input shaft, with no backlash between the drum and the shaft.

Measure the internal diameter of the drum at several points to determine if it is worn or out-of-round **(see illustration)**. If the drum is out-of-round, or if the results are outside the specifications listed at the beginning of this Chapter, replace it with a new one.

**11** Check the amount of friction material remaining on the clutch shoes and compare the results with the specifications **(see illustration)**. Inspect the shoe springs for wear and stretching. Ensure that the shoes are not seized on their pivot pins and that the retaining E-clips are secure in the grooves in the ends of the pins. To fit new shoes, release the three E-clips and remove the back plate **(see illustrations)**. Evenly lever the shoes up off the pins until they can be removed, then separate them and remove the springs **(see illustration)**. Check the condition of the rubber dampers and replace them with new ones if damaged, deformed or deteriorated – they will be either in the cut-out in each shoe or on the pegs on the drive plate **(see illustration)**. Fit the rubber dampers onto the pegs on the drive plate **(see illustration)**. Fit each shoe onto its pin, making sure it is the correct way

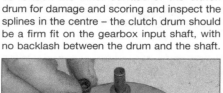

4.11f Fit the dampers onto the pegs

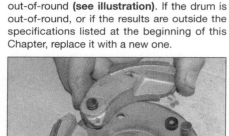

4.11g Fit the shoe onto the pin . . .

4.11h . . . then locate the cut-out over the damper

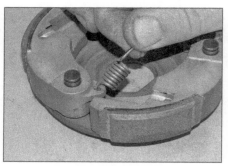

4.11i Fit the springs . . .

4.11j . . . using a cable tie or similar to stretch them into place

round, then pivot it inwards so the cut-out on the underside locates over the rubber damper **(see illustration)**. Fit the springs, making sure each end locates correctly in its hole – use a cable-tie as shown to stretch the springs into their holes, then cut the ties to remove them **(see illustrations)**. Fit the back plate, tapping it down over the pins until the grooves are exposed, then fit the E-clips into the grooves **(see illustrations)**.

**12**  Inspect the inner faces of the driven pulley for signs of overheating or blueing, caused by the pulley running out of alignment. If the pulley has run out of alignment, first check the condition of the bearings in the hub of the pulley inner half (see Step 14), then check the gearbox input shaft for play in the bearings (see Section 6).

**13**  Measure the external diameter of the shaft on the inner half of the pulley and the internal diameter of the boss on the outer half and compare the results to the specifications at the beginning of the Chapter **(see illustration)**. Replace either or both half with a new one if they are worn beyond their limits.

**14**  A needle roller bearing and a sealed ball bearing are fitted in the hub of the pulley inner half **(see illustration)**. Inspect the bearing rollers for flat spots and pitting and check that the ball bearing turns smoothly. If either bearing is worn or damaged replace them both with new ones. First remove the needle bearing using a puller, then remove the circlip retaining the ball bearing and drive the bearing out – refer to the reference section for more information on bearing removal and installation methods and tools.

**15**  Inspect the guide pins and their slots in the pulley outer boss and replace any components that are worn with new ones **(see illustration 4.8b)**.

**16**  Check the condition of the spring. Measure its free length and compare the result with the figure in the Specifications **(see illustration)**. Replace the spring with a new one if it is bent or has sagged to less than the service limit.

4.11k  Make sure the back plate is correctly seated . . .

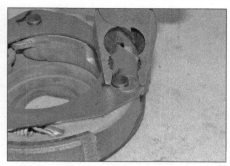
4.11l  . . . then fit the E-clips

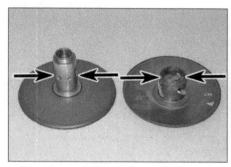
4.13  Measure the shaft and the boss to assess wear

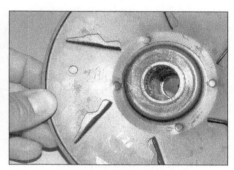
4.14  Check the bearings

### Installation

**17**  Fit new O-rings smeared with grease onto the pulley outer half boss, and fit new oil seals if required **(see illustration)**. Lubricate the oil seal lips with grease.

**18**  Fit the outer half of the pulley onto the inner half **(see illustration 4.8c)**. Make sure the rollers are fitted on the guide pins. Apply grease to the guide pin slots, then fit the guide pins **(see illustration 4.8b)**. Fit the centre sleeve over the boss with its flanged end facing down **(see illustration 4.8a)**.

**19**  Fit the washer, the spring seat, the spring and the collar – the spring seat must be fitted

dished-side up so the base of the spring seats in it **(see illustrations 4.7c, b and a)**.

**20**  Position the clutch assembly over the spring, then press it down to compress the spring, ensuring that the flats on the clutch drive plate are aligned with the flats on the end of the shaft, and hold it there while an assistant threads the nut finger tight onto the shaft **(see illustrations 4.6 and 4.5b)**. Fit the holding tool as on disassembly and tighten the nut to the torque setting specified at the beginning of this Chapter **(see illustration 4.5a)**.

**21**  Lubricate the needle bearing inside the pulley inner half with grease **(see illustration 4.14)**.

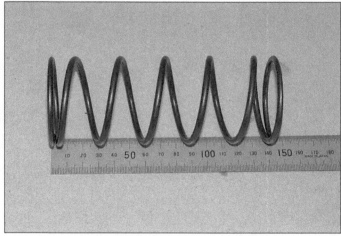
4.16  Measure the spring free length

4.17  Fit new O-rings (A), and seals (B) if required

**4.25 Fit the washer then thread the nut on**

**5.3 Remove the belt from around the driven pulley**

22 Ensure the inner surfaces of both pulley halves and the inside surface of the clutch drum are clean and grease-free.

23 If the drive pulley has not been removed fit the drive belt around the driven pulley halves and ease the belt into the pulley, forcing the halves apart clutch. When there is sufficient slack in the belt, slide the assembly onto the gearbox input shaft. If the drive pulley has been removed the belt can be fitted around the driven pulley after fitting it onto the shaft **(see illustration 4.4)**.

24 Fit the clutch drum, aligning the splines with those on the shaft **(see illustration 4.3b)**.

25 Fit the washer and tighten the nut finger-tight **(see illustration)**. Using the method employed on removal to prevent the clutch turning tighten the nut to the specified torque setting **(see illustration 4.3a)**.

26 Install the drive belt cover (see Section 2).

## 5 Drive belt

### Inspection

1 The belt should be inspected regularly according to the service interval (see Chapter 1). **Note:** *Oil or grease inside the casing will contaminate the belt and prevent it gripping the pulleys. Any evidence of oil inside the casing suggests a worn seal on either the crankshaft or the gearbox input shaft; evidence of grease suggests worn seals in the clutch centre.*

### Renewal

2 Follow the procedure in Section 3 to remove the outer half of the drive pulley. Lift the belt off the shaft.

3 Remove the belt from around the driven pulley **(see illustration)**.

4 Fit the new belt, making sure any directional arrows point in the direction of normal rotation. Ease the belt into the driven pulley to ensure there is sufficient slack to avoid the belt being trapped when the outer half of the drive pulley is installed.

5 Install the outer half of the drive pulley (see Section 3).

6 Install the drive belt cover (see Section 2).

## 6 Gearbox

### Removal

1 Remove the clutch and driven pulley (see Section 4) and the rear wheel (see Chapter 8).

2 Drain the gearbox oil (see Chapter 1).

3 On all drum brake models unscrew the drum brake cable adjustment nut, then draw the cable out of the arm **(see illustrations)**. Remove the bush from the arm, and the spring from between the arm and the case, noting how it locates **(see illustrations)**.

4 Undo the bolts securing the gearbox cover and remove the cover – hold the end of the output shaft to keep it in place so the cover comes away by itself leaving all shafts and

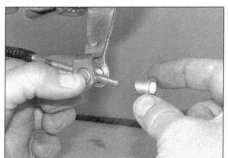

**6.3a Fully unscrew the nut . . .**

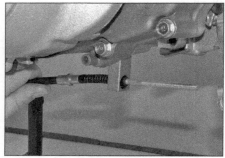

**6.3b . . . then draw the cable out**

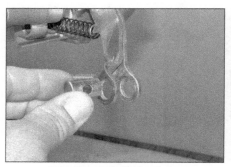

**6.3c Remove the bush . . .**

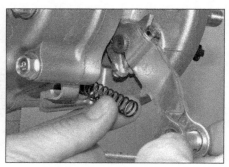

**6.3d . . . and the spring**

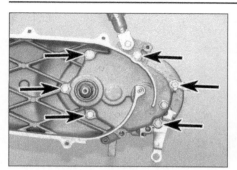

6.4a Unscrew the bolts (arrowed) . . .

6.4b . . . and remove the cover as described

6.4c Cover locating dowels (arrowed)

gears in place (see illustrations). Remove the gasket and discard it as a new one will have to be fitted. Note the location of the dowels and remove them for safekeeping if they are loose (see illustration).

**5** Remove the thrust washer and outer gear from the intermediate shaft, then remove the shaft (see illustrations).

**6** Remove the output shaft (see illustration).

**7** If required, drive the input shaft from the transmission casing using a soft-faced hammer on the shaft end, but note that the bearing and oil seal will have to be replaced with new ones if you do so (see illustration). If there are no signs of oil leakage on the outside of the cover (behind the clutch), and if the shaft turns smoothly and freely with no signs of freeplay in the bearing or between the shaft and the bearing, it is better not to remove it, unless the shaft itself is worn or damaged.

### Inspection

**8** Remove all traces of old gasket from the casing and cover mating surfaces, taking care not to nick or gouge the soft aluminium if a scraper is used. Wash all of the components in clean solvent and dry them off.

**9** Check the pinion teeth for cracking, chipping, pitting and other obvious wear or damage. Check the splines on the shafts for wear and damage. Replace worn or damaged components with new ones.

**10** Check for signs of scoring or bluing on the

6.5a Remove the thrust washer . . .

6.5b . . . the outer gear . . .

pinions and shaft. This could be caused by overheating due to inadequate lubrication.

**11** Note which way round the output shaft oil seal is fitted in the cover, then lever it out and

discard it as a new one must be used (see illustration). Drive the input shaft oil seal out using a socket or driver (see illustration).

**12** Check that all the bearings turn smoothly

6.5c . . . and the intermediate shaft

6.6 Remove the output shaft

6.7 Drive the input shaft out using a soft hammer

6.11a Lever the output shaft oil seal out of the cover . . .

6.11b . . . and drive the input shaft oil seal out of the housing

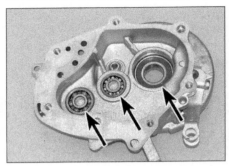

6.12a Check the bearings (arrowed) in the cover . . .

6.12b . . . in the casing . . .

6.12c . . . and on the input shaft

and freely without excessive play between the inner and outer races (see illustrations). The bearings should be a tight fit in the casing; if a bearing is loose, and the casing is not damaged, use a suitable bearing locking compound to hold it in place.

13 The output shaft bearing in the cover can be driven out with a bearing driver or suitably sized socket. The bearing on the input shaft must be removed using a puller or a press. The other bearings in the casing and cover can be removed using an internal expanding puller with slide hammer attachment. To ease removal of the bearings in the casing and cover heat the area around it using a hot-air gun. Install the new bearings into the casing and cover using a bearing driver or socket large enough to contact the outer race of the bearing. Install a new oil seal as required. The new input shaft bearing can either be pressed onto the shaft, or driven on using a suitable tube that bears on the inner race of the bearing.

14 Fit new oil seals and lubricate their lips with grease (see illustrations).

### Installation

15 Fit the input shaft into the casing, then use a drift located against the outer race of the bearing and tap around it until the bearing seats (see illustrations).

16 Fit the output shaft into its bearing in the casing (see illustration 6.6).

17 Fit the intermediate shaft into its bearing in the casing (see illustrations 6.5c). Fit the outer gear and thrust washer onto the shaft (see illustrations 6.5b and a).

18 If removed, fit the dowels, then locate the new gasket onto them (see illustration 6.4c).

19 Install the cover, ensuring the shafts engage fully with their bearings, then tighten the cover bolts evenly and in a criss-cross pattern (see illustration 6.4a). Ensure that the input and output shafts turn freely.

20 Install the clutch and driven pulley (see Section 4) and the rear wheel (see Chapter 8).

21 Fill the gearbox with the specified amount and type of oil (see Chapter 1).

22 On drum brake models locate the brake arm spring between the arm and the case, with the case end in the hole and the arm end over the point (see illustration 6.3d). Fit the bush into the arm, then fit the cable through the bush and thread the nut on (see illustrations 6.3c, b and a). Refer to Chapter 1 and adjust the brake freeplay.

6.14a Fit the new seals . . .

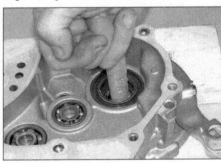

6.14b . . . and lubricate their lips

6.15a Fit the input shaft into the casing . . .

6.15b . . . and tap the bearing in until it seats

# Chapter 4
## Cooling system

## Contents

## Degrees of difficulty

| **Easy,** suitable for novice with little experience 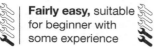 | **Fairly easy,** suitable for beginner with some experience | **Fairly difficult,** suitable for competent DIY mechanic | **Difficult,** suitable for experienced DIY mechanic | **Very difficult,** suitable for expert DIY or professional  |
|---|---|---|---|---|

## Specifications

### Coolant
Mixture type . . . . . . . . . . . . . . . . . . . . . . . . . . . . . . . . . . . . . . . . 50% distilled water, 50% corrosion inhibited ethylene glycol anti-freeze

Coolant capacity
  SH models
    2001 to 2004 . . . . . . . . . . . . . . . . . . . . . . . . . . . . . . . . . . . 1.15 litres
    2005-on . . . . . . . . . . . . . . . . . . . . . . . . . . . . . . . . . . . . . . . 1.35 litres
  Dylan and @ models . . . . . . . . . . . . . . . . . . . . . . . . . . . . . . . 0.95 litres
  PS models . . . . . . . . . . . . . . . . . . . . . . . . . . . . . . . . . . . . . . 1.3 litres
  Pantheon and S-wing models . . . . . . . . . . . . . . . . . . . . . . . . 1.2 litres

### Temperature gauge sensor
SH, Dylan, @ and PS models
  Resistance at 80°C . . . . . . . . . . . . . . . . . . . . . . . . . . . . . . . . 47 to 57 ohms
  Resistance at 120°C . . . . . . . . . . . . . . . . . . . . . . . . . . . . . . . 14 to 18 ohms
Pantheon and S-wing models
  Resistance at 50°C . . . . . . . . . . . . . . . . . . . . . . . . . . . . . . . . 6.8 to 7.4 ohms
  Resistance at 120°C . . . . . . . . . . . . . . . . . . . . . . . . . . . . . . . 0.6 to 0.8 ohms

### Thermostat
Opening temperature . . . . . . . . . . . . . . . . . . . . . . . . . . . . . . . . . 80 to 84°C
Fully open . . . . . . . . . . . . . . . . . . . . . . . . . . . . . . . . . . . . . . . . . 95°C
Valve lift . . . . . . . . . . . . . . . . . . . . . . . . . . . . . . . . . . . . . . . . . . 4.5 mm

### Radiator
Cap valve opening pressure . . . . . . . . . . . . . . . . . . . . . . . . . . . . 16 to 20 psi (1.1 to 1.4 Bar)

### Torque settings
Coolant temperature sensor
  Carburettor models . . . . . . . . . . . . . . . . . . . . . . . . . . . . . . . . 10 Nm
  Fuel injection models . . . . . . . . . . . . . . . . . . . . . . . . . . . . . . . 23 Nm
Cooling fan switch (carburettor models) . . . . . . . . . . . . . . . . . . 18 Nm
Water pump impeller . . . . . . . . . . . . . . . . . . . . . . . . . . . . . . . . . 12 Nm

2.2a Radiator pressure cap (A) and reservoir cap (B) – SH and PS models

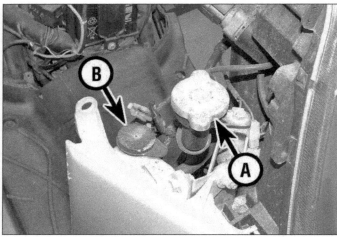

2.2b Radiator pressure cap (A) and reservoir cap (B) – Dylan and @ models

## 1 General information

The cooling system uses a water and anti-freeze coolant mixture to carry away excess heat from the engine and maintain as constant a temperature as possible. The cylinder is surrounded by a water jacket from which the heated coolant is circulated by thermo-syphonic action in conjunction with a water pump, which is driven by the oil pump. The hot coolant from the engine passes via the thermostat to the radiator. The coolant then flows across the core of the radiator, then to the water pump and back to the engine where the cycle is repeated.

A thermostat is fitted in the system to prevent the coolant flowing through the radiator when the engine is cold, therefore accelerating the speed at which the engine reaches normal operating temperature. A temperature sensor mounted in the thermostat housing transmits information to the temperature gauge or warning light (according to model) on the instrument panel, and on fuel injected models also provides engine temperature information to the engine management system. A cooling fan fitted to the back of the radiator aids cooling in extreme conditions by drawing extra air through. The fan motor is controlled on carburettor models by a thermo-switch mounted in the right-hand side of the radiator, or on fuel injection models by a relay that itself is controlled by the engine management system based on the information from the temperature sensor.

The complete cooling system is partially sealed and pressurised, the pressure being controlled by a valve contained in the spring-loaded radiator cap. By pressurising the coolant the boiling point is raised, preventing premature boiling in adverse

conditions. The overflow pipe from the system is connected to a reservoir into which excess coolant is expelled under pressure. The discharged coolant automatically returns to the radiator by the vacuum created when the engine cools.

⚠ *Warning: Do not remove the pressure cap from the radiator when the engine is hot. Scalding hot coolant and steam may be blown out under pressure, which could cause serious injury. When the engine has cooled, place a thick rag, like a towel, over the pressure cap; slowly rotate the cap anti-clockwise to the first stop. This procedure allows any residual pressure to escape. When the steam has stopped escaping, press down on the cap while turning it anti-clockwise and remove it.*
*Caution: Do not allow anti-freeze to come in contact with your skin or painted surfaces of the motorcycle. Rinse off any spills immediately with plenty of water. Anti-freeze is highly toxic if ingested. Never leave anti-freeze lying around in an open container or in puddles on the floor; children and pets are attracted by its sweet smell and may drink it. Check with the local authorities about disposing of used anti-freeze. Many communities will have collection centres which will see that anti-freeze is disposed of safely.*
*Caution: At all times use the specified type of anti-freeze, and always mix it with distilled water in the correct proportion. The anti-freeze contains corrosion inhibitors which are essential to avoid damage to the cooling system. A lack of these inhibitors could lead to a build-up of corrosion which would block the coolant passages, resulting in overheating and severe engine damage. Distilled water must be used as opposed to tap water to avoid a build-up of scale which would also block the passages.*

## 2 Draining, flushing and refilling

⚠ *Warning: Allow the engine to cool completely before performing this maintenance operation. Also, don't allow anti-freeze to come into contact with your skin or the painted surfaces of the motorcycle. Rinse off spills immediately with plenty of water. Anti-freeze is highly toxic if ingested. Never leave anti-freeze lying around in an open container or in puddles on the floor; children and pets are attracted by its sweet smell and may drink it. Check with local authorities (councils) about disposing of anti-freeze. Many communities have collection centres which will see that anti-freeze is disposed of safely. Anti-freeze is also combustible, so don't store it near open flames.*

### Draining

**1** Support the scooter on its centrestand on a level surface. On SH, Dylan, @ and PS models remove the inner front panel, on Pantheon models remove the large maintenance panel in the centre cover, on S-wing models remove the centre cover (see Chapter 9). On @ models you may want to remove the right-hand lower panel for best access to the drain bolt on the water pump. On Pantheon and S-wing models peel back the rubber mat on the left-hand floor panel and remove the access panel to the reservoir cap.
**2** Remove the pressure cap from the filler neck by turning it anti-clockwise until it reaches a stop **(see illustrations)**. If you hear a hissing sound (indicating there is still pressure in the system), wait until it stops. Now press down on the cap and continue turning the cap until it can be removed. Also remove the coolant reservoir cap.
**3** Position a suitable container beneath the

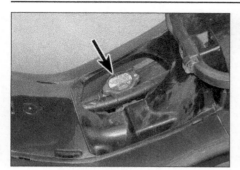

2.2c Radiator pressure cap . . .

2.2d . . . and reservoir cap – Pantheon and S-wing models

2.3 Unscrew the bolt (arrowed) and drain the coolant

water pump on the right-hand side of the engine. Unscrew the drain bolt and allow the coolant to completely drain from the system **(see illustrations)**. If required retain the old sealing washer for use during flushing.

**4** Either remove and drain the reservoir, or draw the coolant out using a siphon pump or syringe (see Section 8).

### Flushing

**5** Flush the system with clean tap water by inserting a hose in the filler neck. Allow the water to run through the system until it is clear and flows out cleanly. If the radiator is extremely corroded, remove it (see Section 6) and have it cleaned by a specialist. Also flush the reservoir.

**6** Clean the drain hole in the water pump then install the drain bolt using the old sealing washer.

**7** Using a suitable funnel inserted in the filler neck, fill the system to the base of the neck with clean water mixed with a flushing compound **(see illustration 2.13a)**. Make sure the flushing compound is compatible with aluminium components, and follow the manufacturer's instructions carefully. Fit the radiator cap and reservoir cap.

**8** Start the engine and allow it to reach normal operating temperature. Let it run for about ten minutes.

**9** Stop the engine. Let it cool for a while, then cover the pressure cap with a heavy rag and turn it anti-clockwise to the first stop, releasing any pressure that may be present

in the system. Once the hissing stops, push down on the cap and remove it completely.

**10** Drain the system once again.

**11** Fill the system with clean water, then fit the radiator cap and repeat the procedure.

### Refilling

**12** Install the drain bolt using a new sealing washer and tighten it.

**13** Using a suitable funnel inserted in the filler neck, fill the system to the base of the neck with the proper coolant mixture (see this Chapter's Specifications) **(see illustration)**. **Note:** *Pour the coolant in slowly to minimise the amount of air entering the system.* Fill the reservoir to the UPPER level line **(see illustration)**. Carefully shake the scooter to dislodge any trapped air.

**14** Start the engine and allow it to idle for 2 to 3 minutes. Flick the throttle twistgrip part open 3 or 4 times, so that the engine speed rises to approximately 4000 to 5000 rpm, then stop the engine. Any air trapped in the system should bleed back to the filler neck.

**15** If necessary, top up the coolant level to the base of the filler neck, then fit the pressure cap. Also top up the coolant reservoir to the UPPER level line if necessary.

**16** Start the engine and allow it to reach normal operating temperature, then shut it off. Let the engine cool then remove the pressure cap. Check that the coolant level is still up to the base of the filler neck. If it's low, add the specified mixture until it reaches the base of the filler neck. Refit the cap.

**17** Check the coolant level in the reservoir and top up if necessary.

**18** Check the system for leaks. Install the body panels (see Chapter 9).

**19** Do not dispose of the old coolant by pouring it down the drain. Instead pour it into a heavy plastic container, cap it tightly and take it into an authorised disposal site or service station – see  at the beginning of this Section.

---

**3  Cooling fan and fan switch or relay**

### Cooling fan

#### Check

**1** If the engine is overheating and the cooling fan isn't coming on, first check the fan fuse (see Chapter 10). If the fuse is good, on carburettor models check the switch and on fuel injection models check the relay, as described below.

**2** To test the cooling fan motor, on SH and PS models remove the front panel, on all other models remove the floor panel (see Chapter 9). Trace the wiring from the fan motor and disconnect it at the connector. On carburettor models also disconnect the wiring connector from the fan switch **(see illustration)**. Using a 12 volt battery and two jumper wires with suitable connectors, connect the battery positive (+) lead to the blue wire terminal on

2.13a Fill the system with coolant . . .

2.13b . . . then fill the reservoir to the UPPER line

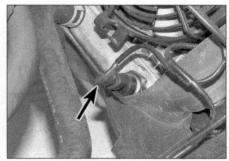

3.2 Fan switch wiring connector (arrowed) – Dylan and @ models

3.5a  Cooling fan bolts (arrowed, bottom one hidden) – SH and PS models

3.5b  Cooling fan bolts (arrowed) – Dylan and @ models

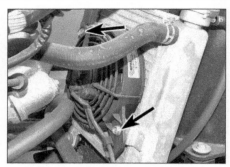

3.5c  Cooling fan bolts (arrowed) – Pantheon and S-wing models

the fan side of the motor wiring connector, and the battery negative (–) lead to the fan switch wire terminal on carburettor models, and to the green wire terminal in the connector on fuel injection models. Once connected the fan should operate. If it does not, and the wiring and connectors are all good, then the fan motor is faulty – replace the fan assembly with a new one.

### Replacement

 **Warning: The engine must be completely cool before carrying out this procedure.**

3 On SH and PS models remove the front panel, on all other models remove the floor panel (see Chapter 9).

4 Trace the wiring from the fan motor and disconnect it at the connector. On carburettor models also disconnect the wiring connector from the fan switch **(see illustration 3.2)**. Release the wiring from any clips or guides not attached to the fan assembly. Where necessary release and move aside the reservoir hose, disconnecting it if required.

5 Undo the bolts securing the fan assembly to the radiator, noting the earth wire secured by the right-hand bolt on carburettor models, and remove the fan assembly **(see illustrations)**.

6 Installation is the reverse of removal.

## Cooling fan switch – carburettor models

### Check

7 If the engine is overheating and the cooling fan isn't coming on, first check the fan motor

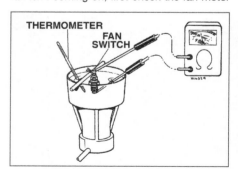

3.10  Fan switch test set-up

fuse (see Chapter 10). If the fuse is blown, check the fan circuit for a short to earth (refer to electrical system fault finding and the wiring diagrams in Chapter 10).

8 If the fuse is good, on SH models remove the front panel, on Dylan and @ models remove the floor panel (see Chapter 9). Disconnect the fan switch wiring connector **(see illustration 3.2)**.

9 With the ignition ON ground the terminal against the radiator body. The fan should come on – if it does the switch is faulty. If it doesn't check the wire from the switch back to the fusebox, via the fan motor, for continuity. Also check that the switch is tight in the radiator, and that the earth wire on the right-hand mounting bolt is secure and clean. Unscrew the earth wire bolt, detach the wire and check that it shows continuity to earth. If it doesn't locate the break or the detached wire or terminal and repair it.

10 If the wiring is good, or if the fan works but is suspected of cutting in at the wrong temperature or is on the whole time, remove the switch (Steps 12 and 13) and test it as follows: fill a small heatproof container with coolant and place it on a stove. Using an ohmmeter or continuity tester, connect the positive (+) probe of the meter to the wire terminal on the switch, and the negative (–) probe to the body of the sensor **(see illustration)**. Using some wire or other support suspend the sensor in the coolant so that just the sensing head up to the threads is submerged, and with the head a minimum of 40 mm above the bottom of the container. Also place a thermometer capable

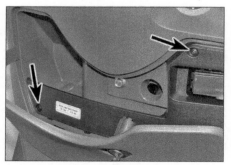

3.16  Undo the screws (arrowed) and remove the inner cover

of reading temperatures up to 130°C in the coolant so that its bulb is close to the sensor. **Note:** *None of the components should be allowed to directly touch the container.*

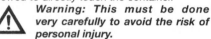 **Warning: This must be done very carefully to avoid the risk of personal injury.**

11 Begin to heat the coolant, stirring it gently. Initially there should be no continuity, showing switch is open or off. When the temperature reaches around 100°C, the switch should close (turn on) and there should be continuity on the meter. Keep heating to a few degrees above 100, then turn off the heat. As the coolant cools to around 100°C the switch should open (turn off) and the meter should show no continuity. If there is more than a 5% error in the temperature at which the switch closes and opens, or if it shows continuity the whole time or no continuity the whole time, replace it with a new one (Steps 12 and 13).

### Replacement

12 The switch is in the radiator – on SH models remove the front panel for access, on Dylan and @ models remove the floor panel (see Chapter 9). Drain the cooling system (see Section 2).

13 Disconnect the wiring connector from the switch **(see illustration 3.2)**. Unscrew the switch. Discard the O-ring as a new one must be used.

14 Installation is the reverse of removal. Fit a new O-ring onto the switch, and tighten it to the torque setting specified at the beginning of the Chapter. Fill the system with the specified coolant (see Section 2). Run the engine and check the switch for leaks before installing the body panel.

## Cooling fan relay – fuel injection models

### Check

15 If the engine is overheating and the cooling fan isn't coming on, first check the cooling fan fuse (see Chapter 10). If the fuse is blown, check the fan circuit for a short to earth (refer to electrical system fault finding and the wiring diagrams in Chapter 10).

16 If the fuse is good, on 2005 to 2008 SH models and PS models remove the glove box inner cover **(see illustration)**. On 2009-on SH

**3.17  Cooling fan relay (arrowed) – Pantheon and S-wing models**

models remove the upper front panel, and on Pantheon and S-wing models remove the storage compartment (see Chapter 9). The relay fits onto a common connector with the main relay on SH and PS models, and with the fuel pump relay on Pantheon and S-wing models – identify which is which by the colour of the wires going into the connector, referring to the wiring diagrams at the end of Chapter 10.

17  Pull the relay off the wiring connector **(see illustration)**. Using a jumper wire short between the blue and black wire terminals on SH and PS models and the black and green wire terminals on Pantheon and S-wing models on the loom side of the connector with the ignition ON – the fan should come on. If it does, the wiring between the relay and the fan and the circuit to earth is all good, so go to Step 18 and check the relay, then if the relay is good to Step 19 to check the power supply to it. If the fan doesn't come on, go to Step 20.

18  Set a multimeter to the ohms x 1 scale and connect it between the adjacent blue and black wire terminals on SH and PS models and the black and green wire terminals on Pantheon and S-wing models. There should be no continuity (infinite resistance). Using a fully-charged 12 volt battery and two insulated jumper wires, connect the positive (+) terminal

of the battery to the blue wire terminal (the other one on SH and PS models) on the relay, and the negative (–) terminal to the black/blue wire terminal. At this point the relay should be heard to click and the multimeter read 0 ohms (continuity). If this is the case the relay is proved good. If the relay does not click when battery voltage is applied and still indicates no continuity (infinite resistance) across its terminals, it is faulty and must be replaced with a new one.

19  If the relay is good, check for battery voltage at the blue wire in the relay wiring connector with the ignition switch ON. If there is no voltage, check the wiring between the relay and the fusebox for continuity, referring to the relevant wiring diagram at the end of Chapter 10.

20  Check that there is continuity in the wiring from the relay wiring connector to the fan wiring connector. If there is no continuity, check all the wiring in the circuit, looking for loose connections and broken wires, referring to electrical system fault finding and the wiring diagrams in Chapter 10.

21  If the fan is on the whole time, pull the relay off its connector. The fan should stop. If it does, the relay is defective and must be replaced with a new one.

22  If the fan works but is suspected of cutting in at the wrong temperature, check the coolant temperature sensor (see Section 4).

**Removal and installation**

23  On 2005 to 2008 SH models and PS models remove the glove box inner cover **(see illustration 3.16)**. On 2009-on SH models remove the upper front panel, and on Pantheon and S-wing models remove the storage compartment (see Chapter 9). The relay fits onto a common connector with the main relay on SH and PS models, and with the fuel pump relay on Pantheon and S-wing models – identify which is which by the colour of the wires going into the connector, referring to the wiring diagrams at the end of Chapter 10.

24  Pull the relay off the wiring connector **(see illustration 3.17)**.
25  Installation is the reverse of removal.

**4    Temperature gauge and coolant temperature sensor**

### *Temperature gauge*

#### Check

1  The circuit consists of the sensor mounted in the thermostat housing and the gauge or warning light (according to model) in the instrument cluster. If the gauge does not work as the engine warms up or the warning light does not come on momentarily when the ignition is switched on first check the fuse, and then on models with a warning light check the bulb in the instrument cluster (see Chapter 10). If the gauge is on H or the light is on all the time that the ignition is on, there is a short circuit in the wire from the instrument cluster to the sensor – locate and repair the break, referring to electrical system fault finding and the wiring diagrams in Chapter 10.

2  Next remove the storage compartment (see Chapter 9). Disconnect the wiring connector from the temperature sensor in the thermostat housing **(see illustrations)**. With the ignition on, ground the wire terminal (green/blue wire on fuel injection models with multi-pin connector) against the engine and check that the needle moves to H on the gauge or the temperature warning light comes on (according to model), then quickly disconnect the wire to avoid damaging the gauge. If the gauge moves or the light comes on check for continuity to earth between the sensor hex and the battery negative (-) terminal. If there is none make sure the earth connectors on the engine and frame are tight. If all is good remove the sensor and check it (Steps 5 to 8).

3  If the gauge does not move or the light does not come on, check the wiring and connectors

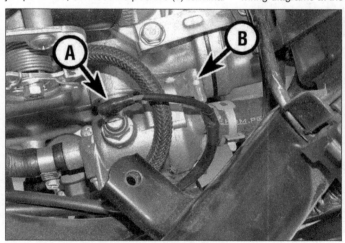

**4.2a  Coolant temperature sensor wiring connector (A) and earth connector (B) – carburettor models**

**4.2b  Coolant temperature sensor wiring connector (arrowed) – fuel injection models**

between the sensor and the instrument cluster for continuity, referring to Chapter 10 for access to the instrument cluster wiring and for the wiring diagrams. If the wiring is good the instrument cluster power circuit or the gauge is faulty. First check the power circuit (see Chapter 10).

### Replacement

4  The temperature gauge is part of the instrument cluster and is covered in Chapter 10.

## *Temperature gauge sensor*

### Check

5  Drain the cooling system (see Section 2).
6  Remove the sensor (see Steps 9 and 10 below).
7  Fill a small heatproof container with coolant and place it on a stove. Using an ohmmeter, connect the positive (+) probe of the meter to the terminal on the sensor (green/blue wire terminal on fuel injection models with multi-pin terminal), and the negative (–) probe to the body of the sensor. Using some wire or other support suspend the sensor in the coolant so that just the sensing head up to the threads is submerged, and with the head a minimum of 40 mm above the bottom of the container **(see illustration 3.10)**. Also place a thermometer capable of reading temperatures up to 130°C in the coolant so that its bulb is close to the sensor. **Note:** *None of the components should be allowed to directly touch the container.*

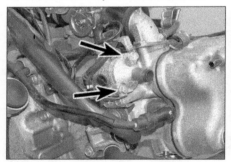
**5.4a  Unscrew the bolts (arrowed) and detach the cover . . .**

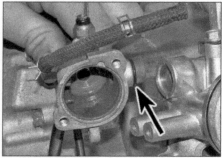
**5.5  Removing the thermostat housing – discard the O-ring (arrowed) and fit a new one**

 *Warning: This must be done very carefully to avoid the risk of personal injury.*

8  Begin to heat the coolant, stirring it gently. When the temperature reaches around 50°C on Pantheon and S-wing models or 80°C on all other models, turn the heat down and maintain the temperature steady for three minutes. The meter reading should be as specified at the beginning of the Chapter. Turn the heat on again. When the temperature reaches around 120°C (or the highest possible without the coolant boiling), again turn the heat down and maintain it for three minutes. The meter reading should again be as specified at the beginning of the Chapter. If the meter readings obtained are different by a margin of 10% or more, then the sensor is faulty and must be replaced with a new one.

### Replacement

 *Warning: The engine must be completely cool before carrying out this procedure.*

9  Drain the cooling system (see Section 2). Remove the storage compartment (see Chapter 9). The sensor is mounted in the thermostat housing **(see illustration 4.2a or b)**.
10  Disconnect the sensor wiring connector. Unscrew and remove the sensor. Where fitted remove and discard the sealing washer – a new one must be used.
11  Apply a suitable sealant to the thread of the sensor, making sure none gets on the sensor head. Install the sensor, using a new sealing washer where fitted, and tighten it to

**5.4b  . . . then remove the thermostat**

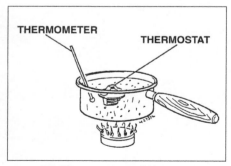
**5.7  Thermostat testing set-up**

the torque setting specified at the beginning of the chapter. Connect the wiring.
12  Install the storage compartment (see Chapter 9). Refill the cooling system (see Section 2).

## 5  Thermostat and housing

1  The thermostat is automatic in operation and should give many years service without requiring attention. In the event of a failure, the valve will probably jam open, in which case the engine will take much longer than normal to warm up. Conversely, if the valve jams shut, the coolant will be unable to circulate and the engine will overheat. Neither condition is acceptable, and the fault must be investigated promptly.

### *Removal*

**Note:** *The complete thermostat housing can be removed without removing the thermostat itself if required.*

 *Warning: The engine must be completely cool before carrying out this procedure.*

2  Drain the coolant (see Section 2). The thermostat housing is on the right-hand side of the engine. Remove the storage compartment and any other panels as required according to model to give the desired amount of access (see Chapter 9).
3  On carburettor models disconnect the temperature sensor earth wire **(see illustration 4.2a)**.
4  To remove the thermostat, unscrew the two bolts securing the cover and detach it from the housing – move any wiring and hoses aside as required **(see illustration)**. Withdraw the thermostat, noting how it fits **(see illustration)**.
5  To remove the thermostat housing, disconnect the temperature sensor wiring connector, and if the thermostat has not been removed on carburettor models disconnect the temperature sensor earth wire **(see illustration 4.2a or b)**. Release the clamps securing the hoses and detach them. Unscrew the bolts securing the housing and remove it – move any wiring and hoses aside as required **(see illustration)**. Discard the O-ring – a new one must be used.

### *Check*

6  Examine the thermostat visually before carrying out the test. If it remains in the open position at room temperature, it should be replaced with a new one. Check the condition of the rubber seal around the thermostat and replace it with a new one if it is damaged, deformed or deteriorated.
7  Suspend the thermostat by a piece of wire in a container of cold water. Place a thermometer capable of reading temperatures up to 110°C in the water so that the bulb is close to the thermostat **(see illustration)**. Heat the water, noting the temperature when the thermostat opens, and compare the result with the Specifications given at the beginning

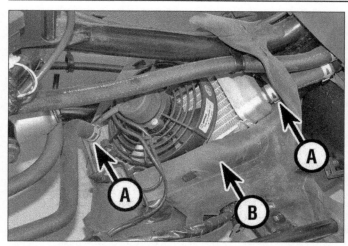

6.3a Radiator hoses (A) and rubber shroud (B) – Dylan and @ models

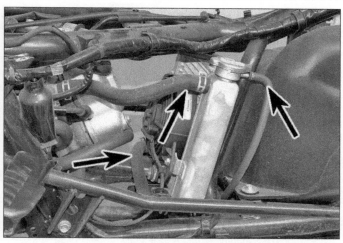

6.3b Radiator hoses (arrowed) – Pantheon and S-wing models

of the Chapter. Also check the amount the valve opens after it has been heated for a few minutes and compare the measurement to the specifications. If the readings obtained differ from those given, the thermostat is faulty and must be replaced with a new one.

**8** In the event of thermostat failure, as an emergency measure only, it can be removed and the machine used without it (this is better than leaving a permanently closed thermostat in, but if it is permanently open, you might as well leave it in). **Note:** *Take care when starting the engine from cold as it will take much longer than usual to warm up.* Ensure that a new unit is installed as soon as possible.

### Installation

**9** To install the thermostat, first make sure the thermostat seal or cover O-ring is fitted and is in good condition, otherwise fit a new one – smear some fresh coolant over it. Install the thermostat with the hole at the top, making sure it locates correctly. Fit the cover onto the housing, then install and tighten the bolts. On carburettor models connect the temperature sensor earth wire **(see illustration 4.2a)**.

**10** Install the thermostat housing using a new O-ring and tighten the bolts **(see illustration 5.5)**. Fit the hoses onto their unions and tighten the hose clamps. Connect the temperature sensor wiring connector, and if the thermostat has not been removed on carburettor models connect the temperature sensor earth wire **(see illustration 4.2a or b)**.

**11** Install the body panels and storage compartment as required according to model (see Chapter 9). Refill the cooling system with fresh coolant (see Section 2).

### 6   Radiator

**Note:** *If the radiator is being removed as part of the engine removal procedure, detach the*

*hoses from their unions on the engine rather than on the radiator and remove the radiator with the hoses attached to it. Note the routing of the hoses.*

### Removal

⚠️ *Warning: The engine must be completely cool before carrying out this procedure.*

**1** On SH and PS models remove the front panel, on all other models remove the floor panel (see Chapter 9). Drain the coolant (see Section 2).

**2** On SH and PS models remove the coolant reservoir (see Section 8) and the cooling fan

6.4a  Radiator lower mounting bolt (arrowed) . . .

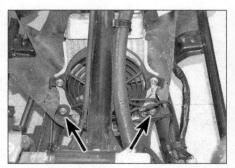

6.4c  Radiator mounting bolts (arrowed) – Dylan and @ models

(see Section 3). On all other models if required remove the cooling fan (see Section 3), otherwise just disconnect the fan motor wiring connector and feed the wiring to the radiator, noting its routing.

**3** Slacken the clamps securing the hoses to the radiator and detach them, noting which fits where **(see illustrations)**. On Dylan and @ models release the rubber shroud.

**4** Unscrew the radiator mounting bolts **(see illustrations)**. Ease the radiator out, noting how it locates. Note the arrangement of the collars and rubber grommets in the radiator mounts, where fitted. Replace the grommets with new ones if they are damaged, deformed or deteriorated.

6.4b  . . . and upper mounting bolts (arrowed) – SH and PS models

6.4d  Radiator mounting bolts (arrowed) – Pantheon and S-wing models

**5** If required and not already done, remove the cooling fan, from the radiator (see Section 3). On SH and PS models remove the radiator shroud. Check the radiator for signs of damage and clear any dirt or debris that might obstruct air flow and inhibit cooling. If the radiator fins are badly damaged or broken the radiator must be replaced with a new one.

### Installation

**6** Installation is the reverse of removal, noting the following.
● Where fitted make sure the rubber grommets are in place and the bolt collars are correctly installed in them.
● Make sure that the fan wiring is correctly connected.
● Ensure the coolant hoses are in good condition (see Chapter 1), and are securely retained by their clamps, using new ones if necessary.
● On completion refill the cooling system with fresh coolant as described in Section 2.

### Pressure cap check

**7** If problems such as overheating or loss of coolant occur, check the entire system as described in Chapter 1. The radiator cap opening pressure should be checked by a Honda dealer with the special tester required to do the job. If the cap is defective, replace it with a new one.

## 7  Water pump

### Check

**1** The water pump is located on the lower right-hand side of the engine. Visually check the area around the pump for signs of leakage.
**2** To prevent leakage of water from the cooling system to the lubrication system and *vice versa*, two seals are fitted on the pump shaft. Below the pump housing there is a drain hole. If either seal fails, the drain allows the coolant or oil to escape and prevents them mixing.
**3** The seal on the water pump side is of the mechanical type which bears on the rear face of the impeller. The second seal, which is mounted behind the mechanical seal, is of the normal feathered lip type. If on inspection the drain shows signs of leakage remove the pump, and fit a new mechanical seal if there is coolant leakage, and a new oil seal as well if there is oil leakage or if the leakage is an emulsion-like mix of coolant and oil.

### Removal

**4** Drain the coolant (see Chapter 1).
**5** If required release the clamps securing the hoses to the pump cover and detach the hoses **(see illustration)**.
**6** Unscrew the pump cover bolts and remove the cover **(see illustration)**. Discard the O-ring as a new one must be used. Remove the cover dowels if they are loose.
**7** Rotate the water pump impeller and wiggle it back-and-forth and in-and-out **(see illustration)**. Also check for corrosion or a build-up of scale in the pump body. If there is excessive noise or roughness when turning the impeller, or excessive movement when wiggling it, remove and disassemble the pump as follows.
**8** Drain the engine oil (see Chapter 1). Refer to Chapter 10 and remove the alternator cover.
**9** Counter-hold the inner end of the pump shaft using a spanner on the flats, then unscrew the impeller – turn it clockwise to unscrew it as it has left-hand threads. Remove the large circlip securing the bearing in the cover **(see illustration)**. Draw the shaft out, bringing the bearing with it.

7.5  Release the clamps (arrowed) and detach the hoses

7.6  Unscrew the bolts (arrowed) and detach the cover

7.7  Check the impeller (arrowed) as described

7.9  Remove the circlip (arrowed)

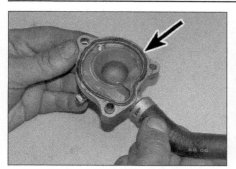

7.17a  Fit a new O-ring (arrowed) into the groove

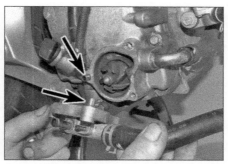

7.17b  Make sure the dowels (arrowed) are in place then fit the cover

## Seal and bearing replacement

**Note:** *Do not remove the seals unless they need to be replaced with new ones – once removed they cannot be re-used.*

**10** To remove the mechanical seal, an expanding knife-edge bearing puller with slide-hammer attachment is useful, if available. Fit the expanding end of the puller behind the seal, then turn the puller to expand it and lock it. Attach the slide hammer to the puller, then operate the slide hammer to jar the seal out. Alternatively drive the seal out using a suitable drift inserted from the inner side of the cover.

**11** Drive the oil seal out using a suitable drift inserted from the inner side of the cover, or use a seal hook from the outside. Note which way round the seal fits.

**12** Fit the new oil seal into the cover and drive it in until it seats using a suitable socket.

**13** Fit the new mechanical seal into the cover and drive it in until it seats using a suitable socket that bears only on the outer flange.

**14** If a new bearing is needed remove the circlip securing it on the shaft, then draw it off and fit a new one in its place. Use a new circlip to secure the bearing, facing its sharp edge away from the bearing.

## Installation

**15** Fit the shaft through the seals, rotating it to ease its passage through, and make sure the bearing seats so the circlip groove is fully exposed. Use a new circlip to secure

the bearing, facing its sharp edge away from the bearing **(see illustration 7.9)**. Thread the impeller onto the shaft, turning it anti-clockwise, and tighten it to the torque setting specified at the beginning of the Chapter, counter-holding the shaft end as before. Rotate the pump by hand to make sure it turns freely (but take into account the grip of the seals).

**16** Refer to Chapter 10 and install the alternator cover.

**17** Smear the new cover O-ring with grease and fit it into its groove in the cover **(see illustration)**. Fit the locating dowels if removed, then fit the cover and tighten the bolts **(see illustration)**. Connect the hoses if detached, and secure them with the clamps **(see illustration 7.5)**.

**18** Fill the engine with the correct amount and type of oil and coolant (see Chapter 1).

8.3a  Reservoir mounting bolt (arrowed) . . .

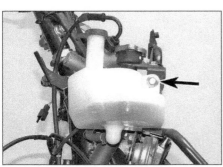

8.3c  Reservoir mounting bolt (arrowed) – Dylan models

8.3d  Reservoir mounting bolt (arrowed) – @ models

## 8  Coolant reservoir

### *Removal*

**1** On SH, Dylan, @ and PS models remove the front panel, and on Pantheon and S-wing models remove the left-hand lower floor panel (see Chapter 9).

**2** Get a suitable container for holding the coolant below the reservoir.

**3** Unscrew the reservoir mounting bolt(s) and manoeuvre the reservoir out, noting how it locates, and detaching the hose when accessible, according to model **(see illustrations)**. Drain the reservoir into the container.

### *Installation*

**4** Installation is the reverse of removal. On completion refill the reservoir to the UPPER level line with the specified coolant mixture (see *Pre-ride checks*).

## 9  Coolant hoses

### *Removal*

**1** Before removing a hose, drain the coolant (see Chapter 1).

**2** Use a screwdriver to slacken the larger-bore

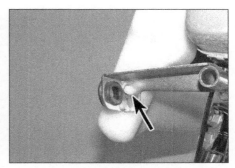

8.3b  . . . and locating peg – SH and PS models

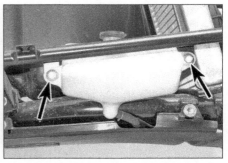

8.3e  Reservoir mounting bolts (arrowed) – Pantheon and S-wing models

hose clamps, then slide them back along the hose and clear of the union spigot. The small-bore hoses are secured by spring clamps which can be expanded by squeezing their ears together with pliers.
**Caution: The radiator unions are fragile. Do not use excessive force when attempting to remove the hoses.**
**3** If a hose proves stubborn, release it by rotating it on its union before working it off. If all else fails, cut the hose with a sharp knife.

Whilst this means replacing the hose with a new one, it is preferable to buying a new radiator.

### Installation

**4** Slide the clamps onto the hose and then work the hose on to its union as far as the spigot where present.
**5** Rotate the hose on its unions to settle it in position before sliding the clamps into place and tightening them securely.

 *If the hose is difficult to push on its union, soften it by soaking it in very hot water, or alternatively a little soapy water on the union can be used as a lubricant.*

**6** Refill the cooling system with fresh coolant (see Section 2).

# Chapter 5A
# Fuel and exhaust systems – carburettor engines

## Contents

## Degrees of difficulty

| Easy, suitable for novice with little experience | 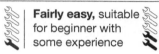 | Fairly easy, suitable for beginner with some experience | | Fairly difficult, suitable for competent DIY mechanic | | Difficult, suitable for experienced DIY mechanic | | Very difficult, suitable for expert DIY or professional |  |

## Specifications

### Fuel
Grade  . . . . . . . . . . . . . . . . . . . . . . . . . . . . . . . . . . . . . . . . . . . . . . Unleaded. Minimum 91 RON (Research Octane Number)
Fuel tank capacity . . . . . . . . . . . . . . . . . . . . . . . . . . . . . . . . . . . . . . see Chapter 1

### Carburettor
Type  . . . . . . . . . . . . . . . . . . . . . . . . . . . . . . . . . . . . . . . . . . . . . . . . CV
ID number
  125 cc engines . . . . . . . . . . . . . . . . . . . . . . . . . . . . . . . . . . . . . VK4AA
  150 cc engines . . . . . . . . . . . . . . . . . . . . . . . . . . . . . . . . . . . . . VK4EA
Pilot screw setting (see text)
  SH models
    125 cc engines . . . . . . . . . . . . . . . . . . . . . . . . . . . . . . . . . 1 1/2 turns out
    150 cc engines . . . . . . . . . . . . . . . . . . . . . . . . . . . . . . . . . 1 1/4 turns out
  Dylan and @ models
    125 cc engines . . . . . . . . . . . . . . . . . . . . . . . . . . . . . . . . . 1 7/8 turns out
    150 cc engines . . . . . . . . . . . . . . . . . . . . . . . . . . . . . . . . . 1 3/4 turns out
Float height
  SH models . . . . . . . . . . . . . . . . . . . . . . . . . . . . . . . . . . . . . . . 18.0 mm
  Dylan and @ models. . . . . . . . . . . . . . . . . . . . . . . . . . . . . . . . 18.2 mm
Idle speed. . . . . . . . . . . . . . . . . . . . . . . . . . . . . . . . . . . . . . . . . . . . see Chapter 1
Pilot jet
  SH models and 2002 Dylan models. . . . . . . . . . . . . . . . . . . . . 38
  2003-on Dylan models and @ models . . . . . . . . . . . . . . . . . . . 35
Main jet . . . . . . . . . . . . . . . . . . . . . . . . . . . . . . . . . . . . . . . . . . . . . . 112

### Automatic choke unit
Resistance . . . . . . . . . . . . . . . . . . . . . . . . . . . . . . . . . . . . . . . . . . . . max. 10 K-ohm

### Fuel level sensor
Sensor resistance. . . . . . . . . . . . . . . . . . . . . . . . . . . . . . . . . . . . . . see table (Section 12)

### PAIR system
Control valve resistance. . . . . . . . . . . . . . . . . . . . . . . . . . . . . . . . . . 20 to 24 ohms 20°C

### Torque settings
Carburettor intake duct bolts . . . . . . . . . . . . . . . . . . . . . . . . . . . . . . 12 Nm
Fuel tap nut . . . . . . . . . . . . . . . . . . . . . . . . . . . . . . . . . . . . . . . . . . . 23 Nm
Exhaust downpipe nuts . . . . . . . . . . . . . . . . . . . . . . . . . . . . . . . . . . 29 Nm
Silencer bolts . . . . . . . . . . . . . . . . . . . . . . . . . . . . . . . . . . . . . . . . . . 49 Nm
PAIR reed valve cover bolts . . . . . . . . . . . . . . . . . . . . . . . . . . . . . . . 5 Nm

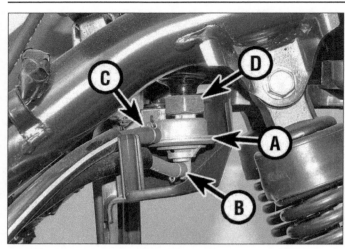

2.1  Fuel tap (A), vacuum hose (B), fuel hose (C), fuel tap nut (D)

2.2  Detach the vacuum hose (arrowed) from the intake duct

## 1  General information and precautions

SH models from 2001 to 2004, all Dylan models and all @ models are fitted with a carburettor. All other models have a fuel injection system (see Chapter 5B).

The fuel system consists of the fuel tank, fuel tap with filter, carburettor, fuel hoses and control cables.

The fuel tap is automatic in operation and is opened by engine vacuum. The fuel filter is fitted inside the fuel tank and is part of the tap.

For cold starting, an electrically-operated automatic choke is fitted in the carburettor. A carburettor heater system passes hot engine coolant through a passage to prevent carburettor icing. A throttle position sensor provides information on throttle position and rate of change to the ECU for optimum ignition timing.

Air is drawn into the carburettor via an air filter and compensation chamber which is housed above the transmission casing. The air filter incorporates a pilot air valve that controls the flow of air to the pilot circuit.

### Precautions

⚠️ *Warning: Petrol is extremely flammable, so take extra pre-cautions when you work on any part of the fuel system. Don't smoke or allow open flames or bare light bulbs near the work area, and don't work in a garage where a natural gas-type appliance is present. If you spill any fuel on your skin, rinse it off immediately with soap and water. When you perform any kind of work on the fuel system, wear safety glasses and have a fire extinguisher suitable for a class B type fire (flammable liquids) on hand.*

Always perform service procedures in a well-ventilated area to prevent a build-up of fumes.

Never work in a building containing a gas appliance with a pilot light, or any other form of naked flame. Ensure that there are no naked light bulbs or any sources of flame or sparks nearby.

Do not smoke (or allow anyone else to smoke) while in the vicinity of petrol or of components containing it. Remember the possible presence of vapour from these sources and move well clear before smoking.

Check all electrical equipment belonging to the house, garage or workshop where work is being undertaken (see the Safety first! section of this manual). Remember that certain electrical appliances such as drills, cutters etc. create sparks in the normal course of operation and must not be used near petrol or any component containing it. Again, remember the possible presence of fumes before using electrical equipment.

Always mop up any spilt fuel and safely dispose of the rag used.

Any stored fuel that is drained off during servicing work must be kept in sealed containers that are suitable for holding petrol, and clearly marked as such; the containers themselves should be kept in a safe place.

Read the Safety first! section of this manual carefully before starting work.

## 2  Fuel tap and filter

⚠️ *Warning: Refer to the precautions given in Section 1 before starting work.*

### Check

1 The fuel tap is located on the underside of the fuel tank at the front, on the right-hand side on SH models and on the left on Dylan and @ models (see illustration). The tap is automatic, operated by a vacuum created when the engine is running which opens a

diaphragm inside the tap. If the tap is faulty, it must be replaced with a new one – it is a sealed unit for which no individual components are available. The most likely problem is a hole or split in the tap diaphragm.

2 To check the tap, remove the storage compartment and the body cover (see Chapter 9). Detach the fuel hose from the carburettor and place the open end in a small container (see illustration 2.1). Detach the vacuum hose from the intake duct (see illustration). Apply a vacuum to it (suck on the hose end). Fuel should flow from the tap and into the container – if it doesn't, the diaphragm is probably split.

3 Before fitting a new tap, check that the vacuum hose is securely attached, and that there are no splits or cracks in it. If in doubt, attach a spare hose to the vacuum union on the tap and again apply a vacuum. If fuel still does not flow, remove the tap and fit a new one.

### Removal

4 The tap should not be removed unnecessarily from the tank.

5 Before removing the tap, detach the fuel hose from the carburettor and draw it out to the side below the tap (see illustration). Place the end in a fuel can with enough capacity to

2.5  Detach the fuel hose (arrowed) from the carburettor

store the fuel in the tank. Detach the vacuum hose from the intake duct **(see illustration 2.2)** and apply a vacuum to it, and allow the tank to fully drain. Reconnect the hoses to the carburettor and duct, and then detach them from the tap **(see illustration 2.1)**.

6 Unscrew the nut and withdraw the tap assembly from the tank **(see illustration 2.1)**. Remove the O-ring and discard it – a new one must be used.

7 Clean the gauze filter to remove all traces of dirt and fuel sediment. Check the gauze for holes. If any are found, fit a new filter.

### Installation

8 Fit the filter if removed, and a new O-ring. Fit the fuel tap into the tank and tighten the nut, to the torque setting specified at the beginning of the Chapter if you have the correct tools **(see illustration 2.1)**.

9 Fit the fuel and vacuum hoses onto their respective unions and secure them with their clips – the fuel hose goes on the upper union and the vacuum hose on the lower one.

## 3  Air filter housing and air compensation chamber

### Air filter housing

#### Removal

1 Remove the storage compartment (see Chapter 9).

2 Release the clamp and detach the idle air control valve hose from its union on the carburettor **(see illustration)**.

3 Slacken the clamp securing the air duct to the compensation chamber, and undo the screws securing the filter housing to the rear hugger and compensation chamber **(see illustration)**.

4 Detach the drain hose from its union on the rear of the housing **(see illustration)**.

3.2  Release the clamp (arrowed) and detach the hose

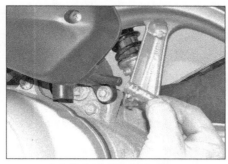

3.4  Detach the drain hose

5 Unscrew the bolts securing the air filter housing to the transmission casing and manoeuvre the housing away, noting how it fits, and detaching the crankcase breather hose from its union when accessible **(see illustrations)**.

#### Installation

6 Installation is the reverse of removal.

### Air compensation chamber

#### Removal

7 Remove the storage compartment (see Chapter 9).

8 Release the clamps and detach the PAIR system air hose and the carburettor vent

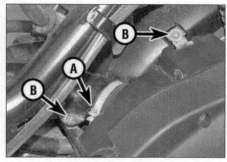

3.3  Slacken the clamp screw (A) and undo the screws (B)

3.5a  Unscrew the bolts (arrowed) . . .

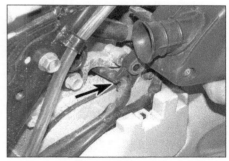

3.5b  . . . release the wiring from its clip on the front mount (arrow) . . .

3.5c  . . . and detach the crankcase breather hose

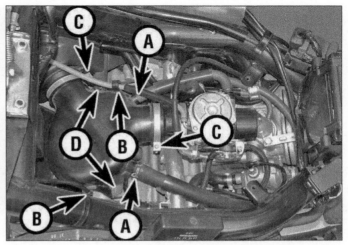

3.8  Detach the hoses (A), release the wiring and hose (B), slacken the clamp screws (C), undo the screw and the bolt (D)

hose from their unions on the chamber **(see illustration)**. Release the wiring from its guide on the right-hand side of the chamber and the idle air control valve hose from the left.

9 Slacken the clamps securing the chamber to the air filter housing and air intake duct on the carburettor.

10 Undo the screw and the bolt and manoeuvre the chamber out.

### Installation

11 Installation is the reverse of removal.

### 4 Idle fuel/air mixture adjustment

**Warning: Adjustment of the pilot screw is made with the engine running. To prevent accidents caused by the rear wheel contacting the ground, ensure that the scooter is on its centrestand and if necessary place a support under the scooter to prevent the rear wheel contacting the ground. Do not run the scooter in an enclosed space.**

1 Idle fuel/air mixture is set using the pilot screw **(see illustration)**. Adjustment of the pilot screw is not normally necessary and should only be performed if the engine is running roughly, stalls continually, or if the pilot screw has been turned or a new pilot screw has been fitted. Before adjusting the pilot screw make sure the spark plugs are clean and in good condition with the correct gap, the air filter is clean, the fuel, air and vacuum hoses are all in good condition and secure at each end, and the carburettor clamps are tight and the ducts in good condition so there are no air leaks, and the intake manifold bolts are tight, and the valve clearances are correct – refer to Chapter 1.

2 If the pilot screw is removed during a carburettor overhaul, record its current setting by turning it in until it seats lightly, counting the number of turns necessary to achieve this, then unscrew it fully. On installation, turn the screw in until it seats lightly, then back it out the number of turns you've recorded. If fitting

a new pilot screw, turn the screw in until it seats, then back it out the number of turns specified at the beginning of the Chapter.

3 Pilot screw adjustment must be made with the engine running and at normal working temperature. Stop the engine and screw the pilot screw in until it seats lightly, then back it out the number of turns specified at the beginning of this Chapter. Start the engine and set the idle speed to the specified amount (see Chapter 1).

4 Now turn the pilot screw outwards by ¼ turn at a time until the idle speed increases. Re-adjust the idle speed.

5 Now turn the pilot screw in until the idle speed drops by 50 rpm, noting exactly the amount of turn it takes. Now turn the pilot screw out by half that amount so it is set between the two parameters. Re-adjust the idle speed.

6 If it is not possible to achieve a satisfactory idle speed after adjusting the pilot screw, take the machine to a scooter dealer and have the fuel/air mixture adjusted with the aid of an exhaust gas analyser. Also bear in mind that it is possible the problem is not down to the fuel system – ignition system causes should also be considered.

### 5 Automatic choke unit and idle air control valve

## *Automatic choke unit*

### Check

1 Poor starting or poor engine performance and an increase in fuel consumption are possible signs that the automatic choke is not working properly.

2 The resistance of the choke unit can be checked with a multimeter after the engine has been warmed to normal operating temperature and then allowed to cool. Remove the storage compartment (see Chapter 9). Trace the wiring from the choke unit on the left-hand side of the carburettor and disconnect it at the connector **(see illustration 5.6)**.

3 Measure the resistance between the terminals on the choke unit side of the connector with

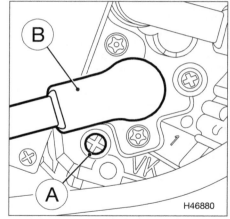

**4.1 The pilot screw (A) is below the throttle position sensor (B)**

the multimeter set to the K-ohms scale. If the result is not as specified at the beginning of the Chapter, replace the choke unit with a new one (see Steps 7 and 8).

4 To check that the plunger is not seized in the choke body, first remove the choke unit from the carburettor (see Section 8). Measure the protrusion of the plunger from the body. Next, use jumper wires to connect a good 12v battery to the choke unit terminals and measure the protrusion again after 5 minutes. If the measurement has not increased by approximately 3 to 6 mm (depending on the type of carburettor) the unit is faulty and should be replaced with a new one.

### Removal and installation

5 Remove the storage compartment (see Chapter 9).

6 Trace the wiring from the choke unit on the left-hand side of the carburettor and disconnect it at the connector **(see illustration)**.

7 Remove the cover from the unit. Undo the screw securing the retaining plate and draw the choke unit out. Remove the plate, noting how it locates. Discard the O-ring – a new one must be used **(see illustration)**.

8 Install the unit using a new O-ring, and make

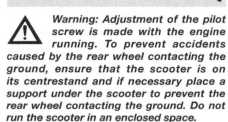

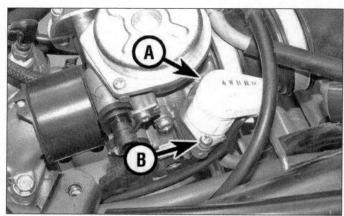

**5.6 Automatic choke unit (A – cover removed), and its mounting plate screw (B)**

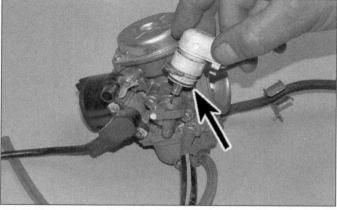

**5.7 Remove the O-ring (arrowed) and fit a new one on installation**

sure the retaining plate is correctly located in its groove.

### Idle air control valve

9 Poor engine performance at temperatures below 15ºC or a rich mixture are possible signs that the idle air control valve is not working properly.
10 Remove the storage compartment (see Chapter 9) and the air filter (see Chapter 1). Check that the valve air hose is securely connected to its union on the carburettor (see illustration 3.2) and to that on the valve (see illustration). Check the hose for splits and cracks and replace it with a new on if necessary.
11 Undo the screw and remove the valve.
12 Get two suitable containers for holding water into which the valve can be suspended. Fill one container with cold water (5°C) and one with warm water (20 to 25°C). Using some wire or other support suspend the sensing portion of the valve in the cold water for at least two minutes, making sure the air inlet and outlet ports are clear of the water. Remove the valve and try to blow through the air ports – the valve should be closed so no air should flow. Repeat the test in the warm water – the valve should now be open allowing air to flow through. If the valve does not perform as described, replace the valve with a new one. The temperature at which the valve should open and close is in the range 10 to 15°C.

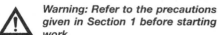

### 6 Carburettor removal and installation

⚠ **Warning: Refer to the precautions given in Section 1 before starting work.**

### Removal

1 Remove the storage compartment (see Chapter 9).
2 Release the clamp and detach the idle air control valve hose from its union on the carburettor (see illustration 3.2). Remove the air compensation chamber (see Section 3).
3 Trace the wiring from the automatic choke unit and throttle position sensor and disconnect it at the connectors (see

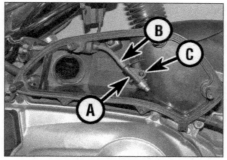

**5.10 Idle air control valve (A) and its hose (B) and screw (C)**

illustration). Free the wiring from any clips or ties.
4 Place a rag under the right-hand side of the carburettor. Clamp the carburettor heater hoses to prevent coolant loss, then detach the hoses from their unions on the carburettor (see illustration).
5 Release the throttle cable from its bracket, then detach the cable end from the pulley (see illustrations 9.2a, b and c).
6 Release the clamp and detach the fuel tap vacuum hose from its union on the intake duct (see illustration 2.2).
7 Have some rag to hand to catch the residual fuel in the fuel hose. Unscrew the bolts securing the intake duct to the engine (see illustration). Lift the carburettor, then release the clamp and detach the fuel hose from its union, catching any fuel in the rag (see illustration 2.5). The breather and drain hoses can be left attached and removed with the carburettor – note the routing of the drain hose as it is withdrawn. Discard the intake duct O-ring – a new one must be used.
8 Loosen the drain screw on the bottom of the carburettor and drain all the fuel into a suitable container.
9 If required slacken the clamps securing the air and intake ducts and detach them from the carburettor, noting how they locate.
**Caution: Stuff clean rag into the intake after removing the carburettor to prevent anything from falling inside.**

### Installation

10 Installation is the reverse of removal, noting the following:

● Make sure the air and intake ducts are correctly positioned and fully engaged with the carburettor and the clamps securely tightened. The duct joint between the carburettor and the intake duct must be fitted with the CARB mark facing the carburettor and the HEAD mark facing the duct.
● Fit a new O-ring into the groove in the mating surface of the intake duct. Tighten the duct bolts to the torque setting specified at the beginning of the Chapter (see illustration 6.7).
● Make sure all hoses and wiring are correctly routed and secured and not trapped or kinked.
● Check the throttle cable adjustment (see Chapter 1).
● If any coolant was lost top-up the cooling system if necessary.
● Check the idle speed and adjust as necessary (see Chapter 1).

### 7 Carburettor overhaul

⚠ **Warning: Refer to the precautions given in Section 1 before proceeding.**

### General information

1 Poor engine performance, difficult starting, stalling, flooding and backfiring are all signs that carburettor maintenance may be required.
2 Keep in mind that many so-called carburettor problems can often be traced to mechanical faults within the engine or ignition system malfunctions. Try to establish for certain that the carburettor is in need of maintenance before beginning a major overhaul.
3 Check the fuel tap and filter, the fuel and vacuum hoses, the intake duct joints, the air filter, the ignition system and the spark plug before assuming that a carburettor overhaul is required.
4 Most carburettor problems are caused by dirt particles, varnish and other deposits which build up in and eventually block the fuel jets and air passages inside the carburettor.

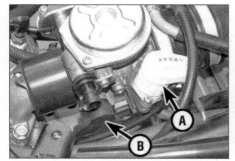

**6.3 Automatic choke unit (A) and throttle position sensor (B)**

**6.4 Clamp the hoses (arrowed), then detach them**

**6.7 Unscrew the intake duct bolts (arrowed)**

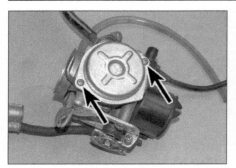

**7.9a  Undo the screws (arrowed) and remove the cover . . .**

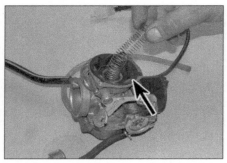

**7.9b  . . . the spring and the diaphragm/ piston assembly (arrowed)**

**7.10a  Release the needle retainer (arrowed) . . .**

Also, in time, gaskets and O-rings deteriorate and cause fuel and air leaks which lead to poor performance.

**5** When overhauling the carburettor, disassemble it completely and clean the parts thoroughly with a carburettor cleaning solvent. If available, blow through the fuel jets and air passages with compressed air to ensure they are clear. Once the cleaning process is complete, reassemble the carburettor using new gaskets and O-rings.

**6** Before disassembling the carburettor, make sure you have the correct carburettor gasket set, some carburettor cleaner, a supply of clean rags, some means of blowing out the carburettor passages and a clean place to work.

## Disassembly

**7** Remove the carburettor (see Section 6). Take care when removing components to note their exact locations and any springs or O-rings that may be fitted.

**8** If required remove the automatic choke unit (see Section 5). If so, and again if required, undo the choke unit housing screws and remove the housing. Discard the sealing-ring as a new one must be fitted. Do not remove the throttle position sensor.

**9** Undo the top cover screws, then lift off the cover and remove the spring from inside the piston **(see illustrations)**. Carefully peel the diaphragm away from its sealing groove in the carburettor and withdraw the diaphragm and piston assembly. Note how the tab on the diaphragm fits in the recess in the carburettor body.

*Caution: Do not use a sharp instrument to displace the diaphragm as it is easily damaged.*

**10** Using a Phillips screwdriver push down lightly on the needle retainer and turn it 90°

anti-clockwise, then lift out the retainer, noting the spring fitted underneath, then push the needle up from the bottom of the piston and withdraw it from the top **(see illustrations)**.

**11** Undo the screws securing the float chamber to the base of the carburettor and remove it **(see illustration)**. Discard the sealing ring as a new one must be used.

**12** Using a pair of thin-nose pliers, carefully withdraw the float pin – if necessary, displace the pin using a small punch or a nail. Remove the float and unhook the float needle valve, noting how it fits onto the tab **(see illustration)**.

**13** Unscrew the pilot jet **(see illustration)**. Unscrew the main jet, which threads into the base of the needle jet, then unscrew the needle jet.

**14** The pilot screw can be removed if required, but note that its setting will be disturbed (see *Haynes Hint*). Unscrew and remove the pilot screw along with its spring, washer and O-ring **(see illustration 4.1)**. **Note:** *Do not remove the screws securing the throttle butterfly to the throttle shaft.*

 **To record the pilot screw's current setting, turn the screw in until it seats lightly, counting the number of turns necessary to achieve this, then unscrew it fully. On installation, turn the screw in until it seats, then back it out the number of turns you've recorded.**

## Cleaning

*Caution: Use only a petroleum-based solvent for carburettor cleaning. Don't use caustic cleaners.*

**15** Use carburettor cleaning solvent to loosen and dissolve the varnish and other deposits on the carburettor body and float chamber; use a nylon-bristled brush to remove the stubborn deposits. Dry the components with compressed air. **Note:** *Avoid soaking the carburettor body in solvent if any O-ring seals remain inside.*

**16** If available, use compressed air to blow out all the fuel jets and the air passages in the carburettor body, not forgetting the passages in the carburettor intake.

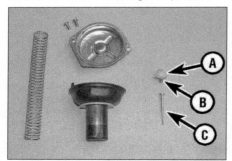

**7.10b  . . . and remove the retainer (A), spring (B) and needle (C) from the piston**

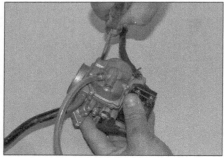

**7.11  Remove the float chamber**

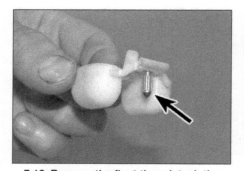

**7.12  Remove the float then detach the needle valve (arrowed) from it**

**7.13  Pilot jet (A), main jet (B)**

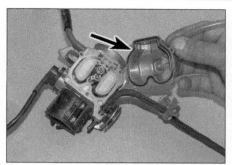

7.28  Fit a new sealing ring (arrowed) into the groove in the chamber

7.30  Make sure the tab (arrowed) is correctly aligned and the diaphragm rim seats properly

8.4  Checking float height

*Caution: Never clean the jets or passages with a piece of wire or a drill bit, as they will be enlarged, causing the fuel and air metering rates to be upset.*

### Inspection

**17**  If removed, check the tapered portion of the pilot screw and the spring for wear or damage. Fit a new O-ring, and replace the screw and/or spring with new ones if necessary.

**18**  Check the carburettor body, float chamber and top cover for cracks, distorted sealing surfaces and other damage. If any defects are found, replace the faulty component, although replacement of the entire carburettor will probably be necessary.

**19**  Inspect the piston diaphragm for splits, holes and general deterioration. Holding it up to a light will help to reveal problems of this nature. Insert the piston in the carburettor body and check that the piston moves up-and-down smoothly in its bore. Check the surface of the piston for wear. If it's worn or scored excessively or doesn't move smoothly, replace the components with new ones as necessary.

**20**  Check the needle is straight by rolling it on a flat surface such as a piece of glass. Fit a new needle if it's bent or if the tip is worn.

**21**  Inspect the tip of the float needle valve. If it has grooves or scratches in it, or is in any way worn, it must be replaced with a new one. If the valve seat is damaged a new carburettor body will have to be fitted.

**22**  Operate the throttle shaft to make sure the throttle butterfly valve opens and closes smoothly. If it doesn't, cleaning the throttle linkage may help. Otherwise, fit a new carburettor.

**23**  Check the float for damage. This will usually be apparent by the presence of fuel inside the float. If the float is damaged, replace it with a new one.

### Reassembly

**Note:** *When reassembling the carburettor, be sure to use new O-rings and seals. Do not overtighten the carburettor jets and screws as they are easily damaged.*

**24**  If removed, install the pilot screw, spring, washer and O-ring **(see illustration 4.1)**. Adjust the screw to the setting as noted on removal (see Step 14). If a new pilot screw is fitted, or if you want to make sure the previous setting was correct, check and adjust the screw after assembling and installing the carburettor (see Section 4).

**25**  Fit the needle jet, then fit the main jet into the bottom of it **(see illustration 7.13)**.

**26**  Fit the pilot jet **(see illustration 7.13)**.

**27**  Hook the float needle valve onto the float tab, then position the float assembly in the carburettor, making sure the needle valve enters its seat **(see illustration 7.12)**. Fit the pin, making sure it is secure. Check the float height (see Section 8).

**28**  Fit a new sealing ring onto the float chamber, making sure it is seated properly in its groove, then fit the chamber onto the carburettor and tighten the screws **(see illustration)**.

**29**  Insert the needle into the piston **(see illustration 7.10b)**. Fit the spring, then fit needle retainer, pressing down lightly on it and turning it 90° clockwise to lock it in place **(see illustration 7.10a)**.

**30**  Align the tab on the diaphragm with the recess in the carburettor body, then fit the piston assembly into the carburettor, ensuring the needle is correctly aligned with the needle jet – keep the piston held up, holding it with your finger inserted in the venturi, and press the rim of the diaphragm into its groove, making sure it is correctly seated **(see illustration)**. Check the diaphragm is not creased, and that the piston moves smoothly up and down in its bore.

**31**  Keeping the piston held up (to prevent the rim of the diaphragm unseating), fit the spring into the piston then fit the top cover, making sure the spring locates over the raised section on the inside of it, then tighten the cover screws **(see illustrations 7.9b and a)**.

**32**  If removed, fit the automatic choke unit housing using a new sealing ring. Install the choke unit (see Section 5).

**33**  Install the carburettor (see Section 7).

**34**  Reset the throttle position sensor. Remove the battery cover and locate the white 2-pin connector near the fusebox. Using a short jumper wire, bridge the two terminals in the connector, then turn the ignition ON. The oil change warning light in the instrument cluster will come on and after a few seconds will blink twice and then stay on – this indicates that the resetting procedure is complete. Turn the ignition OFF and remove the jumper wire.

### 8  Float height check

**1**  If the carburettor floods when the scooter is in use, and the float needle valve and the valve seat are good, the float height should be checked and the result compared to the specification at the beginning of the Chapter.

**2**  If not already done, remove the carburettor (see Section 6).

**3**  Undo the screws securing the float chamber to the base of the carburettor and remove it **(see illustration 7.11)**. Discard the sealing ring as a new one must be used.

**4**  Turn the carburettor on its side so that the float needle valve is just resting against the valve seat and measure the distance between the float chamber gasket face and the bottom of the float **(see illustration)**.

**5**  Compare the result with the specified measurement.

**6**  If the float height is incorrect, carefully bend the float needle valve tab until the float height it is as specified.

**7**  Fit a new sealing ring onto the float chamber, making sure it is seated properly in its groove, then fit the chamber onto the carburettor and tighten the screws **(see illustration 7.28)**.

### 9  Throttle cable

 **Warning: Refer to the precautions given in Section 1 before proceeding.**

### Removal

**Note:** *This procedure covers both carburettor and fuel injection models. On S-wing models the throttle cable pulley is housed in the handlebar switch housing – referrals to the*

9.2a Slacken the nut (arrowed) . . .

9.2b . . . then free the cable elbow from the bracket . . .

9.2c . . . and detach the end from the pulley

throttle pulley housing therefore refer to the switch housing.

1 Remove the body panels as required on your scooter to expose the cable from the handlebar to the carburettor (see Chapter 9).

2 Slacken the nuts on the cable elbow and free the cable from the bracket, noting how it locates (see illustrations). Free the cable end from the pulley on the carburettor (see illustration).

3 Draw the cable out, noting its routing.

4 Unscrew the cable elbow nut from the throttle pulley housing (see illustration). Undo the housing screws and separate the halves (see illustration). Detach the cable end from the pulley, then thread the housing off the cable elbow (see illustrations).

## Installation

5 Thread the throttle pulley housing onto the upper end of the cable elbow without it becoming tight – the elbow must stay loose so that it aligns itself (see illustration 9.4d). Lubricate the cable end with multi-purpose grease and fit it into the throttle pulley (see illustration 9.4c). Assemble the housing onto the handlebar, making sure the pin locates in the hole, then fit the screws and tighten them (see illustration).

6 Feed the cable through to the carburettor, making sure it is correctly routed. The cable must not interfere with any other component and should not be kinked or bent sharply. Now tighten the cable elbow nut on the housing (see illustration 9.4a).

7 Lubricate the cable end with multi-purpose grease and fit it into the pulley (see illustration 9.2c). Locate the elbow in the bracket (see illustration 9.2b), then set the nuts so the cable freeplay is as specified (see Chapter 1).

8 Operate the throttle to check that it opens and closes freely.

9 Turn the handlebars back-and-forth to make sure the cable doesn't cause the steering to bind.

10 Install the body panels (see Chapter 9).

11 Start the engine and check that the idle speed does not rise as the handlebars are turned. If it does, the throttle cable is routed incorrectly. Correct the problem before riding the motorcycle.

## 10 Exhaust system

**Warning: If the engine has been running the exhaust system will be very hot. Allow the system to cool before carrying out any work.**

### Removal

1 Remove the right-hand floor side panel and for best access the belly panel (see Chapter 9).

2 Undo the nuts securing the downpipe to the exhaust port in the head (see illustration).

3 Unscrew the bolts securing the silencer, then support the exhaust system, remove the

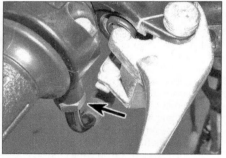

9.4a Unscrew the nut (arrowed) . . .

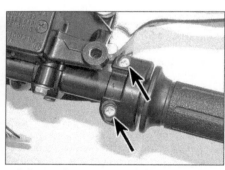

9.4b . . . then undo the housing screws (arrowed)

9.4c Detach the cable end . . .

9.4d . . . then thread the housing off the cable

9.5 Assemble the housing halves, locating the pin in the hole

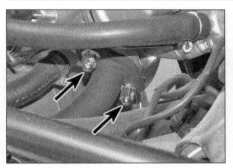

10.2  Undo the nuts (arrowed)

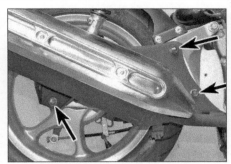

10.3a  Unscrew the bolts (arrowed) . . .

10.3b  . . . and remove the exhaust

bolts, and manoeuvre the exhaust out. **(see illustrations)**

**4** Remove the gasket from the exhaust pipe or port and discard it as a new one must be used **(see illustration 10.5)**.

 **HAYNES HiNT** *Exhaust system fixings tend to become corroded and seized. It is advisable to spray them with penetrating oil before attempting to loosen them.*

### Installation

**5** Installation is the reverse of removal, noting the following:

● Clean the exhaust port studs and lubricate them with a suitable copper-based grease before reassembly.
● Clean the jointing surfaces of the exhaust port and the pipe.
● Use a new gasket and fit it onto the flange of the exhaust header pipe *(see illustration)*.
● Leave the nuts and bolts finger tight until all have been installed, then tighten the exhaust port nuts first, then the bolts, to the torque settings specified at the beginning of the Chapter.
● Run the engine and check that there are no exhaust gas leaks.

### 11  Pulse secondary air (PAIR) system

**Note:** *This system is fitted to all models except the Pantheon*

### General information

**1** To reduce the amount of unburned hydrocarbons released in the exhaust gases, a pulse secondary air (PAIR) system is fitted. The system consists of the control valve (mounted on the right-hand side of the engine), the reed valve (fitted in the valve cover) and the hoses linking them. The control valve is actuated by electronically by the ECU.
**2** Under normal running conditions, the ECU opens up the PAIR control valve which then allows filtered air to be drawn from the compensation chamber through the reed valve and cylinder head passage and into the

exhaust port. The air mixes with the exhaust gases, causing any unburned particles of the fuel in the mixture to be burnt in the exhaust port/pipes. This process changes a considerable amount of hydrocarbons and carbon monoxide into relatively harmless carbon dioxide and water. The reed valve in the valve cover is fitted to prevent the flow of exhaust gases back up the cylinder head passage and into the control valve.

### Testing
#### Control valve

**3** Remove the valve (see Steps 8 to 10).
**4** Check the operation of the control valve by blowing through the air intake hose union – air should flow out through the reed valve hose union. Now connect a 12 volt battery to the terminals in the control valve wiring connector and repeat the check – no air should now flow through the valve if it is functioning correctly. Replace the valve with a new one if faulty.
**5** Connect the probes of a multimeter set to read resistance (ohms) to the terminals in the connector and measure the resistance of the valve windings. If it is not in the range specified at the beginning of the Chapter replace the valve with a new one.

#### Reed valve

**6** Remove the maintenance access panel (see Chapter 9). Disconnect the hose from the reed valve housing **(see illustration 11.13)**. Attach a clean auxiliary hose of the correct bore and about 12 inches long to the union.
**7** Check the valve by blowing and sucking on the auxiliary hose end. Air should flow through the hose only when blown down it and not

10.5  Fit the new gasket onto the exhaust pipe

when sucked back up. If this is not the case the reed valve is faulty, though it is worth removing it (see Steps 12 to 14) and cleaning off any carbon deposits.

### Component renewal
#### Control valve

**8** Remove the storage compartment (See Chapter 9).
**9** Release the clamps and detach the air hoses from the control valve **(see illustration)**. Disconnect the wiring connector. On models with a common sub-loom to the thermostat housing disconnect the wiring from the coolant temperature sensor and its earth terminal **(see illustration)**.
**10** Unscrew the bolts and remove the control valve **(see illustration 11.9a)**. Note the collars in the grommets.
**11** Installation is the reverse of removal. Check the condition of the rubber grommets

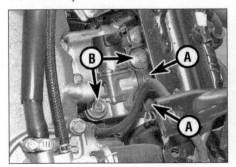

11.9a  PAIR control valve hoses (A) and mounting bolts (B)

11.9b  Disconnect the sensor and earth wiring connectors (arrowed)

**11.13 Release the clamp (arrowed) and detach the hose**

**11.14a Unscrew the bolts (arrowed) and remove the cover . . .**

**11.14b . . . and the reed valve**

and fit new ones if they are damaged, deformed or deteriorated. Make sure the collars are fitted in the grommets. Make sure the hoses are pushed fully onto their unions and secured by their clamps **(see illustration 11.9a)**. Connect the temperature sensor and control valve wiring connectors.

### Reed valve

**12** Remove the storage compartment (See Chapter 9).
**13** Release the clamp and detach the air hose from its union **(see illustration)**.
**14** Unscrew the bolts securing the reed valve cover and remove the cover **(see illustration)**. Remove the reed valve, noting which way around it is fitted **(see illustration)**.
**15** Installation is the reverse of removal. Make sure the reed valve and housing are clean and correctly fitted. Tighten the cover bolts to the torque setting specified at the beginning of the Chapter.

## 12 Fuel gauge and level sensor

### Check

**1** The circuit consists of the level sensor

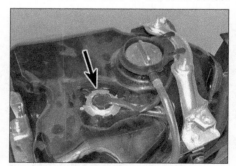

**12.2 Fuel level sensor (arrowed)**

mounted in the top of the fuel tank and the gauge mounted in the instrument cluster. If the instruments malfunction first check the instrument cluster fuse (see Chapter 10).
**2** To check the gauge, remove the storage compartment and the body cover (see Chapter 9). Trace the wiring from the sensor and disconnect it at the wiring connector **(see illustration)**.
**3** Connect a jumper wire between the yellow/white and green wire terminals on the loom side of the connector, then turn the ignition on – the gauge needle should move the FULL position. Detach the jumper wire and turn the ignition off.
**4** If the gauge does not respond as described, remove the handlebar front cover (see Chapter 9). Check the wiring between the sensor connector and the gauge connectors on the back of the instrument cluster for continuity, and check for continuity to earth in the green wire, referring to electrical system testing and the wiring diagrams Chapter 10. If that is good check for voltage at the black/brown wire to the gauge. If the wiring is good the gauge is faulty.
**5** If the gauge and wiring are good, remove the level sensor from the tank (Steps 8 to 10). Check that no fuel has entered the float due to

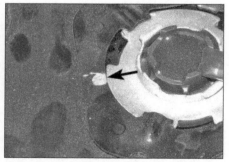

**12.11 Align the retainer so when locked the arrow aligns with the mark**

a leak, and check that the arm moves up and down smoothly.
**6** Connect the probes of an ohmmeter to the specified terminals on the sensor connector as shown in the table and check the resistance of the sensor in both the FULL and EMPTY positions for each connection. If the readings are not as specified, replace the sensor with a new one (Steps 11 and 12).

| | Full position | Empty position |
|---|---|---|
| Green/black – yellow/white | 30 to 45 ohms | 400 to 700 ohms |
| Yellow/white – blue/white | 450 to 750 ohms | 450 to 750 ohms |

### Replacement

**Warning: Refer to the precautions given in Section 1 before starting work.**

**7** The fuel gauge is part of the instrument cluster and is covered in Chapter 10.
**8** To replace the sensor, remove the storage compartment and the body cover (see Chapter 9).
**9** Trace the wiring from the sensor and disconnect it at the connector **(see illustration 12.2)**. Free the wiring from any ties or guides and feed it back to the sensor, noting its routing.
**10** Turn the sensor retainer anti-clockwise and remove it, noting how it locates. Carefully manoeuvre the sensor out of the tank, taking care not to snag the float arm. Discard the sealing-ring as a new one must be used.
**11** Fit a new sealing-ring onto the tank. Fit the sensor into the tank, aligning the tab with the groove. Fit the retainer and turn it clockwise to lock it so that the arrow and mark are aligned **(see illustration)**.
**12** Install the body cover and storage compartment (see Section 2).

# Chapter 5B
# Fuel injection system

## Contents

## Degrees of difficulty

| Easy, suitable for novice with little experience  | Fairly easy, suitable for beginner with some experience | Fairly difficult, suitable for competent DIY mechanic | Difficult, suitable for experienced DIY mechanic | Very difficult, suitable for expert DIY or professional  |
|---|---|---|---|---|

## Specifications

### Fuel
Grade  . . . . . . . . . . . . . . . . . . . . . . . . . . . . . . . . . . . . . . . . . . . . . . Unleaded. Minimum 91 RON (Research Octane Number)
Fuel tank capacity . . . . . . . . . . . . . . . . . . . . . . . . . . . . . . . . . . . . . . . see Chapter 1

### Fuel injection system
Throttle body ID number
   2005 to 2008 SH models and all PS models
      125 cc engines . . . . . . . . . . . . . . . . . . . . . . . . . . . . . . . . . . GQM1A
      150 cc engines . . . . . . . . . . . . . . . . . . . . . . . . . . . . . . . . . . GQM2A
   2009-on SH models
      125 cc engines . . . . . . . . . . . . . . . . . . . . . . . . . . . . . . . . . . GQM8A
      150 cc engines . . . . . . . . . . . . . . . . . . . . . . . . . . . . . . . . . . GQM9A
   Pantheon models
      125 cc engines . . . . . . . . . . . . . . . . . . . . . . . . . . . . . . . . . . GQM0
      150 cc engines . . . . . . . . . . . . . . . . . . . . . . . . . . . . . . . . . . GQN0
   S-wing models
      125 cc engines . . . . . . . . . . . . . . . . . . . . . . . . . . . . . . . . . . GQM4A
      150 cc engines . . . . . . . . . . . . . . . . . . . . . . . . . . . . . . . . . . GQM5A
Idle speed. . . . . . . . . . . . . . . . . . . . . . . . . . . . . . . . . . . . . . . . . . . . . see Chapter 1
Fuel pressure at specified idle speed. . . . . . . . . . . . . . . . . . . . . . . . 43 psi (3.0 Bar)
Minimum fuel flow rate
   SH and PS models . . . . . . . . . . . . . . . . . . . . . . . . . . . . . . . . . . . 22 cc every 10 seconds
   Pantheon and S-wing models . . . . . . . . . . . . . . . . . . . . . . . . . . . 25 cc every 10 seconds

### Fuel injection system test data
**Note:** *Values given are only accurate at 20°C (68°F)*
Engine coolant temperature (ECT) sensor resistance . . . . . . . . . . . . . 2.3 to 2.6 K-ohms
Fuel injector resistance. . . . . . . . . . . . . . . . . . . . . . . . . . . . . . . . . . . 11.1 to 12.3 ohms

### Torque settings
Exhaust downpipe nuts . . . . . . . . . . . . . . . . . . . . . . . . . . . . . . . . . . . 29 Nm
Fuel pump nuts (SH and PS models) . . . . . . . . . . . . . . . . . . . . . . . . . 12 Nm
Fuel pump retainer (Pantheon and S-wing models) . . . . . . . . . . . . . . 50 Nm
Oxygen sensor . . . . . . . . . . . . . . . . . . . . . . . . . . . . . . . . . . . . . . . . . 44 Nm
Silencer bolts . . . . . . . . . . . . . . . . . . . . . . . . . . . . . . . . . . . . . . . . . . 49 Nm

## 1 General information and precautions

### General information

The fuel supply system consists of the fuel tank with internal and integral fuel pump, filter, pressure regulator and level sensor, the fuel hose, the injector, the throttle body, and the throttle cable. The fuel pump is switched on and off with the engine via a relay. Idle speed and fast idle speed for cold starting are set automatically by the electronic control unit (ECU) and the idle air control valve (IACV). The injection system, known as PGM-FI, supplies fuel and air to the engine via a single throttle body with one injector. The injector is operated by the ECU using the information obtained from the various sensors it monitors. The ECU and throttle body are an integrated assembly along with the manifold absolute pressure (MAP) sensor, intake air temperature (IAT) sensor and throttle position (TP) sensor, and the IACV. Refer to Section 3 for more information on the operation of the fuel injection system.

All models have a fuel gauge incorporated in the instrument cluster, actuated by the level sensor inside the fuel tank.

**Note:** *Individual engine management system components can be checked but not repaired. If system troubles occur, and the faulty component can be isolated, the only cure for the problem in most cases is to replace the part with a new one. Keep in mind that most electronic parts, once purchased, cannot be returned. To avoid unnecessary expense, make very sure the faulty component has been positively identified before buying a new part.*

### Precautions

⚠ **Warning: Petrol (gasoline) is extremely flammable, so take extra precautions when you work on any part of the fuel system. Always remove the battery (see Chapter 10). Don't smoke or allow open flames or bare light bulbs near the work area, and don't work in a garage where a natural gas-type appliance is present. If you spill any fuel on your skin, rinse it off immediately with soap and water. When you perform any kind of work on the fuel system, wear safety glasses and have a fire extinguisher suitable for a class B type fire (flammable liquids) on hand.**

With the fuel injection system, some residual pressure will remain in the fuel feed hose and injector after the engine has been stopped. Before disconnecting the fuel hose, ensure the ignition is switched OFF and make sure you have some clean rag to catch and mop up the fuel. It is vital that no dirt or debris is allowed to enter any part of the system while a fuel hose is disconnected. Any foreign matter in the fuel system components could result in injector damage or malfunction. Ensure the ignition is switched OFF before disconnecting or reconnecting any fuel injection system wiring connector. If a connector is disconnected or reconnected with the ignition switched ON, the engine control unit (ECU) may be damaged.

Always perform service procedures in a well-ventilated area to prevent a build-up of fumes.

Never work in a building containing a gas appliance with a pilot light, or any other form of naked flame. Ensure that there are no naked light bulbs or any sources of flame or sparks nearby.

Do not smoke (or allow anyone else to smoke) while in the vicinity of petrol (gasoline) or of components containing it. Remember the possible presence of vapour from these sources and move well clear before smoking.

Check all electrical equipment belonging to the house, garage or workshop where work is being undertaken (see the *Safety first!* section of this manual). Remember that certain electrical appliances such as drills, cutters etc, create sparks in the normal course of operation and must not be used near petrol (gasoline) or any component containing it. Again, remember the possible presence of fumes before using electrical equipment.

Always mop up any spilt fuel and safely dispose of the rag used.

Any stored fuel that is drained off during servicing work must be kept in sealed containers that are suitable for holding petrol (gasoline), and clearly marked as such; the containers themselves should be kept in a safe place. Note that this last point applies equally to the fuel tank if it is removed from the machine; also remember to keep its filler cap closed at all times.

Read the *Safety first!* section of this manual carefully before starting work.

## 2 Air filter housing and air compensation chamber

### Air filter housing – SH and PS models

#### Removal

**1** Slacken the clamp securing the air duct to the compensation chamber, then undo the screws securing the filter housing to the rear hugger and compensation chamber **(see illustration)**.
**2** Detach the drain hose from its union on the rear of the housing.
**3** Unscrew the bolts securing the housing to the transmission casing and manoeuvre the housing away, noting how it fits, and detaching the crankcase breather hose from its union and releasing the starter motor cable from its guide when accessible **(see illustrations)**.

#### Installation

**4** Installation is the reverse of removal.

### Air filter housing – Pantheon and S-wing models

#### Removal

**5** Remove the storage compartment (see Chapter 9).

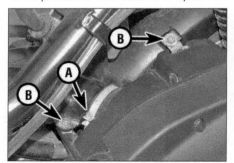

2.1 Slacken the clamp screw (A) and undo the screws (B)

2.3a Unscrew the bolts (arrowed) . . .

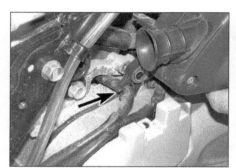

2.3b . . . release the wiring from its clip on the front mount (arrow) . . .

2.3c . . . and detach the crankcase breather hose

**2.6 Slacken the duct clamp (arrowed)**

**2.12 Release the clamp and detach the PAIR hose**

**6** Slacken the clamp securing the air duct to the throttle body **(see illustration)**.
**7** Release the speed sensor wire from its guide on the underside of the housing.
**8** Undo the screw securing the filter housing to the rear hugger.
**9** Unscrew the bolts securing the air filter housing to the transmission casing and manoeuvre the housing away, noting how it fits, and detaching the crankcase breather hose from its union when accessible.

### Installation

**10** Installation is the reverse of removal.

### *Air compensation chamber – SH and PS models*

#### Removal

**11** Remove the storage compartment (see Chapter 9).
**12** Release the clamp and detach the PAIR system air hose from the union on the chamber **(see illustration)**.
**13** Unscrew the fuel hose guide bolt and detach the guide **(see illustration)**.
**14** Slacken the clamps securing the chamber to the air filter housing **(see illustration 2.1)** and air intake rubber on the throttle body **(see illustration)**.
**15** Undo the screw and the bolt and manoeuvre the chamber out.

#### Installation

**16** Installation is the reverse of removal.

### 3 Fuel injection system description

**1** All models covered in this Chapter are equipped with Honda's programmed fuel injection (PGM-FI) system. It is controlled by an electronic control unit (ECU) that operates both the injection and ignition systems.
**2** The engine control unit (ECU) monitors signals from the following sensors:

**2.13 Detach the hose guide, noting how it locates**

● Throttle position (TP) sensor – informs the ECU of the throttle position, and the rate of throttle opening or closing.
● Engine coolant temperature (ECT) sensor – informs the ECU of engine temperature. It also actuates the temperature gauge (see Chapter 4).
● Manifold absolute pressure (MAP) sensor – informs the ECU of the engine load by monitoring the pressure in the throttle body air intake duct.
● Intake air temperature (IAT) sensor – informs the ECU of the temperature of the air entering the throttle body.
● Ignition pulse generator coil – informs the ECU of engine speed and crankshaft position (see Chapter 6).
● Speed sensor – informs the ECU of the speed of the motorcycle (see Chapter 10).
● Lean angle sensor – stops the engine if the bike falls over.
● Oxygen sensor – informs the ECU of the oxygen content of the exhaust gases.
**3** All the information from the sensors is analysed by the ECU, and from that it determines the appropriate ignition and fuelling requirements of the engine. The ECU controls the fuel injector by varying its pulse width – the length of time the injector is held open – to provide more or less fuel, as

**2.14 Air intake duct clamp screw (arrowed)**

appropriate for cold starting, warm up, idle, cruising, and acceleration.
**4** Cold starting and warm up idle speeds are controlled automatically by the ECU and the idle air control valve (IACV).

### 4 Fuel injection system fault diagnosis

**1** When the ignition is switched on the malfunction indicator lamp (MIL) in the instrument cluster will come on for a few seconds, then go out. When the engine is started the fuel injection system automatically performs a self-diagnosis check. If all is good the MIL remains off. If there is an abnormality in any of the readings obtained from any sensor, the ECU enters its back-up mode. If the ECU enters this back-up mode while performing its self-diagnosis check on start-up the MIL will flash. If it enters this back-up mode while riding the MIL will come on. In back-up mode the ECU ignores the abnormal sensor signal, and assumes a pre-programmed value which may, depending on the sensor in question and the fault detected, allow the engine to continue running (albeit at reduced efficiency). Otherwise the engine will stop, or will not be able to be restarted once it has been stopped. In each case the relevant fault code will be stored in the ECU memory. The fault can be identified by reading the fault code or codes as follows.

**2** If the engine can be started, place the motorcycle on its centrestand then start the engine and allow it to idle. Whilst the engine is idling, observe the MIL on the instrument cluster, and go to Step 5.

**3** If the engine cannot be started, place the motorcycle on its centrestand. Turn the engine over on the starter motor for more then ten seconds and observe the MIL on the instrument cluster, and go to Step 5.

**4** Alternatively, and to check for any stored fault codes even though the MIL has not illuminated, on SH and PS models remove the battery access panel in the floor, and on Pantheon and S-wing models remove the seat, then remove the battery access panel in the storage compartment (see Chapter 9), to gain access to the fuel injection system data link connector (DLC), which is a capped 4-pin connector coming out of the wiring loom **(see illustrations)**. Ensure the ignition is switched OFF then remove the cap and either fit the Honda DLC short connector (Part No. 070PZ-ZY30100, available at reasonable cost from your dealer), or make your own using suitable connectors and a piece of wire joining them, between the brown and green wire terminals in the connector. Make sure the kill switch is in the RUN position then turn the ignition ON and observe the warning light. If there are no stored fault codes, the light will come on and stay on. If there are stored fault codes, the light will flash – go to Step 5.

**5** The light emits long (1.3 second) and short (0.5

**4.4a Data link connector (arrowed) – SH and PS models**

**4.4b Data link connector (arrowed) – Pantheon and S-wing models**

second) flashes to give out the fault code. A long flash is used to indicate the first digit of a double digit fault code (i.e. 10 and above). If a single digit fault code is being displayed (i.e. 0 – 9), there will be a number of short flashes equivalent to the code being displayed. For example, two long (1.3 sec) flashes followed by three short (0.5 sec) flashes indicates the fault code number 23. If there is more than one fault code, there will be a gap before the other codes are revealed, and the codes will be revealed in order, starting with the lowest and finishing with the highest. Once all codes have been revealed, the ECU will continuously run through the code(s) stored in its memory, revealing each one in turn with a short gap between them. The fault codes are shown in the table.

**6** Once the fault has been identified and corrected, it will be necessary to reset the system

by removing the fault code from the ECU memory. To do this, ensure the ignition is switched OFF, then either fit the Honda DLC short connector or bridge the brown and green wire terminals of the data link connector (DLC) (see Step 4). Make sure the kill switch is in the RUN position, then turn the ignition switch ON. Disconnect the connector or piece of wire from the DLC. When the wire is disconnected the MIL should come on for about five seconds, during which time the connector or wire must be reconnected. The MIL should start to flash when it is reconnected, indicating that all fault codes have been erased. However if the MIL flashes twenty times the memory has not been erased and the procedure must be repeated. Turn off the ignition then remove the connector or wire. Check the MIL (in some cases it may be necessary to repeat the erasing procedure more than once).

| Fault code (No. of flashes) | Symptoms | Possible causes |
|---|---|---|
| 0 – no code (MIL off) | Engine does not start | Blown ignition/starter motor/fuel pump fuse<br>Faulty power supply to electronic control unit (ECU)<br>Faulty engine stop relay or wiring<br>Faulty engine stop switch/open circuit on switch earth (ground) wire<br>Faulty ignition switch<br>Faulty lean angle sensor or wiring |
| 0 – no code (MIL off) | Engine runs normally | Open or short circuit in warning light wiring<br>Faulty electronic control unit (ECU) |
| 0 – no code (MIL on) | Engine runs normally | Short circuit in data link connector or wiring<br>Faulty electronic control unit (ECU) |
| 1 | Engine runs normally | Faulty manifold absolute pressure (MAP) sensor or wiring |
| 7 | Engine difficult to start at low temperatures | Faulty engine coolant temperature (ECT) sensor or wiring |
| 8 | Poor throttle response | Faulty throttle position (TP) sensor or wiring |
| 9 | Engine runs normally | Faulty intake air temperature (IAT) sensor or wiring |
| 12 | Engine does not start | Faulty injector or wiring |
| 21 | Engine operates normally | Faulty oxygen sensor or wiring |
| 23 | Engine operates normally | Faulty oxygen sensor or wiring, or faulty oxygen sensor heating element |
| 29 | Engine hard to start, stalls, rough idle | Faulty idle air control valve (IACV) or wiring |
| *The following codes are only applicable to Pantheon and S-wing models* | | |
| 11 | Engine operates normally | Faulty speed sensor or wiring |
| 33 | Engine operates normally | Faulty EPROM in ECU |
| *The following code is only applicable to 2009-on models* | | |
| 54 | Engine operates normally | Faulty lean angle sensor or wiring |

## 5  Fuel injection and engine management system components

**Caution: Ensure the ignition is switched OFF before disconnecting/reconnecting any fuel injection system wiring connector. If a connector is disconnected/reconnected with the ignition switched ON the engine control unit (ECU) could be damaged.**

1 If a fault is indicated in any of the system components, first check the wiring and connectors between the appropriate component and the ECU and/or instrument cluster (refer to *Electrical system fault finding* at the beginning of Chapter 10, and to the *Wiring diagrams* at the end of it). A continuity test of all wires will locate a break or short in any circuit. Inspect the terminals inside the wiring connectors and ensure they are not loose, bent or corroded. Spray the inside of the connectors with a proprietary electrical terminal cleaner before reconnection.

### Manifold absolute pressure (MAP) sensor

#### Check

2 The MAP sensor is part of the throttle body/ECU assembly and can only be checked using the Honda diagnostic test pin box.
3 Check the ECU wiring connector (see illustration). If it is good reset the system as described in Section 4, Step 6, then start the engine and check if the same fault code comes up. If it does the sensor is probably faulty. If it doesn't there was probably just a temporary glitch in the system.

#### Removal and installation

4 The MAP sensor is an integral part of the throttle body/ECU assembly and is not available separately. If the sensor is faulty, a complete new throttle body assembly will have to be installed.

### Engine coolant temperature (ECT) sensor

#### Check

5 Remove the storage compartment (see

Chapter 9). Check the wiring and connectors as in Step 1.
6 Disconnect the wiring connector from the sensor (see illustration). With the engine cold, connect an ohmmeter between the pink/white and green/orange wire terminals on the sensor and measure its resistance. Compare the reading obtained to that given in the Specifications, noting that the specified value is valid at 20°C (68°F). If the resistance reading differs greatly from that specified, the sensor is probably faulty.
7 If the sensor appears to be functioning correctly, check its power supply. Connect the positive (+) lead of a voltmeter to the pink/white wire terminal in the sensor wiring connector, then connect the negative (–) lead to a good earth. Turn the ignition switch ON and check that a voltage of 4.75 to 5.25 volts is present. If it isn't, there is a fault in the pink/white wire or the ECU. If voltage was present, now connect the negative lead to the green/orange terminal of the connector and check that the same voltage is present. If it isn't, there is a fault in the green/orange wire or the ECU. If there is voltage, the pink/white wire may be shorted to earth at some point.

⚠️ **Removal and installation**
**Warning: The engine must be completely cool before carrying out this procedure.**
8 Refer to Chapter 4, Section 4.

### Throttle position (TP) sensor

#### Check

9 The TP sensor is part of the throttle body/ECU assembly and can only be checked using the Honda diagnostic test pin box.
10 Check the ECU wiring connector (see illustration 5.3). If it is good reset the system as described in Section 4, Step 6, then start the engine and check if the same fault code comes up. If it does the sensor is probably faulty. If it doesn't there was probably just a temporary glitch in the system.

#### Removal and installation

11 The TP sensor is an integral part of the throttle body/ECU assembly and is not available separately. If the sensor is faulty, a complete new throttle body assembly will

have to be installed.

### Intake air temperature (IAT) sensor

#### Check

12 The IAT sensor is part of the throttle body/ECU assembly and can only be checked using the Honda diagnostic test pin box.
13 Check the ECU wiring connector (see illustration 5.3). If it is good reset the system as described in Section 4, Step 6, then start the engine and check if the same fault code comes up. If it does the sensor is probably faulty. If it doesn't there was probably just a temporary glitch in the system.

#### Removal and installation

14 The IAT sensor is an integral part of the throttle body/ECU assembly and is not available separately. If the sensor is faulty, a complete new throttle body assembly will have to be installed.

### Speed sensor (Pantheon and S-wing models)

#### Check

15 Check the wiring and connectors as in Step 1, checking for continuity in the pink and yellow/red wires to the instrument cluster, in the pink wire to the ECU on Pantheon models, and in the green/black wire to earth – remove the handlebar front cover to access the instrument cluster wiring connector (see Chapter 9).
16 Unscrew the sensor cover bolts and remove the cover (see illustration 5.20). Disconnect the wiring connector from the sensor. Check the connector for loose terminals. With the ignition switch ON, check the input voltage between the yellow/red (+) and green/black (-) wire terminals on the loom side of the connector – there should be 4.75 to 5.25 volts. If there is no voltage, and the wiring is good, the problem could be in the instrument cluster – refer to Chapter 10.
17 If there is voltage, reconnect the wiring connector, then place the machine on its centrestand so the rear wheel is off the ground. Connect a voltmeter between the pink (+) and green/black (-) wire terminals – make sure the probes make good contact when inserted into the connector. With the ignition switch ON, turn the rear wheel by hand and check that a fluctuating voltage reading between 0 and 5 volts is obtained. If no reading is obtained, the speed sensor is faulty and must be replaced with a new one (see Steps 22 to 25).
18 If all is good, refer to Chapter 10 and check the instrument cluster power supply and for continuity to earth in the green/black wire from the instrument cluster. If they are good the printed circuit board (PCB) could be faulty.

#### Removal and installation

19 The speed sensor is mounted on the top of the transmission casing next to the left-hand rear shock absorber.

**5.3  Make sure the wiring connector is securely locked in place and no wires are loose**

**5.6  ECT sensor wiring connector (arrowed)**

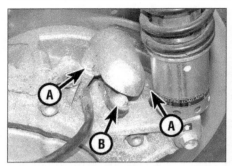

**5.20 Speed sensor cover bolts (A), sensor mounting bolt (B)**

**20** Unscrew the sensor cover bolts and remove the cover **(see illustration)**.
**21** Disconnect the wiring connector from the sensor.
**22** Unscrew the sensor mounting bolt and remove the sensor. Remove the O-ring

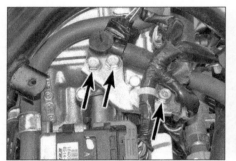

**5.29a Unscrew the bolts (arrowed) and displace the holder . . .**

**5.30a Remove the retainer . . .**

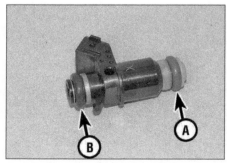

**5.31 Fit new O-rings (arrowed) – orange (A), black (B)**

**5.25a Disconnect the wiring connector from the injector**

and discard it. Plug the sensor orifice with clean rag to prevent anything falling into the engine.
**23** Install the sensor using a new O-ring smeared with clean oil. Make sure the wiring is secure, then fit the cover.

**5.29b . . . then detach the fuel hose**

**5.30b . . . and pull the injector out**

**5.33 Fit the fuel hose holder and bolts**

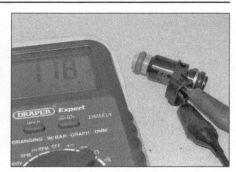

**5.25b Checking injector resistance**

### Fuel injector

⚠ *Warning: Refer to the precautions given in Section 1 before starting work.*

#### Check
**24** Remove the storage compartment (see Chapter 9). Check the wiring and connectors as in Step 1.
**25** Disconnect the wiring connector from the injector **(see illustration)**. Connect an ohmmeter between the terminals and measure the resistance **(see illustration)**. Compare the reading to that given in the Specifications. Also check that there is no continuity to earth on the black/white wire terminal on the injector. If the resistance of the injector differs greatly from that specified, or there is continuity to earth, a new injector should be fitted.
**26** Next check for battery voltage at the black/white wire terminal in the wiring connector with the ignition ON and the kill switch set to RUN. If there is no voltage, check the other components in the power circuit and the wiring and connectors between them, referring to the wiring diagrams at the end of Chapter 10.

#### Removal
**27** Remove the storage compartment (see Chapter 9).
**28** Disconnect the wiring connector from the injector **(see illustration 5.25a)**.
**29** Have some rag to hand to catch residual fuel. Unscrew the fuel supply hose holder bolts and remove the holder, then detach the hose from the top of the injector **(see illustrations)**.
**30** Remove the injector retaining plate, noting how it locates **(see illustration)**. Carefully lift off the injector **(see illustration)**. Discard the O-rings as new ones must be used **(see illustration 5.31)**.

#### Installation
**31** Fit new O-rings lubricated with clean engine oil onto the injector – the orange O-ring fits into the bottom groove and the black one into the top **(see illustration)**.
**32** Ease the injector into the intake duct, making sure the O-ring does not get dislodged, then fit the retaining plate, making sure it locates correctly **(see illustrations 5.30b and a)**.
**33** Fit the fuel hose onto the top of the injector, making sure the O-ring does not get dislodged **(see illustration 5.29b)**. Fit the

holder and tighten its bolts **(see illustration)**.
**34** Connect the wiring connector **(see illustration 5.25a)**.
**35** Run the engine and check there are no leaks from the injector that the fuel system is working correctly before taking the machine out on the road.

### Oxygen sensor

#### Check

**36** The operation of the oxygen sensor itself can only be checked using the Honda diagnostic test pin box.
**37** Refer to Step 40 for access and check the wiring and connectors as in Step 1. If all is good reset the system as described in Section 4, Step 6, then start the engine and check if the same fault code comes up. If it does the sensor is probably faulty. If it doesn't there was probably just a temporary glitch in the system.
**38** To check the sensor heater, disconnect the sensor wiring connector (see Step 40). Connect an ohmmeter between the two white wire terminals on the sensor side of the connector and check that the resistance is below 13 ohms. Also check that there is no continuity to earth (ground) in each white wire. If the resistance is not as specified or if there is continuity to earth, replace the sensor with a new one.
**39** Next check for battery voltage between the black/white (+) wire terminal and earth with the ignition ON. If there is no voltage, check the other components in the power circuit and the wiring and connectors between them, referring to the wiring diagrams at the end of Chapter 10.

#### Removal

**Note:** *The oxygen sensor is delicate and will not work if it is dropped or knocked, or if any cleaning materials are used on it. Ensure the exhaust system is cold before proceeding.*
**40** Unscrew the sensor cover bolts and remove the cover **(see illustrations)**. Free the sensor wiring and connector from its clips and disconnect it **(see illustration)**.
**41** Unscrew and remove the sensor **(see illustration)**. Discard the sealing washer – a new one must be used.

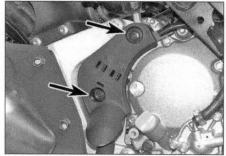

5.40a  Oxygen sensor cover bolts (arrowed) – SH and PS models

5.40c  Release the wiring and connector, and disconnect it

#### Installation

**42** Installation is the reverse of removal. Fit the sensor using a new sealing washer and tighten it to the torque setting specified at the beginning of the Chapter.

### Idle air control valve (IACV)

#### Check

**43** The IACV is part of the throttle body/ECU assembly. Turn the ignition ON and check that the valve makes a beeping sound.
**44** Check the ECU wiring connector **(see illustration 5.3)**. If it is good reset the system as described in Section 4, Step 6, then start the engine and check if the same fault code comes up. If it doesn't there was probably

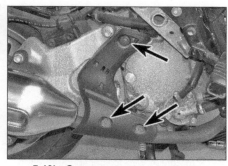

5.40b  Oxygen sensor cover bolts (arrowed) – Pantheon and S-wing models

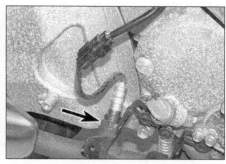

5.41  Unscrew the sensor (arrowed)

just a temporary glitch in the system. If it does have the system tested by a Honda dealer.

#### Removal and installation

**45** The IACV is an integral part of the throttle body/ECU assembly and is not available separately. If the sensor is faulty, a complete new throttle body assembly will have to be installed.

### Lean angle sensor

#### Check – 2005 to 2008 SH models, all PS, Pantheon and S-wing models

**46** Position the scooter on its centrestand so it is level. Remove the body cover (see Chapter 9) – the sensor is mounted at the back of the scooter **(see illustrations)**. On SH

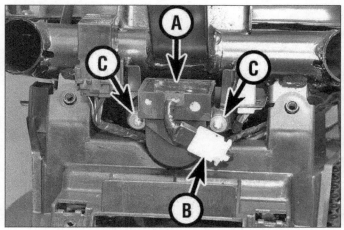

5.46a  Lean angle sensor (A), its wiring connector (B) and mounting screws (C) – PS models

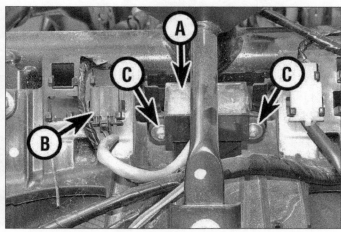

5.46b  Lean angle sensor (A), its wiring connector (B) and mounting screws (C) – S-wing models

models unscrew the three bolts securing the bracket over the sensor and remove it.

**47** With the ignition switch ON and the kill switch set to run, connect the negative (–) lead of a voltmeter to the green wire terminal of the lean angle sensor connector (with the connector still connected). Connect the voltmeter positive (+) lead first to the black wire terminal and check that battery voltage (approximately 12 volts) is present, then connect it to the red/orange wire terminal and check that between 0 to 1 volt is present. Turn the ignition OFF. If there is no voltage check the green wire for continuity to earth – there should be continuity. If battery voltage was not present also check the black wire and connectors between the sensor and the fusebox, referring to the wiring diagrams at the end of Chapter 10. Otherwise check the red/orange wire to the engine stop relay, then check the relay itself (Steps 58 to 60).

**48** Undo the sensor mounting screws and displace the sensor. Hold the sensor horizontal. Set the kill switch to RUN and switch the ignition ON; the engine stop relay (next to the sensor) should click, indicating the power supply is closed (on). Slowly tilt the sensor to the left whilst listening to the engine stop relay; once the sensor reaches an angle of approximately 60° the relay should be heard to click, indicating the power supply is open (off). Switch the ignition OFF and return the sensor to the horizontal, then switch the ignition back ON again (engine stop relay should click again) and tilt the sensor to the right. The engine stop relay should be heard to click again once the sensor reaches an angle of around 60°.

**49** If the relay does not click when the lean angle sensor is tilted the sensor is faulty. If the relay does not click at all it could be faulty.

### Check – 2009-on SH models

**50** Remove the body cover (see Chapter 9). Check the wiring and connectors as in Step 1.

**51** Disconnect the sensor wiring connector.

**52** Connect the positive (+) lead of a voltmeter to the yellow/red wire terminal in the sensor wiring connector, then connect the negative (–) lead to a good earth. Turn the ignition switch ON and check that a voltage of 4.75 to 5.25 volts is present. If it isn't, there is a fault in the yellow/red wire or the ECU. If voltage was present, now connect the negative lead to the green/orange terminal of the connector and check that the same voltage is present. If it isn't, there is a fault in the green/orange wire or the ECU. If there is voltage, there may be a fault in the red/blue wire between the ECU and the lean angle sensor connector.

### Removal

**53** Remove the body cover (see Chapter 9) – the sensor is mounted at the back of the scooter **(see illustration 5.46a)**.

**54** On 2005 to 2008 SH models unscrew the three bolts securing the bracket over the sensor and remove it. Disconnect the lean angle sensor wiring connector. Undo the screws and remove the sensor. Note the collars in the mounting grommets.

**55** On 2009-on SH models displace the fuel pump relay and disconnect the licence plate light wiring connector. Disconnect the lean angle sensor wiring connector. Unscrew the three bolts and remove the bracket. Undo the screws and remove the sensor. Note the collars in the mounting grommets.

**56** On PS, Pantheon and S-wing models disconnect the lean angle sensor wiring connector. Undo the screws and remove the sensor. Note the collars in the mounting grommets.

### Installation

**57** Installation is the reverse of removal. Make sure the collars are in place and the sensor is fitted with its UP mark facing upwards.

## 6 Throttle body

 **Warning: Refer to the precautions given in Section 1 before starting work.**

### *Removal*

**1** On SH and PS models remove the air compensation chamber (see Section 2). On Pantheon and S-wing models remove the air filter housing (see Section 2).

**2** Release the ECU wiring connector clamp and disconnect the connector **(see illustration)**.

**3** Slacken the bottom nut on the cable elbow and free the cable from the bracket, noting how it locates **(see illustrations)**. Free the cable end from the pulley on the throttle body **(see illustration)**.

*Caution: Do not snap the throttle from fully open to fully closed once the cable has been disconnected because this can lead to engine idle speed problems.*

**4** Fully slacken the screws on the intake duct joint piece **(see illustration)**. Ease the throttle body assembly and joint piece off the intake

**6.2 Release the clamp and disconnect the wiring connector**

**6.3a Slacken the nut (arrowed) . . .**

**6.3b . . . then free the cable elbow from the bracket . . .**

**6.3c . . . and detach the end from the pulley**

**6.4a Slacken the screws . . .**

**6.4b . . . and remove the throttle body assembly**

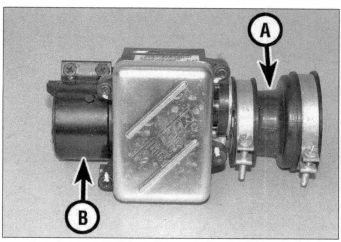

6.5 Remove the air intake rubber (A) and intake duct joint piece (B) if required

6.8 Make sure the tabs locate around the lug (arrow)

duct, noting that it may be quite a tight fit, and remove it (see illustration).
*Caution: Tape over or stuff clean rag into the intake duct after removing the throttle body assembly to prevent anything from falling in.*
**5** If the air intake rubber shows signs of cracking or deterioration a new one must be fitted. Note its orientation and how the clamps locate and are orientated before slackening the clamp and removing it **(see illustration)**. If required also remove the intake duct joint piece by fully undoing its screws and spreading it so it clears the lug on the throttle body.
**6** If required unscrew the intake duct bolts and remove the duct and the joint plate, noting which way round it fits, from the cylinder head. Discard the O-rings – new ones must be used.
*Caution: The throttle body assembly must be treated as a sealed unit. NEVER loosen any of the white-painted nuts/bolts/screws on the assembly as these are pre-set at the factory.*

## Installation

**7** If the intake duct was removed fit new O-rings smeared with oil into the grooves in the joint plate and the duct, and fit the plate with its tab on the right-hand side.
**8** If the intake duct joint piece was removed make sure it is fitted with the THROT BODY mark on the throttle body side and that the tabs locate around the lug on the intake **(see illustration)**, and the hole locates over the peg **(see illustration 6.5)**. Also fit the air intake rubber if removed.
**9** Remove the tape/plug from the intake duct. Lubricate the inside of the joint piece with a light smear of engine oil to aid installation.
**10** Fit the throttle body assembly onto the intake duct, aligning and locating the tabs on each side of the lug, until it is fully engaged **(see illustration 6.4b)**. Tighten the screws **(see illustration 6.4a)**.
**11** Lubricate the throttle cable end with multi-purpose grease and fit it into the pulley. Locate the elbow in the bracket, then set the nuts so the cable freeplay is as specified (see

Chapter 1).
**12** Connect and lock the ECU wiring connector **(see illustrations 6.2 and 5.3)**.
**13** On SH and PS models install the air compensation chamber (see Section 2). On Pantheon and S-wing models install the air filter housing (see Section 2).

### 7 Fuel pressure check

⚠️ *Warning: Refer to the precautions given in Section 1 before starting work.*

**Note:** *A pressure gauge is required for this check. Honda specify the use of their gauge (Pt. No. 07406-0040003) along with an adapter and hose (part Nos. 07ZAJ-S5A0110 and 07ZAJ-S5A0120), that fit between the fuel hose and the fuel pump.*
**1** On SH and PS models remove the storage compartment, on Pantheon models remove the centre cover, and on S-wing models remove the front inner cover (see Chapter 9). Disconnect the battery negative (–) terminal (see Chapter 10).
**2** Lift the rubber seal tab off the top of the fuel hose union on the fuel pump and pull it away from the hose so the sealing ring section is clear of it, and seat the ring around the top of the union to keep it clear **(see illustration 8.8a)**. On SH and PS models release the fuel hose from its clip **(see illustration 8.8b)**. Place some rag around the fuel hose. Press in the tabs on the fuel hose retainer and draw the hose off the union **(see illustration 8.8c)**. Remove the retainer from the union **(see illustration 8.8d)** – Honda specify to use a new one.
**3** Fit the gauge hose and adapter between the fuel supply hose and fuel pump.
**4** Connect the battery negative (–) lead. Start the engine and allow it to idle. Note the pressure present in the fuel system by reading the gauge, then turn the engine off. Compare

the reading obtained to that given in the Specifications.
**5** If the fuel pressure is higher than specified, the fuel pump is faulty and must be replaced with a new one.
**6** If the fuel pressure is lower than specified, likely causes are.
● Leaking fuel hose union
● Blocked fuel strainer
● Faulty fuel pump
If necessary remove the fuel pump (see Section 8) and clean the strainer. If the strainer is clean and there are no leaks evident a new pump assembly must be installed – individual components are not available.
**7** On completion, disconnect the battery negative (–) lead again. Remove the fuel gauge assembly, being prepared to catch the residual fuel. Fit a new hose retainer into the end of the hose, making sure it clicks into place **(see illustration 8.15a)**. Push the hose fully onto the pump union, again until it clicks into place **(see illustration 8.15b)** – check it is secure by trying to pull it off. Relocate the rubber sealing ring in the end of the hose and seat the tab on the top of the union **(see illustration 8.8a)**.
**8** Reconnect the battery then start the engine and check that there is no sign of fuel leakage. If all is well, install the body panels (see Chapter 9).

### 8 Fuel pump, fuel cut-off relay and engine stop relay

⚠️ *Warning: Refer to the precautions given in Section 1 before starting work.*

## Fuel pump

### Check

**1** The fuel pump is fitted into the fuel tank. The fuel pump runs for a few seconds when

8.3a  Disconnecting the pump wiring connector – SH and PS models

the ignition is switched ON to pressurise the fuel system, and then cuts out until the engine is started. Check that it does this. If the pump is thought to be faulty, first check the main fuse and the fuel pump fuse (see Chapter 10). If they are OK proceed as follows.

**2** On SH and PS models remove the storage compartment, on Pantheon models remove the centre cover, and on S-wing models remove the front inner cover (see Chapter 9).

**3** Ensure the ignition is switched OFF then disconnect the fuel pump wiring connector **(see illustrations)**. Connect the positive (+) lead of a voltmeter to the brown wire terminal on the loom side of the connector and the negative (–) lead to the green wire terminal. Switch the ignition ON whilst noting the reading obtained on the meter.

**4** If battery voltage is present for a few seconds, the fuel pump circuit is operating correctly and the fuel pump itself is faulty and must be replaced with a new one.

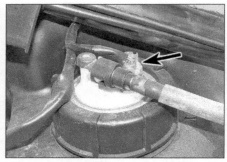

8.3b  Fuel pump wiring connector (arrowed) – Pantheon and S-wing models

**5** If no reading is obtained, check the fuel pump circuit wiring for continuity and make sure all the connectors are free from corrosion and are securely connected. Repair/replace the wiring as necessary and clean the connectors using electrical contact cleaner. If this fails to reveal the fault, check the following components.

● Fuel cut-off relay (see Steps 18 to 20)
● Lean angle sensor (see Section 5)
● Engine stop relay (see Steps 24 to 26)
● Engine control unit (ECU) (see Chapter 6)

## Removal

**Note:** *On SH and PS models the level of the fuel pump mounting is below that of the top of the fuel tank – before removing the pump it is essential to check the level of the fuel in the tank via the filler cap, and if the tank is more than 1/3 full you must siphon out the excess fuel to prevent it coming out of the*

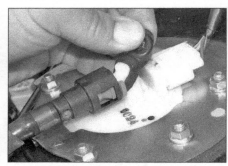

8.8a  Lift and displace the sealing ring as described

*pump orifice as it is removed. Siphon pumps are cheaply available at most car parts and accessories stores. Make sure you store the fuel in a suitable sealable container, and refer to the precautions and warnings given in Section 1 of this Chapter.*

**6** On SH and PS models remove the storage compartment, on Pantheon and S-wing models remove the floor covers (see Chapter 9). Disconnect the battery negative (–) terminal (see Chapter 10).

**7** Disconnect the fuel pump wiring connector **(see illustration 8.3a or b)**.

**8** Lift the rubber seal tab off the top of the fuel hose union on the fuel pump and pull it away from the hose so the sealing ring section is clear of it, and seat the ring around the top of the union to keep it clear **(see illustration)**. On SH and PS models release the fuel hose from its clip **(see illustration)**. Place some rag around the fuel hose. Press in the tabs on the fuel hose retainer and draw the hose off the union **(see illustration)**. Remove the retainer from the union **(see illustration)** – Honda specify to use a new one.

**9** On SH and PS models unscrew the nuts and remove the pump retaining plate **(see illustration)**. Carefully lift the pump out of the tank, taking care not to snag the level sensor float **(see illustration 8.13b)**. Remove the rubber seal from the pump or tank and discard it – a new one must be used **(see illustration 8.13a)**.

**10** On Pantheon and S-wing models unscrew the fuel tank mounting bolts, then tilt the tank to the left and place a support under the right-hand side so the top of the pump is clear of the frame **(see illustration)**. Unscrew

8.8b  Release the fuel hose clip (arrowed)

8.8c  Press the tabs in and draw the hose off

8.8d  Remove the retainer from the union

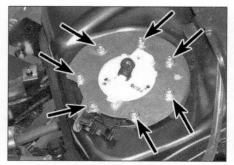

8.9  Unscrew the nuts (arrowed) and remove the plate

8.10a  Unscrew the bolts (arrowed) on each side

8.10b Unscrew the pump retainer (arrowed)

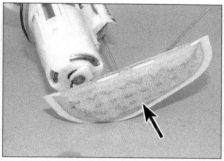

8.12 Check for any debris caught in the strainer (arrowed)

8.13a Fit the new seal . . .

the pump retainer – you will need to use large grips or to drift it round to initially slacken it **(see illustration)**. Note the washer fitted in the retainer. Carefully lift the pump out of the tank, taking care not to snag the level sensor float. Remove the rubber seal and discard it – a new one must be used.

**11** The pump comes as a complete assembly and no individual components are available.

## Installation

**12** Make sure the fuel strainer is clean **(see illustration)**. Clean the mating surfaces of the top of the pump and the fuel tank.

**13** On SH and PS models apply a smear of clean engine oil to the new rubber seal then fit it onto the tank **(see illustration)**. Fit the pump into the tank **(see illustration)**. Fit the retainer plate, aligning the triangular mark with that on the tank, and aligning the pump so its tabs locate in the cut-outs in the plate **(see illustrations)**. Check that the pump, seal and

plate are all evenly seated, then fit the nuts and tighten them finger-tight **(see illustration 8.9)**. Now tighten the nuts evenly and a little at a time in the sequence shown to the torque setting specified at the beginning of the Chapter.

**14** On Pantheon and S-wing models make an alignment mark on the fuel tank of the starting point of the thread for the fuel pump retainer. Now make another mark on the tank 80° anti-clockwise from the first mark. Also make a mark on the outside of the retainer of the starting point of the thread on its inside. Smear clean engine oil onto the upper lip of the new sealing ring, then fit the ring into the pump orifice in the tank, making sure the lip sits flat on the rim. Fit the pump into the tank, aligning the tab with that on the tank, and press it into the seal, making sure the seal lip remains flat on the rim. Make sure the washer is seated in the retainer, then fit the retainer and tighten it to the torque setting specified at the beginning

of the Chapter if the correct tools are available (Honda specify an adapter part No. Miller 6856 that can be used in conjunction with a socket), or to a similar tightness using a pair of grips. Now slacken the retainer by one full turn, then tighten it again to the same torque setting or tightness. Honda say that the important thing is that the retainer has tightened by more than three full turns so the mark made on the outside of the retainer passes that made 80° anti-clockwise from the first mark on the tank. The important thing is that there is no leakage after running the engine and riding the scooter with a full tank. If there is, tighten the retainer some more. Relocate the fuel tank and tighten its bolts **(see illustration 8.10a)**.

**15** Fit a new hose retainer into the end of the hose, making sure it clicks into place **(see illustration)**. Push the hose fully onto the pump union, again until it clicks into place **(see illustration)** – check it is secure by trying

8.13b . . . then manoeuvre the pump into the tank

8.13c Fit the retainer plate . . .

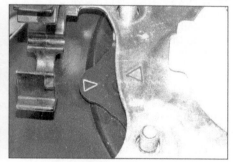

8.13d . . . aligning the marks . . .

8.13e . . . and making sure it locates over the pump tabs

8.15a Fit a new retainer into the hose . . .

8.15b . . then push the hose onto the union

8.22a Fuel cut-off relay (A), engine stop relay (B) – SH and PS models

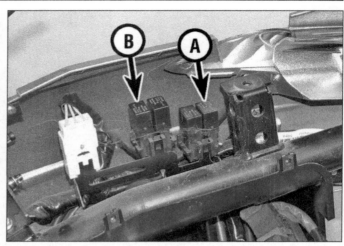

8.22b Fuel cut-off relay (A), engine stop relay (B) – Pantheon and S-wing models

to pull it off. Relocate the rubber sealing ring in the end of the hose and seat the tab on the top of the union **(see illustration 8.8a)**.

16 Connect the fuel pump wiring connector **(see illustration 8.3a or b)**.

17 Connect the battery negative (–) terminal (see Chapter 10). On SH and PS models install the storage compartment, on Pantheon and S-wing models install the floor covers (see Chapter 9).

## *Fuel cut-off relay*

### Check

18 Remove the relay (see below).

19 Connect an ohmmeter between the black/white and adjacent brown wire terminals on the relay. Using a 12 volt battery and auxiliary wires, connect the battery positive (+) terminal to the other black/white wire terminal on the relay and the negative (–) terminal to the brown/black wire terminal and note the meter reading obtained. If the relay is operating correctly there should be continuity (zero resistance) when the battery is connected and no continuity (infinite resistance) when the battery is disconnected. If this is not the case, replace the relay with a new one.

20 If the relay is good check for battery voltage at each black/white wire terminal in the relay wiring connector with the ignition on. If there is no voltage check the wiring to the engine stop relay, then check the relay itself (see below). If all is good check for continuity in the brown wire to the fuel pump and the brown/black wire to the ECU.

### Removal and illustration

21 On SH models remove the body cover (see Chapter 9). On Pantheon and S-wing models remove the storage compartment (see Chapter 9).

22 Pull the relay off its socket **(see illustrations)**.

23 Installation is the reverse of removal.

## *Engine stop relay*

### Check

24 Remove the relay (see below).

25 Connect an ohmmeter between the black and black/white wire terminals on the relay. Using a 12 volt battery and auxiliary wires, connect the battery positive (+) terminal to the other black wire terminal on the relay and the negative (–) terminal to the red/orange wire terminal and note the meter reading obtained. If the relay is operating correctly there should be continuity (zero resistance) when the battery is connected and no continuity (infinite resistance) when the battery is disconnected. If this is not the case, replace the relay with a new one.

26 If the relay is good check for battery voltage at each black wire terminal in the relay wiring connector with the ignition on. If there is no voltage check the wiring to the fusebox, and check the ignition/starter/fuel pump fuse. If all is good check for continuity in the red/orange wire to the lean angle sensor.

### Removal and installation

27 On SH models remove the body cover (see Chapter 9). On Pantheon and S-wing models remove the storage compartment (see Chapter 9).

28 Pull the relay off its socket.

29 Installation is the reverse of removal.

9.3 Undo the nuts (arrowed)

## 9 Exhaust system

> **Warning: If the engine has been running the exhaust system will be very hot. Allow the system to cool before carrying out any work.**

### *Removal*

1 Remove the right-hand floor side panel and for best access the belly panel (see Chapter 9).

2 Unscrew the oxygen sensor cover bolts and remove the cover **(see illustration 5.40a or b)**. Free the sensor wiring and connector from its clips and disconnect the connector **(see illustration 5.40c)**. If required unscrew and remove the sensor **(see illustration 5.41)**. Discard the sealing washer – a new one must be used.

3 Undo the nuts securing the downpipe to the exhaust port in the head **(see illustration)**.

4 Unscrew the bolts securing the silencer, then support the exhaust system, remove the bolts, and manoeuvre the exhaust out **(see illustrations)**.

5 Remove the gasket from the exhaust pipe or port and discard it as a new one must be used **(see illustration 9.6)**.

9.4a Unscrew the bolts (arrowed) . . .

9.4b . . . and remove the exhaust

9.6 Fit the new gasket onto the exhaust pipe

**HAYNES HiNT** *Exhaust system fixings tend to become corroded and seized. It is advisable to spray them with penetrating oil before attempting to loosen them.*

## Installation

**6** Installation is the reverse of removal, noting the following:

- Clean the exhaust port studs and lubricate them with a suitable copper-based grease before reassembly.
- Clean the jointing surfaces of the exhaust port and the pipe.
- Use a new gasket and fit it onto the flange of the exhaust header pipe *(see illustration)*.
- Leave the nuts and bolts finger tight until all have been installed, then tighten the exhaust port nuts first, then the bolts, to the torque settings specified at the beginning of the Chapter.
- Install the oxygen sensor using a new sealing washer and tighten it to the torque setting specified at the beginning of the Chapter.
- Run the engine and check that there are no exhaust gas leaks.

## 10 Fuel gauge and level sensor

### Check

**1** The circuit consists of the level sensor, which is an integral part of the fuel pump assembly in the fuel tank, and the gauge mounted in the instrument cluster. If the instruments malfunction first check the instrument cluster fuse (see Chapter 10).

**2** To check the gauge, on SH and PS models remove the storage compartment, on Pantheon models remove the centre cover, and on S-wing models remove the front inner cover (see Chapter 9). Disconnect the fuel pump assembly wiring connector **(see illustration 8.3a or b)**.

**3** Connect a jumper wire between the yellow/white (SH and PS models) or grey/black (Pantheon and S-wing models) and green/black wire terminals on the loom side of the connector, then turn the ignition on – the gauge needle should move to the FULL position. Detach the jumper wire and turn the ignition off.

**4** If the gauge does not respond as described, remove the handlebar front cover (see Chapter 9). Check the wiring between the sensor connector and the gauge connectors on the back of the instrument cluster on SH and PS models, or the instrument cluster connector on Pantheon and S-wing models, for continuity, and check for continuity to earth in the green/black wire, referring to electrical system testing and the wiring diagrams Chapter 10. If that is good check for voltage at the black wire to the gauge. If the wiring is good the gauge is faulty.

**5** If the gauge and wiring are good, remove the fuel pump (see Section 8). Check that no fuel has entered the float due to a leak, and check that the arm moves up and down smoothly.

**6** Connect the probes of an ohmmeter to the specified terminals on the sensor connector as shown in the table for your model and check the resistance of the sensor in both the FULL and EMPTY positions, on SH and PS models for each connection **(see illustrations)**. If the readings are not as specified, replace the fuel pump assembly with a new one (see Section 8).

| SH and PS models | Full position | Empty position |
|---|---|---|
| Green/black – yellow/white | 25 to 45 ohms | 400 to 700 ohms |
| Yellow/white – gray/black | 450 to 750 ohms | 450 to 750 ohms |

| Pantheon and S-wing models | Full position | Empty position |
|---|---|---|
| Green/black – grey/black | 6 to 8 ohms | 265 to 275 ohms |

### Replacement

⚠️ *Warning: Refer to the precautions given in Section 1 before starting work.*

**7** The fuel gauge is part of the instrument cluster and is covered in Chapter 10.

**8** The fuel level sensor is an integral part of the fuel pump assembly and is covered in Section 8.

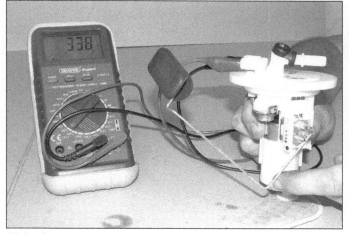

10.6a Checking fuel level sensor resistance in the full position . . .

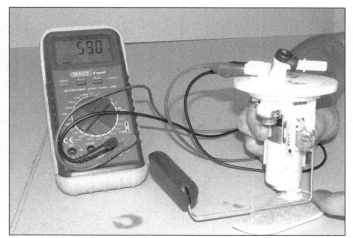

10.6b . . . and in the empty position

## 11 Catalytic converter

### *General information*

**1** A catalytic converter is incorporated in the exhaust system to minimise the level of exhaust pollutants released into the atmosphere.

**2** The catalytic converter consists of a canister containing a fine mesh impregnated with a catalyst material, over which the hot exhaust gases pass. The catalyst speeds up the oxidation of harmful carbon monoxide, unburned hydrocarbons and soot, effectively reducing the quantity of harmful products released into the atmosphere via the exhaust gases.

**3** The catalytic converter is of the closed-loop type with exhaust gas oxygen content information being fed back to the fuel injection system engine control unit (ECU) by the oxygen sensor.

**4** The oxygen sensor contains a heating element which is controlled by the ECU. When the engine is cold, the ECU switches on the heating element which warms the exhaust gases as they pass over the sensor. This brings the catalytic converter quickly up to its normal operating temperature and decreases the level of exhaust pollutants emitted whilst the engine warms up. Once the engine is sufficiently warmed up, the ECU switches off the heating element.

**5** Refer to Section 9 for exhaust system removal and installation, and Section 5 for oxygen sensor removal and installation information.

### *Precautions*

**6** The catalytic converter is a reliable and simple device which needs no maintenance in itself, but there are some facts of which an owner should be aware if the converter is to function properly for its full service life.

● DO NOT use leaded or lead replacement petrol (gasoline) – the additives will coat the precious metals, reducing their converting efficiency and will eventually destroy the catalytic converter.

● Always keep the ignition and fuel systems well-maintained in accordance with the manufacturer's schedule – if the fuel/air mixture is suspected of being incorrect have it checked on an exhaust gas analyser.

● If the engine develops a misfire, do not ride the bike at all (or at least as little as possible) until the fault is cured.

● DO NOT use fuel or engine oil additives – these may contain substances harmful to the catalytic converter.

● DO NOT continue to use the bike if the engine burns oil to the extent of leaving a visible trail of blue smoke.

● Remember that the catalytic converter and oxygen sensor are FRAGILE – do not strike them with tools during servicing work.

# Chapter 6
# Ignition system

## Contents

## Degrees of difficulty

| Easy, suitable for novice with little experience | Fairly easy, suitable for beginner with some experience | Fairly difficult, suitable for competent DIY mechanic | Difficult, suitable for experienced DIY mechanic | Very difficult, suitable for expert DIY or professional |
|---|---|---|---|---|

## Specifications

### General information
Spark plug .......................................... see Chapter 1

### Pulse generator coil
Resistance ......................................... see text
Minimum peak voltage (see text) ............................ 0.7 volts

### Ignition coil
Winding resistance....................................... see text
Spark plug cap resistance ............................... approx 5 K-ohms
Minimum peak voltage (see text) ............................ 100 volts min

### Torque wrench setting
Timing inspection cap ................................... 6 Nm

2.2 Pull the cap off the spark plug

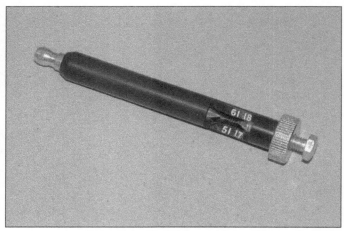

2.4 A typical spark gap testing tool

## 1 General information

All models are fitted with a fully transistorised electronic ignition system which, due to its lack of mechanical parts, is totally maintenance-free. The system comprises a trigger, pulse generator coil, electronic control unit (ECU) and ignition coil (refer to *Wiring Diagrams* at the end of Chapter 10 for details).

The ignition trigger, which is on the alternator rotor on the right-hand end of the crankshaft, magnetically operates the pulse generator coil as the crankshaft rotates. The pulse generator coil sends a signal to the ECU, which then supplies the ignition coil with the power necessary to produce a spark at the plug.

The ECU incorporates an electronic advance system controlled by signals from the ignition trigger and pulse generator coil.

Because of their nature, the individual ignition system components can be checked but not repaired. If ignition system troubles occur, and the faulty component can be isolated, the only cure for the problem is to replace the part with a new one. Keep in mind that most electrical parts, once purchased, cannot be returned. To avoid unnecessary expense, make very sure the faulty component has been positively identified before buying a replacement part.

Note that there is no provision for adjusting the ignition timing.

## 2 Ignition system check

⚠ **Warning: The energy levels in electronic systems can be very high. On no account should the**

*ignition be switched on whilst the plug or plug cap is being held. Shocks from the HT circuit can be most unpleasant. Secondly, it is vital that the engine is not turned over or run with the plug cap removed, and that the plug is soundly earthed (grounded) when the system is checked for sparking. The ignition system components can be seriously damaged if the HT circuit becomes isolated.*

1 As no means of adjustment is available, any failure of the system can be traced to failure of a system component or a simple wiring fault. Of the two possibilities, the latter is by far the most likely. In the event of failure, check the system in a logical fashion, as described below.

2 Put the scooter on its centrestand, making sure the rear wheel is clear of the ground. Remove the maintenance access panel to the spark plug (see Chapter 9). Pull the cap off the spark plug **(see illustration)**. Fit a spare spark plug that is known to be good into the cap and lay the plug against the cylinder head with the threads contacting it. If necessary, hold the spark plug with an insulated tool.

⚠ **Warning: Do not remove the spark plug from the engine to perform this check – atomised fuel being pumped out of the open spark plug hole could ignite, causing severe injury! Make sure the plug is securely held against the engine – if it is not earthed when the engine is turned over, the ignition control unit could be damaged.**

3 Turn the ignition switch ON, and turn the engine over on the starter motor. If the system is in good condition a regular, fat blue spark should be seen at the plug electrodes. If the spark appears thin or yellowish, or is non-existent, further investigation is necessary.

4 The ignition system must be able to produce a spark which is capable of jumping a particular size gap – Honda do not give a specification, but a healthy system should

produce a spark capable of jumping at least 6 mm. Simple ignition spark gap testing tools are commercially available – follow the manufacturer's instructions **(see illustration)**.

5 If the test results are good the entire ignition system can be considered good.

6 Ignition faults can be divided into two categories, namely those where the ignition system has failed completely, and those which are due to a partial failure. The likely faults are listed below, starting with the most probable source. Work through the list systematically, referring to the subsequent sections for full details of the necessary checks and tests, to electrical system fault finding at the beginning of Chapter 10 and to the *Wiring Diagrams* at the end of it. **Note:** *Before checking the following items ensure that the battery is fully charged and that all fuses are in good condition.*

  a) *Loose, corroded or damaged wiring and connectors, broken or shorted wiring between any of the component parts of the ignition system (see Chapter 10).*

  b) *Faulty HT lead or spark plug cap, faulty spark plug, dirty, worn or corroded plug electrodes, or incorrect gap between electrodes.*

  c) *Faulty pulse generator coil or damaged trigger.*

  d) *Faulty ignition coil.*

  e) *Faulty ignition switch (see Chapter 10).*

  f) *Faulty sidestand switch (where fitted) (see Chapter 10).*

  g) *Faulty main relay (see Chapter 10).*

  h) *Faulty engine stop relay (fuel injection models – see Chapter 5B).*

  i) *Faulty lean angle sensor (fuel injection models – see Chapter 5B).*

  j) *Faulty electronic control unit (ECU).*

7 If the above checks don't reveal the cause of the problem, have the ignition system tested by a Honda dealer.

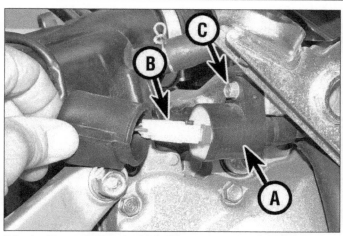

3.1a  Ignition coil (A); primary wiring connectors (B), mounting bolt (C) – 2001 to 2004 SH, Dylan and @ models

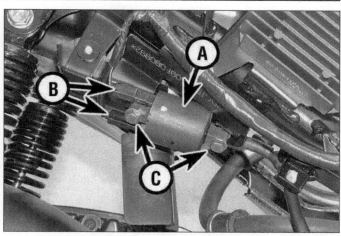

3.1b  Ignition coil (A); primary wiring connectors (B), mounting bolts (C) – 2005-on SH and all PS models

## 3  Ignition coil

### Check

**1** On 2001 to 2004 SH, and all Dylan and @ models the coil is mounted above the alternator cover on the right-hand side of the engine **(see illustration)**. On 2005-on SH and all PS models the coil is mounted under the frame forward of the right-hand shock absorber **(see illustration)**. On Pantheon and S-wing models the coil is mounted on the right-hand frame rail **(see illustration)** – remove the storage compartment (see Chapter 9). Check the coil visually for loose or damaged connectors and terminals, cracks and other damage.

**2** Make sure the ignition is off. Remove the maintenance access panel (see Chapter 9).

**3** Disconnect the primary wiring connectors from the coil **(see illustration 3.1a, b or c)**. Pull the cap off the spark plug **(see illustration 2.2)**.

**4** Set an ohmmeter or multimeter to the ohms x 1 scale and measure the resistance between the primary terminals on the coil **(see illustration)**. This will give a resistance reading of the primary windings of the coil – Honda do not specify a value, but you should get a figure of a few ohms (an S-wing coil measured 2.8 ohms when tested). The important thing is that you do not get a zero or infinite reading.

**5** Now set the meter to the K-ohm scale. Connect one meter probe to one of the primary terminals on the coil, and insert the other in the end of the spark plug cap, making sure the probe is long enough to make contact **(see illustration)**. This will give a resistance reading of the secondary windings of the coil – you should get a figure of several K-ohms (the S-wing coil measured 15 K-ohms). The important thing is that you do not get a zero reading.

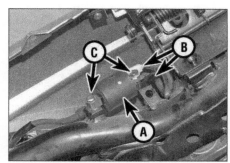

3.1c  Ignition coil (A); primary wiring connectors (B), mounting bolts (C) – Pantheon and S-wing models

**6** If the reading is not as described, unscrew the plug cap from the end of the HT lead. Measure the resistance of the spark plug cap by connecting the meter probes between the HT lead socket and the spark plug contact

3.4  To test the coil primary resistance, connect the multimeter leads between the primary circuit terminals

3.5  To test the coil secondary resistance connect the multimeter leads between a primary circuit terminal and the spark plug cap

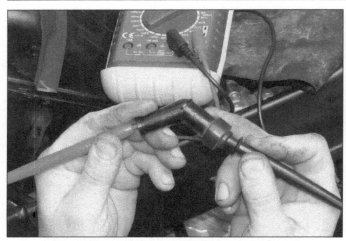

3.6  Measuring the resistance of the spark plug cap

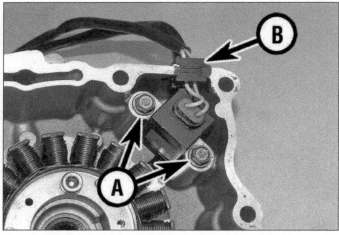

4.6  Unscrew the bolts (A) and free the wiring grommet (B)

(see illustration). The reading should be around 5 K-ohms. If not replace the spark plug cap with a new one.

7 If the primary and secondary resistance readings obtained are not as described, it is possible that the coil is defective. To confirm this, it must be tested as follows using the specified equipment, or by a Honda dealer. Honda specify their own Imrie diagnostic tester (model 625), or the peak voltage adapter (Pt. No. 07HGJ-0020100) with an aftermarket digital multimeter having an impedance of 10 M-ohm/DCV minimum, for a complete test. If this equipment is available, reconnect the wiring connectors to the coil. Connect the cap to a new spark plug and lay the plug on the engine with the threads contacting it. If necessary, hold the spark plug with an insulated tool. Connect the positive (+) lead of the voltmeter and peak voltage adapter arrangement to the black/yellow primary wire terminal on the coil on carburettor models, or to the black/white wire terminal on fuel injection models, with the wiring connector still connected, and connect the negative (–) lead to a suitable earth (ground) point.

8 Turn the ignition switch ON. Check that there is battery voltage reading on the meter, then turn the engine over on the starter motor and note the peak voltage reading on the meter. Once both readings have been noted, turn the ignition switch off and disconnect the meter.

9 If the peak voltage readings are lower than the specified minimum then a fault is present somewhere else in the ignition system circuit (see Section 2).

10 If the initial and peak voltage readings are as specified and the plug does not spark, then the coil is faulty and must be replaced with a new one.

### Removal and installation

11 On all models remove the maintenance access panel to the spark plug (see Chapter 9). On 2001 to 2004 SH, and all Dylan

and @ models the coil is mounted above the alternator cover on the right-hand side of the engine (see illustration 3.1a) – the coil is accessible, but remove the body panels as required according to model for better access if required. On 2005-on SH and all PS models the coil is mounted under the frame forward of the right-hand shock absorber (see illustration 3.1b) – the coil is accessible, but remove the body cover for better access if required. On Pantheon and S-wing models the coil is mounted on the right-hand frame rail (see illustration 3.1c) – remove the storage compartment (see Chapter 9).

12 Disconnect the primary wiring connectors from the coil (see illustration 3.1a, b or c). Pull the cap off the spark plug (see illustration 2.2).

13 Unscrew the bolt(s) and remove the coil (see illustration 3.1a, b or c).

14 Installation is the reverse of removal.

### 4  Pulse generator coil

### Check

1 Trace the 2-wire lead from the top of the alternator cover on the right-hand side of the engine and disconnect it at the connector – remove the body panels as required according to your model for access to the connector (see Chapter 9).

2 Using a multimeter set to the ohms x 10 scale, measure the resistance between the white/yellow and yellow wire terminals on the alternator side of the connector – Honda do not specify a figure for any of the models covered, but you should get a figure of a few ohms. The important thing is that you do not get a zero or infinite reading. If the reading obtained is not as described, it is possible that the coil is defective.

3 To confirm this, it must be tested as described below using the specified equipment

and with the connector still connected, or by a Honda dealer. Honda specify their own Imrie diagnostic tester (model 625), or the peak voltage adapter (Pt. No. 07HGJ-0020100) with an aftermarket digital multimeter having an impedance of 10 M-ohm/DCV minimum, for a complete test. If this equipment is available, on carburettor models connect the positive (+) lead of the voltmeter and peak voltage adapter arrangement to the white/yellow wire terminal in the wiring connector, and the negative (–) lead to the yellow wire terminal, and on fuel injection models connect the positive (+) lead to the yellow wire terminal in the wiring connector, and the negative (–) lead to the white/yellow wire terminal.

4 Turn the ignition switch ON, turn the engine over on the starter motor and note the peak voltage reading on the meter. If the peak voltage reading is lower than the specified minimum, the pulse generator coil is faulty.

5 If the ignition pulse generator coil functions correctly then the fault must be in the wiring harness to the electronic control unit. Check the wiring for continuity, referring to electrical system fault finding at the beginning of Chapter 10 and to the Wiring Diagrams at the end of it. If the wiring is good, the ECU could be faulty.

### Removal and installation

6 Remove the alternator cover (see Chapter 10). Unscrew the pulse generator coil bolts, then free the wiring grommet from the cover and remove the coil (see illustration).

7 Installation is the reverse of removal. Apply some sealant to the wiring grommet.

### 5  Electronic control unit (ECU)

### Check

1 If the tests shown in the preceding or following Sections have failed to isolate the

5.2a  ECU (arrowed) – Dylan and @ models

5.2b  On fuel injection models release the connector lock . . .

5.2c  . . . then pull the connector off

cause of an ignition fault, it is possible that the electronic control unit (ECU) itself is faulty. No test details are available with which the unit can be tested. On carburettor models the best way to determine whether it is faulty is to substitute it with a known good one, if available. On fuel injection models, where the ECU is an integral part of the throttle body assembly, take the unit to a Honda dealer for assessment.

**2** Before condemning the ECU make sure the wiring connector is secure and the terminals are clean and none of the wires have broken. For access, on 2001 to 2004 SH models remove the body cover – the ECU is at the back of the scooter. On Dylan models remove the body cover, and on @ models remove the right-hand side panel – the ECU is on the right-hand side **(see illustration)**. On all fuel injection models remove the storage compartment (see Chapter 9) **(see illustrations)**. Make sure the ignition is off before disconnecting the wiring connector.

**3** Also make sure the power supply and earth wires are good – with the ignition off disconnect the wiring connector, then check for battery voltage at the black wire (carburettor models) or black/white wire (fuel injection models) terminal of the connector using a voltmeter, with the ignition on. Also check for continuity to earth in the green wire(s).

### Removal and installation

**4** Make sure the ignition is off.

6.4  Unscrew the inspection cap

**5** On 2001 to 2004 SH and Dylan models remove the body cover, on @ models remove the right-hand side panel (see Chapter 9). Disconnect the wiring connector and remove the ECU.

**6** On fuel injection models remove the throttle body assembly – the ECU is an integral part of it.

**7** Installation is the reverse of removal. Make sure the wiring connector is securely connected.

---

## 6  Ignition timing

### General information

**1** Since no provision exists for adjusting the ignition timing and since no component is subject to mechanical wear, there is no need for regular checks: only if investigating a fault such as a loss of power or a misfire, should the ignition timing be checked.

**2** The ignition timing is checked dynamically (engine running) using a stroboscopic lamp. The inexpensive neon lamps should be adequate in theory, but in practice may produce a pulse of such low intensity that the timing mark remains indistinct. If possible, one of the more precise xenon

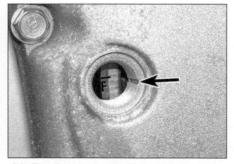

6.5  The line above the F should align with the notch (arrowed)

tube lamps should be used, powered by an external source of the appropriate voltage. **Note:** *Do not use the machine's own battery, as an incorrect reading may result from stray impulses within the machine's electrical system.*

### Check

**3** Warm the engine up to normal operating temperature, then stop it.

**4** Unscrew the timing inspection cap from the alternator cover on the right-hand side of the engine **(see illustration)**.

**5** The mark on the timing rotor which indicates the firing point at idle speed is a line next to an F **(see illustration)**. The static timing mark with which this should align is the notch in the inspection hole.

> **HAYNES HiNT** *The timing marks can be highlighted with white paint to make them more visible under the stroboscope light.*

**6** Connect the timing light to the coil HT lead as described in the manufacturer's instructions.

**7** Start the engine and aim the light at the inspection hole.

**8** With the machine idling, the F mark should align with the static timing mark.

**9** Slowly increase the engine speed whilst observing the F mark. The mark should appear to move until it reaches full advance (no identification mark).

**10** As already stated, there is no means of adjustment of the ignition timing on these machines. If the ignition timing is incorrect, or suspected of being incorrect, one of the ignition system components is at fault, and the system must be tested as described in the preceding Sections of this Chapter.

**11** Install the timing inspection cap using a new O-ring if required, and smear the O-ring and the cap threads with clean oil. Tighten the cap to the torque setting specified at the beginning of the Chapter.

**Notes**

# Chapter 7
# Frame and suspension

## Contents

## Degrees of difficulty

| Easy, suitable for novice with little experience | Fairly easy, suitable for beginner with some experience | Fairly difficult, suitable for competent DIY mechanic | Difficult, suitable for experienced DIY mechanic | Very difficult, suitable for expert DIY or professional |
|---|---|---|---|---|

## Specifications

**Front forks**

**2001 to 2004 SH models**

| | |
|---|---|
| Fork oil type ........................................ | 10W fork oil |
| Fork oil capacity .................................... | 100 cc each leg |
| Fork oil level* ....................................... | 64 mm |
| Spring free length | |
|   Standard ......................................... | 233.5 mm |
|   Service limit (min) .................................. | 228.8 mm |
| Fork inner tube runout .............................. | 0.2 mm |

**2005-on SH models**

| | |
|---|---|
| Fork oil type ........................................ | 10W fork oil |
| Fork oil capacity .................................... | 99 to 101 cc each leg |
| Fork oil level* ....................................... | 106 mm |
| Spring free length | |
|   Standard ......................................... | 257.2 mm |
|   Service limit (min) .................................. | 252 mm |
| Fork inner tube runout .............................. | 0.2 mm |

**Dylan and @ models**

| | |
|---|---|
| Fork oil type ........................................ | 10W fork oil |
| Fork oil capacity .................................... | 108 cc each leg |
| Fork oil level* ....................................... | 50 mm |
| Spring free length | |
|   Standard ......................................... | 233.5 mm |
|   Service limit (min) .................................. | 228.8 mm |
| Fork inner tube runout .............................. | 0.2 mm |

**PS models**

| | |
|---|---|
| Fork oil type ........................................ | 10W fork oil |
| Fork oil capacity .................................... | 113 to 115 cc each leg |
| Fork oil level* ....................................... | 82 mm |
| Spring free length | |
|   Standard ......................................... | 250.2 mm |
|   Service limit (min) .................................. | 245 mm |
| Fork inner tube runout .............................. | 0.2 mm |

## Front forks (continued)

Pantheon models
    Fork oil type . . . . . . . . . . . . . . . . . . . . . . . . . . . . . . . . . . . . . . . . . . . . .   10W fork oil
    Fork oil capacity . . . . . . . . . . . . . . . . . . . . . . . . . . . . . . . . . . . . . . . . .   133 to 135 cc each leg
    Fork oil level* . . . . . . . . . . . . . . . . . . . . . . . . . . . . . . . . . . . . . . . . . . .   93 mm
    Spring free length
        Standard . . . . . . . . . . . . . . . . . . . . . . . . . . . . . . . . . . . . . . . . .   290.7 mm
        Service limit (min) . . . . . . . . . . . . . . . . . . . . . . . . . . . . . . . . . . .   284.9 mm
    Fork inner tube runout . . . . . . . . . . . . . . . . . . . . . . . . . . . . . . . . .   0.2 mm
S-wing models
    Fork oil type . . . . . . . . . . . . . . . . . . . . . . . . . . . . . . . . . . . . . . . . . . . . .   10W fork oil
    Fork oil capacity . . . . . . . . . . . . . . . . . . . . . . . . . . . . . . . . . . . . . . . . .   129.5 to 132.5 cc each leg
    Fork oil level* . . . . . . . . . . . . . . . . . . . . . . . . . . . . . . . . . . . . . . . . . . .   97 mm
    Spring free length
        Standard . . . . . . . . . . . . . . . . . . . . . . . . . . . . . . . . . . . . . . . . .   296.7 mm
        Service limit (min) . . . . . . . . . . . . . . . . . . . . . . . . . . . . . . . . . . .   290.8 mm
    Fork inner tube runout . . . . . . . . . . . . . . . . . . . . . . . . . . . . . . . . .   0.2 mm
*measured from top of fork tube, leg fully compressed*

## Torque settings

Fork damper rod bolt . . . . . . . . . . . . . . . . . . . . . . . . . . . . . . . . . . . . .   20 Nm
Handlebar locating bolt
    S-wing models . . . . . . . . . . . . . . . . . . . . . . . . . . . . . . . . . . . . . . . .   44 Nm
    All other models . . . . . . . . . . . . . . . . . . . . . . . . . . . . . . . . . . . . . . .   39 Nm
Rear axle nut . . . . . . . . . . . . . . . . . . . . . . . . . . . . . . . . . . . . . . . . . . . .   118 Nm
Sidestand pivot bolt . . . . . . . . . . . . . . . . . . . . . . . . . . . . . . . . . . . . .   10 Nm
Sidestand pivot bolt nut . . . . . . . . . . . . . . . . . . . . . . . . . . . . . . . . . .   29 Nm

### 1 General information

All scooters covered by this manual are fitted with a tubular steel one-piece frame.

Front suspension is by conventional telescopic forks, and is not adjustable on any model.

At the rear, twin oil damped shock absorbers with adjustable spring pre-load are mounted between the engine/transmission unit and the frame on the left-hand side and between the swingarm and the frame on the right. The engine unit pivots on a hanger bracket with Silentbloc bushes between the engine and the bracket and between the bracket and the frame.

Ancillary items such as stands and handlebars are covered in this Chapter.

### 2 Frame

1 The frame should not require attention unless accident damage has occurred. In most cases, fitting a new frame is the only satisfactory remedy for such damage. A few frame specialists have the jigs and other equipment necessary for straightening the frame to the required standard of accuracy, but even then there is no simple way of assessing to what extent the frame may have been over-stressed.

2 After a high mileage, the frame should be examined closely for signs of cracking or splitting at the welded joints. Loose engine mount and suspension bolts can cause ovaling or fracturing of the mounting points. Minor damage can often be repaired by specialist welding, depending on the extent and nature of the damage.

3 Remember that a frame which is out of alignment will cause handling problems. If misalignment is suspected as the result of an accident, it will be necessary to strip the machine completely so the frame can be thoroughly checked (see Chapter 8 for wheel alignment checks).

### 3 Stand(s)

#### Centrestand

1 The centrestand is fixed directly to the underside of the engine. Support the scooter securely in an upright position using an auxiliary stand. **Note:** *Do not rest the weight of the machine on the bodywork – if necessary, remove the belly panel to expose the frame (see Chapter 9).*

2 Note which way round the stand springs fit and how they locate. With the stand retracted (UP position) carefully lever one end of each spring off using a large screwdriver or steel rod.

3 Unscrew the bolt on each side and remove the stand, retrieving the collars

between it and the mounting lugs, and noting which fits where **(see illustration)**.

4 Thoroughly clean the stand and inspect all components, replacing any that are worn or damaged with new ones.

5 Installation is the reverse of removal, noting the following:
● Apply grease to the pivot points.
● Make sure that the springs hold the stand up securely when it is not in use – an accident is almost certain to occur if the stand extends while the machine is moving. If necessary, fit new springs.

#### Sidestand

6 A sidestand is fitted as standard to @, Pantheon and S-wing models, but may be fitted to other models as an optional extra. Support the scooter on its centre stand.

7 Remove the left-hand lower panel (see Chapter 9).

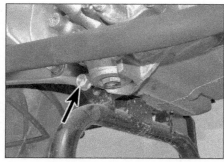

3.3 Unscrew the bolt (arrowed) on each side

**8** Unscrew the sidestand switch bolt and displace the switch, noting how it locates **(see illustration)**.

**9** Unhook the stand springs, noting how they fit **(see illustration)**.

**10** Unscrew the nut on the stand pivot bolt, then unscrew the bolt and remove the stand **(see illustration 3.9)**.

**11** Installation is the reverse of removal, noting the following:

● Apply grease to the pivot bolt shank.
● Tighten the pivot bolt to the torque setting specified at the beginning of the Chapter, then fit the nut and tighten that to the specified torque.
● Make sure that the springs hold the stand up securely when it is not in use – an accident is almost certain to occur if the stand extends while the machine is moving. If necessary, fit new springs.
● Make sure the sidestand switch locates correctly.

## 4 Handlebars and levers

### *Handlebars*

#### Removal

**Note:** *If required, the handlebars can be displaced from the steering head for access to the bearings without having to detach any cables or remove the front and rear brake levers and/or brake master cylinder(s). If this is the case, ignore the Steps which do not apply. If you are removing the handlebars completely, carefully note the routing of all cables and wiring before freeing it.*

**1** Remove the handlebar covers and any other panels required according to model (see Chapter 9).

**2** Displace the front and rear brake lever and master cylinder assemblies from the handlebars (see Chapter 8). Make sure not strain is placed on the hose(s) and/or cables, according to model. Keep the brake fluid reservoir(s) upright to prevent air entering the system.

**3** On S-wing models displace the switch

**3.8 Unscrew the bolt (arrowed) and displace the switch**

housings from the handlebars (see Chapter 10) – there is no need to disconnect the wiring connectors. Undo the handlebar end-weight screws and remove the weights **(see illustration)**.

**4** Detach the throttle cable from the twistgrip (see Chapter 5A). Slide the twistgrip off the end of the handlebar **(see illustration)**.

**5** Remove the left-hand grip. It may be possible to pull the grip off the end of the bar, if necessary cut it off.

**6** Release the cables/hoses/wiring from any guides and ties on the handlebar as required according to model, noting their routing.

**7** Undo the handlebar retaining bolt nut and remove the spacer, noting which way round it fits **(see illustration)**. Withdraw the bolt with its spacer, then ease the handlebars up off the stem, taking care not to strain any cables, wiring and hoses that have been left in position if only displacing the handlebars **(see**

**4.3 Handlebar end-weight screw (arrowed)**

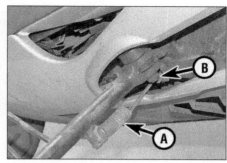

**3.9 Unhook the springs (A). Pivot bolt nut (B)**

**illustrations)**. Fit the spacers and nut in the correct order and way round back onto the bolt to avoid confusion on installation.

**8** If the handlebars are just being displaced, position and support them so that no strain is placed on any of the cables or hoses still attached.

#### Installation

**9** Installation is the reverse of removal, noting the following.

● Make sure the spacers are the correct way round with the rounded side against the steering stem.
● Tighten the handlebar locating bolt nut to the torque settings specified at the beginning of this Chapter.
● Make sure all cables, hoses and wiring are correctly routed and secured.
● Check the throttle cable adjustment (see Chapter 1).

**4.4 Slide the throttle twistgrip off**

**4.7a Unscrew the nut (arrowed) and remove the spacer . . .**

**4.7b . . . then withdraw the bolt . . .**

**4.7c . . . and lift the handlebars off the steering stem**

4.11 Unscrew the locknut (A) then unscrew the pivot bolt (B) and remove the lever

4.12a Unscrew the locknut then unscrew the pivot bolt . . .

4.12b . . . remove it with its spring . . .

4.12c . . . then remove the lever . . .

4.12d . . . and if required the connecting cable arm . . .

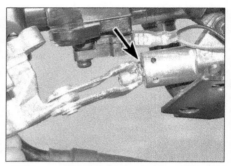

4.12e . . . detaching it from the cable and removing the spring (arrowed)

● Check the operation of the brakes and switches before riding the scooter.

### Brake levers

#### Removal

10 Remove the handlebar covers as required according to model for access to the lever pivots (see Chapter 9).
11 On Pantheon and S-wing models unscrew the lever pivot bolt locknut, then unscrew the pivot bolt and remove the lever (see illustration).
12 To remove the front brake lever on all except Pantheon and S-wing models, unscrew the lever pivot bolt locknut, then unscrew the pivot bolt and remove the spring, noting how its ends locate (see illustrations). Draw the lever and connecting cable arm out and separate them, noting how they fit (see

illustrations). If required detach the arm from the cable, noting and retrieving the spring over the cable end (see illustration).
13 To remove the rear brake lever on all except Pantheon and S-wing models, undo the screw securing the lever to the cable linkage rod (see illustration). Unscrew the lever pivot bolt locknut, then unscrew the pivot bolt and remove the lever (see illustration).

#### Installation

14 Installation is the reverse of removal. Apply a smear grease or other suitable lubricant to the pivot bolt shank and the contact areas between the lever and its bracket. Tighten the pivot bolt lightly, then tighten the locknut. Check that the lever doesn't bind in its bracket. When fitting the front brake lever on all except Pantheon and S-wing models

make sure the spring is fitted over the end of the connecting cable, and apply a smear of grease to the cable end before fitting it into the arm (see illustration 4.12e). Make sure the ends of the spring under the pivot bolt locate correctly (see illustration). Make sure the brakes function correctly before riding the scooter.

### 5 Steering stem

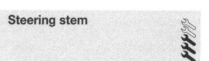

#### Removal

1 Remove or displace the handlebars (see Section 4).
2 Remove the front forks (see Section 7).

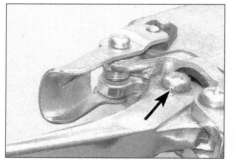

4.13a Undo the cable linkage rod screw (arrowed) . . .

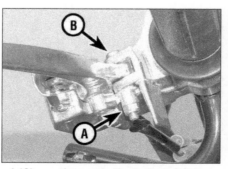

4.13b . . . then undo the locknut (A) then the pivot bolt (B)

4.14 Make sure the spring ends are correctly located

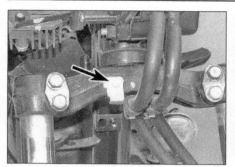

5.4a Unscrew the brake hose guide bolt (arrowed – S-wing shown, other models vary in position)

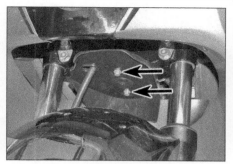

5.4b Unscrew the bolts (arrowed) and displace the shield

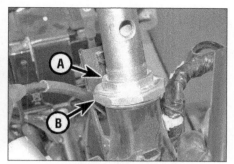

5.5 Locknut (A) and adjuster nut (B)

5.6 Lower the steering stem out of the head

5.8a Remove the upper bearing . . .

5.8b . . . and the lower bearing

**3** On SH models remove the front mudguard (see Chapter 9).

**4** Unscrew the bolt securing the brake hose guide to the fork yoke (see illustration). On Dylan, @ and PS models also displace the deflector shield (see illustration).

**5** Counter-hold the bearing adjuster nut, then unscrew and remove the locknut (see illustration). Where fitted remove the washer, noting how it locates.

**6** Support the steering stem, then unscrew the bearing adjuster nut and carefully lower the stem out of the steering head (see illustration).

**7** On Pantheon and S-wing models lift out the upper bearing inner race – on all other models the inner race is formed into the underside of the adjuster nut.

**8** Remove the upper bearing from the top of the steering head and the lower bearing from the steering stem (see illustrations).

**9** Remove all traces of old grease from the bearings and races and check them for wear or damage as described in Section 6. **Note:** *Do not attempt to remove the outer races from the frame or the lower bearing inner race from the steering stem unless they are to be replaced with new ones.*

## Installation

**10** Smear a liberal quantity of grease on the bearings and races. Fit the lower bearing onto the steering stem (see illustration 5.8b).

**11** Carefully lift the steering stem up through the steering head and hold it in position (see illustration 5.6). Fit the upper bearing (see illustration), then on Pantheon and S-wing models fit the upper race. On all models

thread the adjuster nut onto the steering stem and tighten it finger-tight (see illustration).

**12** Tighten the adjuster nut initially to settle the bearings, then slacken it, then re-tighten until all freeplay is removed. Check that the steering still turns freely from side-to-side with no front-to-rear movement. The object is to set the adjuster nut so that the bearings are under a very light loading, just enough to remove any freeplay.

*Caution: Take great care not to apply excessive pressure because this will cause premature failure of the bearings.*

**13** Where removed fit the lockwasher, locating its tab in the groove. Fit the locknut and tighten it tight (see illustration) – where no lock washer is fitted between the locknut and adjuster nut make sure the adjuster nut does not turn as you tighten the locknut (see

5.11a Fit the upper bearing over the stem

5.11b Thread the adjuster nut on finger-tight

5.13a Thread the locknut tightly against the adjuster nut . . .

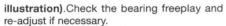

**5.13b ... where no washer is fitted counter-holding the adjuster nut to prevent it turning**

**6.3 Check the races for wear and damage**

**6.6a Drive the bearing races out with a brass drift ...**

illustration).Check the bearing freeplay and re-adjust if necessary.

**14** Install the remaining components in the reverse order of removal. Check the bearing freeplay according to the procedure in Chapter 1 and re-adjust if necessary.

## 6 Steering head bearing overhaul

### Inspection

**1** Remove the steering stem (see Section 5).
**2** Remove all traces of old grease from the bearings and races and check them for wear or damage.
**3** The races should be polished and free from indentations. The outer races are in the steering head, the upper inner race rests

on top of the upper bearing on Pantheon and S-wing models, and is formed into the underside of the adjuster nut on all other models, and the lower inner race is on the bottom of the steering stem **(see illustration)**.
**4** Inspect the bearings for signs of wear, pitting or corrosion, and for cracks in the ball cage.
**5** If there are any signs of wear or damage on any of the above components both upper and lower bearing assemblies should be replaced as a set. Only remove the races from the steering head and the stem if new ones are to be fitted – do not re-use them once they have been removed.

### Renewal

**6** The outer races are an interference fit in the frame and can be tapped from position using a suitable drift located against the inner rim **(see illustrations)**. Tap firmly and evenly around each race to ensure that it is driven out squarely. It may prove advantageous to curve the end of the drift slightly to improve access.
**7** Alternatively, the races can be pulled out using a slide-hammer with internal expanding extractor.
**8** The new outer races can be pressed into the frame using a drawbolt arrangement **(see illustration)**, or by using a large diameter tubular drift which bears only on the outer edge of the race. Ensure that the drawbolt washer or drift (as applicable) bears only on the outer edge of the race and does not contact the working surface.

**6.6b ... locating it against the exposed rim (arrowed)**

 **HAYNES HiNT** *Installation of new bearing outer races is made much easier if the races are left overnight in the freezer. This causes them to contract slightly making them a looser fit.*

**9** To remove the lower inner race from the steering stem, first drive a chisel between the base of the race and the fork yoke **(see illustration)**. Work the chisel around the race to ensure it lifts squarely. Once there is clearance beneath the race, use two levers placed on opposite sides of the race to work it free, using blocks of wood to improve leverage and protect the yoke **(see illustration)**. If the race is firmly in place it can drawn off using a puller **(see**

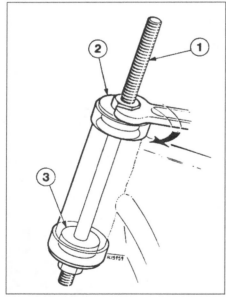

**6.8 Drawbolt arrangement for fitting steering stem bearing races**

1 Long bolt or threaded bar
2 Thick washer
3 Guide for lower race

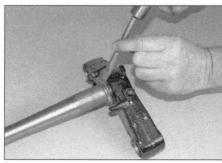

**6.9a Remove the lower bearing race using a cold chisel ...**

**6.9b ... and screwdrivers ...**

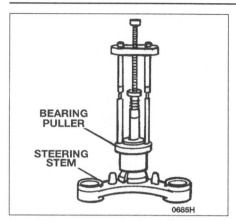

6.9c . . . or a puller if necessary

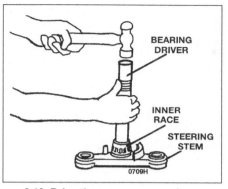

6.10 Drive the new race on using a suitable bearing driver or a length of pipe that bears only against the inner edge

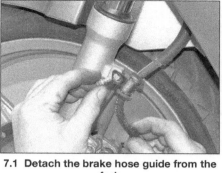

7.1 Detach the brake hose guide from the fork

illustration). Remove the dust seal and replace it with a new one.

10 Fit the new lower inner race bearing onto the steering stem. A length of tubing with an internal diameter slightly larger than the steering stem will be needed to tap the new race into position (see illustration). Ensure that the tube bears only on the inner edge of the race and does not contact its working surface.

11 Install the steering stem (see Section 5).

## 7 Front forks

**Note:** *Always dismantle each fork separately and store all components in separate, clearly marked containers to avoid interchanging parts. Check the availability of replacement parts and the type and quantity of fork oil required before disassembling the forks.*

### Removal

1 Remove the front wheel (see Chapter 8). Unscrew the bolt securing the brake hose guide to the left-hand fork and secure the brake caliper with a cable-tie to avoid straining the hose (see illustration).

2 Remove the front mudguard (see Chapter 9). If required remove the lower front panel for improved access to the top of the fork (see Chapter 9).

3 Work on one fork at a time. Unscrew and remove the upper clamp bolt (see illustration). On 2001 to 2004 SH models and all Dylan and @ models, if the fork oil is being changed or the fork is being disassembled, slacken the top bolt now while the inner tube is still clamped in the yoke. Hold the fork and slacken the lower clamp bolt, then remove the fork leg by twisting it and pulling it downwards (see illustration).

**HAYNES HINT** *If the fork legs are seized in the yoke, spray the area with penetrating oil and allow time for it to soak in before trying again.*

### Installation

4 Remove all traces of corrosion from the fork inner tubes and in the yoke. Install each fork separately.

5 Slide the fork up into the yoke and align the groove in the top of the inner tube with the upper clamp bolt hole in the yoke (see illustration 7.3b). Insert the bolt and tighten it (see illustration 7.3a). Tighten the lower

clamp bolt. On 2001 to 2004 SH models and all Dylan and @ models, if the fork oil has been changed or the fork was disassembled, slacken the upper clamp bolt and tighten the fork top bolt now, then retighten the clamp bolt.

6 Install the remaining components in the reverse order of removal. Check the operation of the front forks before riding the scooter.

### Oil change

7 Remove the fork (see Steps 1 to 3). Always dismantle each fork separately to avoid interchanging parts. Store all components in separate, clearly marked containers.

8 On 2001 to 2004 SH models and all Dylan and @ models unscrew the fork top bolt, noting that it is under pressure from the fork spring (see illustration) – using a ratchet tool enables you to maintain a constant downward pressure while unscrewing the bolt, then to release the pressure slowly.

⚠ *Warning: The fork spring is pressing on the fork top bolt or plug with considerable pressure. It is advisable to wear some form of eye and face protection when carrying out this operation.*

9 On 2005-on SH models, and all PS, Pantheon and S-wing models remove the fork top cap, then press the top plug down against the tension of the fork spring and remove the

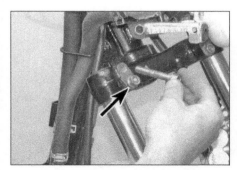

7.3a Remove the top clamp bolt and slacken the lower one (arrowed) . . .

7.3b . . . then draw the fork out of the yoke

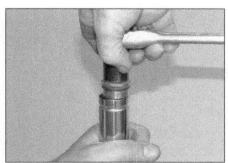

7.8 Unscrewing the fork top bolt using a ratchet tool

**7.9a Remove the cap . . .**

**7.9b . . . then press down on the top plug and remove the retaining ring . . .**

**7.9c . . . then release and remove the plug**

retaining ring **(see illustrations)**. Ease the plug out carefully **(see illustration)**.

**10** Slide the inner tube down into the outer tube and withdraw the spring, noting which way up it is fitted – some models have closer-wound coils at one end **(see illustration)**.

**11** Invert the fork over a suitable container and pump it to expel as much oil as possible **(see illustration)**.

**12** Slowly pour in the correct quantity of the specified grade of fork oil and carefully pump the fork to distribute the oil evenly. Support the

fork upright and allow the oil to settle for a few minutes, then measure the oil level from the top of the tube with it fully compressed **(see illustrations)**. Add or extract oil as necessary to ensure the level is correct.

**13** Pull the inner tube out and install the spring **(see illustration 7.10)**. Note that if the spring coils are closer together at one end, this end should be uppermost.

**14** If necessary, fit a new O-ring onto the fork top bolt or plug and lubricate it with clean fork oil **(see illustration)**.

**15** On 2001 to 2004 SH models and all Dylan and @ models, keeping the fork leg fully extended, fit the top bolt, pressing down onto the spring, and thread it into the tube, again using a ratchet tool if possible to maintain downward pressure **(see illustration 7.8)**. Tighten the bolt as much as possible – it can be fully tightened after the fork has been installed (see Step 5).

> ⚠ **Warning: Compressing the spring with the fork top bolt or plug is a potentially dangerous operation and should be performed with care, using an assistant if necessary. Wipe off any excess oil beforehand to prevent the possibility of slipping.**

**16** On 2005-on SH models, and all PS, Pantheon and S-wing models, keeping the fork fully extended, press the plug down onto the spring until the retaining ring groove is visible and fit the ring **(see illustrations)**. Make sure the ring is correctly located in its groove, then slowly release pressure so the plug seats on the underside of the ring. Fit the top cap **(see illustration 7.9a)**.

**17** Install the fork (see Steps 4 to 6).

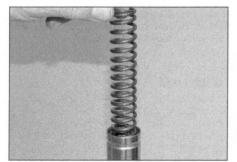

**7.10 Lift the spring out of the fork**

**7.11 Invert the fork over a container and tip the oil out**

**7.12a Pour the oil into the top of the tube, and distribute and bleed it as described . . .**

**7.12b . . . then measure the level**

**7.14 Check the O-ring (arrowed) and fit a new one if necessary**

**7.16a Fit the plug . . .**

**7.16b . . . the press it down and fit the retaining ring into its groove**

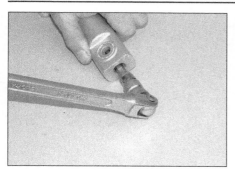

7.19 Slacken the damper rod bolt

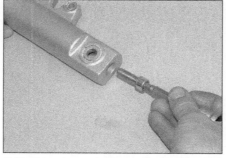

7.21 Unscrew and remove the damper rod bolt

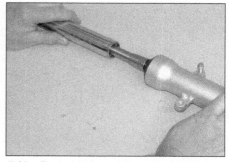

7.22a Draw the inner tube out of the outer tube . . .

## Disassembly

**18** Remove the fork (see Steps 1 to 3).

**19** Turn the fork upside down and compress it so that the spring exerts maximum pressure on the damper rod head, then loosen the damper rod bolt in the base of the fork outer tube, then lightly retighten it to prevent oil leaking from around it **(see illustration)**.

**20** Drain the oil from the fork (see Steps 7 to 11).

**21** Lay the fork flat and unscrew the damper rod bolt **(see illustration)**. Discard the sealing washer as a new one must be used on reassembly.

**22** Pull the inner tube and damper rod out of the outer tube **(see illustration)**. The damper rod seat may come out on the bottom of the rod, in which case remove it, then tip the damper rod out of the top the inner tube **(see**

illustration). If the seat was not on the bottom of the rod tip it out of the outer tube.

**23** Carefully lever the dust seal out of the top of the outer tube **(see illustration)**.

**24** Prise out the oil seal retaining clip **(see illustration)**. Remove the oil seal using an internal expanding puller with slide hammer attachment **(see illustration)**. Discard the oil and dust seals as new ones must be used on reassembly.

## Inspection

**25** Clean all parts in a suitable solvent and dry them with compressed air, if available.

**26** Inspect the fork inner tubes for score marks, pitting or flaking of the chrome finish and excessive or abnormal wear. Check each tube is straight by laying a straight-edge along it. If any bend is evident check the amount of runout using V-blocks and a dial gauge. If

either of the tubes is damaged or worn, or the amount of runout exceeds the limit specified at the beginning of the Chapter, replace both inner tubes with new ones.

**27** Check the condition of the bush in the top of the outer tube **(see illustration)** – if the grey Teflon surface has worn to expose the copper underneath over more than 3/4 of the surface area, or if the surface is scratched or otherwise damaged, remove it using the same puller and slide hammer arrangement used for the oil seal.

**28** Inspect the fork springs for cracks, wear and other damage. Over an extended period, the springs will sag – measure the spring free length, and check they are both the same length **(see illustration)**. If one spring is defective, or if the springs have sagged, replace the springs with a new pair.

**29** Check the condition of the damper rod

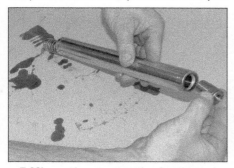

7.22b . . . then remove the damper rod seat and tip the rod out

7.23 Prise out the dust seal using a flat bladed screwdriver

7.24a Prise out the retaining clip using a flat bladed screwdriver

7.24b Locate the puller under the oil seal and jar the seal out using the slide-hammer attachment

7.27 Check the bush (arrowed) for wear

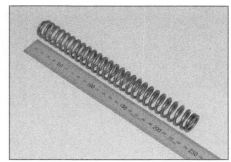

7.28 Measure the free length of the spring

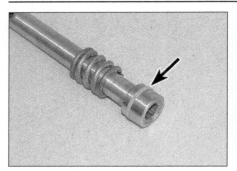

**7.29  Check the rod for damage and the ring (arrowed) for wear**

**7.30  Drive the bush into place until it seats**

**7.31a  Fit the oil seal . . .**

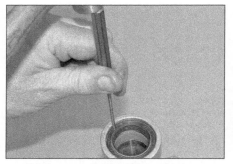

**7.31b  . . . and drive it into place . . .**

illustrations). The markings on the seal should face upwards. When the seal is fully seated secure it with the circlip **(see illustration)**. Make sure the clip is correctly located in its groove.

**32** If removed fit the rebound spring onto the damper rod, and the piston ring into the groove in its head **(see illustration 7.29)**. Fit the damper rod into the top of the inner tube and slide it down so that it protrudes from the bottom **(see illustration)**. Fit the seat onto the bottom of the rod, then push it up into the bottom of the tube **(see illustrations)**.

**33** Lubricate the fork oil seal with the specified fork oil, then slide the inner tube fully into the outer tube, taking care not to damage the lips of the seal **(see illustrations)**. Temporarily fit the fork spring to hold the damper rod in position **(see illustration 7.10)**.

**34** Fit a new sealing washer to the damper bolt and apply a few drops of a suitable, non-permanent thread-locking compound **(see illustration)**. Thread the bolt into the

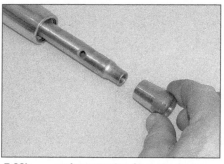

**7.31c  Fit the seal retaining clip into its groove**

the top of the outer tube, then drive it into place using suitable drift, making sure it enters squarely, until seated **(see illustration)**.

**31** Press a new oil seal into place in the outer tube, using a driver or suitably-sized socket that bears on the outer edge of the seal only **(see**

and its rebound spring **(see illustration)**. Check the piston ring in the groove in the top of the rod for wear and replace it with a new one if necessary.

### Reassembly

**30** If a new bush is being fitted, locate it in

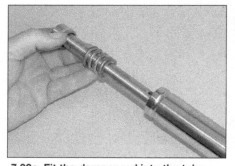

**7.32a  Fit the damper rod into the tube . . .**

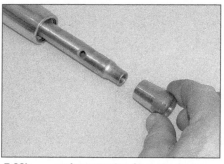

**7.32b  . . . so it protrudes from the bottom, then fit the seat . . .**

**7.32c  . . . and locate it in the bottom of the tube**

**7.33a  Lubricate the seal lips . . .**

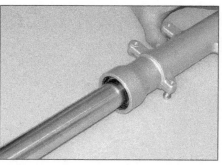

**7.33b  . . . then fit the inner tube into the outer tube**

**7.34  Fit the bolt using threadlock and a new sealing washer**

**7.35 Fit the dust seal into the top of the outer tube**

**8.3a Shock absorber mounting bolts (arrowed) . . .**

**8.3b . . . draw the shock back off the mount after removing the bottom bolt**

bottom of the damper rod via the hole in the bottom of the outer tube and tighten it to the torque setting specified at the beginning of the chapter **(see illustration 7.19)**. If the damper rotates inside the tube, wait until the fork is fully assembled then hold it with spring pressure as on disassembly.

**35** Lubricate the inside of the new dust seal then slide it down the fork tube and press it into position **(see illustration)**.

**36** Add the recommended quantity of oil then finish rebuilding the fork – see Steps 12 to 17. Do not forget to tighten the damper rod bolt if necessary.

## 8 Rear shock absorbers

### *Removal*

**1** Support the scooter on its centre stand, then position a support under the rear wheel so that the engine does not drop when the second shock absorber is removed. Check that the weight of the machine is off the rear suspension so that the shock is not compressed.

**2** Remove the body cover (see Chapter 9). On SH, Dylan, @ and PS models remove the air filter housing to access the left-hand shock absorber. On all models remove the exhaust system to access the right-hand one (see Chapter 5A or B).

**3** Undo the bolt securing the lower end of the shock and pull the shock away from its mounting **(see illustrations)**.

**4** Undo the bolt securing the upper end of the shock, then support the shock and withdraw the bolt. Lift the shock absorber off.

### *Inspection*

**5** Inspect the shock absorber for obvious physical damage. Check the coil spring for looseness, cracks or signs of fatigue.

**6** Inspect the damper rod for signs of bending, pitting and oil leaks **(see illustration)**.

**7** Inspect the upper mounting bush in the top of the shock absorber and the lower mounting bush in either the transmission casing or the swingarm for wear, and replace them with new ones if necessary **(see illustration 8.3b)**.

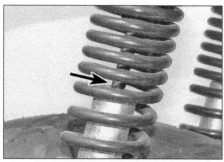

**8.6 Check for oil leaks around the rod (arrowed)**

Inspect the mounting bolts and bolt holes for wear.

**8** With the exception of the bushes and mounting hardware, individual components are not available for the shock. If any parts are worn or damaged, a new shock must be fitted – it is best to replace them as a pair.

### *Installation*

**9** Installation is the reverse of removal.

### *Adjustment*

**10** The rear shock absorbers are adjustable for spring pre-load. On Pantheon and S-wing models there are five settings, and on all other models there are three.

**11** Adjustment is made by turning the spring seat on the bottom of the shock absorber, using a pin spanner **(see illustration)**.

**12** On Pantheon and S-wing models the standard setting is in position 3. Positions 1 and 2 are for lighter loads and smooth roads, and positions 4 and 5 for heavy loads.

**8.11 Turn the spring seat (arrowed) to adjust pre-load – Pantheon/S-wing type shown**

**13** On all other models the standard setting is in position 1, with the spring seat on the highest point so the spring is at its least compressed. Positions 2 and 3 are for heavier loads.

**14** Always make sure both shock absorbers are set to the same position.

## 9 Swingarm

### *Removal*

**1** Remove the exhaust system (see Chapter 5A or B). Remove the rear mudguard (see Chapter 9).

**2** Lock the wheel using a piece of wood between a spoke and the transmission casing **(see illustration 9.10b)**, then slacken the rear wheel nut and thread it off the axle **(see illustration)**. Also remove the spacer **(see illustration)**.

**9.2a Unscrew the rear wheel nut . . .**

**9.2b . . . and remove the spacer**

9.5a Unscrew the bolts (arrowed)

9.5b Draw the swingarm off . . .

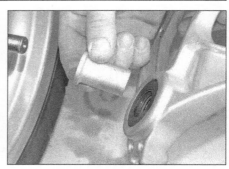

9.5c . . . and remove the inner spacer

3 On 2009-on SH models with a rear disc brake, and all Pantheon and S-wing models, displace the rear brake caliper and hose and tie it clear of the swingarm (see Chapter 8). On S-wing models with ABS remove the rear wheel speed sensor cover and displace the sensor and wiring from the swingarm (see Chapter 8).

4 Undo the bottom bolt securing the right-hand shock absorber to the swingarm, then pivot it back and secure it clear (see illustration 8.3b).

5 Unscrew the bolts securing the swingarm to the engine, noting the washers (see illustration). Grasp the swingarm and draw it off the rear axle (see illustration). Remove the inner spacer – it may have stayed on the axle (see illustration).

## Inspection

6 Thoroughly clean all components, removing all traces of dirt, corrosion and grease.

7 Inspect the swingarm, looking for cracks or distortion due to accident damage.

8 Check the condition of the rear axle bearing and its grease seals (see illustration). If necessary lever out the seals using a flat bladed screwdriver or seal hook – discard them and use new ones.

9 If the bearing is worn, remove the circlip securing it, then drive it out from the other side using a driver or suitable socket. Drive the new bearing in until it seats using a driver or socket that bears only on the outer race. Secure the bearing with a new circlip – if the circlip has a chamfered edge face it towards the bearing. Fit a new seal

into each side, setting them flush with their housing rim.

## Installation

10 Installation is the reverse of removal. Apply grease to the inside of the spacers and to the seal lips. Fit the shouldered spacer into the seal on the inside of the swingarm and the plain spacer into that in the outside. Make sure the washers are fitted with the bolts (see illustration). Tighten the rear axle nut to the torque setting specified at the beginning of the Chapter, locking the rear wheel as before (see illustration).

11 Check the operation of the rear brake and suspension before riding the scooter.

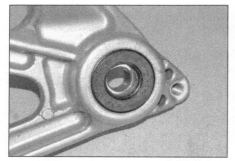

9.8 Check the seal on each side and the bearing

9.10a Fit the bolts with their washers

9.10b Tighten the axle nut to the specified torque

# Chapter 8
# Brakes, wheels and tyres

## Contents

## Degrees of difficulty

| **Easy,** suitable for novice with little experience | **Fairly easy,** suitable for beginner with some experience | **Fairly difficult,** suitable for competent DIY mechanic  | **Difficult,** suitable for experienced DIY mechanic  | **Very difficult,** suitable for expert DIY or professional  |
|---|---|---|---|---|

## Specifications

### Front disc brake

**2001 to 2008 SH models, 2009-on SH models with rear drum brake, all Dylan, @ and PS models**

| | | |
|---|---|---|
| Brake fluid type | DOT 4 | |
| | **Standard** | **Service limit** |
| Caliper bore ID | 27.000 to 27.050 mm | 27.060 mm |
| Caliper piston OD | 26.918 to 26.968 mm | 26.910 mm |
| Master cylinder bore ID | 12.700 to 12.743 mm | 12.755 mm |
| Master cylinder piston OD | 12.657 to 12.684 mm | 12.645 mm |
| Disc thickness | 3.8 to 4.2 mm | 3.5 mm |
| Disc maximum runout | – | 0.30 mm |

**2009-on SH models with rear disc brake**

| | | |
|---|---|---|
| Brake fluid type | DOT 4 | |
| Caliper bore ID | **Standard** | **Service limit** |
| Upper and lower bores | 25.400 to 25.450 mm | 25.460 mm |
| Middle bore | 22.650 to 22.700 mm | 22.710 mm |
| Caliper piston OD | | |
| Upper and lower bores | 25.335 to 25.368 mm | 25.310 mm |
| Middle bore | 22.585 to 22.618 mm | 22.56 mm |
| Master cylinder bore ID | 11.000 to 11.043 mm | 11.055 mm |
| Master cylinder piston OD | 10.957 to 10.984 mm | 10.945 mm |
| Disc thickness | 3.8 to 4.2 mm | 3.5 mm |
| Disc maximum runout | – | 0.30 mm |

## Front disc brake (continued)

### Pantheon and S-wing models

| | Standard | Service limit |
|---|---|---|
| Brake fluid type | DOT 4 | |
| Caliper bore ID | | |
|   Upper and lower bores | 27.000 to 27.050 mm | 27.060 mm |
|   Middle bore | 22.650 to 22.700 mm | 22.710 mm |
| Caliper piston OD | | |
|   Upper and lower bores | 26.918 to 26.968 mm | 26.910 mm |
|   Middle bore | 22.585 to 22.618 mm | 22.560 mm |
| Master cylinder bore ID | 12.700 to 12.743 mm | 12.755 mm |
| Master cylinder piston OD | 12.657 to 12.684 mm | 12.645 mm |
| Disc thickness | 4.0 mm | 3.5 mm |
| Disc maximum runout | – | 0.25 mm |

## Rear drum brake

| Drum internal diameter | |
|---|---|
|   Standard | 130.0 mm |
|   Service limit | 131.0 mm |

## Rear disc brake

### 2009-on SH models

| | Standard | Service limit |
|---|---|---|
| Brake fluid type | DOT 4 | |
| Caliper bore ID | 38.180 to 38.230 mm | 38.240 mm |
| Caliper piston OD | 38.115 to 38.148 mm | 38.09 mm |
| Master cylinder bore ID | 14.000 to 14.043 mm | 14.055 mm |
| Master cylinder piston OD | 13.957 to 13.984 mm | 13.945 mm |
| Disc thickness | 4.8 to 5.2 mm | 4.0 mm |
| Disc maximum runout | – | 0.30 mm |

### Pantheon models

| | Standard | Service limit |
|---|---|---|
| Brake fluid type | DOT 4 | |
| Caliper bore ID | 33.960 to 34.010 mm | 34.020 mm |
| Caliper piston OD | 33.878 to 33.928 mm | 33.870 mm |
| Master cylinder bore ID | 14.000 to 14.043 mm | 14.055 mm |
| Master cylinder piston OD | 13.957 to 13.984 mm | 13.945 mm |
| Disc thickness | 5.0 mm | 4.0 mm |
| Disc maximum runout | – | 0.25 mm |

### S-wing models

| | Standard | Service limit |
|---|---|---|
| Brake fluid type | DOT 4 | |
| Caliper bore ID | 38.180 to 38.230 mm | 38.240 mm |
| Caliper piston OD | 38.098 to 38.148 mm | 38.09 mm |
| Master cylinder bore ID | 14.000 to 14.043 mm | 14.055 mm |
| Master cylinder piston OD | 13.957 to 13.984 mm | 13.945 mm |
| Disc thickness | 5.0 mm | 4.0 mm |
| Disc maximum runout | – | 0.25 mm |

## ABS (S-wing A models)

| Wheel speed sensor air gap | 0.2 to 1.2 mm |
|---|---|

## Wheels

| Maximum wheel runout (front and rear) | |
|---|---|
|   Axial (side-to-side) | 2.0 mm |
|   Radial (out-of-round) | 2.0 mm |
| Maximum axle runout (front) | 0.20 mm |

## Tyres

| | Front | Rear |
|---|---|---|
| Tyre pressures | see *Pre-ride* checks | |
| Tyre sizes* | | |
|   SH models | 100/80-16M/C (50P) | 120/80-16M/C (60P) |
|   Dylan, @ and PS models | 110/90-13M/C (56L) | 130/70-13M/C (57L) |
|   Pantheon and S-wing models | 110/90-13M/C (56L) | 130/70-12M/C (62L) |

*Refer to the owners handbook or the tyre information label on the swingarm for approved tyre brands.*

## Torque settings

| | |
|---|---|
| Brake caliper bleed valves | 6 Nm |
| Brake disc bolts | 42 Nm |
| Brake hose banjo bolts | 34 Nm |
| Brake pipe gland nuts | 14 Nm |
| Front axle nut | |
|    SH, Dylan, @ and PS models | 68 Nm |
|    Pantheon and S-wing models | 59 Nm |
| Front brake caliper body bolts (Pantheon models) | 32 Nm |
| Front brake caliper mounting bolts | 30 Nm |
| Front brake pad retaining pin(s) | 17 Nm |
| Front wheel pulse ring (S-wing A models) | 8 Nm |
| Master cylinder clamp bolts | 12 Nm |
| Rear brake caliper mounting bolts | 30 Nm |
| Rear brake caliper slider pin bolt (SH and S-wing models) | 30 Nm |
| Rear brake caliper slider pin (Pantheon models | 22 Nm |
| Rear brake pad retaining pin (Pantheon models) | 18 Nm |
| Rear wheel pulse ring (S-wing A models) | 8 Nm |

## 1 General information

All models covered in this manual have an hydraulically operated front disc brake, with a twin piston sliding caliper on models that have a rear drum brake, and a triple piston sliding caliper on models with a rear disc brake. All models with a rear disc brake have a sliding rear caliper with a single piston.

All models have a linked braking system, whereby the rear brake lever also actuates the front brake. On models with a rear drum brake the front brake is actuated via a twin cable system, with the connecting cable pulling on an arm mounted under the front brake lever. On models with a rear disc brake the rear brake lever actuates the middle piston in the front brake caliper via a delay valve (the front brake lever actuates the upper and lower pistons).

S-wing A models are fitted with an anti-lock braking system (ABS), that prevents the wheels from locking under heavy braking.

All models are fitted with cast alloy wheels designed for tubeless tyres only.

*Caution: Disc brake components rarely require disassembly. Do not disassemble components unless absolutely necessary. If an hydraulic brake hose is loosened or disconnected, the union sealing washers must be renewed and the system bled upon reassembly. Do not use solvents on internal brake components. Solvents will cause the seals to swell and distort. Use only clean DOT 4 brake fluid for cleaning. Use care when working with brake fluid as it can injure your eyes and it will damage painted surfaces and plastic parts.*

## 2 Front brake pads

⚠ *Warning: The dust created by the brake system is harmful to your health. Never blow it out with compressed air and don't inhale any of it. An approved filtering mask should be worn when working on the brakes.*

### Removal

**2001 to 2008 SH models, 2009-on SH models with rear drum brake, all Dylan, @ and PS models**

**1** Unscrew the pad retaining pin plugs, then slacken the pad retaining pins **(see illustration)**.

**2** Unscrew the caliper mounting bolts and slide the caliper off the disc **(see illustration)**. Free the brake hose from the front fork to give more freedom of movement if required **(see illustration 3.2)**.

**3** Unscrew and remove the pad pins, then remove the pads, noting how they fit **(see illustrations)**. **Note:** *Do not operate either brake lever while the pads are out of the caliper.*

**2009-on SH models with rear disc brake, Pantheon and S-wing models**

**4** On Pantheon models remove the pad retaining pin plug.

**5** On S-wing models with ABS unscrew the wheel speed sensor mounting bolts and wiring guide bolt and displace the sensor from the caliper bracket.

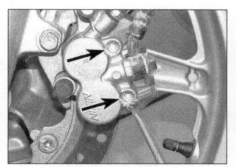

2.1 Remove the plugs, then slacken the pins (arrowed)

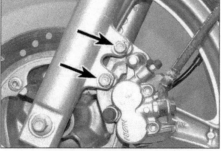

2.2 Unscrew the bolts (arrowed) and displace the caliper

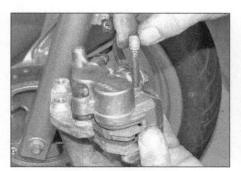

2.3a Unscrew the pins . . .

2.3b . . . and remove the pads

2.6 Slacken the pin (arrowed)

2.7 Unscrew the bolts (arrowed) and displace the caliper

2.8a Unscrew the pin . . .

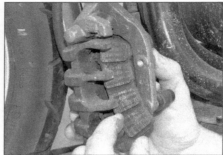

2.8b . . . and remove the pads

**6** Slacken the pad retaining pin **(see illustration)**.

**7** Unscrew the caliper mounting bolts and slide the caliper off the disc **(see illustration)**. Free the brake hose from the front fork to give more freedom of movement if required **(see illustration 3.2)**.

**8** Unscrew and remove the pad pin, then remove the pads, noting how they fit **(see illustrations)**. **Note:** *Do not operate either brake lever while the pads are out of the caliper.*

### Inspection

**9** Inspect the surface of each pad for contamination and check that the friction material has not worn beyond its service limit (see Chapter 1). If either pad is worn down to, or beyond, the service limit wear indicator, is fouled with oil or grease, or heavily scored or damaged, fit a set

of new pads. **Note:** *It is not possible to degrease the friction material; if the pads are contaminated in any way they must be replaced with new ones.*

**10** If the pads are in good condition clean them carefully, using a fine wire brush which is completely free of oil and grease to remove all traces of road dirt and corrosion. Using a pointed instrument, dig out any embedded particles of foreign matter. If available, spray with a dedicated brake cleaner to remove any dust.

**11** Check the condition of the brake disc (see Section 4).

**12** Remove all traces of corrosion from the pad pin(s) and check for wear and damage. Where fitted check the condition of the O-ring on its inner end and replace it with a new one if necessary.

**13** Slide the caliper off the bracket **(see illustration)**. Clean around the exposed

section of each piston to remove any dirt or debris that could cause the seals to be damaged. If new pads are being fitted, push the pistons all the way back into the caliper to create room for them; if the old pads are still serviceable push the pistons in a little way. To push the pistons back use finger pressure or a piece of wood as leverage, or place the old pads back in the caliper and use a metal bar or a screwdriver inserted between them, or use grips and a piece of wood, with rag or card to protect the caliper body **(see illustration)**. Alternatively obtain a proper piston-pushing tool from a good tool supplier **(see illustration)**. If there is too much brake fluid in the reservoir it may be necessary to remove the master cylinder reservoir cover, plate and diaphragm and siphon some out (see *Pre-ride checks*). If the pistons are difficult to push back, remove the bleed valve cap, then attach a length of clear hose to the bleed valve and place the open end in a suitable container, then open the valve and try again (see Section 14). Take great care not to draw any air into the system. If in doubt, bleed the brake afterwards.

**14** If a piston appears seized, first block or hold the other piston(s) using wood or cable ties, then apply the brake lever and check whether the piston in question moves at all. If it moves out but can't be pushed back in the chances are there is some hidden corrosion stopping it. If it doesn't move at all, or to fully clean and inspect the pistons, disassemble and overhaul the caliper (see Section 3).

**15** Clean off all traces of corrosion and hardened grease from the slider pins and boots. Replace the rubber boots with new ones if they are damaged, deformed or deteriorated **(see illustration 3.8)**. Make sure the slider pins are tight. Apply a smear of silicone-based grease to the boots and slider pins, and where fitted to the O-ring on the pad retaining pin.

### Installation

**Note:** *Honda specify to use new caliper mounting bolts, which come pre-treated with a thread locking compound. If preferred, clean the old locking compound off the original bolts and apply fresh compound just before fitting them.*

2.13a Slide the caliper off the bracket

2.13b Push the pistons in using one of the methods described . . .

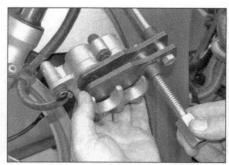

2.13c . . . this is a piston pushing tool

2.16a  Correct fitting of the pad spring . . .

2.16b  . . . and pad guide

2.16c  Make sure the boot lip locates correctly

**2001 to 2008 SH models, 2009-on SH models with rear drum brake, all Dylan, @ and PS models**

16  Make sure the pad spring is correctly located in the caliper, and the pad guide is correctly located on the bracket **(see illustrations)**. Slide the caliper onto the bracket **(see illustration 2.13a)** – make sure the rim of each boot locates correctly around the base of its slider pin **(see illustration)**.

17  Lightly smear the back and the front edge of the pad backing material with copper-based grease, making sure that none gets on the friction material.

18  Fit the pads into the caliper, making sure they locate correctly **(see illustration)**.

Smear some copper grease over the pad retaining pins. Insert the pins and tighten them finger-tight **(see illustration)**.

19  Slide the caliper onto the disc making sure the pads locate correctly on each side **(see illustration)**. Install the caliper mounting bolts (see **Note** above) and tighten them to the torque setting specified at the beginning of the Chapter. Fit the brake hose onto the front fork if displaced.

20  Tighten the pad pins to the torque setting specified at the beginning of this Chapter **(see illustration 2.1)**. Fit the pad pin plugs.

21  Operate the brake lever until the pads contact the disc. Check the level of fluid in the hydraulic reservoir and top-up if necessary (see *Pre-ride checks*).

22  Check the operation of the front brake before riding the motorcycle.

**2009-on SH models with rear disc brake, Pantheon and S-wing models**

23  Make sure the pad spring is correctly located in the caliper, and the pad guide is correctly located on the bracket **(see illustrations)**. Slide the caliper onto the bracket **(see illustration)** – make sure the rim of each boot locates correctly around the base of its slider pin **(see illustration 2.16c)**.

24  Lightly smear the back and the front edge of the pad backing material with copper-based grease, making sure that none gets on the friction material.

25  Fit the pads into the caliper, making sure

2.18a  Fit the pads into the caliper . . .

2.18b  . . . then fit the pins and tighten finger-tight

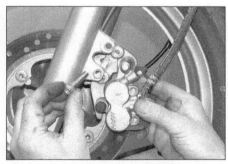

2.19  Slide the caliper onto the disc and fit the bolts

2.23a  Correct fitting of the pad spring . . .

2.23b  . . . and pad guide

2.23c  Slide the caliper onto the bracket

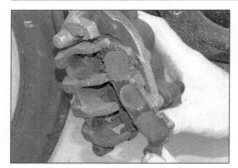

2.25 Fit the pads into the caliper

2.26 Slide the caliper onto the disc and fit the bolts

3.2 Unscrew the bolt and free the hose from the fork

they locate correctly **(see illustration)**. Smear some copper grease over the pad retaining pin. Push the pads up against the spring to align the holes and insert the pin, then tighten it finger-tight **(see illustration 2.8a)**.

26 Slide the caliper onto the disc making sure the pads locate correctly on each side **(see illustration)**. Install the caliper mounting bolts (see **Note** above) and tighten them to the torque setting specified at the beginning of the Chapter. Fit the brake hose onto the front fork if displaced.

27 Tighten the pad pin to the torque setting specified at the beginning of this Chapter **(see illustration 2.6)**. On Pantheon models fit the pad pin plug.

28 On S-wing models with ABS fit the wheel speed sensor and its wiring guide onto the caliper bracket.

29 Operate the brake lever until the pads contact the disc. Check the level of fluid in the hydraulic reservoir and top-up if necessary (see *Pre-ride checks*).

30 Check the operation of the front brake before riding the motorcycle.

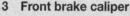
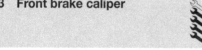

## 3  Front brake caliper

⚠ *Warning: If the caliper is in need of an overhaul all old brake fluid should be flushed from the system. Also, the dust created by the brake system may contain asbestos, which is harmful to your health. Never blow it out*

with compressed air and do not inhale any of it. An approved filtering mask should be worn when working on the brakes. Overhaul of the brake caliper must be done in a spotlessly clean work area to avoid contamination and possible failure of the brake hydraulic system components. Do not, under any circumstances, use petroleum-based solvents to clean brake parts. Use clean DOT 4 brake fluid, dedicated brake cleaner or denatured alcohol only, as described. To prevent damage from spilled brake fluid, always cover paintwork when working on the braking system.

### Removal

*Note: If the caliper is being overhauled (usually due to sticking pistons or fluid leaks) read through the entire procedure first and make sure that you have obtained all the new parts required, including some new DOT 4 brake fluid.*

1 If the caliper is being overhauled, remove the pad retaining pin plug(s) where fitted then slacken the brake pad retaining pin(s) **(see illustration 2.1 or 2.6)**. If the caliper is just being displaced from the forks as part of the wheel removal procedure, the brake pads can be left in place.

2 Free the brake hose(s) from the front fork to give more freedom of movement if required **(see illustration)**.

3 On S-wing models with ABS unscrew the wheel speed sensor mounting bolts and wiring guide bolt and displace the sensor from the caliper bracket.

4 If the caliper is being completely removed or overhauled, unscrew the brake hose banjo bolt(s) and detach the hose(s), noting the alignment with the caliper **(see illustrations)**. Wrap plastic foodwrap around the banjo union(s) and secure the hose(s) in an upright position to minimise fluid loss. Discard the sealing washers, as new ones must be fitted on reassembly.

5 Unscrew the caliper mounting bolts and slide the caliper off the disc **(see illustration 2.2 or 2.7)**. If the caliper is just being displaced, secure it to the motorcycle with a cable-tie to avoid straining the brake hose. **Note:** *Do not operate either brake lever while the caliper is off the disc.*

6 If the caliper is being overhauled, remove the brake pads (see Section 2). Also remove the pad spring, noting how it fits **(see illustration 2.16a or 2.23a)**.

### Overhaul

7 Slide the caliper off the bracket **(see illustration 2.13a or 2.23c)**. On Pantheon models unscrew the caliper body bolts and remove the rear section.

8 Clean the exterior of the caliper and bracket with denatured alcohol or brake system cleaner. Have some clean rag ready to catch any spilled brake fluid. Clean off all traces of corrosion and hardened grease from the slider pins and their rubber boots. Replace the rubber boots with new ones if they are damaged, deformed or deteriorated **(see illustration)**. Make sure the slider pins are tight.

3.4a Brake hose banjo bolt (arrowed) – twin piston calipers

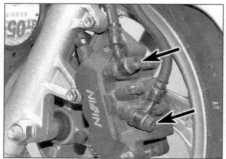

3.4b Brake hose banjo bolts (arrowed) – triple piston calipers

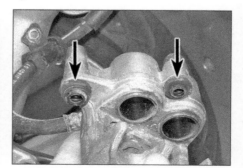

3.8 Check the condition of the boots (arrowed) and fit new ones if necessary

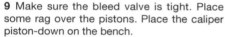
3.10a  Apply compressed air to the fluid passage . . .

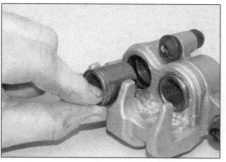
3.10b  . . . until the piston is displaced

3.12  Remove the seals and discard them

**9** Make sure the bleed valve is tight. Place some rag over the pistons. Place the caliper piston-down on the bench.

**10** Apply compressed air gradually and progressively, starting with a fairly low pressure, to the fluid inlet in the caliper and allow the pistons to ease out of their bores, blocking them as required using a piece of wood if one is moving out more than another, so they are expelled equally **(see illustrations)**.

**11** If a piston is stuck in its bore due to corrosion, block the fluid inlet banjo bolt bore(s) using suitable bolt(s), then unscrew the bleed valve and apply the air to this in the same way – the narrower bore will allow more air pressure to be applied to the pistons as less air can escape. Do not try to remove a piston by levering it out or by using pliers or other grips. If the piston has completely seized you may have to replace the caliper with a new one. Mark each piston and bore so they can be returned to their original location.

**12** Remove the dust seals and the piston seals from the piston bores using a soft wooden or plastic tool to avoid scratching the bores **(see illustration)**. Discard the seals as new ones must be fitted.

**13** Clean the pistons and bores with clean brake fluid. Blow through the fluid galleries in the caliper with compressed air to ensure they are clear.

*Caution: Do not, under any circumstances, use a petroleum-based solvent to clean brake parts.*

**14** Inspect the pistons and bores for signs of corrosion, nicks and burrs and loss of plating. If surface defects are present, the pistons and/or the caliper assembly must be replaced with new ones. If the necessary measuring equipment is available, compare the dimensions of the caliper bore and piston to those specified at the beginning of this Chapter, and obtain new pistons or a new caliper if necessary.

**15** Lubricate the new piston seals with clean brake fluid and fit them into the inner (large) grooves in the caliper bore **(see illustrations)**. On models with triple pistons make sure the correct size seals are fitted to the correct bores – the middle piston and bore is smaller.

**16** Lubricate the new dust seals with silicone

grease and fit them into the outer grooves in the caliper bore **(see illustration)**.

**17** Lubricate the pistons with clean brake fluid and fit them, closed-end first, into the caliper bores, taking care not to displace the seals **(see illustration)**. Using your thumbs, push the pistons all the way in, making sure they enter the bore squarely.

**18** On Pantheon models fit the rear section of the caliper body and tighten the bolts to the torque setting specified at the beginning of the Chapter.

**19** Apply a smear of silicone-based grease to the boots and slider pins. Slide the caliper onto the bracket **(see illustration 2.13a or 2.23c)**.

### Installation

**Note:** *Honda specify to use new caliper mounting bolts, which come pre-treated with a thread locking compound. If preferred, clean*

3.15a  Lubricate the new piston seal with brake fluid . . .

3.16  . . . followed by the new dust seal

*the old locking compound off the original bolts and apply fresh compound just before fitting them.*

**20** If the caliper has not been overhauled, refer to Steps 8 and 19 and clean, check and re-grease the slider pins and boots.

**21** Fit the pad spring into the caliper, making sure it locates correctly, and check the pad guide is correctly located on the bracket **(see illustrations 2.16a and b or 2.23a and b)**. Slide the caliper onto the bracket, making sure rim of each boot locates correctly around the base of its slider pin **(see illustration 2.13a or 2.23c, and 2.16c)**.

**22** If removed, inspect and install the brake pads (see Section 2).

**23** Slide the caliper onto the disc, making sure the pads locate correctly on each side **(see illustration 2.19 or 2.26)**.

**24** Install the caliper mounting bolts (see **Note** above) and tighten them to the torque

3.15b  . . . then fit it into its groove

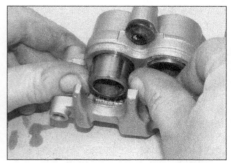
3.17  Fit the piston and push it all the way in

4.2 Measure the thickness of the disc

4.3 Checking disc runout with a dial gauge

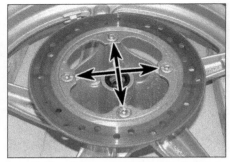

4.5 The disc is secured by four bolts (arrowed)

setting specified at the beginning of the Chapter. If necessary tighten the pad pin(s) to the torque setting specified at the beginning of this Chapter **(see illustration 2.1 or 2.6)**. Fit the pad pin plug(s) where removed.

**25** If removed, connect the brake hose(s) to the caliper, making sure they are correctly aligned, and using new sealing washers on each side of the banjo fitting(s) **(see illustration 3.4a or b)**. Tighten the banjo bolt(s) to the specified torque setting.

**26** Fit the brake hose(s) onto the front fork if displaced **(see illustration 3.2)**.

**27** On S-wing models with ABS fit the wheel speed sensor and its wiring guide onto the caliper bracket.

**28** Top up the hydraulic reservoir with DOT 4 brake fluid (see *Pre-ride checks*) and bleed the system as described in Section 14. Check that there are no fluid leaks and test the operation of the brake before riding the motorcycle.

## 4  Front brake disc

### Inspection

**1** Inspect the surface of the disc for score marks and other damage. Light scratches are normal after use and won't affect brake operation, but deep grooves and heavy score marks will reduce braking efficiency and accelerate pad wear. If a disc is badly grooved it must be replaced with a new one.

**2** The disc must not be machined or allowed to wear down to a thickness less than the service limit listed in this Chapter's Specifications. The minimum thickness should also be stamped on the disc. Check the thickness of the disc with a Vernier gauge or micrometer and replace it with a new one if necessary **(see illustration)**.

**3** To check if the disc is warped, position the bike on an auxiliary stand with the front wheel raised off the ground and turned to one side. Mount a dial gauge to the fork leg, with the gauge plunger touching the surface of the disc about 10 mm from the outer edge **(see illustration)**. Hold the handlebars against the stop then rotate the wheel and watch

the gauge needle, comparing the reading with the limit listed in the Specifications at the beginning of this Chapter. If the runout is greater than the service limit, check the wheel bearings for play (see Chapter 1). If the bearings are worn, install new ones (see Section 16) and repeat this check. If the disc runout is still excessive, a new disc will have to be fitted.

### Removal

**4** Remove the wheel (see Section 18).
*Caution: Don't lay the wheel down and allow it to rest on the disc – the disc could become warped. Set the wheel on wood blocks so the wheel rim supports the weight of the wheel.*

**5** If you are not replacing the disc with a new one, mark the relationship of the disc to the wheel, so it can be installed in the same position. Unscrew the disc retaining bolts, loosening them evenly and a little at a time in a criss-cross pattern to avoid distorting the disc, then remove the disc **(see illustration)**.

### Installation

**Note:** *Honda specify to use new disc mounting bolts, which come pre-treated with a thread locking compound. If preferred, clean the old locking compound off the original bolts and apply fresh compound just before fitting them.*

**6** Before installing the disc, make sure there is no dirt or corrosion where the disc seats on the hub. If the disc does not sit flat when it is bolted down, it will appear to be warped when checked or when the front brake is used.

**7** Fit the disc on the wheel with its marked side facing out, aligning the previously applied matchmarks (if you're reinstalling the original disc).

**8** Install the mounting bolts (see **Note** above) and tighten them evenly and a little at a time in a criss-cross pattern to the torque setting specified at the beginning of this Chapter. Clean the disc using acetone or brake system cleaner. If a new disc has been installed, remove any protective coating from its working surfaces and fit new brake pads.

**9** Install the front wheel (see Section 18).

**10** Operate the brake lever several times to bring the pads into contact with the disc.

Check the operation of the brake before riding the motorcycle.

## 5  Front brake master cylinder

⚠ *Warning: If the brake master cylinder is in need of an overhaul all old brake fluid should be flushed from the system. Overhaul must be done in a spotlessly clean work area to avoid contamination and possible failure of the brake hydraulic system components. Do not, under any circumstances, use petroleum-based solvents to clean brake parts. Use clean DOT 4 brake fluid, dedicated brake cleaner or denatured alcohol only, as described. To prevent damage from spilled brake fluid, always cover paintwork when working on the braking system.*

### Removal

**Note:** *If the master cylinder is being overhauled (usually due to sticking or poor action, or fluid leaks) read through the entire procedure first and make sure that you have obtained all the new parts required, including some new DOT 4 brake fluid.*

**1** Remove the handlebar covers, and then if not already done (according to model), remove the mirror (see Chapter 9).

**2** Disconnect the wiring connectors from the brake light switch **(see illustration)**.

**3** If the master cylinder is being overhauled,

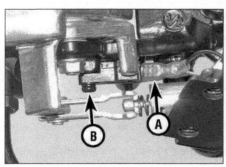

5.2 Disconnect the brake light switch wires (A). Brake light switch screw (B)

**5.3 Unscrew the bolts (arrowed) and remove the master cylinder and its clamp**

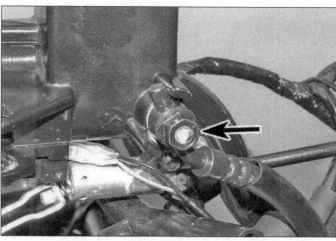

**5.4 Brake hose banjo bolt (arrowed) – note its alignment**

follow Steps 4 to 9. If the master cylinder is just being displaced, follow this Step only: unscrew the master cylinder clamp bolts and remove the back of the clamp, noting how it fits, then position the master cylinder assembly clear of the handlebar **(see illustration)**. Ensure no strain is placed on the hydraulic hose. Keep the reservoir upright to prevent air entering the system.

**4** Unscrew the brake hose banjo bolt and detach the banjo union, noting its alignment with the master cylinder **(see illustration)**. Wrap plastic foodwrap around the banjo union and secure the hose in an upright position to minimise fluid loss. Discard the sealing washers as new ones must be fitted on reassembly.

**5** Remove the brake lever (see Chapter 7). On models with a rear drum brake, undo the screw securing the connecting cable holder and displace the holder, noting how it locates **(see illustration)**.

**6** Slacken the reservoir cover screws.

**7** Unscrew the master cylinder clamp bolts and remove the back of the clamp, noting how it fits, then lift the master cylinder and reservoir away from the handlebar **(see illustration 5.3)**.

**8** Remove the reservoir cover, diaphragm plate and diaphragm. Drain the brake fluid from the master cylinder and reservoir into a suitable container. Wipe any remaining fluid out of the reservoir with a clean rag.

**9** If required, undo the screw securing the brake light switch to the bottom of the master cylinder and remove the switch **(see illustration 5.2)**.

### Overhaul

**10** Carefully remove the rubber boot from the master cylinder **(see illustration)**.

**11** Depress the piston and use circlip pliers to remove the circlip, and on 2009-on SH models remove the washer **(see illustration)**. Slide out the piston assembly and the spring, noting how they fit **(see illustration)**. If they are difficult to remove, apply low pressure compressed air to the brake fluid outlet. Lay

the parts out in the proper order to prevent confusion during reassembly.

**12** Clean the master cylinder bore with clean brake fluid. If compressed air is available, blow it through the fluid galleries to ensure they are clear (make sure the air is filtered and unlubricated).

*Caution: Do not, under any circumstances, use a petroleum-based solvent to clean brake parts.*

**13** Check the master cylinder bore for corrosion, scratches, nicks and score marks. If the necessary measuring equipment is available, compare the dimensions of the piston and bore to those given in the Specifications

**5.5 Undo the screw (arrowed) and displace the cable holder**

**5.11a Release the circlip . . .**

at the beginning of this Chapter. If damage or wear is evident, the master cylinder must be replaced with a new one. If the master cylinder is in poor condition, then the caliper should be checked as well.

**14** The dust boot, circlip, washer (where fitted), piston, seal, cup and spring are all included in the master cylinder rebuild kit. Use all of the new parts, regardless of the apparent condition of the old ones.

**15** Smear the cup and seal with new brake fluid. If not already assembled fit them into their grooves in the piston so their flared ends will fit into the master cylinder first, according

**5.10 Remove the boot**

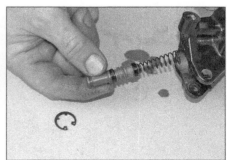

**5.11b . . . then draw out the piston assembly and the spring**

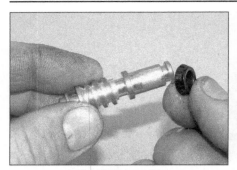

5.15a Fit the seal . . .

5.15b . . . and the cup onto the piston . . .

5.15c . . . making sure they are as shown

to the layout of the removed assembly **(see illustrations)**.

**16** Fit the spring onto the end of the piston, twisting it slightly clockwise to spread the coils if necessary **(see illustration)**.

**17** Lubricate the piston and the master

5.16 Fit the spring onto the end of the piston

cylinder bore with new brake fluid and slide the assembly into the master cylinder **(see illustration)**. Make sure the lips on the cup and seal do not turn inside out. On 2009-on SH models fit the washer. Fit the circlip, with its chamfered side facing in, over the end of the

5.17a Fit the assembly into the cylinder . . .

piston, then push the piston in to compress the spring and fit the circlip into its groove, making sure it locates correctly **(see illustrations)**.

**18** Smear some silicone grease onto the lips and inside of the rubber boot. Fit the rubber boot on the piston so its outer end lips locate in the groove and press the boot into place in the end of the cylinder **(see illustrations)**.

**19** Inspect the reservoir diaphragm and fit a new one if it is damaged or deteriorated.

### Installation

**20** If removed, fit the brake light switch onto the bottom of the master cylinder, making sure the pin locates in the hole, and tighten the screw.

**21** Attach the master cylinder to the handlebar, aligning the clamp joint with the punch mark on the top of the handlebar, then fit the back of the clamp with its UP mark facing up **(see illustration)**. Tighten the upper bolt first, then

5.17b . . . making sure the lips do not turn inside out

5.17c Fit the circlip . . .

5.17d . . . and push it into its groove

5.18a Fit the rubber boot . . .

5.18b . . . locating it as shown

5.21 Align the mating surfaces of the clamp with the punch mark (arrowed)

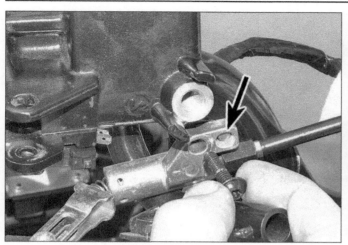

5.22  Fit the hole (arrowed) onto the pin

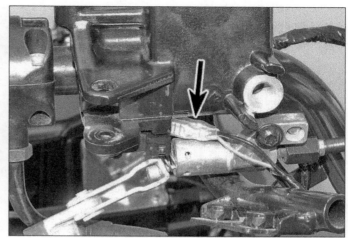

5.23  Connect the brake light switch wiring (arrowed)

the lower bolt, to the torque setting specified at the beginning of the Chapter.

**22**  On drum brake models fit the connecting cable holder, locating the hole over the pin **(see illustration)**.

**23**  Connect the brake light switch wiring **(see illustration)**.

**24**  Install the brake lever (see Chapter 7).

**25**  Connect the brake hose to the master cylinder, aligning it as noted on removal, and using new sealing washers on each side of the banjo fitting **(see illustration)**. Tighten the banjo bolt to the torque setting specified at the beginning of this Chapter.

**26**  Fill the fluid reservoir with new DOT 4 brake fluid (see *Pre-ride checks*). Refer to Section 14 and bleed the air from the system.

**27**  Install the mirror and handlebar covers (see Chapter 9). Check the operation of the brake before riding the motorcycle.

### 6  Rear drum brake

 *Warning: The dust created by the brake system may contain asbestos, which is harmful to your health. Never blow it out with*

*compressed air and don't inhale any of it. An approved filtering mask should be worn when working on the brakes.*

### Check

**1**  Remove the rear wheel (see Section 19).

**2**  Inspect the surface of the friction material on each shoe for contamination **(see illustration)**. If either shoe is fouled with oil or grease, or heavily scored or damaged by dirt and debris, both shoes must be replaced as a set. Note that it is not possible to degrease the friction material; if the shoes are contaminated in any way they must be replaced.

**3**  If the shoes are in good condition clean them carefully, using a fine wire brush which is completely free of oil and grease, some sandpaper, to remove all traces of road dirt and corrosion. Using a pointed instrument, dig out any embedded particles of foreign matter. If the material appears glazed, roughen up the surface using course sandpaper, bearing in mind the *Warning* above.

**4**  Check the condition of the brake shoe springs and replace them if they appear weak or are obviously deformed or damaged.

**5**  Clean the brake drum lining using brake cleaner or a rag soaked in solvent. Examine

the surface of the brake drum lining for scoring and excessive wear. While light scratches are expected, any heavy scoring or cracks will impair braking and there is no satisfactory way of removing them – the wheel should be replaced with a new one. Measure the internal diameter of the drum and replace the wheel with a new one if it has worn below the service limit specified at the beginning of the Chapter **(see illustration)**.

**6**  Check that the brake cam operates smoothly and to its full limits of travel by operating the lever arm. Clean off all traces of old and hardened grease from the cam and pivot post – remove the shoes to do this. If the bearing surfaces of the cam are worn or damaged it should be replaced with a new one. Remove the cable arm from the cam shaft, noting or marking its alignment, then draw the cam out, noting the washer.

**7**  Check the cables (see Section 7).

### Shoe replacement

**8**  Remove the wheel (see Section 19).

**9**  Grasp the outer edge of each shoe and fold them upwards and inwards to form a 'V', noting that they are under the pressure of the springs, then remove them, noting how they

5.25  Always use new sealing washers

6.2  Check the friction material on each shoe

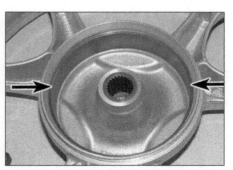

6.5  Check the drum lining, and measure the diameter to determine the extent of wear

**6.9 Removing the brake shoes**

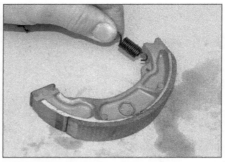

**6.11a Fit the springs into one shoe . . .**

flat ends together. Position the shoes so that the rounded end of each shoe fits around the pivot post and the flat end against the flats on the cam **(see illustration)**. Fold the shoes flat, making sure they sit correctly on each side of the pivot and the cam and the springs remain in place **(see illustration 6.9)**. Operate the lever arm to check that the cam and shoes work correctly.

**12** Install the wheel (see Section 19). Check the operation of the brake before riding the scooter.

<table>
<tr><td>

**7** **Rear drum brake cables and equalizer mechanism**

</td><td></td></tr>
</table>

**Note:** *For details of cable adjustment and lubrication see Chapter 1.*

**1** Remove the front handlebar covers (see Chapter 9).

**2** Undo the bolt securing the cable guide on the underside of the drive belt cover **(see illustration)**.

**3** Fully unscrew the adjuster nut on the brake drum end of the cable, then draw the cable out of the brake arm and the holder on the underside of the drive belt cover **(see illustrations)**. Remove the bush from the arm and the return spring from between the arm and casing, noting how it locates **(see illustrations)**.

**4** Undo the screw securing the rear brake lever to the cable linkage rod **(see illustration)**. Either undo the screw and remove the brake locking lever grommet, or remove the circlip

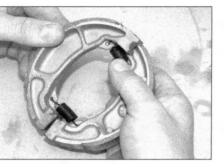

**6.11b . . . then connect them to the other**

locate around the cam and the pivot post **(see illustration)**. Remove the springs from the shoes.

**10** Check the shoes and the drum as outlined above.

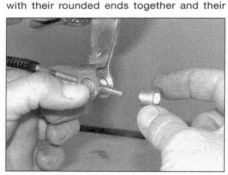

**6.11c Locate the shoes around the post then against the cam**

**11** Apply some copper grease to the bearing surfaces on the cam and pivot post. Fit the springs onto the shoes **(see illustrations)** – make sure the shoes are the same way round, with their rounded ends together and their

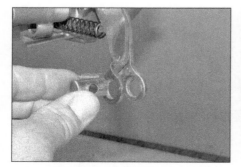

**7.2 Unscrew the bolt and detach the guide**

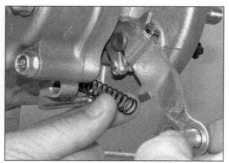

**7.3a Unscrew the nut . . .**

**7.3b . . . and draw the cable out**

**7.3c Remove the bush . . .**

**7.3d . . . and the spring**

**7.4a Undo the screw (arrowed)**

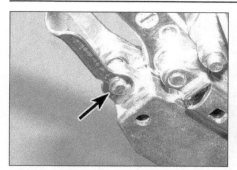

7.4b  Remove the circlip (arrowed) . . .

7.4c  . . . then withdraw the pin and remove the spring and lever . . .

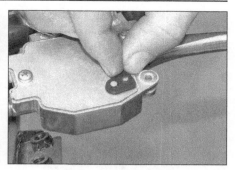

7.4d  . . . and the seal

7.5a  Undo the screws (arrowed) and remove the cover

7.5b  Remove the brake lock arm (arrowed) and spring – Dylan type shown

from the lever pivot pin, withdraw the pin and remove the return spring, lever and seal, according to the mechanism fitted to your model **(see illustrations)**.

**5** Undo the screws and remove the equalizer mechanism cover **(see illustration)**. Remove the brake lock arm and its spring, noting how they fit **(see illustration)**.

**6** Create some slack in the connecting cable using the adjuster on the cable holder under the front brake master cylinder **(see illustration)**. Release the cable end from the arm and remove the spring, then draw the cable out of the holder.

**7** Release both cable ends from the equalizer housing, then draw the connector out and detach the cable ends from it **(see illustration)**. Check the condition of the connector boot in the housing, and replace it with a new one if necessary.

**8** Remove the front panel, floor or belly panels as required according to model to gain access to the cable run (see Chapter 9). Free the cable from any clips or ties, then withdraw it carefully, noting its routing and any guides it passes through.

**9** Install the new cables in a reverse of the removal procedure (see *Haynes Hint*). Apply

some grease to the ends of the inner cables before fitting them, and to the lever and arm pivot points.

**10** Adjust the cable freeplay (see Chapter 1). Check the operation of the brakes before riding the scooter.

> **HAYNES HiNT**  *When fitting a new cable, tape the lower end of the new cable to the upper end of the old cable before removing it from the machine. Slowly pull the lower end of the old cable out, guiding the new cable down into position. Using this method will ensure the cable is routed correctly.*

## 8  Rear brake pads

> ⚠ *Warning: The dust created by the brake system may contain asbestos, which is harmful to your health. Never blow it out with compressed air and don't inhale any of it. An approved filtering mask should be worn when working on the brakes.*

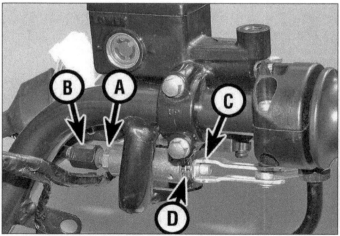

7.6  Slacken the locknut (A) and turn the adjuster (B) in. Release the cable from the arm (C) and remove the spring (D)

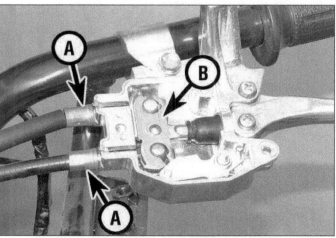

7.7  Draw the cables (A) out of the housing then remove and detach the connector (B)

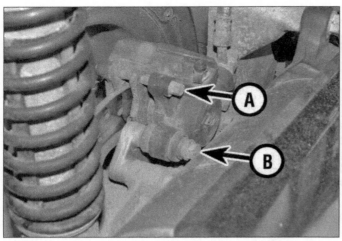

8.2 Slacken the retaining pin (A), then unscrew the slider pin (B)

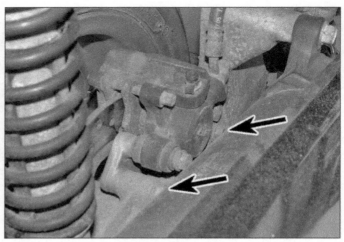

8.4 Caliper mounting bolts (arrowed)

## Removal

1 Remove the exhaust system (see Chapter 5B).

### Pantheon models

2 Slacken the pad retaining pin **(see illustration)**. Unscrew the rear slider pin.

3 Unscrew and remove the pad pin, then remove the pads, noting how they fit. **Note:** *Do not operate the brake lever while the pads are out of the caliper.*

4 Unscrew the caliper mounting bolts and slide the caliper off the disc **(see illustration)**. Slide the caliper off the bracket.

### SH and S-wing models

5 Counter-hold the hex on the caliper bracket slider pin and slacken the slider pin bolt **(see illustration)**.

6 Unscrew the caliper mounting bolts and slide the caliper off the disc **(see illustration)**.

7 Unscrew and remove the slider pin bolt, then pivot the caliper up and slide it off the bracket **(see illustrations)**. Remove the pads from the bracket, noting how they fit **(see illustration)**. **Note:** *Do not operate the brake lever while the pads are out of the caliper.*

## Inspection

8 Inspect the surface of each pad for contamination and check that the friction material has not worn beyond its service limit (see Chapter 1). If either pad is worn down to, or beyond, the service limit wear indicator, is fouled with oil or grease, or heavily scored or damaged, fit a set of new pads. **Note:** *It is not possible to degrease the friction material; if the pads are contaminated in any way they must be replaced with new ones.*

9 If the pads are in good condition clean them carefully, using a fine wire brush which

8.5 Counter-hold the hex and slacken the bolt

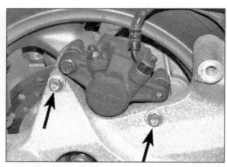

8.6 Unscrew the bolts (arrowed) and slide the caliper off the disc

8.7a Unscrew the slider pin bolt . . .

8.7b . . . then pivot the caliper up . . .

8.7c . . . and slide it off the bracket

8.7d Remove the pads from the bracket

is completely free of oil and grease to remove all traces of road dirt and corrosion. Using a pointed instrument, dig out any embedded particles of foreign matter. If available, spray with a dedicated brake cleaner to remove any dust.

**10** Check the condition of the brake disc (see Section 9).

**11**On Pantheon models remove all traces of corrosion from the pad pin and check it for wear and damage. Check the condition of the O-ring on its inner end and replace it with a new one if necessary.

**12** Clean around the exposed section of the piston to remove any dirt or debris that could cause the seals to be damaged. If new pads are being fitted, push the piston all the way back into the caliper to create room for them; if the old pads are still serviceable push the piston in a little way. To push the piston back use finger pressure or a piece of wood as leverage, or two pieces of wood and a metal bar or a screwdriver inserted between them, or use grips and a piece of wood, with rag or card to protect the caliper body **(see illustration)**. Alternatively obtain a proper piston-pushing tool from a good tool supplier **(see illustration 2.13c)**. If there is too much brake fluid in the reservoir it may be necessary to remove the master cylinder reservoir cover, plate and diaphragm and siphon some out (see *Pre-ride checks*). If the piston is difficult to push back, remove the bleed valve cap, then attach a length of clear hose to the bleed valve and place the open end in a suitable container, then open the valve and try again (see Section 14). Take great care not to draw any air into the system. If in doubt, bleed the brake afterwards.

**13** If the piston appears seized, apply the brake lever and check whether the piston moves at all. If it moves out but can't be pushed back in the chances are there is some hidden corrosion stopping it. If it doesn't move at all, or to fully clean and inspect the piston, disassemble and overhaul the caliper (see Section 9).

**14** Clean off all traces of corrosion and hardened grease from the slider pins and boots. Replace the rubber boots with new ones if they are damaged, deformed or deteriorated **(see illustration 9.6)**. Make sure the fitted slider pin is are tight. Apply a smear of silicone-based grease to the boots and slider pins, and on Pantheon models to the O-ring on the pad retaining pin.

### Installation

**Note:** *Honda specify to use new caliper mounting bolts, which come pre-treated with a thread locking compound. If preferred, clean the old locking compound off the original bolts and apply fresh compound just before fitting them.*

### Pantheon models

**15** Clean the threads of the slider pin. Make sure the pad spring is correctly located in

**8.12  Push the piston into the caliper**

**8.23  Make sure the pads locate correctly against the guides**

the caliper, and the pad guide is correctly located on the bracket. Slide the caliper onto the bracket, making sure the rim of each boot locates correctly around the base of its slider pin.

**16** Slide the caliper onto the disc. Install the caliper mounting bolts (see **Note** above) and tighten them to the torque setting specified at the beginning of the Chapter **(see illustration 8.4)**.

**17** Lightly smear the back and the front edge of the pad backing material with copper-based grease, making sure that none gets on the friction material.

**18** Fit the pads into the caliper, making sure they locate correctly. Smear some copper grease over the pad retaining pin. Insert the pin, pushing the pads up against the spring to align the holes, and tighten it finger-tight.

**19** Apply some fresh threadlock to the rear slider pin threads and tighten it to the specified torque **(see illustration 8.2)**. Tighten the pad pin to the specified torque.

**20** Operate the brake lever until the pads contact the disc. Check the level of fluid in the hydraulic reservoir and top-up if necessary (see *Pre-ride checks*).

**21** Check the operation of the rear brake before riding the motorcycle.

### SH and S-wing models

**22** Clean the threads of the slider pin bolt. Make sure the pad guides are correctly located on the bracket **(see illustration)**.

**23** Lightly smear the back and the front edge of the pad backing material with copper-based grease, making sure that none

**8.22  Make sure the guides are correctly fitted**

**8.25  Slide the caliper onto the disc**

gets on the friction material. Fit the pads into the bracket **(see illustration 8.7d)**, making sure they locate correctly **(see illustration)**.

**24** Slide the caliper onto the bracket, making sure rim of the boot locates correctly around the base of its slider pin **(see illustration 8.7c)**. Pivot the caliper down onto the bracket **(see illustration 8.7b)**. Apply some fresh threadlock to the slider pin bolt threads and tighten it finger-tight **(see illustration 8.7a)**.

**25** Slide the caliper onto the disc making sure the pads locate correctly on each side **(see illustration)**. Install the caliper mounting bolts (see **Note** above) and tighten them to the torque setting specified at the beginning of the Chapter. Counter-hold the hex on the caliper bracket slider pin and tighten the slider pin bolt to the specified torque **(see illustration 8.5)**.

**26** Operate the brake lever until the pads contact the disc. Check the level of fluid in the hydraulic reservoir and top-up if necessary (see *Pre-ride checks*).

**27** Check the operation of the front brake before riding the motorcycle.

### 9  Rear brake caliper

**Warning: If the caliper is in need of an overhaul all old brake fluid should be flushed from the system. Also, the dust created by the brake system may contain asbestos, which is harmful to your health. Never blow it out with compressed**

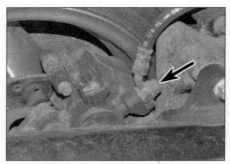

**9.4a Brake hose banjo bolt (arrowed) – Pantheon**

**9.4b Brake hose banjo bolt (arrowed) – SH and S-wing**

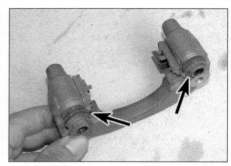

**9.6 Check the condition of the boots (arrowed) and fit new ones if necessary**

*air and do not inhale any of it. An approved filtering mask should be worn when working on the brakes. Overhaul must be done in a spotlessly clean work area to avoid contamination and possible failure of the brake hydraulic system components. Do not, under any circumstances, use petroleum-based solvents to clean brake parts. Use clean DOT 4 brake fluid, dedicated brake cleaner or denatured alcohol only, as described. To prevent damage from spilled brake fluid, always cover paintwork when working on the braking system.*

### Removal

**Note:** *If the caliper is being overhauled (usually due to a sticking piston or fluid leak) read through the entire procedure first and make sure that you have obtained all the new parts required, including some new DOT 4 brake fluid.*

**1** Remove the exhaust system (see Chapter 5A).

**2** If required unscrew the brake hose guide bolts and displace it from the swingarm.

**3** If the caliper is just being displaced, unscrew the caliper mounting bolts and slide the caliper off the disc **(see illustration 8.6)**. Tie or support it clear, making sure no strain is placed on the hose. **Note:** *Do not operate the brake lever while the caliper is off the disc.*

**4** If the caliper is being completely removed or overhauled, unscrew the brake hose banjo bolt and detach the banjo union, noting its alignment with the caliper **(see illustrations)**. Wrap plastic foodwrap around the banjo union and secure the hose in an upright position to minimise fluid loss. Discard the sealing washers as new ones must be fitted on reassembly.

**5** If the caliper is being overhauled, remove the brake pads (see Section 8, Steps 2 to 4 for Pantheon models and Steps 5 to 7 for SH and S-wing models).

### Overhaul

**6** Clean the exterior of the caliper and bracket with denatured alcohol or brake system cleaner. Have some clean rag ready to catch any spilled brake fluid. Clean off all traces of corrosion and hardened grease from the slider pins on the bracket and from the boots in the caliper. Replace the rubber boots with

new ones if they are damaged, deformed or deteriorated **(see illustration)**. Make sure the rear slider pin is tight.

**7** Place a wad of rag over the piston and hold the caliper piston down on the bench. Apply compressed air gradually and progressively, starting with a fairly low pressure, to the fluid inlet on the caliper body and allow the piston to ease out of its bore **(see illustrations 3.10a and b)**.

**8** If the piston is stuck in its bore due to corrosion, find a suitable bolt to block the fluid inlet banjo bolt bore and thread it in, then unscrew the bleed valve and apply the air to this in the same way – the narrower bore will allow more air pressure to be applied to the piston as less can escape. Do not try to remove the piston by levering it out or by using pliers or other grips. If the piston has completely seized you may have to replace the caliper with a new one.

**9** Remove the dust seal and the piston seal from the piston bore using a soft wooden or plastic tool to avoid scratching the bores **(see illustration 3.12)**. Discard the seals as new ones must be fitted.

**10** Clean the piston and bore with clean brake fluid of the specified type. Blow through the fluid galleries in the caliper to ensure they are clear.

**Caution: Do not, under any circumstances, use a petroleum-based solvent to clean brake parts.**

**11** Inspect the caliper bore and piston for signs of corrosion, nicks and burrs and loss of plating. If surface defects are present, the piston and/or the caliper assembly must be replaced with new ones. If the necessary measuring equipment is available, compare the dimensions of the caliper bore and piston to those specified at the beginning of this Chapter, and obtain a new piston or a new caliper if necessary.

**12** Lubricate the new piston seal with clean brake fluid and fit it into the inner (large) groove in the caliper bore **(see illustrations 3.15a and b)**.

**13** Lubricate the new dust seal with silicone grease and fit it into the outer groove in the caliper bore **(see illustration 3.16)**.

**14** Lubricate the piston with clean brake fluid and fit it, closed-end first, into the caliper

bore, taking care not to displace the seals **(see illustration 3.17)**. Using your thumbs, push the piston all the way in, making sure it enters the bore squarely.

**15** Apply a smear of silicone-based grease to the boots and slider pins **(see illustration 9.6)**.

### Installation

**Note:** *Honda specify to use new caliper mounting bolts, which come pre-treated with a thread locking compound. If preferred, clean the old locking compound off the original bolts and apply fresh compound just before fitting them.*

**16** If the caliper was just displaced, refer to the relevant steps in Section 8 for your model and make sure the pads and all caliper components are in good functioning order. Slide the caliper onto the disc making sure the pads locate correctly on each side **(see illustration 8.25)**. Install the caliper mounting bolts (see **Note** above) and tighten them to the torque setting specified at the beginning of the Chapter.

**17** If the caliper has been overhauled refer to Section 8, Steps 15 to 21 for Pantheon models and Steps 22 to 27 for SH and S-wing models, and install the brake pads (see Section 8).

**18** If detached, connect the brake hose to the caliper, aligning it as noted on removal, and using new sealing washers on each side of the fitting. Tighten the banjo bolt to the torque setting specified at the beginning of the Chapter **(see illustration 9.4a or b)**.

**19** If detached fit the rear brake hose guide onto the swingarm.

**20** Top up the hydraulic reservoir with DOT 4 brake fluid (see *Pre-ride checks*) and bleed the system as described in Section 14. Check that there are no fluid leaks and test the operation of the brake before riding the motorcycle.

### 10 Rear brake disc

### Inspection

**1** Refer to Section 4 of this Chapter, noting that the dial gauge should be attached to the swingarm.

## Removal

**2** Remove the wheel (see Section 19).
*Caution: Don't lay the wheel down and allow it to rest on the disc – it could become warped. Set the wheel on wood blocks so the wheel rim supports the weight of the wheel.*
**3** If you are not replacing the disc with a new one, mark the relationship of the disc to the wheel so it can be installed in the same position. Unscrew the disc retaining bolts, loosening them evenly and a little at a time in a criss-cross pattern to avoid distorting the disc, then remove the disc.

## Installation

**Note:** *Honda specify to use new disc mounting bolts, which come pre-treated with a thread locking compound. If preferred, clean the old locking compound off the original bolts and apply fresh compound just before fitting them.*
**4** Before installing the disc, make sure there is no dirt or corrosion where the disc seats on the hub. If the disc does not sit flat when it is bolted down, it will appear to be warped when checked or when the rear brake is used.
**5** Install the disc on the wheel with its marked side facing out, aligning the previously applied matchmarks (if you're reinstalling the original disc).
**6** Install the mounting bolts (see **Note** above) and tighten them evenly and a little at a time in a criss-cross pattern to the torque setting specified at the beginning of this Chapter. Clean the disc using acetone or brake system cleaner. If a new disc has been installed, remove any protective coating from its working surfaces and fit new brake pads.
**7** Install the rear wheel (see Section 19).
**8** Operate the brake lever several times to bring the pads into contact with the disc. Check the operation of the brake before riding the motorcycle.

## 11 Rear brake master cylinder

**Warning: If the brake master cylinder is in need of an overhaul all old brake fluid should be flushed from the system. Overhaul must be done in a spotlessly clean work area to avoid contamination and possible failure of the brake hydraulic system components. Do not, under any circumstances, use petroleum-based solvents to clean brake parts. Use clean DOT 4 brake fluid, dedicated brake cleaner or denatured alcohol only, as described. To prevent damage from spilled brake fluid, always cover paintwork when working on the braking system.**

## Removal

**Note:** *If the master cylinder is being overhauled (usually due to sticking or poor action, or fluid leaks) read through the entire procedure first and make sure that you have*

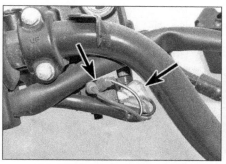

**11.2 Disconnect the four wiring connectors (arrowed)**

obtained all the new parts required, including some new DOT 4 brake fluid.
**1** Remove the handlebar covers, and then if not already done (according to model) remove the mirror (see Chapter 9).
**2** Disconnect the wiring connectors from the brake light switch and starter inhibitor switch **(see illustration)**.
**3** If the master cylinder is being overhauled, follow Steps 4 to 9. If the master cylinder is just being displaced, follow this Step only: unscrew the master cylinder clamp bolts and remove the back of the clamp, noting how it fits, then position the master cylinder assembly clear of the handlebar **(see illustration)**. Ensure no strain is placed on the hydraulic hose. Keep the reservoir upright to prevent air entering the system.
**4** Remove the brake lever (see Chapter 7).
**5** Slacken the reservoir cover screws.
**6** Unscrew the brake hose banjo bolt and detach the banjo union, noting its alignment with the master cylinder **(see illustration 5.4)**. Wrap plastic foodwrap around the banjo union and secure the hose in an upright position to minimise fluid loss. Discard the sealing washers as new ones must be fitted on reassembly.
**7** Unscrew the master cylinder clamp bolts and remove the back of the clamp, noting how it fits, then lift the master cylinder and reservoir away from the handlebar **(see illustration 11.3)**.
**8** Remove the reservoir cover, diaphragm plate and diaphragm. Drain the brake fluid from the master cylinder and reservoir into a suitable container. Wipe any remaining fluid out of the reservoir with a clean rag.
**9** If required, undo the screws securing the brake light/inhibitor switch to the bottom of the master cylinder and remove the switch.

## Overhaul

**10** Carefully remove the rubber boot from the master cylinder **(see illustration 5.10)**.
**11** Depress the piston and use circlip pliers to remove the circlip **(see illustration 5.11a)**. Slide out the piston assembly and the spring, noting how they fit. If they are difficult to remove, apply low pressure compressed air to the brake fluid outlet. Lay the parts out in the proper order to prevent confusion during reassembly.
**12** Clean the master cylinder bore with clean

**11.3 Unscrew the bolts (arrowed) and remove the master cylinder and its clamp**

brake fluid. If compressed air is available, blow it through the fluid galleries to ensure they are clear (make sure the air is filtered and unlubricated).
*Caution: Do not, under any circumstances, use a petroleum-based solvent to clean brake parts.*
**13** Check the master cylinder bore for corrosion, scratches, nicks and score marks. If the necessary measuring equipment is available, compare the dimensions of the piston and bore to those given in the Specifications at the beginning of this Chapter. If damage or wear is evident, the master cylinder must be replaced with a new one. If the master cylinder is in poor condition, then the caliper should be checked as well.
**14** The dust boot, circlip, piston, seal, cup and spring are all included in the master cylinder rebuild kit. Use all of the new parts, regardless of the apparent condition of the old ones.
**15** Smear the cup and seal with new brake fluid. If not already assembled fit the seal into its groove in the piston so its flared ends will fit into the master cylinder first, according to the layout of the removed assembly.
**16** Lubricate the piston and the master cylinder bore with new brake fluid
**17** Fit the dished side of the cup onto the narrow end of the spring. Fit the wide end of the spring into the master cylinder. Locate the end of the piston against the cup and push the cup and piston in, making sure the cup and seal lips do not turn inside out. Fit the circlip, with its chamfered side facing in, over the end of the piston, and fit it into its groove in the master cylinder, making sure it locates correctly **(see illustrations 5.17c and d)**.
**18** Smear some silicone grease onto the lips and inside of the rubber boot. Fit the rubber boot onto the piston so its outer end lips locate in the groove and press the boot into place in the end of the cylinder **(see illustrations 5.18a and b)**.
**19** Inspect the reservoir diaphragm and fit a new one it if it is damaged or deteriorated.

## Installation

**20** If removed, fit the brake light/inhibitor switch onto the bottom of the master cylinder and tighten the screws.
**21** Attach the master cylinder to the

12.1a Delay valve (arrowed) – Pantheon

12.1b Delay valve (arrowed) – S-wing

14.2 Set-up for bleeding the brakes

handlebar, aligning the clamp joint with the punch mark on the top of the handlebar, then fit the back of the clamp with its UP mark facing up **(see illustration 11.3)**. Tighten the upper bolt first, then the lower bolt, to the torque setting specified at the beginning of the Chapter.

**22** Connect the brake hose to the master cylinder, aligning it as noted on removal, and using new sealing washers on each side of the banjo fitting. Tighten the banjo bolt to the torque setting specified at the beginning of this Chapter.

**23** Install the brake lever (see Chapter 7).

**24** Connect the brake light/inhibitor switch wiring **(see illustration 11.2)**.

**25** Fill the fluid reservoir with new DOT 4 brake fluid (see *Pre-ride checks*). Refer to Section 14 and bleed the air from the system.

**26** Install the mirror and handlebar covers (see Chapter 9). Check the operation of the brake before riding the motorcycle.

## 12 Hydraulic system delay valve

**1** The delay valve is fitted to models with an hydraulic rear brake and is part of the linked braking system **(see illustrations)**. It receives the hydraulic pressure from the rear master cylinder and distributes it to the rear and front calipers. The only maintenance is to check for leaks around the hose and pipe unions.

### Removal

**2** On 2009-on SH models remove the front inner cover (see Chapter 9). On Pantheon models remove the headlight cover (see Chapter 9). On S-wing models remove the front cover (see Chapter 9).

**3** Place a wad of rag under and around the delay valve to catch any spilled brake fluid.

**4** Unscrew the brake hose banjo bolt(s) and brake pipe gland nut and detach the brake hose(s) and pipe from the valve. Wrap plastic foodwrap around the banjo union(s) and pipe end and secure the hose(s) in an upright position to minimise fluid loss. Discard the hose sealing washers as new ones must be fitted on reassembly.

**5** Unscrew the valve mounting bolts and

remove the valve.

### Installation

**6** Installation is the reverse of removal. Use a new sealing washer on each side of each brake hose union and make sure the hoses are correctly aligned. Tighten the brake hose banjo bolts and the pipe union nut to the specified torque, noting that to tighten the nuts you will need a special bit that is like the end of an open spanner with a socket to attach the torque wrench.

**7** Bleed the hydraulic system following the procedure in Section 14. Check the operation of both front and rear brakes carefully before riding the motorcycle.

## 13 Brake hoses, pipes and fittings

### Inspection

**1** see Chapter 1, Section 4.

### Removal and installation

**2** The brake hoses have a banjo union on each end. Cover the surrounding area with plenty of rags and unscrew the banjo bolt at each end of the hose, noting the alignment of the union **(see illustrations 3.4a or b, 5.4, and 9.4a or b)**. Free the hose from any clips or guides and remove it, noting its routing. Discard the sealing washers. **Note:** *Do not operate the brake lever or pedal while a brake hose is disconnected.*

**3** Position the new hose, making sure it isn't twisted or otherwise strained, and ensure that it is correctly routed through any clips or guides and is clear of all moving components.

**4** Check that the fittings align correctly, then install the banjo bolts, using a new sealing washer on each side of the union **(see illustration 5.25)**. Tighten the banjo bolts to the torque setting specified at the beginning of this Chapter.

**5** On models with a rear disc brake, and on S-wing models with ABS, the hoses join to pipes that connect the system components. The joints between the hoses and pipes, and where the pipes connect to the delay valve and ABS unit are held by nuts **(see illustrations**

**12.1a and b)**. There are no sealing washers. Unscrew the nuts to separates the hoses from the pipes and to detach the pipes. When refitting them tighten the nuts to the specified torque setting if the correct tools are available.

**6** Flush the old brake fluid from the system, refill with new DOT 4 brake fluid (see *Pre-ride checks*) and bleed the air from the system (see Section 14).

**7** Check the operation of the brakes before riding the motorcycle.

## 14 Brake system bleeding and fluid change

**Note:** *If required use a commercially available vacuum-type brake bleeding tool. If bleeding the system using the conventional method does not work sufficiently well, it is advisable to obtain a bleeder and repeat the procedure detailed below, following the manufacturers instructions for using the tool.*

### Bleeding

**1** Bleeding the brakes is simply the process of removing air from the brake fluid reservoir, the hoses/pipes and the brake caliper(s). Bleeding is necessary whenever a brake system hydraulic connection is loosened, after a component or hose is replaced with a new one, or when the master cylinder or caliper is overhauled. Leaks in the system may also allow air to enter, but leaking brake fluid will reveal their presence and warn you of the need for repair.

**2** To bleed the brakes, you will need some new DOT 4 brake fluid, a length of clear flexible hose, a small container partially filled with clean brake fluid, some rags, a spanner to fit the brake caliper bleed valve, and help from an assistant **(see illustration)**. Bleeding kits that include the hose, a one-way valve and a container are available relatively cheaply from a good auto store, and simplify the task.

**3** Cover painted components to prevent damage in the event that brake fluid is spilled.

**4** Refer to *Pre-ride checks* and remove the reservoir cover, diaphragm plate and diaphragm and slowly pump the brake lever a few times, until no air bubbles can be seen

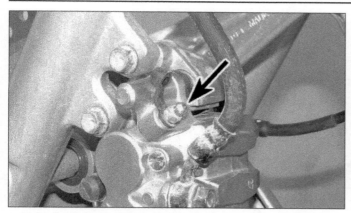

**14.6a  Front brake caliper bleed valve (arrowed) – models with rear drum brake**

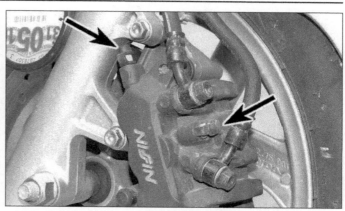

**14.6b  Front brake caliper bleed valves (arrowed) – models with rear disc brake**

floating up from the holes in the bottom of the reservoir. This bleeds the air from the master cylinder end of the line. Temporarily refit the reservoir cover.

**5** On models with a rear disc brake, when bleeding the front brake system do so via the upper bleed valve on the front caliper, and when bleeding the rear/combined system do so via the lower bleed valve on the front caliper and the bleed valve on the rear caliper. Note that when pumping the rear brake lever some resistance may be felt – this is due to the function of the delay valve and is not a problem, but make sure to overcome the resistance and pull the lever all the way back.

**6** Pull the dust cap off the bleed valve **(see illustrations)**. If using a ring spanner fit it onto the valve **(see illustration)**. Attach one end of the hose to the bleed valve and, if not using a kit, submerge the other end in the clean brake fluid in the container **(see illustration 14.2)**.

**7** Check the fluid level in the reservoir. Do not

**14.6c  Rear brake caliper bleed valve (arrowed)**

**14.6d  Fit a ring spanner onto the valve**

> **HAYNES HINT**
> *To avoid damaging the bleed valve during the procedure, loosen it and then tighten it temporarily with a ring spanner before attaching the hose. With the hose attached, the valve can then be opened and closed either with an open-ended spanner, or by leaving the ring spanner located on the valve and fitting the hose above it.*

allow the fluid level to drop below the lower mark during the procedure.

**8** Carefully pump the brake lever three or four times and hold it in while opening the bleed valve. When the valve is opened, brake fluid will flow out of the caliper into the clear tubing, and the lever will move toward the handlebar. If there is air in the system there will be air bubbles in the brake fluid coming out of the caliper.

**9** Tighten the bleed valve, then release the brake lever gradually. Repeat the process until no air bubbles are visible in the brake fluid leaving the caliper, and the lever is firm when applied, topping the reservoir up when

necessary. On completion, disconnect the hose, then tighten the bleed valve to the torque setting specified at the beginning of this Chapter and fit the dust cap.

**10** Top-up the reservoir, then install the

> **HAYNES HINT**
> *If it is not possible to produce a firm feel to the lever, the fluid may be aerated. Let the brake fluid in the system stabilise for a few hours and then repeat the procedure when the tiny bubbles in the system have settled out.*

diaphragm, diaphragm plate, and cover (see *Pre-ride checks*). Wipe up any spilled brake fluid. Check the entire system for fluid leaks.

**11** Check the operation of the brakes before riding the motorcycle.

### Fluid change

**12** Changing the brake fluid is a similar process to bleeding the brakes and requires the same materials plus a suitable tool (such as a syringe) for siphoning the fluid out of the reservoir. Also ensure that the container is large enough to take all the old fluid when it is flushed out of the system.

**13** Follow Steps 3 and 6, then remove the reservoir cap, diaphragm plate and diaphragm and siphon the old fluid out of the reservoir. Wipe the reservoir clean. Fill the reservoir with new brake fluid, then carefully pump the brake

lever three or four times and hold it in while opening the caliper bleed valve (see Step 5). When the valve is opened, brake fluid will flow out of the caliper into the clear tubing, and the lever will move toward the handlebar, or the pedal will move down.

**14** Tighten the bleed valve, then release the brake lever gradually. Keep the reservoir topped-up with new fluid to above the LOWER level at all times or air may enter the system and greatly increase the length of the task. Repeat the process until new fluid can be seen emerging from the caliper bleed valve.

> **HAYNES HINT**
> *Old brake fluid is invariably much darker in colour than new fluid, making it easy to see when all old fluid has been expelled from the system.*

**15** Disconnect the hose, then tighten the bleed valve to the specified torque setting and fit the dust cap.

**16** Top-up the reservoir, then install the diaphragm, diaphragm plate, and cover (see *Pre-ride checks*). Wipe up any spilled brake fluid. Check the entire system for fluid leaks.

**17** Check the operation of the brakes before riding the motorcycle.

### Draining the system for overhaul

**18** Draining the brake fluid is again a similar

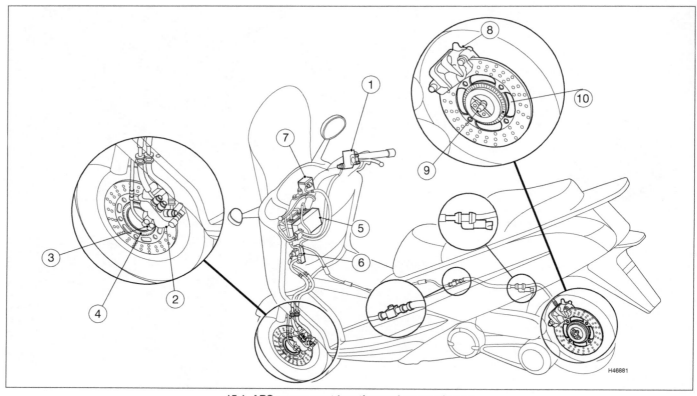

**15.1 ABS component location and system layout**

| | | | |
|---|---|---|---|
| *1 Front brake master cylinder* | *4 Front wheel pulse ring* | *7 Rear brake master cylinder* | *9 Rear wheel speed senor* |
| *2 Front brake caliper* | *5 ABS control unit* | *8 Rear brake caliper* | *10 Rear wheel pulse ring* |
| *3 Front wheel speed sensor* | *6 Delay valve* | | |

process to bleeding the brakes. The quickest and easiest way is to use a commercially available vacuum-type brake bleeding tool – follow the manufacturer's instructions. Otherwise follow the procedure described above for changing the fluid, but quite simply do not put any new fluid into the reservoir – the system fills itself with air instead.

## 15 ABS (Anti-lock brake system)

### *Operation and fault finding*

**1** The ABS prevents the wheels from locking up under hard braking or on uneven road surfaces **(see illustration)**. A sensor on each wheel transmits information about the speed of rotation to the ABS control unit; if the unit senses that a wheel is about to lock, it releases brake pressure to that wheel momentarily, preventing a skid.

**2** The ABS is self-checking and is activated when the ignition switch is turned on – the ABS indicator light in the instrument cluster will come on and will remain on until road speed increases above 6 mph (10 kph) at which point, if the ABS is normal, the light will go off. **Note:** *If the ABS indicator light does not come on initially there could be a fault in the instrument cluster – see Chapter 10.*

**3** If the indicator light remains on, or starts flashing while the machine is being ridden, there is a fault in the system and the ABS function will be switched off – the brakes will still function but in normal mode.

**4** If a fault is indicated, a fault code will be stored in the control unit's memory. The memory is only capable of recording one fault at a time – if there are multiple faults the first one must be diagnosed, rectified and the code erased before the next one will be indicated. However it can store and display more than one fault code if these are generated at different instances of the bike being used.

**5** Access the fault code or codes as follows. Make sure the ignition switch is OFF. Remove the maintenance access panel to the battery and fusebox (see Chapter 9).

**6** Locate the ABS service check connector and connect a jump wire between the brown/white and green/black wire terminals **(see illustration)**. Turn the ignition switch ON and observe the warning light in the instrument cluster. The warning light comes on for 2 seconds, then goes out for 3.6 seconds. After that, if there are no stored fault codes, the light will come on and stay on. If there are one or more stored fault codes, the light will flash.

**7** The light emits long (1.3 second) and short (0.3 second) flashes to give out the fault code. A long flash is used to indicate the first digit of the

double digit fault code. For example, two long (1.3 sec) flashes followed by three short (0.3 sec) flashes indicates the fault code number 23. If there is more than one fault code stored, there will be a 3.6 second gap before the other codes are revealed, and the codes will be revealed in order, starting with the lowest and finishing with the highest. Once all codes have been revealed, the ECU will continuously run through the code(s) stored in its memory, revealing each one in turn with a short gap between them. The fault codes are shown in the table.

**8** Turn the ignition OFF and remove the jump wire when the code or codes have been recorded.

**9** Once the fault has been corrected, erase

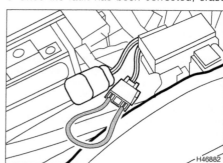

**15.6 Bridge the connector terminals in the ABS service check connector (arrowed) as shown to access fault codes**

the fault code(s) as follows: connect the jump wire between the brown/white and green/black wire terminals in the ABS service check connector as before. Turn the ignition witch ON while squeezing the front brake lever. The ABS light should come on for 2 seconds, then go out. When the light goes out release the brake lever immediately. The light should come on again. When the light comes on squeeze the brake lever immediately. The light should go out. When the light goes out release the brake lever immediately. The code(s) should now be erased, and the light should flash twice then stay on. If it does not flash code erasure has not been successful, in which case try again. If the light continues to flash the system is faulty.

**10** Turn the ignition switch OFF and remove the jump wire when the code or codes have been erased. Fit the access panel and install the seat (see Chapter 9). Check that the ABS is operating normally (see Step 2).

**Note:** *The ABS indicator may diagnose a fault if tyre sizes other than those specified by Honda are fitted, if the tyre pressures are incorrect, if there is tyre or wheel damage, if the machine has been run continuously over bumpy roads, if the front wheel is raised whilst riding (wheelie) or if, for some reason, the machine is on an auxiliary stand with the engine running and the rear wheel turning. Strong electromagnetic radio wave interference can also cause a problem.*

### System checks

**11** If a fault is indicated in the ABS, first check that the battery is fully charged, then check the ABS fuses (see Chapter 10).

**12** The ABS unit is a sealed component containing the modulator (with motor and solenoid valves) and the electronic control unit. Individual components are not available and no repairs can be made.

**13** Refer to Chapter 10, Section 2, for general electrical fault finding procedures and equipment.

**14** If, after a thorough check, the source of a fault has not been identified, have the ABS system tested by a Honda dealer.

| Fault code/flashes | Faulty component or system | Possible causes |
|---|---|---|
| **No code displayed** | Indicator light does not come on with ignition switch | No voltage at instrument cluster<br>Faulty wiring or wiring connector<br>Faulty ABS indicator light<br>Faulty ABS unit |
| **No code displayed** | Indicator light stays on after self diagnosis | No voltage at control unit<br>Blown ABS main fuse<br>Faulty wiring or wiring connector<br>Faulty ABS unit<br>Faulty instrument cluster or wiring |
| **11 and 12** | Front wheel speed sensor | Faulty wiring or wiring connector<br>Faulty sensor<br>Electromagnetic interference |
| **13 and 14** | Rear wheel speed sensor | Faulty wiring or wiring connector<br>Faulty sensor<br>Electromagnetic interference |
| **21** | Front wheel speed sensor<br>Front wheel pulse ring | Faulty wiring or wiring connector<br>Damaged pulse ring<br>Faulty sensor |
| **23** | Rear wheel speed sensor<br>Rear wheel pulse ring | Faulty wiring or wiring connector<br>Damaged pulse ring<br>Faulty sensor |
| **31, 32, 33, 34, 37 and 38** | Modulator solenoid valve | Faulty ABS unit |
| **41** | Front wheel lock | Riding conditions (see Note after Step 10) |
| **42** | Front wheel lock (wheelie) | Riding conditions (see Note after Step 10) |
| **43** | Rear wheel lock | Riding conditions (see Note after Step 10) |
| **51** | ABS motor lock | Blown ABS fuse<br>Faulty wiring or wiring connector<br>Faulty ABS unit |
| **52** | ABS motor stuck off | Blown ABS fuse<br>Faulty wiring or wiring connector<br>Faulty ABS unit |
| **53** | ABS motor stuck on | Blown ABS fuse<br>Faulty wiring or wiring connector<br>Faulty ABS unit |
| **54** | Fail safe relay circuit | Blown ABS fuse<br>Faulty wiring or wiring connector |
| **61** | Power circuit – input voltage too low | Blown ABS fuse<br>Faulty wiring or wiring connector<br>Faulty ABS unit |
| **62** | Power circuit – input voltage too high | Blown ABS fuse<br>Faulty wiring or wiring connector<br>Faulty ABS unit |
| **71** | Tyre(s) | Wrong tyre size(s), pressures, or tyre/wheel damage (see Note after Step 10) |
| **81** | Faulty ABS electronic control unit (ECU) | Faulty ABS unit |

## No code displayed – indicator light does not come on

**15** First check the instrument cluster wiring connector, power supply and earth connection (see Chapter 10).

**16** Remove the front fairing panel (see Chapter 9). Disconnect the ABS unit wiring connector. Turn the ignition switch ON, and check the ABS indicator light – if the light comes on the control unit is faulty and must be replaced with a new one.

**17** If the light does not come on, disconnect the instrument cluster wiring connector and check for continuity in the red/black wire between the control unit and instrument wiring connectors. If there is no continuity locate and repair the break in the wire or the connector terminal. If there is continuity the instrument cluster is faulty (see Chapter 10).

## No code displayed – indicator light stays on

**18** First check the ABS main (10A) fuse (see Chapter 10). If the main fuse has blown remove the fuse and check for continuity to earth in the black/yellow wire from the fusebox. If there is continuity a short circuit has blown the fuse – locate and repair the break in the wire or the connector terminal. If not it is possible the fuse has blown for no reason other than it had had enough. Replace the fuse with a new one

**19** If the fuse is good remove the front fairing panel (see Chapter 9). Disconnect the ABS unit wiring connector. Turn the ignition switch ON, and check for battery voltage between the black/yellow and green wire terminals in the loom side of the connector. If there is no voltage check the black/yellow wire between the connector and the fusebox for continuity, then check for continuity to earth in the green wire. There should be continuity in each case – if not locate and repair the break in the wire or the connector terminal.

**20** If there is voltage turn the ignition switch OFF and check for continuity in the brown/white wire between the ABS unit connector and the service check connector. There should be continuity – if not locate and repair the break in the wire or the connector terminal.

**21** If there is continuity short between the red/black wire terminal in the instrument cluster wiring connector, with it still connected, and ground using a jumper wire, then turn the ignition switch ON and check the indicator light. If the light does not go out the instrument cluster is faulty (see Chapter 10).

**22** If the light goes out, turn the ignition OFF and remove the jumper wire. disconnect the instrument cluster and ABS unit wiring connectors and check for continuity in the red/black wire between them. If there is no continuity locate and repair the break in the wire or the connector terminal. If there is continuity the ABS unit is faulty.

## Fault codes 11, 12, 21, 41 and 42

**Note:** *Before carrying out any of the checks,*

*follow the procedure in Step 9 to reset the control unit memory, then activate the self-checking procedure. If the fault code is the result of unusual riding or conditions and the ABS is normal, the indicator light will go off. Otherwise perform the following checks.*

**23** Measure the air gap between the front wheel speed sensor and the pulse ring with a feeler gauge, then compare the result with the Specification at the beginning of this Chapter. The gap is not adjustable – if it is outside the specification, check that the sensor and pulse ring fixings are tight, that the components are not damaged and that there is no dirt or anything else on the sensor tip or between the slots in the pulse ring. If any of the components are damaged they must be replaced with new ones.

**24** If all is good so far remove the front fairing panel and the inner cover panel (see Chapter 9). Disconnect the ABS unit wiring connector. Trace the wheel sensor wiring to the green connector and disconnect it. Check for continuity first in the pink/black wire between the control unit wiring connector and the sensor wiring connector and then in the green/orange wire – there should be continuity in each wire. If not locate and repair the break.

**25** If there is continuity in the wiring next check for continuity between each terminal on the sensor side of the connector and earth (ground). If there is continuity in either of the wires the sensor is faulty and must be replaced with a new one.

**26** If all the checks have failed to identify the fault, replace the wheel sensor with a known good one. Connect all wiring connectors then follow the procedure in Step 9 to reset the control unit memory, then activate the self-checking procedure. If the indicator light is no longer flashing, the original sensor was faulty. If the fault code reappears the ABS unit is faulty.

## Fault codes 13, 14, 23, and 43

**Note:** *Before carrying out any of the checks, follow the procedure in Step 9 to reset the control unit memory, then activate the self-checking procedure. If the fault code is the result of unusual riding or conditions and the ABS is normal, the indicator light will go off. Otherwise perform the following checks.*

**27** Measure the air gap between the rear wheel speed sensor and the pulse ring with a feeler gauge, then compare the result with the Specification at the beginning of this Chapter. The gap is not adjustable – if it is outside the specification, check that the sensor and pulse ring fixings are tight, that the components are not damaged and that there is no dirt or anything else on the sensor tip or between the slots in the pulse ring. If any of the components are damaged they must be replaced with new ones.

**28** If all is good so far remove the front fairing panel (see Chapter 9). Disconnect the ABS unit wiring connector. Unscrew the oxygen

sensor cover bolts and remove the cover. Trace the wheel sensor wiring to the connector and disconnect it. Check for continuity first in the pink/green wire between the control unit wiring connector and the sensor wiring connector and then in the green/red wire – there should be continuity in each wire. If not locate and repair the break.

**29** If there is continuity in the wiring next check for continuity between each terminal on the sensor side of the connector and earth (ground). If there is continuity in either of the wires the sensor is faulty and must be replaced with a new one.

**30** If all the checks have failed to identify the fault, replace the wheel sensor with a known good one. Connect all wiring connectors then follow the procedure in Step 9 to reset the control unit memory, then activate the self-checking procedure. If the indicator light is no longer flashing, the original sensor was faulty. If the fault code reappears the ABS unit is faulty.

## Fault codes 31, 32, 33, 34, 37 and 38

**31** Erase the fault code (see Step 9). Start the engine and go for a short ride so the ABS system performs its self-diagnosis. If the ABS indicator light stays off, the fault was temporary. If the fault code is displayed again the ABS unit is faulty.

## Fault codes 51, 52 or 53

**32** First check the ABS motor (30A) fuse (see Chapter 10). If the fuse has blown remove the fuse and check for continuity to earth in the red wire from the fusebox. If there is continuity a short circuit has blown the fuse – locate and repair the break in the wire or the connector terminal. If not it is possible the fuse has blown for no reason other than it had had enough. Replace the fuse with a new one.

**33** If the fuse is good remove the front fairing panel (see Chapter 9). Disconnect the ABS unit wiring connector. Check there is battery voltage at all times (i.e. with the ignition On and OFF) between the red and green wire terminals in the loom side of the connector. If there is no voltage check the red wire between the connector and the battery for continuity, then check for continuity to earth in the green wire. There should be continuity in each case – if not locate and repair the break in the wire or the connector terminal.

**34** If there is voltage erase the fault code (see Step 9). Start the engine and go for a short ride so the ABS system performs its self-diagnosis. If the ABS indicator light stays off, the fault was temporary. If the fault code is displayed again the ABS unit is faulty.

## Fault code 56

**35** First check the ABS FSR (30A) fuse (see Chapter 10). If the fuse has blown remove the fuse and check for continuity to earth in the black wire from the fusebox. If there is continuity a short circuit has blown the fuse – locate and repair the break in the wire or the connector terminal. If not it is possible the fuse has blown for no reason other than it had had enough. Replace the fuse with a new one.

**36** If the fuse is good remove the front fairing panel (see Chapter 9). Disconnect the ABS unit wiring connector. Check there is battery voltage at all times (i.e. with the ignition On and OFF) between the black and green wire terminals in the loom side of the connector. If there is no voltage check the black wire between the connector and the fusebox and the red wire between the fusebox and the battery for continuity, then check for continuity to earth in the green wire. There should be continuity in each case – if not locate and repair the break in the wire or the connector terminal.

**37** If there is voltage erase the fault code (see Step 9). Start the engine and go for a short ride so the ABS system performs its self-diagnosis. If the ABS indicator light stays off, the fault was temporary. If the fault code is displayed again the ABS unit is faulty.

### Fault codes 61 and 62

**38** First check the ABS main (10A) fuse (see Chapter 10). If the main fuse has blown remove the fuse and check for continuity to earth in the black/yellow wire from the fusebox. If there is continuity a short circuit has blown the fuse – locate and repair the break in the wire or the connector terminal. If not it is possible the fuse has blown for no reason other than it had had enough. Replace the fuse with a new one

**39** If the fuse is good remove the front fairing panel (see Chapter 9). Disconnect the ABS unit wiring connector. Turn the ignition switch ON, and check for battery voltage between the black/yellow and green wire terminals in the loom side of the connector. If there is no voltage check the black/yellow wire between the connector and the fusebox for continuity, then check for continuity to earth in the green wire. There should be continuity in each case – if not locate and repair the break in the wire or the connector terminal.

**40** If there is voltage erase the fault code (see Step 9). Start the engine and go for a short ride so the ABS system performs its self-diagnosis. If the ABS indicator light stays off, the fault was temporary. If the fault code is displayed again the ABS unit is faulty.

### Fault code 71

**41** First check the air pressure in each tyre (see *Pre-ride checks*). Next check that the correct size tyres are fitted, referring to the Specifications at the beginning of the Chapter. Finally check for damage and deformation to the tyres and wheels.

**42** If all appears good erase the fault code (see Step 9). Start the engine and go for a short ride so the ABS system performs its self-diagnosis. If the ABS indicator light stays off, the fault was temporary. If the fault code is displayed again the ABS unit is faulty.

### Fault code 81

**43** Erase the fault code (see Step 9). Start the engine and go for a short ride so the ABS system performs its self-diagnosis. If the ABS indicator light stays off, the fault was temporary. If the fault code is displayed again the ABS unit is faulty.

## Component removal and installation

### Front wheel speed sensor

**44** Remove the front cover (see Chapter 9). Unscrew the cable guard bolts, then release and remove the guard, noting how it locates.

**45** Trace the wheel sensor wiring to the green connector and disconnect it. Undo the bolts securing the sensor wiring guides, and release the wiring from any other clips or ties, then feed it down to the sensor, noting its routing.

**46** Unscrew the sensor bolts and remove it from the caliper bracket.

**47** Clean the sensor head and check it for damage.

**48** Install the sensor and tighten the mounting bolts. Feed the wiring up to the connector, routing and securing it as noted on removal. Install the cable guide

**49** Check the air gap (see Step 23). Install the front cover (see Chapter 9).

### Front pulse ring

**50** Remove the front wheel (see Section 18).

**51** Undo the bolts securing the ring and lift it off.

**52** Ensure there is no dirt or corrosion where the ring seats on the hub – if the ring does not sit flat when it is installed the sensor air gap will be incorrect. Clean the threads of the bolts and apply a non-permanent thread locking compound (or alternatively use new bolts from Honda which come pre-treated) and tighten them to the torque setting specified at the beginning of the Chapter.

**53** Install the front wheel (see Section 18). Check the sensor air gap (see Step 23).

### Rear wheel speed sensor

**54** Unscrew the oxygen sensor cover bolts and remove the cover.

**55** Undo the wheel sensor cover plate bolts on the swingarm and remove the plate.

**56** Trace the wheel sensor wiring to the connector and disconnect it. Undo the bolts securing the sensor wiring guides, and release the wiring from any other clips or ties, then feed it down to the sensor, noting its routing

**57** Unscrew the sensor bolts and remove it from the swingarm.

**58** Clean the sensor head and check it for damage.

**59** Install the sensor and tighten the mounting bolts. Feed the wiring up to the connector, routing and securing it as noted on removal.

**60** Check the air gap (see Step 27). Install the covers.

### Rear pulse ring

**61** Remove the rear wheel (see Section 19).

**62** Undo the bolts securing the ring and lift it off.

**63** Ensure there is no dirt or corrosion where the ring seats on the hub – if the ring does not sit flat when it is installed the sensor air gap will be incorrect. Clean the threads of the bolts and apply a non-permanent thread locking compound (or alternatively use new bolts from Honda which come pre-treated) and tighten them to the torque setting specified at the beginning of the Chapter.

**64** Install the rear wheel (see Section 19). Check the speed sensor air gap (see Step 27).

### ABS unit

**Note:** *Before the modulator can be removed from the bike, the brake fluid must be drained from the hydraulic system. When refilling and bleeding the ABS-equipped brake system it is essential to use a vacuum-type brake bleeder kit. Alternatively, removal and installation of the control unit should be entrusted to a Honda dealer.*

**65** Remove the front cover (see Chapter 9).

**66** Refer to the procedure in Section 14 and drain the brake fluid – siphon the fluid out of the front and rear reservoirs and pump any residual fluid out through the brake calipers, but do not refill the system at this stage.

**67** Pull the wiring connector lock up and disconnect the connector.

**68** Cover the area around the modulator with clean rag to catch any brake fluid.

**69** Unscrew the five brake pipe gland nuts.

**70** Unscrew the modulator mounting bolts. Remove the modulator, taking care not to bend any of the pipes. Cover the ends of the pipes in plastic foodwrap to prevent fluid drips and contamination of the system.

**71** Installation is the reverse of removal, noting the following:
- If the correct tools are available tighten the brake pipe gland nuts to the torque setting specified at the beginning of the Chapter.
- Ensure the wiring connector is secure.
- Follow the procedure in Section 14 to refill and bleed the brake system.

## 16 Wheel inspection and repair

**1** In order to carry out a proper inspection of the wheels, it is necessary to support the scooter upright so that the wheel being inspected is raised off the ground. Clean the wheels thoroughly to remove mud and dirt that may interfere with the inspection procedure or mask defects. Make a general check of the wheels (see Chapter 1) and tyres (see *Pre-ride checks*).

**2** Attach a dial gauge to the fork or the swingarm and position its tip against the side

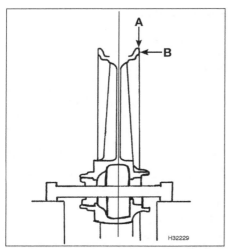

**16.2  Check the wheel for radial (out-of-round) runout (A) and axial (side-to-side) runout (B)**

of the wheel rim. Spin the wheel slowly and check the axial (side-to-side) runout of the rim **(see illustration)**.

3 In order to accurately check radial (out of round) runout with the dial gauge, remove the wheel from the machine, and the tyre from the wheel. With the axle clamped in a vice and the dial gauge positioned on the top of the rim, the wheel can be rotated to check the runout **(see illustration 16.2)**.

4 An easier, though slightly less accurate, method is to attach a stiff wire pointer to the fork or the swingarm and position the end a fraction of an inch from the wheel rim where the wheel and tyre join. If the wheel is true, the distance from the pointer to the rim will be constant as the wheel is rotated. **Note:** *If wheel runout is excessive, check the wheel bearings very carefully before renewing the wheel.*

5 The wheels should also be inspected for cracks, flat spots on the rim and other damage. Look very closely for dents in the area where the tyre bead contacts the rim. Dents in this area may prevent complete sealing of the tyre against the rim, which leads to deflation of the tyre over a period of time. If damage is evident, or if runout in either direction is excessive, the

wheel will have to be renewed. Never attempt to repair a damaged cast alloy wheel.

## 17 Wheel alignment check

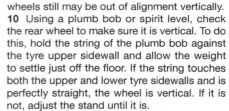

1 Misalignment of the wheels due to a bent frame, engine hanger or forks can cause strange and possibly serious handling problems. If the frame or forks are at fault, repair by a specialist or renewal are the only options.

2 To check wheel alignment you will need an assistant, a length of string or a perfectly straight piece of wood and a ruler. A plumb bob or spirit level for checking that the wheels are vertical will also be required.

3 In order to make a proper check of the wheels it is necessary to support the scooter in an upright position, using an auxiliary stand. First measure the width of both tyres at their widest points. Subtract the smaller measurement from the larger measurement, then divide the difference by two. The result is the amount of offset that should exist between the front and rear tyres on both sides of the machine.

4 If a string is used, have your assistant hold one end of it about halfway between the floor and the rear axle, with the string touching the back edge of the rear tyre sidewall.

5 Run the other end of the string forward and pull it tight so that it is roughly parallel to the floor **(see illustration)**. Slowly bring the string into contact with the front edge of the rear tyre sidewall, then turn the front wheel until it is parallel with the string. Measure the distance from the front tyre sidewall to the string.

6 Repeat the procedure on the other side of the scooter. The distance from the front tyre sidewall to the string should be equal on both sides.

7 As previously mentioned, a perfectly straight length of wood or metal bar may be substituted for the string **(see illustration)**.

8 If the distance between the string and tyre is greater on one side, or if the rear wheel appears to be out of alignment, have your machine checked by a Honda dealer or frame specialist.

9 If the front-to-back alignment is correct, the

wheels still may be out of alignment vertically.

10 Using a plumb bob or spirit level, check the rear wheel to make sure it is vertical. To do this, hold the string of the plumb bob against the tyre upper sidewall and allow the weight to settle just off the floor. If the string touches both the upper and lower tyre sidewalls and is perfectly straight, the wheel is vertical. If it is not, adjust the stand until it is.

11 Once the rear wheel is vertical, check the front wheel in the same manner. If both wheels are not perfectly vertical, the frame and/or major suspension components are bent.

## 18 Front wheel

### *Removal*

1 Position the motorcycle on its centrestand. Remove the belly pan (see Chapter 9).

2 Displace the front brake caliper (see Section 3). Support the caliper with a cable-tie or a bungee cord so that no strain is placed

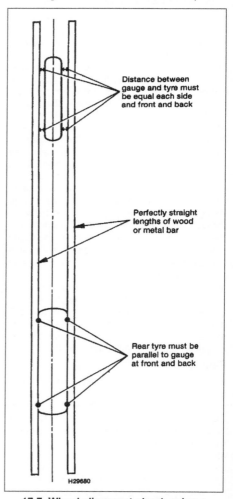

Distance between gauge and tyre must be equal each side and front and back

Perfectly straight lengths of wood or metal bar

Rear tyre must be parallel to gauge at front and back

**17.7  Wheel alignment check using a straight edge**

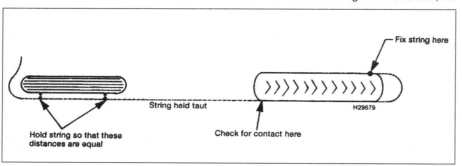

Fix string here

String held taut

Hold string so that these distances are equal

Check for contact here

**17.5  Wheel alignment check using string**

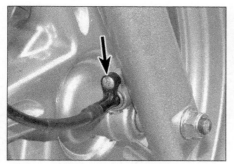

**18.3 Speedometer cable retaining screw (arrowed)**

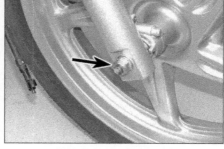

**18.4 Axle nut (arrowed)**

**18.5 Withdraw the axle and remove the wheel**

on the hydraulic hose. There is no need to disconnect the hose from the caliper. **Note**: *Do not operate the front brake lever with the caliper removed.*

**3** On all except Pantheon and S-wing models undo the screw securing the speedometer cable or speed sensor wiring (according to model) in the drive housing and draw the cable or sensor out **(see illustration)**.

**4** Where fitted remove the axle nut cap. Slacken the axle nut **(see illustration)**. Place a support under the frame so the front wheel is off the ground. Make sure the scooter is secure. Unscrew and remove the axle nut.

**5** Take the weight of the wheel, then withdraw the axle **(see illustration)**. Carefully lower the wheel and draw it forwards.

**6** On all except Pantheon and S-wing models remove the speedometer drive housing from the right-hand side of the wheel, noting how it fits, and the spacer from the left-hand side **(see illustrations)**. On Pantheon and S-wing models

remove the spacer from each side of the wheel. Clean all old grease of the spacer(s), drive housing (where fitted), axle and bearing seals.

***Caution: Don't lay the wheel down and allow it to rest on the disc – it could become warped. Set the wheel on wood blocks so the disc doesn't support the weight of the wheel.***

**7** Check the axle is straight by rolling it on a flat surface such as a piece of plate glass (first remove any corrosion using wire wool or a suitable alternative). If the equipment is available, place the axle in V-blocks and measure the runout using a dial gauge. If the axle is bent or the runout exceeds the limit specified, replace it with a new one.

**8** Check the condition of the grease seals and wheel bearings (see Section 20).

### Installation

**Note:** *If a new tyre has been fitted, make sure the directional arrow on the tyre is pointing in*

*the direction of normal rotation of the wheel.*

**9** On all except Pantheon and S-wing models apply a smear of grease to the inside of the wheel spacer and to the speedometer drive housing, and also to the seal lips. Make sure the gear and the washers behind it are correctly located in the speedometer drive housing **(see illustration)**. Make sure the drive plate is correctly located in the wheel hub. Fit the spacer into the left-hand side of the wheel **(see illustration 18.6b)**. Fit the drive housing into the right-hand side, locating the raised tabs on the drive plate in the cut-outs in the housing **(see illustration 18.6a)**.

**10** On Pantheon and S-wing models apply a smear of grease to the inside of each wheel spacer and to the seal lips. Fit the spacer into each side of the wheel.

**11** Manoeuvre the wheel into position between the forks, making sure the brake disc is on the left-hand side. Apply a thin coat of grease to the axle.

**12** Lift the wheel into place, making sure the spacer(s) and/or speedometer drive housing (where fitted) remain in position, and that the lug on the speedometer drive housing (where fitted) locates against the correct side of the stopper on the bottom of the right-hand fork, i.e. so in the normal direction of rotation of the wheel the lug is effectively forced against the stopper **(see illustration)**. Slide the axle through **(see illustration 18.5)**.

**13** Fit the axle nut and tighten it to the torque setting specified at the beginning of the Chapter **(see illustration)**. Counter-hold the axle head if necessary.

**18.6a Remove the drive housing . . .**

**18.6b . . . and the spacer**

**18.9 Check and lubricate the drive housing**

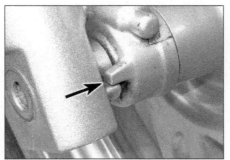

**18.12 Butt the lug (arrowed) against the stopper as shown – cable drive type shown**

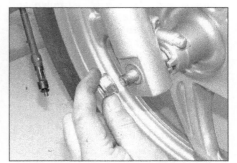

**18.13 Fit the axle nut and tighten to the specified torque**

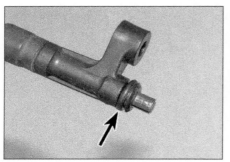

18.15a Make sure the O-ring (arrowed) is fitted . . .

18.15b . . . then fit the cable or sensor

19.2 Draw the wheel off the axle

14 Lower the front wheel to the ground, then install the brake caliper (see Section 3).
15 On all except Pantheon and S-wing models, make sure the O-ring on the end of the speedometer cable or sensor is fitted and in good condition (replace it with a new one if necessary), and smear it with grease. Fit the cable or sensor into the drive housing and secure it with the screw (see illustrations).
16 Apply the front brake a few times to bring the pads back into contact with the disc.
17 Check for correct operation of the front brake before riding the motorcycle.

## 19 Rear wheel

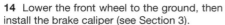

### Removal

1 Remove the swingarm (see Chapter 7).
2 Draw the wheel off the axle (see illustration).

### Installation

Note: If a new tyre has been fitted, make sure the directional arrow on the tyre is pointing in the direction of normal rotation of the wheel.
3 Installation is the reverse of removal. Check the condition of the splines on the axle and in the wheel and smear them with grease.

## 20 Wheel bearings

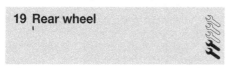

Caution: Don't lay the wheel down and allow it to rest on the disc – it could become warped. Set the wheel on wood blocks so the wheel rim supports the weight of the wheel, or keep the wheel upright. Don't operate the brake lever with the wheel removed.
Note: Always renew the wheel bearings in sets, never individually. Avoid using a high pressure cleaner on the wheel bearing area.

### Front wheel bearings

1 Remove the wheel (see Section 18).
2 On all except Pantheon and S-wing models lever out the bearing seal from the left-hand side of the hub using a flat-bladed

screwdriver or a seal hook, and the speedometer driveplate/seal from the right (see illustrations). On Pantheon and S-wing models lever out the bearing seal from each side of the hub using a flat-bladed screwdriver or a seal hook. Take care not to damage the hub. Discard the seals as new ones must be fitted on reassembly.
3 Inspect the bearings – check that the inner race turns smoothly, quietly and freely and that the outer race is a tight fit in the hub.
Note: Honda recommends that the bearings are not removed unless they are going to be replaced with new ones.
4 If the bearings are worn, remove them using an internal expanding puller with slide-hammer attachment. Remove the spacer which fits between the bearings.
5 Thoroughly clean the hub area of the wheel with a suitable solvent and inspect the bearing seats for scoring and wear. If the seats are damaged, consult a Honda dealer before reassembling the wheel.

20.2a Lever out the bearing seal . . .

20.6 Using a socket to drive the bearing in

6 The new bearings can be installed in the hub using a drawbolt arrangement or by using a bearing driver or suitable socket (see illustration). Ensure that the drawbolt washer or driver (as applicable) bears only on the outer race and does not contact the bearing housing walls. If the bearings are open-sided pack them with bearing grease.
7 Install the left-hand bearing first, with the marked or sealed side facing outwards. Ensure the bearing is fitted squarely and all the way into its seat.
8 Turn the wheel over then install the bearing spacer and the other new bearing.
9 On all except Pantheon and S-wing models fit the new speedometer drive plate/seal into the right-hand side, and a new seal into the left-hand side (see illustration). On Pantheon and S-wing models fit a new seal into each side of the hub. Press the seals in using your fingers or a suitable driver. Level the seals with the rim of the hub with a small block of wood. Apply a smear of grease to the seal lips.

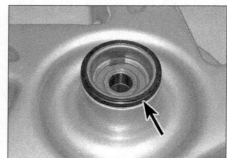

20.2b . . . and the driveplate/seal

20.9 Press or drive the seal into place

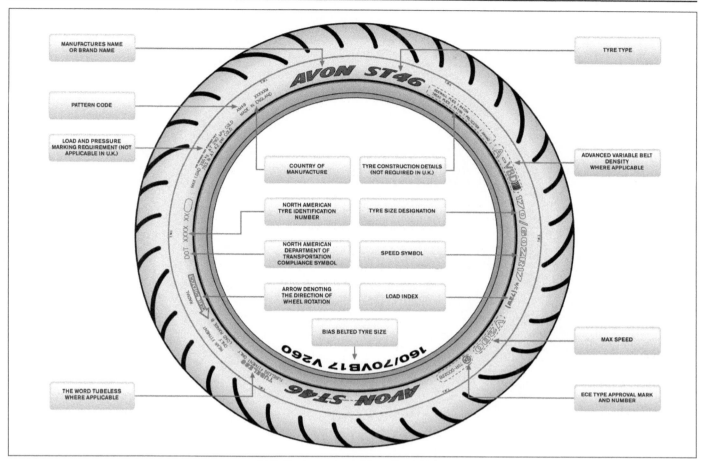

**21.3  Common tyre sidewall markings**

**10** Clean the brake disc using acetone or brake system cleaner, then install the wheel (see Section 18).

### Rear wheel bearings

**11** The bearings for the rear wheel axle are fitted on the output shaft in the gearbox (see Chapter 3), and in the swingarm (see Chapter 7).

### General information

**1** The wheels fitted to all models are designed to take tubeless tyres only. Tyre sizes are given in the Specifications at the beginning of this Chapter.

**2** Refer to the *Pre-ride checks* listed at the beginning of this manual for tyre maintenance.

### Fitting new tyres

**3** When selecting new tyres, refer to the tyre information in the Owner's Handbook. Ensure that front and rear tyre types are compatible, the correct size and correct speed rating; if necessary seek advice from a Honda dealer or tyre fitting specialist **(see illustration)**.

**4** It is recommended that tyres are fitted by a scooter tyre specialist rather than attempted in the home workshop. This is particularly relevant in the case of tubeless tyres because the force required to break the seal between the wheel rim and tyre bead is substantial, and is usually beyond the capabilities of an individual working with normal tyre levers. Additionally, the specialist will be able to balance the wheels after tyre fitting.

**5** Note that punctured tubeless tyres can in some cases be repaired – seek advice first. Repairs must be carried out by a tyre fitting specialist.

# Notes

# Chapter 9
# Bodywork

## Contents

## Degrees of difficulty

| **Easy,** suitable for novice with little experience  | **Fairly easy,** suitable for beginner with some experience | **Fairly difficult,** suitable for competent DIY mechanic | **Difficult,** suitable for experienced DIY mechanic | **Very difficult,** suitable for expert DIY or professional  |
|---|---|---|---|---|

## 1 General information

Almost all the functional components of the scooters covered by this manual are enclosed by body panels, making removal of relevant panels a necessary part of most servicing and maintenance procedures.

Before attempting to remove any body panel, study it closely, noting any fasteners and associated fittings. Most panels are retained by screws and inter-locking tabs, and in some places trim clips are used, while on later models snap-fit clips are used.

To release trim clips, push the centre of the clip into the body, then draw the body out of the panel. Reset the clip by pulling the centre out of the body. To install the clip, push the body into the hole in the panel, then push the centre into the body.

The snap-fit clips can be quite hard to release, and must be done so by pulling the panel straight back from its position, not tilting or angling it, so as not to damage the clip or panel. The panel will probably come out a little bit then feel tight as the clip compresses fully – at this point you will probably start to worry about the amount of force that may be needed, especially if there is any corrosion on the metal clip part, but there is no alternative. Be especially careful where there is more than one clip to be released – if one clip releases before the other the panel will tilt. Try to release them evenly. You can use a spray lubricant when there is a little gap to squirt it in, and with care a taped-up flat bladed screwdriver can be used to apply some gentle and even leverage, but take care not to damage the paintwork. Special panel release tools made out of plastic are available from good automotive suppliers, but these are generally geared towards car interior panels and so should be selected and used with care.

Once the evident fasteners have been removed, try to remove the panel as described but DO NOT FORCE IT – if it will not release, check that all fasteners have been removed and try again. Where a panel engages another by means of tabs, be careful not to break the tab or its mating slot. Remember that a few moments of patience at this stage will save you a lot of money in replacing broken body panels!

When installing a body panel, check the fasteners and associated fittings removed with it, to be sure of returning everything to its correct place. Ensure all the fasteners are in good condition, including all trim clips and grommets; any of these should be replaced with new ones if faulty before the panel is reassembled. Check also that all mounting brackets are straight and repair or replace them if necessary before attempting to install the panel. Where assistance was required to remove a panel, make sure your assistant is on hand to install it.

Tighten the fasteners securely, but be careful not to overtighten any of them or the panel may break (not always immediately) due to the uneven stress. Where quick-release fasteners are fitted, turn them 90° anti-clockwise to release them, and 90° clockwise to secure them.

> **HAYNES HiNT** *Note that a small amount of lubricant or grease applied to rubber mounting grommets and over the metal clip part of the snap-fit clips will ease installation and make removal the next time that much easier.*

In the case of damage to the body parts, it is usually necessary to remove the broken component and replace it with a new (or used) one. There are however some shops that specialise in 'plastic welding', so it may be worthwhile seeking the advice of one of these specialists before consigning an expensive component to the bin. Additionally, proprietary repair kits can be obtained for repair of small components **(see illustration)**.

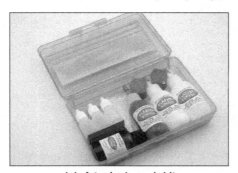

**1.1 A typical repair kit**

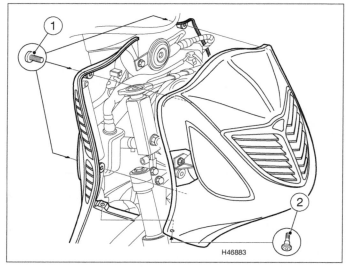

**2.32 Upper front panel removal**

*1 Inner panel screw – 4 off*　　*2 Front panel bolt – 2 off*

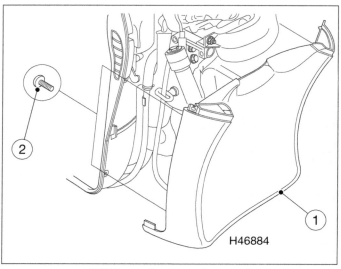

**2.37 Lower front panel removal**

*1 Lower panel*　　*2 Panel screws – 4 off*

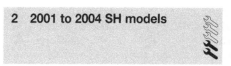

## 2　2001 to 2004 SH models

### Seat

**1** Unlock the seat and swing it up (see illustration 3.1).
**2** Undo the nuts securing the seat to the hinge and remove the seat (see illustration 3.2).
**3** Installation is the reverse of removal.

### Storage compartment

**4** Remove the seat.
**5** Undo the screw at the front (see illustration 3.5).
**6** Unscrew the four bolts inside the compartment, noting which fits where (see illustration 3.6).
**7** Lift the storage compartment out, noting how it locates (see illustration 3.7b).
**8** Installation is the reverse of removal.

### Maintenance panel

**9** Undo the screw at the front and the screw on each side (see illustration 3.9).
**10** Release the tabs from the body cover on each side then the floor panel at the front, and remove the panel (see illustration 3.10).
**11** Installation is the reverse of removal.

### Luggage rack

**12** Unlock the seat and swing it up.
**13** Unscrew the bolts and remove the rack (see illustration 3.13a and b).
**14** Installation is the reverse of removal.

### Body cover

**15** Remove the storage compartment.
**16** Remove the maintenance panel.
**17** Remove the luggage rack.
**18** Undo the screw on each side (see illustration 3.19a).
**19** Release the body cover sections from the floor panel on each side and from each other at the front and draw the assembly back a little (see illustration 3.20a). Disconnect the tail light assembly wiring connector, release the seat lock cable, and remove the body cover (see illustration 3.20d).
**20** Installation is the reverse of removal. Make sure the wiring connector is securely connected, and check the operation of the turn signals, brake light and tail light before riding the scooter.

### Belly panel

**21** Undo the two screws on each side (see illustration 3.22).
**22** Release the tabs from the floor panel and remove the belly panel out from under the scooter.
**23** Installation is the reverse of removal.

### Floor panel

**24** Remove the maintenance panel.
**25** Remove the belly panel.
**26** Remove the body cover.
**27** Remove the inner front panel.
**28** Remove the battery (see Chapter 10). Release the battery leads and starter relay from the floor panel, noting their routing (see illustration 3.29).
**29** Lower the passenger footrests and undo the screws behind them.
**30** Unscrew the floor panel bolts and remove the panel (see illustration 3.31a and b).
**31** Installation is the reverse of removal.

### Upper front panel

**32** Undo the four screws on the inner panel (see illustration).
**33** Unscrew the bolt on each side.
**34** Release the front panel from the inner panel, then disconnect the turn signal wiring connectors and remove the panel.
**35** Installation is the reverse of removal.

### Lower front panel

**36** Remove the upper front panel.
**37** Undo the screws on the inner panel and floor cover (see illustration).
**38** Release the panel and slide it down.
**39** Installation is the reverse of removal.

### Inner front panel

**40** Remove the upper and lower front panels.
**41** Remove the handlebar covers – although not strictly necessary it makes removing the panel a lot easier.
**42** Disconnect the white 3-pin and black 6-pin wiring connectors on the right-hand side.
**43** Release the ignition switch cover by turning it anti-clockwise and draw it off the switch, noting how it locates – it may need to be eased off the tabs on the switch using a screwdriver (see illustration).
**44** Undo the shopping bag hook screws and remove the hook.
**45** Open the glove compartment and unscrew the bolt.
**46** Release the panel from the floor panel, and if not removed draw it out from under the handlebar covers – if difficulty is encountered removing the panel from under the handlebar covers, remove them.
**47** Installation is the reverse of removal.

### Mirrors

**48** Lift the rubber boot (see illustration 3.51). Hold the mirror stem and slacken the locknut, then unscrew the mirror.
**49** Installation is the reverse of removal – position the mirror as required, then hold it in place and tighten the locknut.

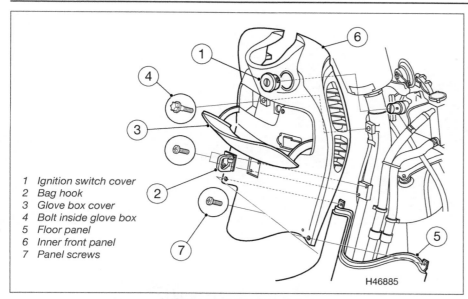

1 Ignition switch cover
2 Bag hook
3 Glove box cover
4 Bolt inside glove box
5 Floor panel
6 Inner front panel
7 Panel screws

2.43 Inner front panel removal

### Front handlebar cover

**50** Remove the upper front panel.
**51** Undo the screws in the bottom of the front cover and the two in the rear cover, then release the front cover from the rear cover at each end, draw the cover forwards and disconnect the headlight wiring connector **(see illustration)**.
**52** Installation is the reverse of removal. Make sure the wiring connector is securely connected, and check the operation of the headlight before riding the scooter.

### Rear handlebar cover

**53** Remove the front handlebar cover.
**54** Remove the mirrors.
**55** Disconnect the speedometer cable.
**56** Disconnect the instrument cluster/handlebar switch loom wiring connectors.
**57** Disconnect the brake light switch wiring connectors on each side **(see illustration)**.
**58** Undo the screws and remove the cover along with the instrument cluster and sub-loom, noting its routing as you draw it out **(see illustration)**.
**59** Installation is the reverse of removal. Make sure the wiring connectors are correctly and securely connected, and check the operation of all instruments, warning lights and switches before riding the scooter.

### Front mudguard

**60** Remove the front wheel (see Chapter 8).
**61** Unscrew the bolts securing the mudguard, then draw it down, freeing the cable from the guide **(see illustrations 3.63a and b)**.
**62** Installation is the reverse of removal.

### Rear hugger

**63** Undo the screw securing the left-hand side of the hugger to the air filter housing **(see illustration 3.65)**.
**64** Unscrew the bolts securing the right-hand side of the hugger to the swingarm and manoeuvre the hugger out.
**65** Installation is the reverse of removal.

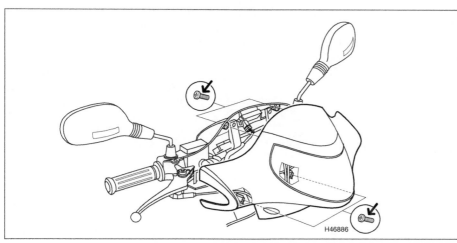

2.51 Front handlebar cover screws (arrowed)

2.57 Disconnect the brake light switch connectors (arrowed)

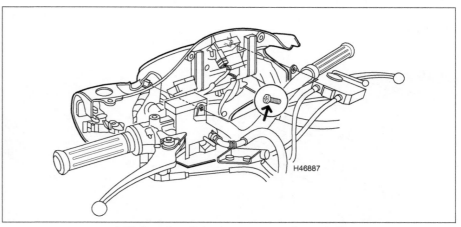

2.58 Rear handlebar cover screws (arrowed8

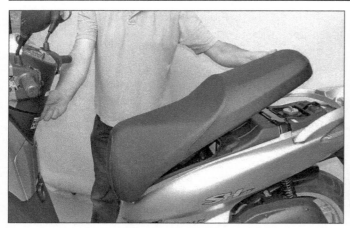

3.1 Unlock and raise the seat

3.2 Unscrew the two nuts (arrowed)

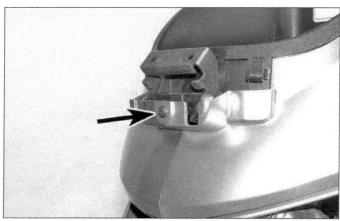

3.5 Undo the screw (arrowed) . . .

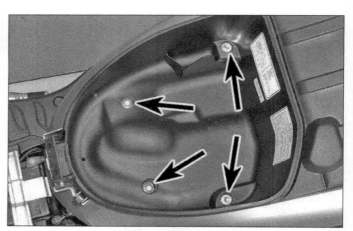

3.6 . . . and the four bolts (arrowed) . . .

## 3  2005 to 2008 SH models

### Seat

1 Unlock the seat and swing it up **(see illustration)**.
2 Undo the nuts securing the seat to the hinge and remove the seat **(see illustration)**.
3 Installation is the reverse of removal.

### Storage compartment

4 Remove the seat.
5 Undo the screw at the front **(see illustration)**.
6 Unscrew the four bolts inside the compartment, noting which fits where **(see illustration)**.
7 Lift the front of the storage compartment and release the two tabs at the back from the frame cross-piece, then lift the compartment out **(see illustrations)**. Note the washer on the support lug and remove it for safekeeping **(see illustration)**.
8 Installation is the reverse of removal.

3.7a Release the tabs . . .

3.7b . . . and remove the storage compartment

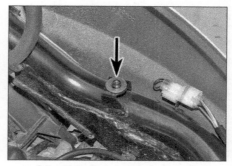

3.7c Note the washer (arrowed)

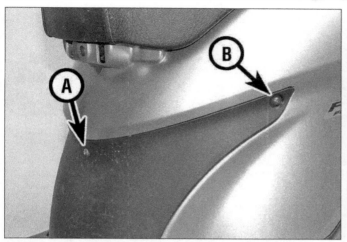

3.9  Undo the screw (A) at the front and the screw (B) on each side

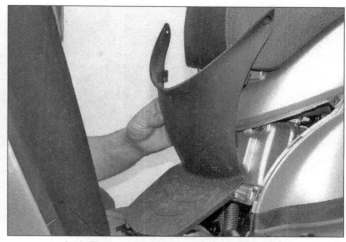

3.10  Release the tabs and remove the panel

## Maintenance panel

**9**  Undo the screw at the front and the screw on each side **(see illustration)**.
**10**  Release the tabs from the body cover on each side then the floor panel at the front, and remove the panel **(see illustration)**.
**11**  Installation is the reverse of removal.

## Luggage rack

**12**  Unlock the seat and swing it up **(see illustration 3.1)**.
**13**  Unscrew the bolts and remove the rack **(see illustrations)**.
**14**  Installation is the reverse of removal.

## Body cover

**15**  Remove the storage compartment.
**16**  Remove the maintenance panel.
**17**  Remove the luggage rack.
**18**  Undo the two screws on the fuel tank cover **(see illustration)**. Undo the fuel filler cap, then lift the tank cover, noting how the tabs along the front locate, and detach the fuel drain hose **(see illustrations)**. Refit the filler cap.
**19**  Undo the screw and release the trim clip on each side **(see illustrations)**.
**20**  Release the body cover sections from the

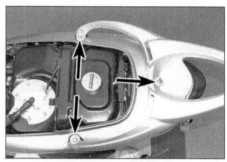

3.13a  Unscrew the bolts (arrowed) . . .

3.13b  . . . and remove the rack

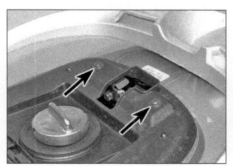

3.18a  Undo the screws (arrowed)

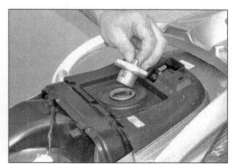

3.18b  Remove the filler cap . . .

3.18c  . . . then lift the cover and detach the drain hose

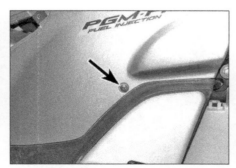

3.19a  Undo the screw (arrowed) on each side . . .

3.19b  . . . and release the trim clip (arrowed) on each side

3.20a Release the tabs from the floor panel on each side . . .

3.20b . . . and separate the sections at the front . . .

3.20c . . . then draw the cover back, disconnect the wiring connector . . .

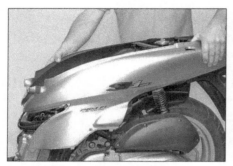

3.20d . . . and remove the cover

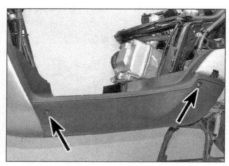

3.22 Undo the screws (arrowed) on each side

3.23 Detach the drain hose (arrowed) as you remove the panel

3.29 Free the leads and displace the relay

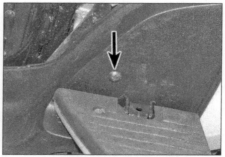

3.30a Undo the screw (arrowed) behind each footrest . . .

3.30b . . . and the two at the front on each side

floor panel on each side and from each other at the front and draw the assembly back a little **(see illustrations)**. Disconnect the tail light assembly wiring connector and remove the body cover **(see illustrations)**.

21 Installation is the reverse of removal. Make sure the wiring connector is securely

connected, and check the operation of the turn signals, brake light and tail light before riding the scooter.

### Belly panel

22 Undo the two screws on each side **(see illustration)**.

23 Release the tabs from the floor panel, then detach the fuel drain hose and remove the belly panel out from under the scooter **(see illustration)**.

24 Installation is the reverse of removal.

### Floor panel

25 Remove the maintenance panel.
26 Remove the belly panel.
27 Remove the body cover.
28 Remove the inner front panel.
29 Remove the battery (see Chapter 10). Release the battery leads and starter relay from the floor panel, noting their routing **(see illustration)**.
30 Lower the passenger footrests and undo the screw behind each one **(see illustration)**. Undo the four screws along the front of the panel **(see illustration)**.
31 Unscrew the floor panel bolts and remove the panel **(see illustrations)**.
32 Installation is the reverse of removal.

3.31a Unscrew the bolts (arrowed) . . .

3.31b . . . and remove the floor panel

3.33a Undo the upper screws (arrowed) . . .

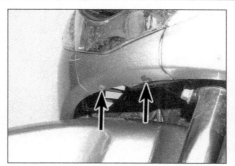

3.33b . . . and the lower screws (arrowed) . . .

3.34 . . . and remove the panel

## Upper front panel

**33** Undo the two screws at the top and the two on the underside **(see illustrations)**.
**34** Release and remove the panel **(see illustration)**.
**35** Installation is the reverse of removal.

## Lower front panel

**36** Remove the upper front panel.
**37** Remove the inner front panel.
**38** Remove the front wheel (see Chapter 8). Remove the front mudguard.
**39** Undo the front screw on each side of the belly panel and the four screws along the front of the floor panel **(see illustrations 3.22 and 3.30b)**.
**40** Disconnect the turn signal wiring connectors and free the wiring and the fan wiring from the guides.
**41** Unscrew the bolt in the front **(see illustration)**. Carefully pull the panel forwards to release the pegs from the grommets at each end of the coolant reservoir, then lift the panel to release the hook, then slide it down under the forks **(see illustrations)**.
**42** Installation is the reverse of removal.

## Inner front panel

**43** Remove the handlebar covers.
**44** Remove the four screws on each side of the panel **(see illustration)**.
**45** Remove the in-fill panel at the front by sliding it forwards **(see illustration)**.

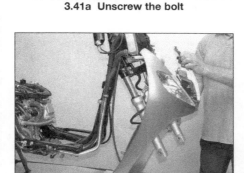

3.41a Unscrew the bolt

3.41b Release the pegs and the hook . . .

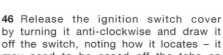

3.41c . . . and remove the panel

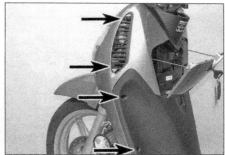

3.44 Undo the screws (arrowed) on each side

**46** Release the ignition switch cover by turning it anti-clockwise and draw it off the switch, noting how it locates – it may need to be eased off the tabs on

the switch using a screwdriver **(see illustration)**.
**47** Undo the shopping bag hook screws and remove the hook **(see illustration)**.

3.45 Release and remove the in-fill panel

3.46 Twist the cover anticlockwise over the tabs and draw it off the switch

3.47 Undo the screws (arrowed) and remove the hook

3.48 Unscrew the bolt (arrowed)

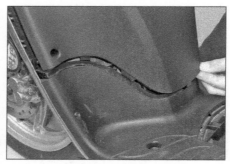

3.49a Release the panel from the floor . . .

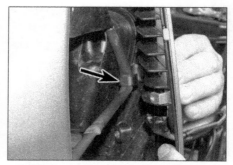

3.49b . . . free the wiring from the hook (arrowed) on each side . . .

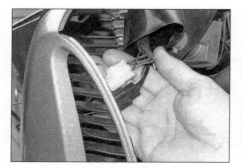

3.49c . . . disconnect the wiring connectors . . .

3.49d . . . and remove the panel

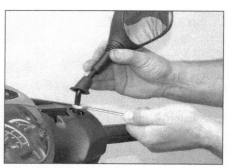

3.51 Lift the boot, slacken the locknut and unscrew the mirror

**48** Open the glove compartment and unscrew the bolt **(see illustration)**.

**49** Release the panel from the floor panel, then draw it out from under the handlebars, free the wiring from the hook on each side, disconnect the white 4-pin and black 6-pin wiring connectors, and remove the panel **(see illustrations)**.

**50** Installation is the reverse of removal.

### Mirrors

**51** Lift the rubber boot **(see illustration)**. Hold the mirror stem and slacken the locknut, then unscrew the mirror.

**52** Installation is the reverse of removal – position the mirror as required, then hold it in place and tighten the locknut.

### Front handlebar cover

**53** Remove the upper front panel.

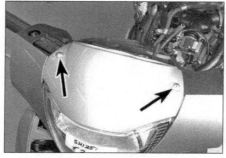

3.54a Undo the screws (arrowed) . . .

**54** Undo the screws securing the top section, then lift the top of it and draw it forwards to release the hooks **(see illustrations)**.

**55** Undo the screws in the bottom of the front cover, then release the front cover from

3.54b . . . then release the hooks

the rear cover at each end, draw the cover forwards to free the pegs from the grommets, and disconnect the headlight wiring connector **(see illustrations)**.

**56** Installation is the reverse of removal.

3.55a Undo the screws (arrowed)

3.55b Release the pegs from the holes at each end . . .

3.55c . . . free the pegs from the grommets . . .

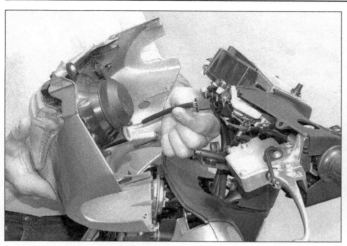

3.55d ... disconnect the wiring connector and remove the cover

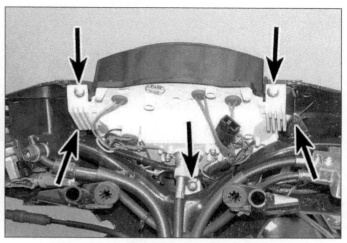

3.59a Undo the screws (arrowed) at the front ...

3.59b ... and the screw (arrowed) at the back ...

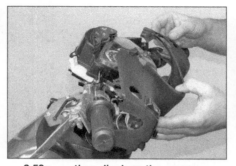

3.59c ... then displace the cover ...

3.60 ... and disconnect the switch wiring connectors

Make sure the wiring connector is securely connected, and check the operation of the headlight before riding the scooter.

### Rear handlebar cover

**57** Remove the front handlebar cover.
**58** Remove the mirrors.
**59** Undo the five screws from the front and the single screw from the back and displace the cover **(see illustrations)**.
**60** Disconnect the wiring connectors for the handlebar switches, noting where they fit **(see illustration)**. **Note:** *When disconnecting*

*the wiring, it is advisable to mark or tag the connectors as a reminder of where they connect.* Ensure all the wiring has been disconnected and remove the cover.
**61** Installation is the reverse of removal. Make sure the wiring connectors are correctly and securely connected, and check the operation of all instruments, warning lights and switches before riding the scooter.

### Front mudguard

**62** Remove the front wheel (see Chapter 8).

**63** Unscrew the bolts securing the mudguard, then draw it down, freeing the cable from the guide **(see illustrations)**.
**64** Installation is the reverse of removal.

### Rear hugger

**65** Undo the screw securing the left-hand side of the hugger to the air filter housing **(see illustration)**.
**66** Unscrew the bolts securing the right-hand side of the hugger to the swingarm and manoeuvre the hugger out.
**67** Installation is the reverse of removal.

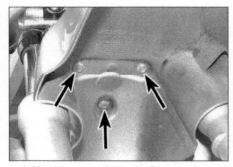

3.63a Unscrew the bolts (arrowed) ...

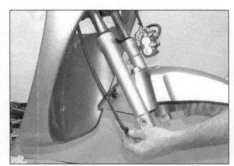

3.63b ... and remove the mudguard

3.65 Undo the screw (arrowed)

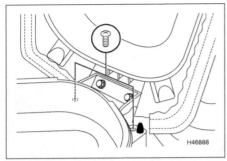

4.9 Undo the two screws under the seat (arrowed)

## 4 2009-on SH models

### Seat

1 Unlock the seat and swing it up **(see illustration 3.1)**.
2 Undo the nuts securing the seat to the hinge and remove the seat **(see illustration 3.2)**.
3 Installation is the reverse of removal.

### Storage compartment

4 Remove the seat.
5 Undo the two screws at the front **(see illustration 3.9)** and the two to the rear of the fuel filler cap **(see illustration 7.6b)**.
6 Unscrew the four bolts inside the compartment, noting which fits where **(see illustration 3.6)**.
7 Lift the storage compartment and remove it. Note the washer on the support lug and remove it for safekeeping **(see illustration 3.7c)**.
8 Installation is the reverse of removal.

### Maintenance panel

9 Unlock the seat and swing it up **(see illustration 3.1)**. Undo the screws on the top of the panel **(see illustration)**. Close the seat.
10 Release the tabs from the body cover on each side then the floor panel at the front and sides, and remove the panel **(see illustration 3.10)**.
11 Installation is the reverse of removal.

### Luggage rack

12 Unlock the seat and swing it up **(see illustration 3.1)**.

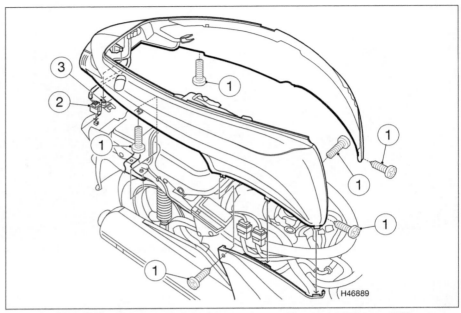

4.18 Body cover screws (1), tail light connect (2) and mounting stud (3)

13 Unscrew the bolts and remove the rack **(see illustrations 3.13a and b)**.
14 Installation is the reverse of removal.

### Body cover

15 Remove the maintenance panel.
16 Remove the storage compartment.
17 Remove the luggage rack.
18 Undo the three screws on each side **(see illustration)**.
19 Release the body cover sections from the floor panel on each side and from the lug at the back and draw the assembly back a little. Disconnect the tail light assembly wiring connector and remove the body cover.
20 Installation is the reverse of removal. Make sure the wiring connector is securely connected, and check the operation of the turn signals, brake light and tail light before riding the scooter.

### Belly panel

21 Undo the three screws on each side, noting which fits where **(see illustration)**.
22 Release the tabs from the floor panel by sliding the panel forwards, then detach the fuel drain hose and remove the belly panel out from under the scooter **(see illustration 3.23)**.
23 Installation is the reverse of removal.

### Floor panel

24 Remove the maintenance panel.
25 Remove the belly panel.
26 Remove the body cover.
27 Remove the inner front panel.
28 Remove the battery (see Chapter 10). Release the battery leads and starter relay from the floor panel, noting their routing **(see illustration 3.29)**.
29 Lower the passenger footrests and

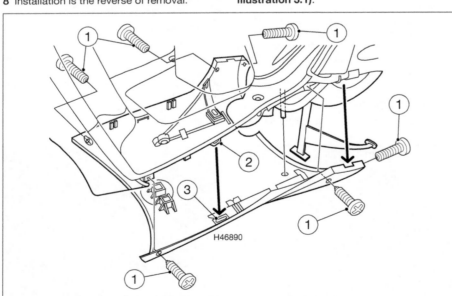

4.21 Belly panel screws (1), tab (2) and tab slot (3)

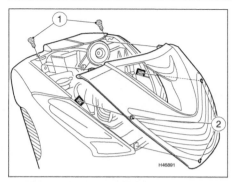

**4.32 Upper front panel screws (1) and snap-fit clip locations (2)**

undo the screw behind each one **(see illustration 3.30a)**.

**30** Unscrew the floor panel bolts, then lift the panel at the front and manoeuvre it up over the footrests **(see illustration 3.31a)**.

**31** Installation is the reverse of removal.

## Upper front panel

**32** Undo the two screws at the top **(see illustration)**.

**33** Release the three snap-fit clips, one on each side and one at the bottom, and remove the panel.

**34** Installation is the reverse of removal.

## Lower front panel

**35** Remove the upper front panel.

**36** Remove the trim panels from the inner front panel by undoing the screw and releasing the tabs securing each one.

**37** Remove the front wheel (see Chapter 8). Remove the front mudguard.

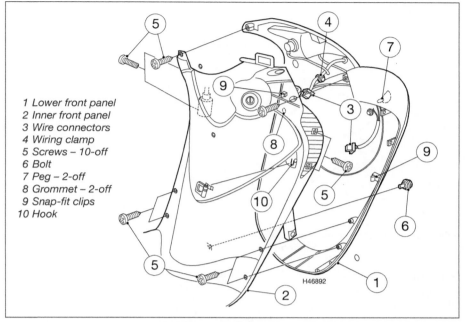

1 Lower front panel
2 Inner front panel
3 Wire connectors
4 Wiring clamp
5 Screws – 10-off
6 Bolt
7 Peg – 2-off
8 Grommet – 2-off
9 Snap-fit clips
10 Hook

**4.39 Lower front panel**

**38** Disconnect the turn signal/sidelight wiring connectors and free the wiring from the guides.

**39** Undo the five screws up each side of the inner front panel **(see illustration)**.

**40** Unscrew the bolt in the front. Carefully pull the panel forwards to release the two pegs from the grommets and the two snap-fit clips, then lift the panel to release the hook, then slide it down under the forks.

**41** Installation is the reverse of removal.

## Inner front panel

**42** Remove the trim panels from the inner front panel by undoing the screw and releasing the tabs securing each one.

**43** Remove the handlebar covers.

**44** Remove the four screws on each side of the panel **(see illustration)**.

**45** Remove the in-fill panel at the front by sliding it rearwards.

**46** Release the ignition switch cover by turning it anti-clockwise and draw it off the switch, noting how it locates – it may need to be eased off the tabs on the switch using a screwdriver **(see illustration)**.

**47** Undo the shopping bag hook screws and remove the hook.

**48** Undo the centre screw.

**49** Release the panel from the floor panel, then draw it back to release the two snap-fit clips, and out from under the handlebars, and remove the panel.

**50** Installation is the reverse of removal.

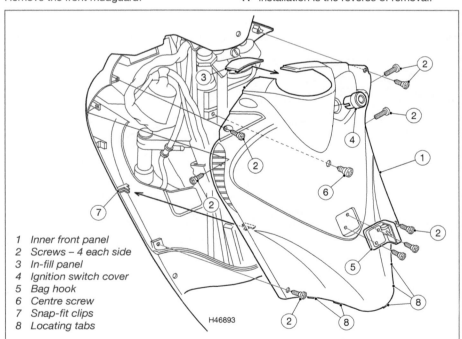

1 Inner front panel
2 Screws – 4 each side
3 In-fill panel
4 Ignition switch cover
5 Bag hook
6 Centre screw
7 Snap-fit clips
8 Locating tabs

**4.44 Inner front panel**

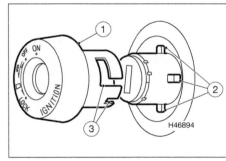

**4.46 Ignition switch cover (1) locks into place over tabs (2) on switch body. Rotate the cover anti-clockwise to release its slots (3) from the tabs**

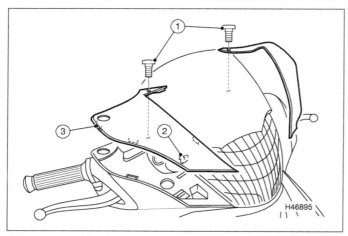

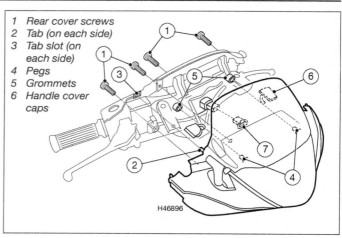

1  Rear cover screws
2  Tab (on each side)
3  Tab slot (on each side)
4  Pegs
5  Grommets
6  Handle cover caps

**4.56 Front handlebar cover trim panel screws (1), snap-fit clips (2) and tab (3)**

**4.57 Front handlebar cover mountings**

## Mirrors

**51** Lift the rubber boot.

**52** To remove the mirror from the adapters, hold the adaptor and unscrew the mirror, turning the right-hand one anti-clockwise and the left-hand clockwise. Now if required unscrew the adapters, turning the right-hand one clockwise and the left-hand anti-clockwise.

**53** To remove the mirror and adapters together, unscrew the adapter, turning the right-hand one clockwise and the left-hand anti-clockwise.

**54** Installation is the reverse of removal – if the mirrors and adapters were separated, thread the adapter in tight, then thread the mirror in and position it as required on the adapter.

## Front handlebar cover

**55** Remove the mirrors.

**56** Remove the trim panels from the cover by undoing the screw and releasing the tab and the snap-fit clip securing each one **(see illustration)**.

**57** Undo the four self-tapping screws in the rear handlebar cover **(see illustration)**.

**58** Release the front cover tabs from the rear cover, draw the cover forwards to free the pegs from the grommets, remove the handle cover caps, and disconnect the headlight wiring connector.

**59** Installation is the reverse of removal. Make sure the wiring connector is securely connected, and check the operation of the headlight before riding the scooter.

## Rear handlebar cover

**60** Remove the front handlebar cover.

**61** Undo the five screws from the front which retain the handlebar and instrument cluster

to the handlebar cover. Also remove the single screw from the back of the cover, then withdraw the cover **(see illustration)**.

**62** Disconnect the wiring connectors for the handlebar switches, noting where they fit. **Note:** *When disconnecting the wiring, it is advisable to mark or tag the connectors as a reminder of where they connect.* Ensure all the wiring has been disconnected and remove the cover.

**63** Installation is the reverse of removal. Make sure the wiring connectors are correctly and securely connected, and check the operation of all instruments, warning lights and switches before riding the scooter.

## Front mudguard

**64** Remove the front wheel (see Chapter 8).

**65** Unscrew the bolts securing the mudguard,

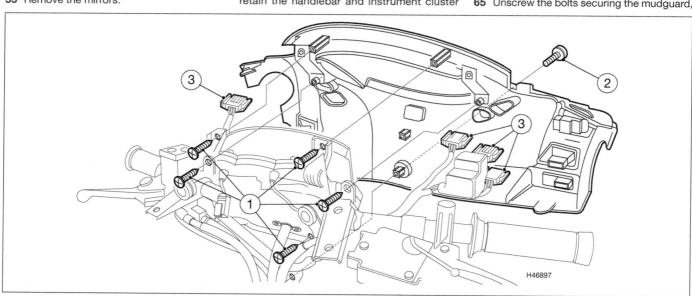

**4.61 Rear handlebar cover**

1  Front screws          2  Rear screw          3  Wiring connectors

then draw it down, freeing the cable from the guide **(see illustrations 3.63a and b)**.
66 Installation is the reverse of removal.

### Rear hugger

67 Undo the screw securing the left-hand side of the hugger to the air filter housing **(see illustration 3.65)**.
68 Unscrew the bolts securing the right-hand side of the hugger to the swingarm, on models with a rear disc brake noting how they secure the brake hose guide, and manoeuvre the hugger out, noting how the slit locates over the tab on the air filter housing.
69 Installation is the reverse of removal.

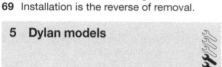

## 5  Dylan models

### Seat

1 Unlock the seat and swing it up **(see illustration)**.
2 Undo the nuts securing the seat to the hinge and remove the seat **(see illustration)**.
3 Installation is the reverse of removal.

### Storage compartment

4 Remove the seat.
5 Undo the screw at the front **(see illustration)**.
6 Unscrew the two bolts and the four nuts, removing their washers **(see illustrations)**.
7 Lift the storage compartment and remove it **(see illustration)**.
8 Installation is the reverse of removal.

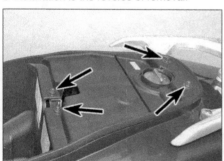

5.6b ... and the nuts (arrowed) ...

5.9b ... and remove the panel

5.1  Unlock and raise the seat

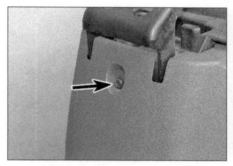

5.5  Undo the screw (arrowed)

### Maintenance panels

9 To remove the small access panel to the spark plug undo the screw, then release the tabs and remove the panel **(see illustrations)**.
10 To remove the large access panel to the battery/fusebox/starter relay, first remove the

5.7  ... and lift the compartment out

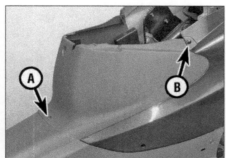

5.10a  Undo the screw (A) and release the trim clip (B) on each side ...

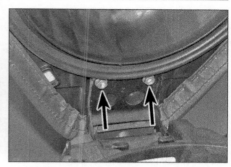

5.2  Unscrew the two nuts (arrowed)

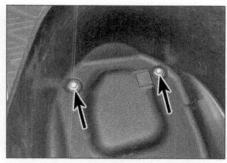

5.6a  Unscrew the bolts (arrowed) ...

storage compartment. Undo the screw at the front and release the trim clip on each side **(see illustration)**. Release the tabs from the body cover on each side then the floor panel at the front and sides, and remove the panel **(see illustration)**.
11 Installation is the reverse of removal.

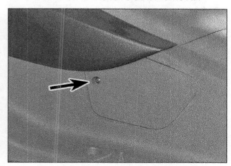

5.9a  Undo the screw (arrowed) ...

5.10b  ... and remove the panel

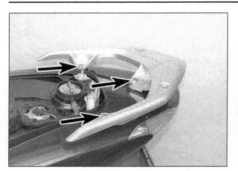

5.13a Unscrew the bolts (arrowed)

5.13b Remove the rack and the spacer

5.18a Undo the screw (arrowed) on each side . . .

5.18b . . . and release the trim clip (arrowed) on each side

### Luggage rack

**12** Unlock the seat and swing it up **(see illustration 5.1)**.
**13** Unscrew the bolts, noting the spacer under the rear one, and remove the rack **(see illustrations)**.
**14** Installation is the reverse of removal.

### Body cover

**15** Remove the storage compartment.
**16** Remove the large maintenance panel.
**17** Remove the luggage rack.
**18** Undo the screw and release the trim clip on each side **(see illustrations)**.
**19** Release the body cover sections from the floor panel on each side and from the lug at the back and draw the assembly back a little **(see illustration)**. Disconnect the tail light assembly wiring connector and remove the body cover **(see illustrations)**.
**20** Installation is the reverse of removal. Make sure the wiring connector is securely connected, and check the operation of the turn signals, brake light and tail light before riding the scooter.

### Lower covers

**21** Unscrew the bolt and release the trim clip at the front, then undo the screw and the bolt at the back **(see illustrations)**.
**22** Release the tabs from the floor panel by sliding the cover back – when removing the left-hand cover on models fitted with a sidestand, move the stand as required as you remove the cover **(see illustration)**.
**23** Installation is the reverse of removal.

5.19a Release the tabs from the floor panel

5.19b Disconnect the wiring connector . . .

5.19c . . . and remove the cover

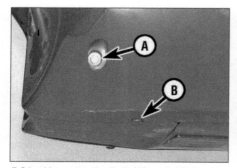

5.21a Unscrew the bolt (A) and release the trim clip (B)

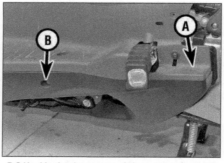

5.21b Undo the screw (A) and the bolt (B)

5.22 Release and remove the cover

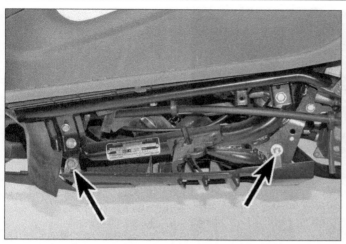

5.25a Unscrew the bolts (arrowed) on each side . . .

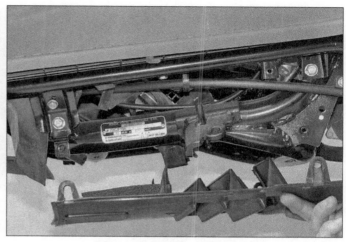

5.25b . . . and remove the panel

## Belly panel

24 Remove the lower covers.
25 Unscrew the two bolts on each side and remove the belly panel out from under the scooter **(see illustrations)**.
26 Installation is the reverse of removal.

## Floor panel

27 Remove the body cover.
28 Remove the lower covers.
29 Unscrew the passenger footrest bracket bolts and remove each footrest assembly **(see illustrations)**.

30 Undo the three screws and two floor panel bolts on each side **(see illustration)**.
31 Pull the bottom of the inner front panel away and release the floor panel from it, then remove the floor panel **(see illustrations)**.
32 Installation is the reverse of removal.

## Upper front panel

33 Undo the two screws on the inner front panel **(see illustration)**.
34 Draw the panel down and remove it **(see illustration)**.
35 Installation is the reverse of removal.

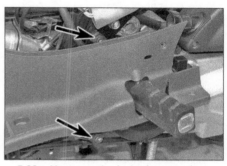

5.29a Unscrew the bolts (arrowed) . . .

5.29b . . . and remove the footrest assembly

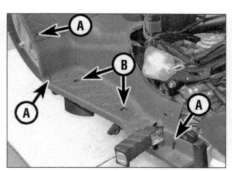

5.30 Undo the screws (A) and the bolts (B) . . .

5.31a . . . then release the front of the floor panel . . .

5.31b . . . and remove it

5.33 Undo the screws (arrowed) . . .

5.34 . . . and remove the panel

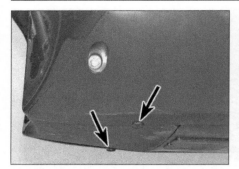

5.38a Release the trim clips (arrowed)

5.38b Undo the screws . . .

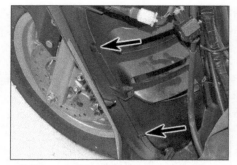

5.38c . . . release the tabs (arrowed) on each side . . .

5.38d . . . and draw the centre section out

5.39 Disconnect the headlight wiring connector and the turn signal connector on each side

**39** Disconnect the headlight and turn signal wiring connectors (**see illustration**).

**40** Undo the two screws on the underside of the nose and the two bolts at the top (**see illustration**). Draw the panel forwards to release the pegs from the grommets (**see illustrations**).

**41** Installation is the reverse of removal.

### Inner front panel

**42** Remove the upper front panel.

**43** Remove the handlebar covers.

**44** Release the ignition switch cover by turning it anti-clockwise and draw it off the switch, noting how it locates (**see illustration**) – it may need to be eased off the tabs on the switch using a screwdriver.

**45** Undo the shopping bag hook screws and remove the hook (**see illustration**).

**46** Release the wiring from the ties (**see illustration**).

### Lower front panel

**36** Remove the upper front panel.

**37** Remove the inner front panel.

**38** Release the two trim clips on the underside of the centre section, then undo the three screws on each side, release its tabs and draw it out to one side (**see illustrations**).

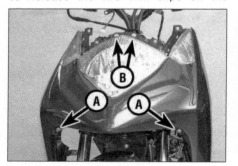

5.40a Undo the screws (A) and the bolts (B) . . .

5.40b . . . then free the pegs from the grommets . . .

5.40c . . . and remove the panel

5.44 Twist the cover anticlockwise over the tabs and draw it off the switch

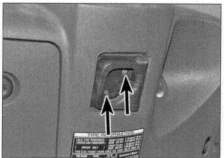

5.45 Undo the screws (arrowed) and remove the hook

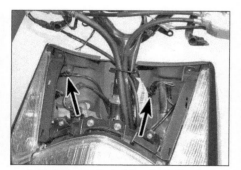

5.46 Release the wiring from the ties (arrowed)

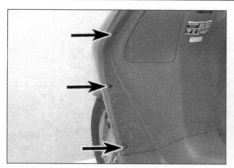

**5.47 Undo the screws (arrowed) on each side**

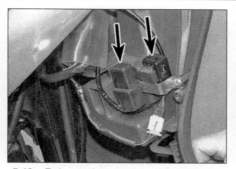

**5.48a Release the panel and displace the relays (arrowed) . . .**

**5.48b . . . and remove the panel**

**47** Undo the three screws on each side of the panel **(see illustration)**.
**48** Release the panel from the lower front panel and floor panel and displace the turn signal and starter relays from their bracket, then remove the panel **(see illustrations)**.
**49** Installation is the reverse of removal.

### Mirrors

**50** Lift the rubber boot **(see illustration)**. Hold the mirror stem and slacken the locknut, then unscrew the mirror.
**51** Installation is the reverse of removal – position the mirror as required, then hold it in place and tighten the locknut.

### Front handlebar cover

**52** Remove the upper front panel.
**53** Undo the two screws in the rear handlebar cover and the two on the underside of the front **(see illustrations)**.

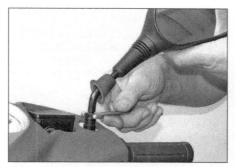

**5.50 Lift the boot, slacken the locknut and unscrew the mirror**

**54** Release the tabs from the rear cover and draw the cover forwards **(see illustrations)**.
**55** Installation is the reverse of removal.

### Rear handlebar cover

**56** Remove the front handlebar cover.

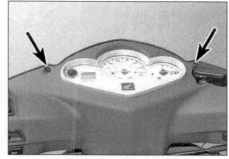

**5.53a Undo the rear screws (arrowed) . . .**

**57** Remove the mirrors.
**58** Disconnect the instrument cluster wiring connector **(see illustration)**.
**59** Undo the two screws from the front and the single screw from the back and displace the cover **(see illustrations)**.

**5.53b . . . and the front screws (arrowed)**

**5.54a Release the pegs from the holes at each end . . .**

**5.54b . . . and remove the cover**

**5.58 Disconnect the wiring connector**

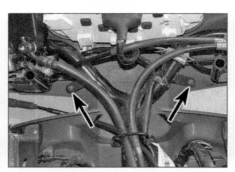

**5.59a Undo the front screws (arrowed) . . .**

**5.59b . . . and rear screw (arrowed) . . .**

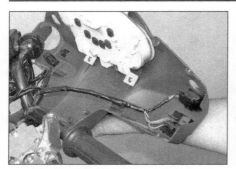

5.60 . . . then displace the cover and disconnect the switch connectors

5.62 Undo the screws (arrowed) on each side

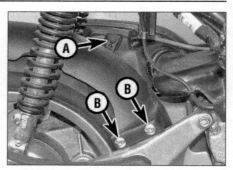

5.64 Undo the screw (A) and the bolts (B)

60 Disconnect the wiring connectors for the handlebar switches, noting where they fit (see illustration). Note: *When disconnecting the wiring, it is advisable to mark or tag the connectors as a reminder of where they connect.* Ensure all the wiring has been disconnected and remove the cover. Remove the instrument cluster from it if required.

61 Installation is the reverse of removal. Make sure the wiring connectors are correctly and securely connected, and check the operation of all instruments, warning lights and switches before riding the scooter.

### Front mudguard

62 Undo the two screws on each side and draw the mudguard forwards (see illustration).

63 Installation is the reverse of removal.

### Rear hugger

64 Undo the screw securing the left-hand side of the hugger to the air filter housing and the bolts securing the right-hand side to the swingarm and manoeuvre the hugger out (see illustration).

65 Installation is the reverse of removal.

## 6   @ models

### Seat

1 Unlock the seat and swing it up (see illustration).

2 Undo the nuts securing the seat to the hinge and remove the seat (see illustration).

3 Installation is the reverse of removal.

### Storage compartment

4 Remove the seat.

5 Undo the screw at the front (see illustration).

6 Unscrew the two bolts and the four nuts, removing their washers (see illustration).

7 Lift the storage compartment out (see illustration).

8 Installation is the reverse of removal.

### Maintenance panels

9 To remove the small access panel to the spark plug undo the screw, then release the tabs and remove the panel (see illustrations 5.9a and b).

10 To remove the large access panel to the battery/fusebox/starter relay, first remove the storage compartment. Release the trim clip on each side (see illustration). Release the tabs

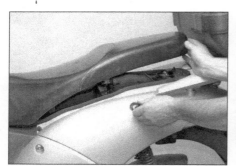

6.1 Unlock and raise the seat

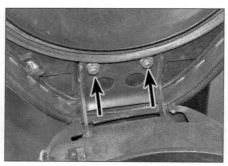

6.2 Unscrew the two nuts (arrowed)

6.5 Undo the screw (arrowed)

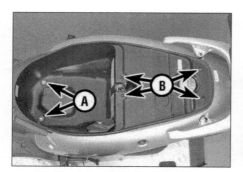

6.6 Unscrew the bolts (A) and the nuts (B) . . .

6.7 . . . and lift the compartment out

6.10a Release the trim clip (arrowed) on each side . . .

6.10b . . . and remove the panel

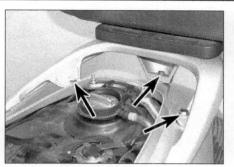

6.13 Unscrew the bolts (arrowed) and remove the rack

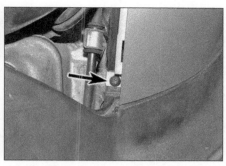

6.16a Undo the screw (arrowed) at the front . . .

from the body cover on each side then the floor panel at the front and sides, and remove the panel **(see illustration)**.

11 Installation is the reverse of removal.

### Luggage rack

12 Unlock the seat and swing it up **(see illustration 6.1)**.
13 Unscrew the bolts and remove the rack **(see illustration)**. Remove the spacers, noting which fits where.
14 Installation is the reverse of removal.

### Side covers

15 Remove the large maintenance panel.
16 Undo the screw at the front and the screw and two bolts on the side and release the cover from the floor panel **(see illustrations)**.
17 Installation is the reverse of removal.

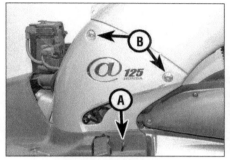

6.16b . . . the screw (A) and the bolts (B) on the side . . .

6.16c . . . and remove the cover

### Body cover

18 Remove the side covers.
19 Remove the luggage rack.
20 Undo the screw on each side **(see illustration)**.

21 Release the seat lock cable from the locking mechanism **(see illustration)**.
22 Lift the rear of the cover to release the pegs from the grommets on the tail light, and remove the cover **(see illustration)**.
23 Installation is the reverse of removal.

### Lower covers

24 Undo the screw at the back and the bolts on the side **(see illustrations)**.
25 Release the tabs from the floor panel – when removing the left-hand cover, move the stand as required as you remove the cover.
26 Installation is the reverse of removal.

### Belly panel

27 Remove the lower covers.
28 Unscrew the two bolts on each side and remove the belly panel out from under the scooter **(see illustration 5.25a and b)**.
29 Installation is the reverse of removal.

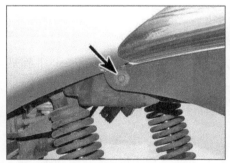

6.20 Undo the screw (arrowed) on each side

6.21 Release the cable

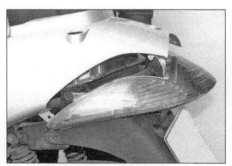

6.22 Release and remove the cover

6.24a Undo the screw (arrowed) . . .

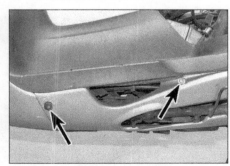

6.24b . . . and the bolts (arrowed)

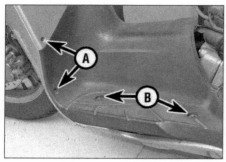

6.33 Undo the screws (A) and the bolts (B)

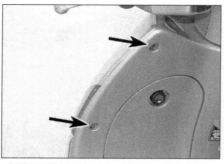

6.36 Undo the screws (arrowed) on each side

6.37a Release the tabs . . .

6.37b . . . then disconnect the wiring connector and remove the panel

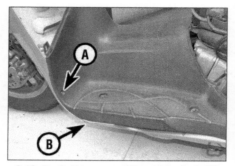

6.43 Undo the screw (A) and the bolt (B) on each side

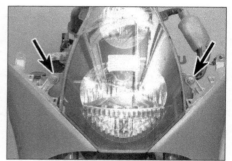

6.44 Undo the nuts (arrowed) and remove the panel

### Floor panel

**30** Remove the side covers.
**31** Remove the lower covers.
**32** Unscrew the passenger footrest bracket bolts and remove each footrest assembly (**see illustrations 5.29a and b**).
**33** Undo the two screws and the two floor panel bolts on each side (**see illustration**).
**34** Release the floor panel from bottom of the inner front panel and remove the floor panel.
**35** Installation is the reverse of removal.

### Upper front panel

**36** Undo the two upper screws on each side of the inner front panel (**see illustration**).
**37** Release the tabs from the lower front panel

on each side, then disconnect the turn signal wiring connectors and remove the panel (**see illustrations**).
**38** Installation is the reverse of removal.

### Lower front panel

**39** Remove the upper front panel.
**40** Remove the inner front panel.
**41** Remove the front wheel (see Chapter 8). Remove the front mudguard.
**42** Remove the deflector from the underside of the bottom yoke.
**43** Undo the screw in the floor panel and the bolt in the lower cover on each side (**see illustration**).
**44** Unscrew the two nuts and remove

the washers, then draw the panel down from around the forks and remove it (**see illustration**).
**45** Installation is the reverse of removal.

### Inner front panel

**46** Remove the upper front panel.
**47** Either remove the handlebar covers or the floor panel – the handlebar covers require less work, but if you are removing the floor panel anyway and not the handlebar covers, do it that way.
**48** Undo the shopping bag hook screws and remove the hook (**see illustration**).
**49** Undo the two screws on each side of the panel (**see illustration**).

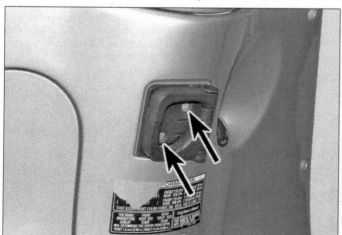

6.48 Undo the screws (arrowed) and remove the hook

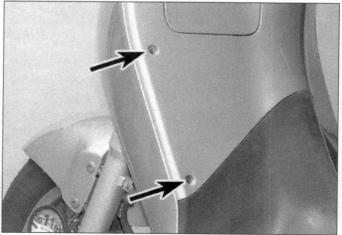

6.49 Undo the screws (arrowed) on each side

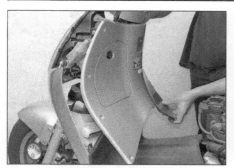

6.50a Release the panel . . .

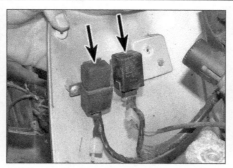

6.50b . . . displace the relays (arrowed) . . .

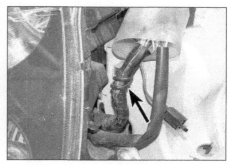

6.50c . . . and release the wiring clip (arrowed)

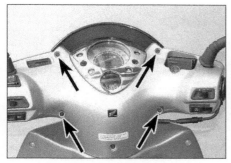

6.54 Undo the screws (arrowed)

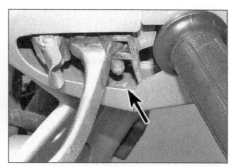

6.55a Release the pegs from the holes at each end . . .

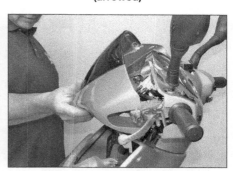

6.55b . . . and remove the cover

**50** Release the panel from the lower front panel and floor panel if not removed, then displace the turn signal and starter relays from their bracket, release the wiring clip, and remove the panel **(see illustrations)**.
**51** Installation is the reverse of removal.

### Mirrors

**52** Lift the rubber boot **(see illustration 5.50)**. Hold the mirror stem and slacken the locknut, then unscrew the mirror.
**53** Installation is the reverse of removal – position the mirror as required, then hold it in place and tighten the locknut.

### Front handlebar cover

**54** Undo the four screws in the rear handlebar cover **(see illustration)**.
**55** Release the tabs from the rear cover and draw the cover forwards **(see illustrations)**.
**56** Installation is the reverse of removal.

### Rear handlebar cover

**57** Remove the front handlebar cover.
**58** Remove the mirrors.
**59** Undo the five screws from the front and the single screw from the back and displace the cover **(see illustrations)**.
**60** Disconnect the wiring connectors for the handlebar switches, noting where they fit.

**Note:** *When disconnecting the wiring, it is advisable to mark or tag the connectors as a reminder of where they connect.* Ensure all the wiring has been disconnected and remove the cover.
**61** Installation is the reverse of removal. Make sure the wiring connectors are correctly and securely connected, and check the operation of all instruments, warning lights and switches before riding the scooter.

### Front mudguard

**62** Either free the speedometer cable guide from the mudguard, or undo the screw securing the cable to its drive housing on the front wheel and draw the cable out.

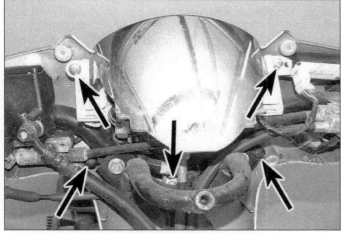

6.59a Undo the front screws (arrowed) . . .

6.59b . . . and rear screw (arrowed)

**63** Undo the two screws on each side and draw the mudguard forwards **(see illustration 5.62)**.

**64** Installation is the reverse of removal.

### Rear hugger

**65** Undo the screw securing the left-hand side of the hugger to the air filter housing and the bolts securing the right-hand side to the swingarm and manoeuvre the hugger out **(see illustration 5.64)**.

**66** Installation is the reverse of removal.

## 7  PS models

### Seat

**1** Unlock the seat and swing it up **(see illustration)**.

**2** Undo the nuts securing the seat to the hinge and remove the seat **(see illustration)**.

**3** Installation is the reverse of removal.

### Storage compartment

**4** Remove the seat.

**5** Undo the screw at the front **(see illustration)**.

**6** Unscrew the four bolts inside the

**7.1  Unlock and raise the seat**

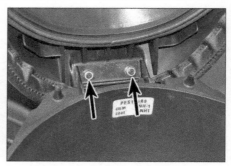

**7.2  Unscrew the two nuts (arrowed)**

compartment, noting which fits where, and the two bolts to the rear of the fuel filler cap **(see illustrations)**.

**7** Lift the storage compartment out **(see illustration)**. Note the washer on the support lug and remove it for safekeeping **(see illustration)**.

**8** Installation is the reverse of removal.

### Maintenance panels

**9** To remove the small access panel to the spark plug undo the screw, then release the tabs and remove the panel **(see illustrations)**.

**10** To remove the large access panel to the battery/starter relay, undo the screw, then

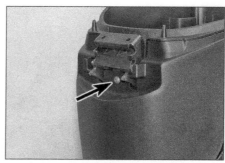

**7.5  Undo the screw (arrowed) . . .**

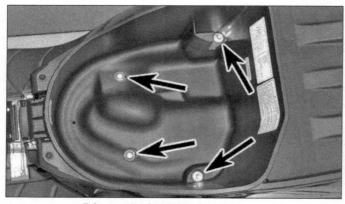

**7.6a  . . . the four bolts (arrowed) . . .**

**7.6b  . . . and the two bolts (arrowed) . . .**

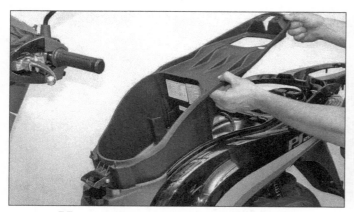

**7.7a  . . . and remove the storage compartment**

**7.7b  Note the washer (arrowed)**

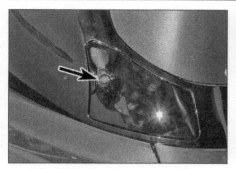

7.9a Undo the screw (arrowed) . . .

7.9b . . . and release the panel

7.10a Undo the screw (arrowed) . . .

release the tabs from the floor panel at the front and sides, and remove the panel (see illustrations).

11 Installation is the reverse of removal.

## Luggage rack

12 Unlock the seat and swing it up (see illustration 7.1).
13 Unscrew the bolts and remove the rack (see illustration).
14 Installation is the reverse of removal.

## Body cover

15 Remove the storage compartment.
16 Undo the three screws securing the centre section, noting which fits where, then release the tabs from the body cover and remove it (see illustrations).
17 Remove the large maintenance panel.
18 Remove the luggage rack.

7.10b . . . and release the panel

19 Undo the two screws on each side (see illustration).
20 Release the body cover from the floor panel on each side and from the lug at the back and draw the assembly back a little

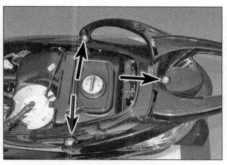

7.13 Unscrew the bolts (arrowed) and remove the rack

(see illustrations). Disconnect the tail light assembly wiring connector and remove the body cover (see illustration).
21 Installation is the reverse of removal. Make sure the wiring connector is securely

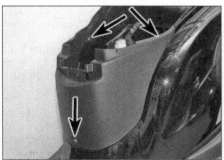

7.16a Undo the screws (arrowed) . . .

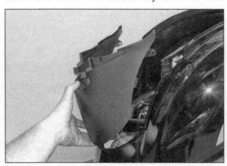

7.16b . . . and remove the centre section

7.19 Undo the screws (arrowed) on each side

7.20a Release the tabs from the floor panel on each side . . .

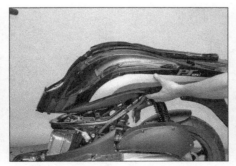

7.20b . . . then draw the cover back . . .

7.20c . . . and disconnect the wiring connector

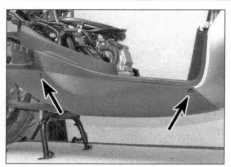

7.22a Undo the screws (arrowed) on each side . . .

7.22b . . . and the screw (arrowed) at the back

7.23a Detach the drain hose (arrowed) . . .

7.23b . . . then release the hooks by sliding the panel back . . .

7.23c . . . and remove it

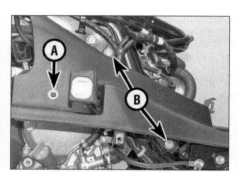

7.28 Undo the screw (A) on each side. Footrest bracket bolts (B)

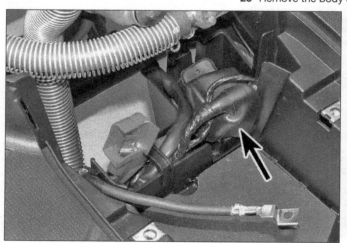

7.29 Lift the panel and manoeuvre the footrest out

connected, and check the operation of the turn signals, brake light and tail light before riding the scooter.

## Belly panel

22 Undo the two screws on each side and the screw at the back (see illustrations).
23 Detach the fuel drain hose (see illustration). Slide the panel back to release it from the floor panel hooks, then remove the belly panel out from under the scooter (see illustrations).
24 Installation is the reverse of removal.

## Floor panel

25 Remove the body cover.

26 Remove the belly panel.
27 Remove the inner front panel.
28 Undo the screw on each side at the back (see illustration).
29 Unscrew the passenger footrest bracket bolts on one side (see illustration 7.28). Lift the floor panel and remove the one footrest assembly (see illustration) – remove both if required, but there is no need.
30 Remove the battery (see Chapter 10). Release the battery leads and starter relay from the floor panel, noting their routing (see illustration).
31 Undo the four screws along the front of the panel (see illustration).
32 Unscrew the floor panel bolts and

7.30 Free the leads and displace the relay (arrowed)

7.31 Undo the screws (arrowed) on each side

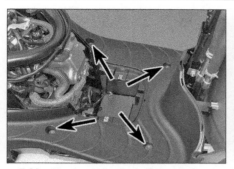

7.32a Unscrew the bolts (arrowed) . . .

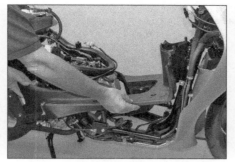

7.32b . . . and remove the floor panel

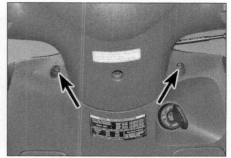

7.34a Undo the upper screws
(arrowed) . . .

remove the panel, manoeuvring it around the remaining passenger footrest if not removed **(see illustrations)**.

**33** Installation is the reverse of removal.

### Upper front panel

**34** Undo the two screws at the top and the two on the underside **(see illustrations)**. Release and remove the panel **(see illustration)**.

**35** Installation is the reverse of removal.

### Lower front panel

**36** Remove the upper front panel.

**37** Remove the inner front panel.

**38** Remove the front wheel (see Chapter 8). Remove the front mudguard.

**39** Undo the front screw on each side of the

belly panel **(see illustration 7.22a)** and the four screws along the front of the floor panel **(see illustration 7.31)**.

**40** Disconnect the turn signal wiring connectors **(see illustration)**.

**41** Unscrew the bolt in the front **(see illustration)**. Carefully pull the panel forwards to release the pegs from the grommets at each end of the coolant reservoir **(see illustration)**, then lift the panel to release the hook **(see illustration)**, then slide it down under the forks.

**42** Installation is the reverse of removal.

### Inner front panel

**43** Remove the upper front panel.

**44** Remove the handlebar covers.

**45** Remove the five screws on each side of the panel **(see illustration)**.

7.34b . . . and the lower screws
(arrowed) . . .

**46** Release the ignition switch cover by turning it anti-clockwise and draw it off the switch, noting how it locates **(see illus-**

7.34c . . . and remove the panel

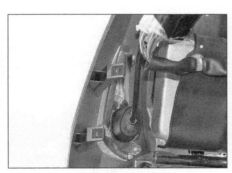

7.40 Disconnect the turn signal wiring
connectors

7.41a Unscrew the bolt

7.41b Release the pegs (arrowed) . . .

7.41c . . . and the hook (arrowed) and
remove the panel

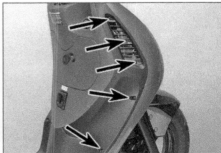

7.45 Undo the screws (arrowed) on each
side

7.46 Twist the cover anticlockwise over the tabs and draw it off the switch

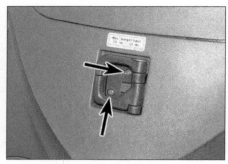

7.47 Undo the screws (arrowed) and remove the hook

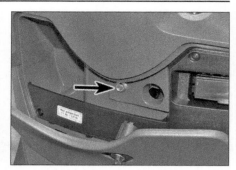

7.48 Unscrew the bolt (arrowed)

7.49a Undo the screws (arrowed)

7.49b Release the panel at the top . . .

tration) – it may need to be eased off the tabs on the switch using a screwdriver.

47 Undo the shopping bag hook screws and remove the hook (see illustration).

48 Open the storage compartment and unscrew the bolt (see illustration).

49 Undo the two screws at the front (see illustration). Release the panel at the top, then draw it out from under the handlebars and disconnect the white 4-pin and black 6-pin wiring connectors (see illustrations). Release it from the floor panel, and remove the panel (see illustration).

50 Installation is the reverse of removal.

## Mirrors

51 Lift the rubber boot (see illustration). Hold the mirror stem and slacken the locknut, then unscrew the mirror, turning the right-hand mirror clockwise and the left one anti-clockwise.

52 Installation is the reverse of removal – position the mirror as required, then hold it in place and tighten the locknut.

## Front handlebar cover

53 Undo the screws in the rear cover (see illustration).

54 Undo the screws in the bottom of the front cover (see illustration). Release the front cover from the rear cover at each end, draw the cover forwards to free the pegs from

7.49c . . . and from the floor . . .

7.49d . . . and disconnect the wiring connectors

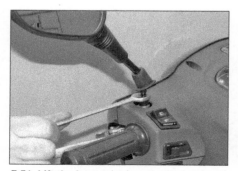

7.51 Lift the boot, slacken the locknut and unscrew the mirror

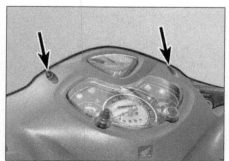

7.53 Undo the screws (arrowed)

7.54a Undo the screws (arrowed)

7.54b Release the pegs from the holes at each end . . .

7.54c . . . free the pegs from the grommets . . .

7.54d . . . disconnect the wiring connector and remove the cover

the grommets, and disconnect the headlight wiring connector **(see illustrations)**.

**55** Installation is the reverse of removal. Make sure the wiring connector is securely connected, and check the operation of the headlight before riding the scooter.

### Rear handlebar cover

**56** Remove the front handlebar cover.
**57** Remove the mirrors.
**58** Undo the five screws from the front and the single screw from the back and displace the cover **(see illustrations)**.
**59** Disconnect the wiring connectors for the handlebar switches, noting where they fit **(see illustration)**. **Note:** *When disconnecting the wiring, it is advisable to mark or tag the connectors as a reminder of where they connect.* Ensure all the wiring has been disconnected and remove the cover.
**60** Installation is the reverse of removal. Make sure the wiring connectors are correctly and securely connected, and check the operation of all instruments, warning lights and switches before riding the scooter.

### Front mudguard

**61** Either free the speedometer cable guide from the mudguard, or undo the screw securing the cable to its drive housing on the front wheel and draw the cable out.
**62** Unscrew the bolts securing the mudguard and draw it forwards **(see illustration)**.
**63** Installation is the reverse of removal.

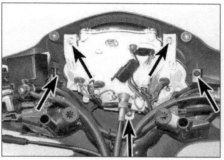

7.58a Undo the screws (arrowed) at the front . . .

### Rear hugger

**64** Undo the screw securing the left-hand side of the hugger to the air filter housing and the bolts securing the right-hand side to the swingarm and manoeuvre the hugger out **(see illustration)**.
**65** Installation is the reverse of removal.

### 8  Pantheon models

### Seat

**1** Unlock the seat and swing it up **(see illustration 9.1)**.

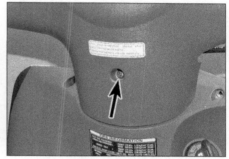

7.58b . . . and the screw (arrowed) at the back . . .

**2** Undo the nuts securing the seat to the hinge and remove the seat **(see illustration 9.2)**.
**3** Installation is the reverse of removal.

### Storage compartment

**4** Remove the seat. Remove the carpet **(see illustration 9.4)**.
**5** Undo the tail light bulb access panel screws and displace the panel, then disconnect the power socket and storage compartment light wiring connectors **(see illustrations 9.5a and b)**. Also disconnect the storage compartment light switch wiring connector.
**6** Remove the battery (see Chapter 10). Displace the fusebox and starter relay from their mounts **(see illustration 9.6)**.
**7** Release the seat lock cable cover trim clip

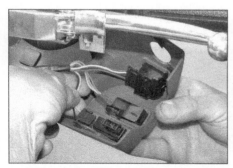

7.59 . . . then displace the cover and disconnect the switch wiring connectors

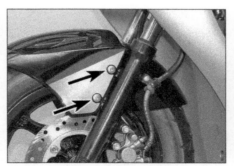

7.62 Unscrew the bolts (arrowed) and remove the mudguard

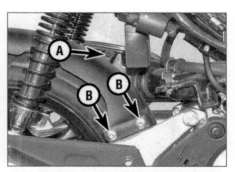

7.64 Undo the screw (A) and the bolts (B)

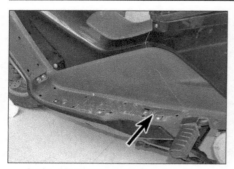

8.13a Undo the screw (arrowed) . . .

8.13b . . . and remove the panel

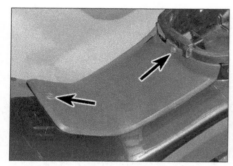

8.14a Undo the screws (arrowed) . . .

8.14b . . . then release the tabs and remove the panel

and remove the cover **(see illustration 9.7a)**. Detach the cable from the lock mechanism **(see illustration 9.7b)**.

8 Unscrew the two bolts on the outside of the battery case **(see illustration 9.8)**.

9 Undo the three screws around the front of the compartment.

10 Unscrew the seven bolts inside the compartment **(see illustration 9.10)**.

11 Lift the storage compartment and draw

the seat lock cable out **(see illustrations 9.11a and b)**.

12 Installation is the reverse of removal.

## Maintenance panels

13 To remove the small access panel to the engine in each floor panel, undo the screw, then release the tabs and remove the panel **(see illustrations)**.

14 To remove the large access panel to the radiator in the centre cover, unlock the seat and swing it up **(see illustration 9.1)**. Undo the two screws, then release the tabs from the centre cover and remove the panel **(see illustrations)**.

15 To remove the access panel to the battery/fusebox/starter relay in the storage compartment, unlock and raise the seat **(see illustration 9.1)**, then remove the carpet **(see illustration 9.4)**. Undo the screws and remove the panel **(see illustration 9.13)**.

16 Installation is the reverse of removal.

## Luggage rack

17 Unlock the seat and swing it up **(see illustration 9.1)**.

18 Unscrew the bolts and remove the washers, then lift the rack away and remove the spacers, noting which fits where **(see illustration 9.19)**.

19 Installation is the reverse of removal.

## Body cover

20 Remove the seat.

21 Remove the luggage rack.

22 Remove the storage compartment.

23 Undo the two screws above the licence plate and the two screws on each side **(see illustrations)**.

24 Unscrew the bolt near the seat hinge. Remove the seat hinge.

25 Release the body cover from the floor panel on each side and draw the assembly back a little. Disconnect the tail light assembly wiring connectors and remove the body cover.

26 Installation is the reverse of removal. Make sure the wiring connectors are securely connected, and check the operation of the turn signals, brake light and tail light before riding the scooter.

## Centre cover

27 Remove the seat.

28 Remove the storage compartment.

29 Remove the large maintenance panel to the radiator.

30 Unscrew the bolt near the seat hinge. Undo the screw on each side of the front of the body cover **(see illustration 8.23c)**.

31 Raise the fuel filler cap cover. Undo the screws and remove the cover from the hinge **(see illustration)**. Unscrew the bolt next to the hinge.

8.23a Undo the screws (arrowed) . . .

8.23b . . . the screw (arrowed) . . .

8.23c . . . and the screw (arrowed)

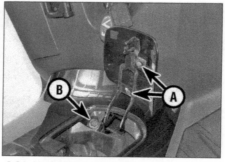

8.31 Undo the screws (A) and remove the cover, then unscrew the bolt (B)

8.32 Undo the screws (arrowed) on each side

8.33 Undo the screw (arrowed) on each side

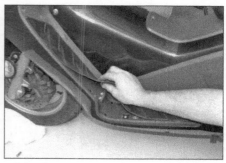

8.35 Release and remove the floor mat

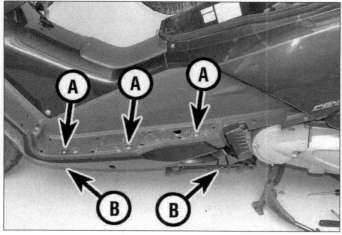

8.36 Undo the screws (A) and the bolts (B)

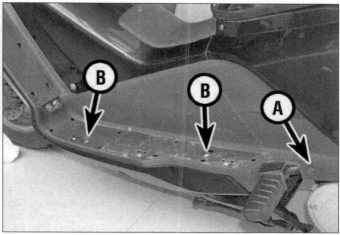

8.47 Undo the screw (A) and the bolts (B)

32 Undo the two screws on each side of the centre cover (see illustration).

33 Release the body cover from the floor panel on each side to expose the rear screws for the centre cover, then undo the screws (see illustration). Draw the centre cover back to release the tabs from the floor covers, and remove the cover.

34 Installation is the reverse of removal. Make sure the wiring connectors are securely connected, and check the operation of the turn signals, brake light and tail light before riding the scooter.

### Lower covers

35 Release the floor mat locating pegs from the floor covers and remove the mats (see illustration).

36 Undo the three screws along the top and the two bolts on the side (see illustration).

37 Release the tabs from the floor panel and the lower front cover and remove the cover – when removing the left-hand cover, move the sidestand as required.

38 Installation is the reverse of removal.

### Belly panel

39 Remove the lower covers.

40 Unscrew the two bolts on each side (see illustration 9.35).

41 Slide the panel back to release the tab at the front, then detach the fuel drain hose and remove the belly panel out from under the scooter.

42 Installation is the reverse of removal.

### Floor panels

43 Remove the body cover.

44 Remove the centre cover.

45 Remove the lower covers.

46 Remove the inner front panel.

47 Undo the screw at the back and the two bolts (see illustration). Release the panel from the frame and remove the panel.

48 Installation is the reverse of removal.

### Upper front panel

49 Undo the two screws at the top and the two on the underside (see illustrations).

50 Draw the panel forwards to free the pegs from the grommets, then disconnect the headlight wiring connector and remove

8.49a Undo the screw (arrowed) on each side . . .

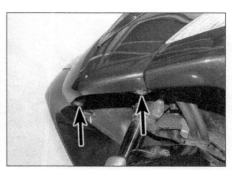

8.49b . . . and the screws (arrowed) on the underside . . .

8.50a . . . then release the panel . . .

8.50b . . . and disconnect the headlight wiring connector (arrowed)

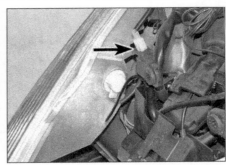

8.54 Disconnect the wiring connector (arrowed) on each side

the panel along with the headlight **(see illustrations)**.
51 Installation is the reverse of removal.

### Lower front panel

52 Remove the upper front panel.
53 Remove the front mudguard. Remove the front wheel (see Chapter 8).
54 Disconnect the turn signal wiring connectors **(see illustration)**.
55 Undo the two screws in the front **(see illustration 9.49a)**, and the five screws on each side of the inner front panel **(see illustration)**.
56 Unscrew the bolt on each side at the bottom **(see illustration 9.50a)** and the two bolts in the front **(see illustration 9.50b)**.
57 Carefully pull the panel forwards to release the pegs from the grommets and the bottom of the panel from the belly panel tab, then slide it down under the forks.

58 Installation is the reverse of removal.

### Inner front panel

59 Remove the centre cover.
60 Remove the upper front panel.
61 Remove the rear handlebar cover.
62 Release the ignition switch cover by turning it anti-clockwise and draw it off the switch, noting how it locates **(see illustration 9.57)** – it may need to be eased off the tabs on the switch using a screwdriver.
63 Release the wiring from the clamp.
64 Release the floor mat locating pegs from the floor covers and remove the mats **(see illustration 8.35)**.
65 Undo the two screws in the front of the lower front panel **(see illustration 9.49a)**.
66 Unscrew the two bolts on each side at the bottom **(see illustration 9.63)**.
67 Undo the five screws on each side of the panel **(see illustration 8.55)**.

68 Undo the shopping bag hook screws and remove the hook **(see illustration 9.66)**.
69 Release the panel from the top of the lower front panel, then draw it out from under the handlebars and release it from the floor panel and remove the panel.
70 Installation is the reverse of removal.

### Mirrors

71 Lift the rubber boot **(see illustration 7.51)**. Hold the mirror stem and slacken the locknut, then unscrew the mirror, turning the right-hand mirror clockwise and the left one anti-clockwise.
72 Installation is the reverse of removal – position the mirror as required, then hold it in place and tighten the locknut.

### Handlebar covers, windshield and instrument cover

73 To remove the front handlebar cover undo the six screws in the rear cover and remove the front cover **(see illustrations)**.
74 To remove the windshield, remove the front handlebar cover, then undo the four screws and remove the windshield **(see illustration)**.
75 To remove the inner front cover, remove the front handlebar cover and windshield, then undo the three screws and remove the cover **(see illustration)**.
76 To remove the instrument cover, remove the front handlebar cover, windshield, inner front cover and the mirrors. Disconnect the instrument cluster wiring connector and displace the turn signal relay, then undo the screws and displace the cover, disconnect the dimmer switch wiring

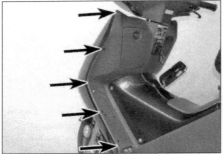

8.55 Undo the screws (arrowed) on each side

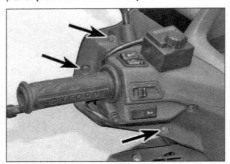

8.73a Undo the screws (arrowed) on each side . . .

8.73b . . . and remove the cover

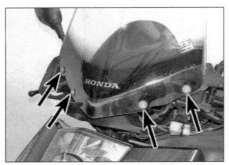

8.74 Windshield screws (arrowed)

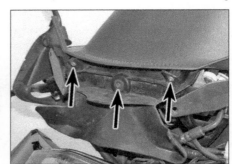

8.75 Undo the screws (arrowed) and remove the cover

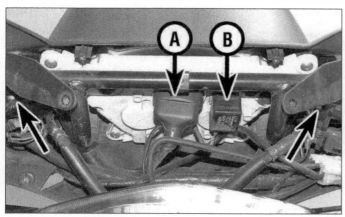

8.76a Disconnect the wiring connector (A) and displace the relay (B), then undo the front screws (arrowed) . . .

8.76b . . . and the rear screws (arrowed)

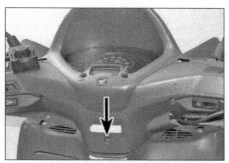

8.77 Undo the screw (arrowed) and remove the cover – note the routing of the throttle cable

connector, and remove the cover along with the instrument cluster (see illustrations).

77 To remove the rear handlebar cover, remove the front handlebar cover, windshield and inner front cover. Detach the throttle cable from the throttle pulley and housing (see Chapter 5A). Disconnect the wiring connectors for the handlebar switches, noting where they fit. **Note:** *When disconnecting the wiring, it is advisable to mark or tag the connectors as a reminder of where they connect.* Undo the screw and remove the cover, drawing it off the throttle cable (see illustration).

78 Installation is the reverse of removal.

### Front mudguard

79 Unscrew the bolts securing the mudguard

and draw it forwards (see illustration 9.85).
80 Installation is the reverse of removal.

### Rear hugger

81 Undo the screw securing the left-hand side of the hugger to the back of the air filter housing (see illustration 9.87).
82 Unscrew the bolts securing the right-hand side of the hugger to the swingarm, noting how they secure the brake hose guide, and manoeuvre the hugger out (see illustration 9.88).
83 Installation is the reverse of removal.

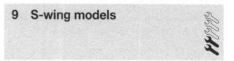

**9    S-wing models**

### Seat

1 Unlock the seat and swing it up (see illustration).
2 Undo the nuts securing the seat to the hinge and remove the seat (see illustration).
3 Installation is the reverse of removal.

### Storage compartment

4 Remove the seat. Remove the carpet (see illustration).
5 Undo the tail light bulb access panel screws and displace the panel, then disconnect the power socket and storage compartment light wiring connectors (see illustrations).

9.1 Unlock and raise the seat

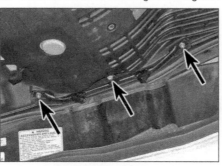

9.2 Unscrew the nuts (arrowed) and remove the seat

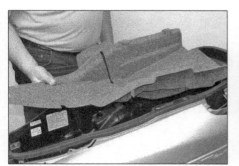

9.4 Lift the carpet out

9.5a Undo the screws (arrowed) and displace the panel . . .

9.5b . . . and disconnect the wiring from it

9.6 Displace the fusebox and relay

9.7a Release the trim clip (arrowed) and remove the cover . . .

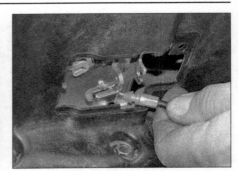

9.7b . . . then detach the cable

Also disconnect the storage compartment light switch wiring connector – do this after displacing the storage compartment for easier access if necessary.

6 Remove the battery (see Chapter 10). Displace the fusebox and starter relay from their mounts (see illustration).
7 Release the seat lock cable cover trim

clip and remove the cover (see illustration). Detach the cable from the lock mechanism (see illustration).
8 Unscrew the two bolts on the outside of the battery case (see illustration).
9 Remove the centre cover (Steps 14 to 16). Undo the two screws around the front of the compartment (see illustration).
10 Unscrew the seven bolts inside the compartment (see illustration).
11 Lift the storage compartment and draw the seat lock cable out (see illustrations).
12 Installation is the reverse of removal.

### Maintenance panel

13 To remove the access panel to the battery/fusebox/starter relay in the storage compartment, unlock and raise the seat, then remove the carpet (see illustrations 9.1 and 9.4). Undo the screws and remove the panel (see illustration). Installation is the reverse of removal.

### Centre cover

14 Unlock the seat and swing it up (see illustration 9.1).
15 Undo the screw and release the trim clip on each side (see illustration).
16 Release the tabs on each side at the back of the cover from the body cover, then release the tabs along the front and slide the cover back to release the hooks along each side from the slots in the

9.8 Unscrew the bolts (arrowed)

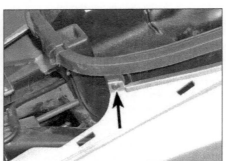

9.9 Undo the screw (arrowed) on each side

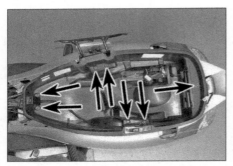

9.10 Unscrew the bolts (arrowed) . . .

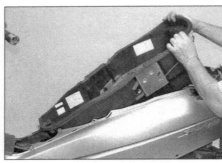

9.11a . . . then lift the storage compartment out . . .

9.11b . . . and draw the cable out

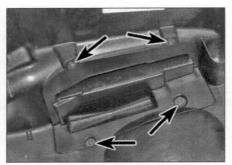

9.13 Undo the screws (arrowed) and remove the panel

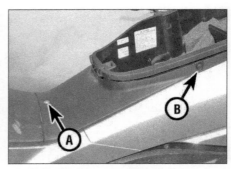

9.15 Undo the screw (A) and release the trim clip (B) on each side . . .

9.16 . . . then release the tabs and remove the cover

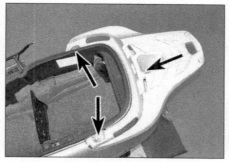

9.19 Unscrew the bolts (arrowed) and remove the rack

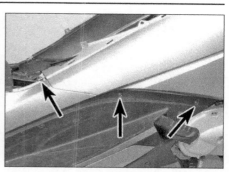

9.26a Undo the screws (arrowed) on each side . . .

9.26b . . . and the screw (arrowed) on each side . . .

9.27 . . . and the two bolts (arrowed)

body cover and remove the panel **(see illustration)**.

17 Installation is the reverse of removal.

### Luggage rack

18 Unlock the seat and swing it up **(see illustration 9.1)**.

19 Unscrew the bolts and remove the washers, then lift the rack away **(see illustration)**.

20 Installation is the reverse of removal.

### Body cover

21 Remove the seat.
22 Remove the luggage rack.
23 Remove the storage compartment.
24 Remove the centre cover.
25 Remove the seat hinge.
26 Undo the three screws on each side at the front and the screw on each side at the back **(see illustrations)**.
27 Unscrew the two bolts on the top **(see illustration)**.
28 Release the body cover from the front inner cover and floor panel on each side, then pull each side out to free the screw lugs and draw the assembly back a little **(see illustrations)**. Disconnect the tail light assembly wiring connectors and remove the body cover.
29 Installation is the reverse of removal. Make sure the wiring connectors are securely connected, and check the operation of the turn signals, brake light and tail light before riding the scooter.

### Lower covers

30 Release the floor mat locating pegs from the floor covers and remove the mats **(see illustration)**.
31 Undo the three screws along the top,

the screw to the rear of the passenger footrest, and the two bolts on the side **(see illustrations)**.
32 Release the tabs from the floor panel and the lower front cover and remove the

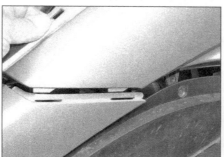

9.28a Release the tabs . . .

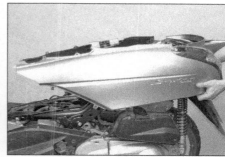

9.28b . . . and remove the cover

9.30 Release and remove the floor mat

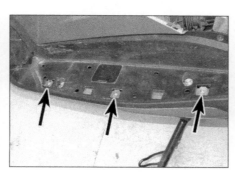

9.31a Undo the screws (arrowed) . . .

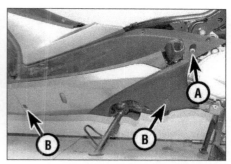

9.31b . . . the screw (A) and the bolts (B)

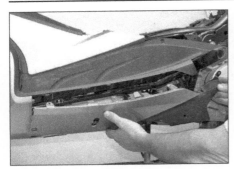

9.32 Release the tabs and remove the cover

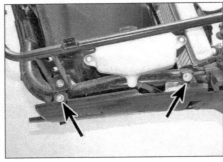

9.35 Unscrew the bolts (arrowed) on each side

9.41a Unscrew the bolts (arrowed)

9.41b Release and remove the panel

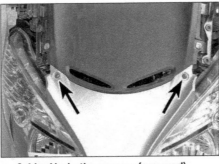

9.44a Undo the screws (arrowed) . . .

9.44b . . . then pull the panel off

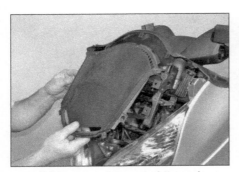

9.45a Undo the screws (arrowed) . . .

9.45b . . . and remove the panel

9.48 Release and remove the floor mat on each side

9.49a Undo the screw (arrowed) on each side . . .

cover **(see illustration)** – when removing the left-hand cover, move the sidestand as required.

33 Installation is the reverse of removal.

## Belly panel

34 Remove the lower covers.
35 Unscrew the two bolts on each side **(see illustration)**.
36 Slide the panel back to release the tab at the front, then detach the fuel drain hose and remove the belly panel out from under the scooter.
37 Installation is the reverse of removal.

## Floor panels

38 Remove the centre cover.
39 Remove the lower covers.
40 Remove the inner front panel.
41 Undo the two screws at the back **(see illustration 9.26a)**. Unscrew the two bolts **(see illustration)**. Release the panel from the frame and remove it **(see illustration)**.
42 Installation is the reverse of removal.

## Upper front panels

43 Remove the windshield (Steps 72 and 73).
44 Undo the two screws at the top of the headlight trim panel, then pull the panel away to release the snap-fit clips **(see illustrations)**.
45 Undo the two screws, then release the panel from the instrument cover **(see illustrations)**.
46 Installation is the reverse of removal.

## Lower front panel

47 Remove the headlight trim panel (Steps 43 and 44).
48 Release the floor mat locating pegs from the inner front panel and remove the mats **(see illustration)**.
49 Undo the two screws in the front, and the four screws on each side of the inner front panel **(see illustrations)**.

9.49b . . . and the four screws (arrowed) on each side

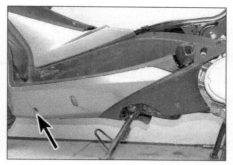

9.50a Unscrew the bolt (arrowed) on each side . . .

9.50b . . . and the bolts (arrowed) at the front

50 Unscrew the bolt on each side at the bottom and the two bolts in the front **(see illustrations)**.
51 Carefully pull the panel forwards to release the snap-fit clips, and the bottom of the panel from the belly panel tab, then manoeuvre it down and out from between the forks and the frame **(see illustration)**.
52 Installation is the reverse of removal.

### Inner front panel

53 Remove the instrument cover.
54 Remove the centre cover.
55 Undo the four screws on each side of the body cover securing it to the storage compartment, inner front panel and floor covers **(see illustrations 9.26a and b)**. Carefully release the body cover from the inner front panel and floor covers on each side **(see illustration 9.28a)**.
56 Raise the fuel filler cap cover. Unscrew the bolt next to the hinge **(see illustration)**.
57 Release the ignition switch cover by turning it anti-clockwise and draw it off the switch, noting how it locates **(see illustration)** – it may need to be eased off the tabs on the switch using a screwdriver.
58 Release the fuel hose guide peg from the grommet **(see illustration)**.
59 Release the wiring guide **(see illustration)**.
60 Release the floor mat locating pegs and remove the mats **(see illustration 9.48)**.
61 Undo the two screws in the front of the

lower front panel **(see illustration 9.49a)**.
62 Undo the two screws on each side at the back of the panel **(see illustration)**.

9.51 Release and remove the panel as described

9.57 Twist the cover anticlockwise over the tabs and draw it off the switch

63 Unscrew the two bolts on each side at the bottom **(see illustration)**.
64 Undo the three screws securing the

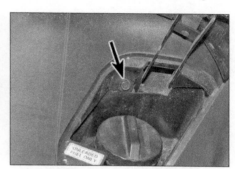

9.56 Unscrew the bolt (arrowed)

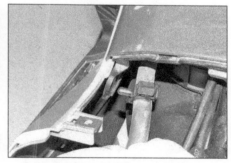

9.58 Release the fuel hose guide . . .

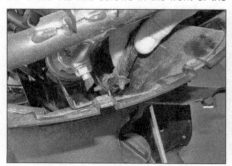

9.59 . . . and the wiring guide

9.62 Undo the screws (arrowed)

9.63 Unscrew the bolts (arrowed) on each side

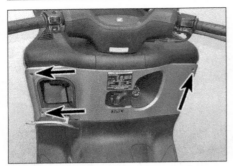

9.64a  Undo the screws (arrowed) . . .

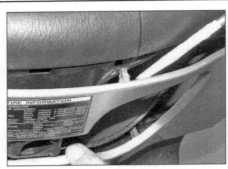

9.64b  . . . then release the snap-fit clips as
described and remove the panel

9.66  Undo the screws (arrowed) and
remove the hook

9.67a  Release the tabs and hooks . . .

9.67b  . . . and remove the panel

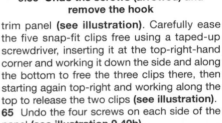

9.69  Unscrew the bolts (arrowed) and
remove the mirror

9.70a  Undo the screws (arrowed) . . .

trim panel **(see illustration)**. Carefully ease
the five snap-fit clips free using a taped-up
screwdriver, inserting it at the top-right-hand
corner and working it down the side and along
the bottom to free the three clips there, then
starting again top-right and working along the
top to release the two clips **(see illustration)**.
65  Undo the four screws on each side of the
panel **(see illustration 9.49b)**.
66  Undo the shopping bag hook screws and
remove the hook **(see illustration)**.
67  Slightly spread the front of the body cover
on each side, then draw the inner front panel
back to free its tabs and hooks from the floor
panels and remove it **(see illustrations)**.
68  Installation is the reverse of removal.

### Mirrors and mirror covers
69  Lift the rubber boot, then unscrew the two
bolts and remove the mirror **(see illustration)**.
70  Undo the two screws securing the cover,
then release the tabs and remove the cover
**(see illustrations)**.
71  Installation is the reverse of removal. To
re-position the mirror as required, slacken the
upper nut on the mirror stem, move the mirror,
then hold it and tighten the nut.

### Windshield
72  Remove the mirrors and mirror covers.
73  Undo the six screws, noting the plastic
washers, and remove the windshield **(see
illustration)**.
74  Installation is the reverse of removal.

9.70b  . . . and remove the cover

9.73  Windshield screws (arrowed)

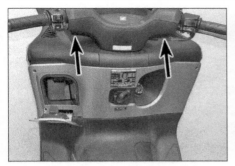

9.75a Undo the screws (arrowed)

9.75b Release the tabs and the clip and remove the cover

9.76a Undo the screws (arrowed)

## Handlebar covers

75 To remove the lower handlebar cover undo the two screws, then release the tab on each end and the snap-fit clip in the centre from the upper cover, and remove the cover (see illustrations).

76 To remove the upper handlebar cover, remove the lower cover. Undo the two screws on the underside, then release the peg from the grommet and remove the cover (see illustrations).

## Instrument cover

77 Remove the lower and upper handlebar covers and the upper front panel.

78 Refer to Step 64 and remove the trim panel from the inner front panel.

79 Unscrew the bolts and remove the bracket cross-piece (see illustration).

80 Disconnect the instrument cluster wiring connector (see illustration).

81 Undo the five screws along the back of the cover (see illustration). Release the centre section tabs and remove it (see illustration).

82 Release the two snap-fit clips on each side, then release the screw tabs along the

back from the inner front panel and remove the cover along with the instrument cluster, noting how its pegs locate in the grommets (see illustrations).

83 Installation is the reverse of removal.

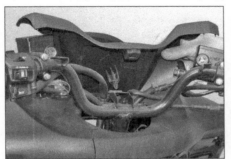

9.76b Release the peg and remove the cover

9.79 Unscrew the bolts (arrowed) and remove the cross-piece

9.80 Disconnect the wiring connector

9.81a Undo the screws (arrowed)

9.81b Remove the centre section

9.82a Release the snap-fit clips . . .

9.82b . . . and remove the cover . . .

9.82c . . . noting how the instrument cluster peg (arrowed) on each side locates

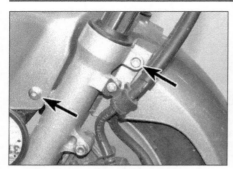

9.85 Front mudguard bolts (arrowed)

9.87 Undo the screw (arrowed) . . .

9.88 . . . and the bolts (arrowed)

### Front mudguard

84 Remove the front wheel (see Chapter 8).
85 Unscrew the bolts and manoeuvre the mudguard out **(see illustration)**.
86 Installation is the reverse of removal.

### Rear hugger

87 Undo the screw securing the left-hand side of the hugger to the back of the air filter housing **(see illustration)**.
88 Unscrew the bolts securing the right-hand side of the hugger to the swingarm, noting how they secure the brake hose guide, and manoeuvre the hugger out **(see illustration)**.
89 Installation is the reverse of removal.

# Chapter 10
# Electrical system

## Contents

## Degrees of difficulty

| | | | | |
|---|---|---|---|---|
| **Easy,** suitable for novice with little experience  | **Fairly easy,** suitable for beginner with some experience | **Fairly difficult,** suitable for competent DIY mechanic | **Difficult,** suitable for experienced DIY mechanic | **Very difficult,** suitable for expert DIY or professional  |

## Specifications

### Battery

| | |
|---|---|
| Capacity | 12 V, 6 Ah |
| Voltage | |
| Fully-charged | 13.0 to 13.2 V |
| Uncharged | below 12.3 V |
| Charging rate | |
| Normal | 0.6 A for 5 to 10 hrs |
| Quick | 3.0 A for 1 hr |

### Charging system

| | |
|---|---|
| Current leakage | |
| 2001 to 2004 SH, Dylan and @ models | 1.0 mA (max) |
| 2005-on SH and PS models | 0.2 mA (max) |
| Pantheon and S-wing models | 0.1 mA (max) |
| Alternator stator coil resistance | 0.1 to 0.5 ohms |
| Alternator output | |
| 2001 to 2004 SH, Dylan and @ models | 230 W @ 5000 rpm |
| 2005-on SH, PS, Pantheon and S-wing models | 300 W @ 5000 rpm |
| Regulated voltage output | 14.5 to 15.3 V @ 5000 rpm |

### Starter motor

| | |
|---|---|
| Brush length | |
| Standard | 10 to 10.5 mm |
| Service limit (min) | 6.5 mm |

## Fuses

| | | |
|---|---|---|
| Main | . . . . . . . . . . . . . . . . . . . . . . . . . . . . . . . . . . . . . . | 30 A |
| Others | . . . . . . . . . . . . . . . . . . . . . . . . . . . . . . . . . . . . . . | 15 A or 10 A (see Section 5) |

## Bulbs

| | | |
|---|---|---|
| Headlight | | |
| @, Pantheon and S-wing models . . . . . . . . . . . . . . . . . . . . . . . . . | 55 W x 2 |
| SH, Dylan and PS models . . . . . . . . . . . . . . . . . . . . . . . . | 60/55 W x 1 |
| Sidelight . . . . . . . . . . . . . . . . . . . . . . . . . . . . . . . . . . . . . | 5 W |
| Brake/tail light . . . . . . . . . . . . . . . . . . . . . . . . . . . . . . . . . | 21/5 W |
| Licence plate light . . . . . . . . . . . . . . . . . . . . . . . . . . . . . . . | 5 W |
| Turn signal lights. . . . . . . . . . . . . . . . . . . . . . . . . . . . . . . . | 21 W x 4 |

## Torque settings

| | | |
|---|---|---|
| Alternator rotor nut. . . . . . . . . . . . . . . . . . . . . . . . . . . . . . . . | 116 Nm |
| Alternator stator bolts. . . . . . . . . . . . . . . . . . . . . . . . . . . . . . | 12 Nm |

## 1 General information

All models have a 12 volt electrical system charged by a three-phase alternator with a separate regulator/rectifier.

The regulator maintains the charging system output within the specified range to prevent overcharging, and the rectifier converts the ac (alternating current) output of the alternator to dc (direct current) to power the lights and other electrical systems and components and to charge the battery. The alternator rotor is mounted on the right-hand end of the crankshaft.

The starter motor is mounted on the top of the crankcase. The starting system includes the motor, the battery, the relay and the various wires and switches. A safety system, either using the brake light switch(es) or a separate inhibitor switch (depending on model), prevents the engine from being started unless the rear brake lever, or on some models either brake lever, is pulled in. On models with a sidestand, the sidestand switch prevents the engine from being started if it is down.

**Note:** *Keep in mind that electrical parts, once purchased, often cannot be returned. To avoid unnecessary expense, make very sure the faulty component has been positively identified before buying a replacement part.*

## 2 Electrical system fault finding

**1** A typical electrical circuit consists of an electrical component, the switches, relays, etc, related to that component and the wiring and connectors that link the component to the battery and the frame.

**2** Before tackling any troublesome electrical circuit, first study the wiring diagram thoroughly to get a complete picture of what makes up that individual circuit. Trouble spots, for instance, can often be narrowed down by noting if other components related to that circuit are operating properly or not. If several components or circuits fail at one time, chances are the fault lies either in the fuse or in the common earth (ground) connection, as several circuits are often routed through the same fuse and earth (ground) connections.

**3** Electrical problems often stem from simple causes, such as loose or corroded connections or a blown fuse. Prior to any electrical fault finding, always visually check the condition of the fuse, wires and connections in the problem circuit. Intermittent failures can be especially frustrating, since you can't always duplicate the failure when it's convenient to test. In such situations, a good practice is to clean all connections in the affected circuit, whether or not they appear to be good – where possible use a dedicated electrical cleaning spray along with sandpaper, wire wool or other abrasive material to remove corrosion, and a dedicated electrical protection spray to prevent further problems. All of the connections and wires should also be wiggled to check for looseness which can cause intermittent failure.

**4** If you don't have a multimeter it is highly advisable to obtain one – they are not expensive and will enable a full range of electrical tests to be made. Go for a modern digital one with LCD display as they are easier to use. A continuity tester and/or test light are useful for certain electrical checks as an alternative, though are limited in their usefulness compared to a multimeter **(see illustrations)**.

### Continuity checks

**5** The term continuity describes the uninterrupted flow of electricity through an electrical circuit. Continuity can be checked with a multimeter set either to its continuity function (a beep is emitted when continuity is found), or to the resistance (ohms / $\Omega$) function, or with a dedicated continuity tester. Both instruments are powered by an internal battery, therefore the checks are made with the ignition OFF. As a safety precaution, always disconnect the battery negative (-) lead before making continuity checks, particularly if ignition switch checks are being made.

**6** If using a multimeter, select the continuity function if it has one, or the resistance (ohms)

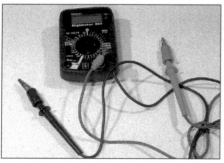

**2.4a A digital multimeter can be used for all electrical tests**

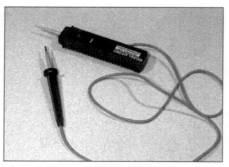

**2.4b A battery-powered continuity tester**

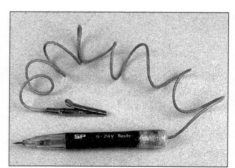

**2.4c A simple test light is useful for voltage tests**

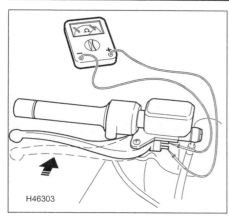

2.10 Continuity should be indicated across switch terminals when lever is operated

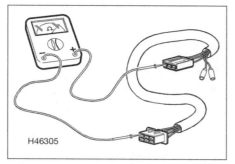

2.12 Wiring continuity check. Connect the meter probes across each end of the same wire

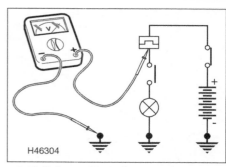

2.15 Voltage check. Connect the meter positive probe to the component and the negative probe to earth

function. Touch the meter probes together and check that a beep is emitted or the meter reads zero, which indicates continuity. If there is no continuity there will be no beep or the meter will show infinite resistance. After using the meter, always switch it OFF to conserve its battery.

7 A continuity tester can be used in the same way – its light should come on or it should beep to indicate continuity in the switch ON position, but should be off or silent in the OFF position.

8 Note that the polarity of the test probes doesn't matter for continuity checks, although care should be taken to follow specific test procedures if a diode or solid-state component is being checked.

### Switch continuity checks

9 If a switch is at fault, trace its wiring to the wiring connectors. Separate the connectors and inspect them for security and condition. A build-up of dirt or corrosion here will most likely be the cause of the problem – clean up and apply a water dispersant such as WD40, or alternatively use a dedicated contact cleaner and protection spray.

10 If using a multimeter, select the continuity function if it has one, or the resistance (ohms) function, and connect its probes to the terminals in the connector (see illustration). Simple ON/OFF type switches, such as brake light switches, only have two wires whereas combination switches, like the handlebar switches, have many wires. Study the wiring diagram to ensure that you are connecting to the correct pair of wires. Continuity should be indicated with the switch ON and no continuity with it OFF.

### Wiring continuity checks

11 Many electrical faults are caused by damaged wiring, often due to incorrect routing or chaffing on frame components. Loose, wet or corroded wire connectors can also be the cause of electrical problems.

12 A continuity check can be made on a single length of wire by disconnecting it at each end and connecting the meter or continuity tester probes to each end of the

wire (see illustration). Continuity (low or no resistance – 0 ohms) should be indicated if the wire is good. If no continuity (high resistance) is shown, suspect a broken wire.

13 To check for continuity to earth in any earth wire connect one probe of your meter or tester to the earth wire terminal in the connector and the other to the frame, engine, or battery earth (-) terminal. Continuity (low or no resistance – 0 ohms) should be indicated if the wire is good. If no continuity (high resistance) is shown, suspect a broken wire or corroded or loose earth point (see below).

### Voltage checks

14 A voltage check can determine whether power is reaching a component. Use a multimeter set to the dc voltage scale, or a test light. The test light is the cheaper component, but the meter has the advantage of being able to give a voltage reading.

15 Connect the meter or test light in parallel, i.e. across the load (see illustration).

16 First identify the relevant wiring circuit by referring to the wiring diagram at the end of this manual. If other electrical components share the same power supply (i.e. are fed from the same fuse), take note whether they are working correctly – this is useful information in deciding where to start checking the circuit.

17 If using a meter, check first that the meter leads are plugged into the correct terminals on the meter (red to positive (+), black to negative (-). Set the meter to the dc volts function, where necessary at a range suitable for the battery voltage – 0 to 20 vdc. Connect the meter red probe (+) to the power supply wire and the black probe to a good metal earth (ground) on the scooter's frame or directly to the battery negative terminal. Battery voltage should be shown on the meter with the ignition switch, and if necessary any other relevant switch, ON.

18 If using a test light, connect its positive (+) probe to the power supply terminal and its negative (-) probe to a good earth (ground) on the scooter's frame. With the switch, and if necessary any other relevant switch, ON, the test light should illuminate.

19 If no voltage is indicated, work back towards the fuse continuing to check for voltage. When you reach a point where there

is voltage, you know the problem lies between that point and your last check point.

### Earth (ground) checks

20 Earth connections are made either directly to the engine or frame via the mounting of the component, or by a separate wire into the earth circuit of the wiring harness. Alternatively a short earth wire is sometimes run from the component directly to the scooter's frame.

21 Corrosion is a common cause of a poor earth connection, as is a loose earth terminal fastener.

22 If total or multiple component failure is experienced, check the security of the main earth lead from the negative (-) terminal of the battery, the earth lead bolted to the engine, and the main earth point(s) on the frame. If corroded, dismantle the connection and clean all surfaces back to bare metal. Remake the connection and prevent further corrosion from forming by smearing battery terminal grease over the connection.

23 To check the earth of a component, use an insulated jumper wire to temporarily bypass its earth connection (see illustration) – connect one end of the jumper wire to the earth terminal or metal body of the component and the other end to the scooter's frame. If the circuit works with the jumper wire installed, the earth circuit is faulty.

24 To check an earth wire first check for corroded or loose connections, then check the wiring for continuity (Step 13) between each connector in the circuit in turn, and then to its earth point, to locate the break.

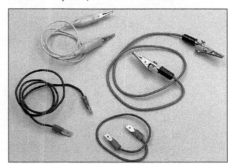

2.23 A selection of insulated jumper wires

3.2a Undo the screws (arrowed) and remove the retainer

3.2b Disconnect the negative lead first, then disconnect the positive lead (arrowed) . . .

3.2c . . . and lift the battery out

## 3 Battery removal, installation and inspection

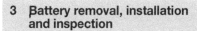

**Caution: Be extremely careful when handling or working around the battery. The electrolyte is very caustic and an explosive gas (hydrogen) is given off when the battery is charging.**

### Removal and installation

1 Make sure the ignition is switched OFF. Remove the maintenance access panel to the battery (see Chapter 9).
2 On SH and PS models undo the screws and remove the battery retainer **(see illustration)**.

3.3a On Dylan and @ models disconnect the negative lead (A) first, then disconnect the positive lead (B)

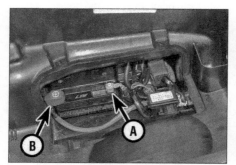

3.4a On Pantheon and S-wing models disconnect the negative lead (A) first, then disconnect the positive lead (B) . . .

Unscrew the negative (–) terminal bolt first and disconnect the lead from the battery **(see illustration)**. Lift up the red insulating cover to access the positive (+) terminal, then unscrew the bolt and disconnect the lead. Lift the battery out **(see illustration)**.
3 On Dylan and @ models unscrew the negative (–) terminal bolt first and disconnect the lead from the battery **(see illustration)**. Lift up the red insulating cover to access the positive (+) terminal, then unscrew the bolt and disconnect the lead. Unscrew the battery retainer bolt and remove the battery **(see illustration)**.
4 On Pantheon and S-wing models unscrew the negative (–) terminal bolt first and disconnect the lead from the battery **(see illustration)**. Lift up the red insulating cover to

3.3b Unscrew the bolt (arrowed) and remove the retainer, then remove the battery

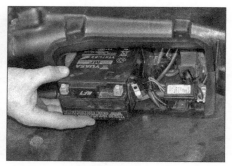

3.4b . . . and draw the battery out

access the positive (+) terminal, then unscrew the bolt and disconnect the lead. Draw the battery out **(see illustration)**.
5 On installation, clean the battery terminals and lead ends with a wire brush, fine sandpaper or steel wool. Reconnect the leads, connecting the positive (+) terminal first.

> **HAYNES HiNT** *Battery corrosion can be kept to a minimum by applying a layer of battery terminal grease or petroleum jelly (Vaseline) to the terminals after the leads have been connected. DO NOT use a mineral based grease.*

6 Where removed fit the battery retainer **(see illustration 3.2a or 3.3b)**. Install the maintenance access panel (see Chapter 9).

### Inspection

7 The battery fitted to all models covered in this manual is of the maintenance-free (sealed) type, therefore requiring no regular maintenance. However, the following checks should still be performed.
8 Check the battery terminals and leads are tight and free of corrosion. If corrosion is evident, clean the terminals as described above, then protect them from further corrosion (see **Haynes Hint**).
9 Keep the battery case clean to prevent current leakage, which can discharge the battery over a period of time (especially when it sits unused). Wash the outside of the case with a solution of baking soda and water. Rinse the battery thoroughly, then dry it.
10 Look for cracks in the case and replace the battery with a new one if any are found. If acid has been spilled on the frame or battery box, neutralise it with a baking soda and water solution, dry it thoroughly, then touch up any damaged paint.
11 If the scooter sits unused for long periods of time, disconnect the cables from the battery terminals, negative (–) terminal first. Refer to Section 4 and charge the battery once every month to six weeks.
12 Check the condition of the battery by measuring the voltage present at the battery

terminals **(see illustration)**. Connect the voltmeter positive (+) probe to the battery positive (+) terminal, and the negative (–) probe to the battery negative (–) terminal. When fully-charged there should be 13.0 to 13.2 volts present. If the voltage falls below 12.3 volts remove the battery (see above), and recharge it as described below in Section 4.

## 4  Battery charging

*Caution: Be extremely careful when handling or working around the battery. The electrolyte is very caustic and an explosive gas (hydrogen) is given off when the battery is charging.*

**1** Remove the battery (see Section 3). Connect the charger to the battery, making sure that the positive (+) lead on the charger is connected to the positive (+) terminal on the battery, and the negative (–) lead is connected to the negative (–) terminal **(see illustration)**.

**2** Honda recommend that the battery is charged at the normal rate specified at the beginning of the Chapter. Exceeding this figure can cause the battery to overheat, buckling the plates and rendering it useless. Few owners will have access to an expensive current controlled charger, so if a normal domestic charger is used check that after a possible initial peak, the charge rate falls to a safe level. If the battery becomes hot during charging **stop**. Further charging will cause damage. **Note:** *In emergencies the battery can be charged at the quick rate specified. However, this is not recommended and the normal charging rate is by far the safer method of charging the battery.*

**3** If the recharged battery discharges rapidly if left disconnected it is likely that an internal short caused by physical damage or sulphation has occurred. A new battery will

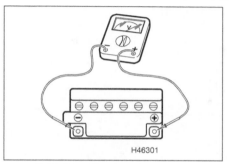

**3.12  Checking battery voltage**

be required. A sound item will tend to lose its charge at about 1% per day.

**4** Install the battery (see Section 3).

**5** If the scooter sits unused for long periods of time, charge the battery once every month to six weeks and leave it disconnected.

## 5  Fuses and main relay

**1** If one particular electrical circuit or component fails to work, i.e. the brake lights or the horn, check the individual fuse for that

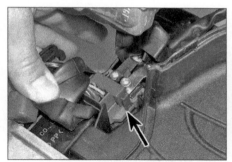

**5.3a  Starter relay (arrowed) – SH and PS models . . .**

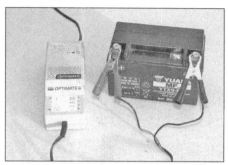

**4.1  Battery connected to a charger**

circuit. If the complete lighting circuits fail at the same time, check the main relay. If there are no electrical systems working at all, check the main fuse.

### Fuses

**2** The electrical system is protected by fuses of different ratings. The main fuse is integral with the starter relay. The other fuses are all housed in the fusebox.

**3** To access the main fuse remove the maintenance access panel to the battery (see Chapter 9). Disconnect the starter relay wiring connector **(see illustrations)**.

**4** To access the fusebox, on 2001 to 2008 SH

**5.3b  . . . disconnect the relay wiring connector to access the main fuse (arrowed)**

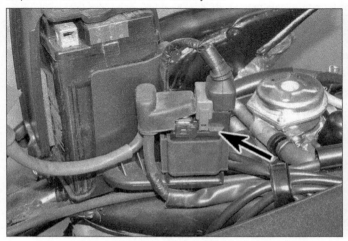

**5.3c  Starter relay (arrowed) – Dylan and @ models**

**5.3d  Starter relay (arrowed) – Pantheon and S-wing models**

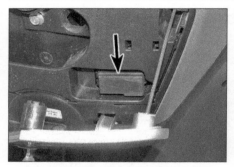

5.4a Fusebox (arrowed) – SH and PS models . . .

5.4b . . . unclip the lid to access the fuses

5.4c Fusebox (arrowed) – Dylan and @ models . . .

5.4d . . . unclip the lid to access the fuses

5.4e Fusebox (arrowed) – Pantheon and S-wing models

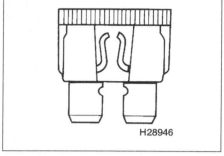

5.5 A blown fuse can be identified by a break in its element

models and PS models open the glove box, on later SH models remove the upper front panel (see Chapter 9), and on Dylan, @, Pantheon and S-wing models remove the maintenance access panel to the battery (see Chapter 9) **(see illustrations)**. On S-wing models with ABS there are two fuseboxes. Unclip the fusebox lid to expose the fuses – the location, identity and rating of each fuse is marked on a s ticker on the lid.

**5** The fuses can be removed and checked visually. If you can't pull the fuse out with your fingertips, use a pair of suitable pliers. A blown fuse is easily identified by a break in the element **(see illustration)**. Each fuse is clearly marked with its rating and must only be replaced by a fuse of the correct rating. A spare fuse of each rating is housed in the box. If a spare fuse is used, always replace it with

a new one so that a spare of each rating is carried on the bike at all times.

 *Warning: Never put in a fuse of a higher rating or bridge the terminals with any other substitute, however temporary it may be. Serious damage may be done to the circuit, or a fire may start.*

**6** If the new fuse blows immediately check the wiring circuit very carefully for evidence of a short-circuit. Look for bare wires and chafed, melted or burned insulation.

**7** Occasionally a fuse will blow or cause an open-circuit for no obvious reason. Corrosion of the fuse ends and fusebox terminals may occur and cause poor fuse contact. If this happens, remove the corrosion with a wire brush or emery paper, then spray the fuse end and terminals with electrical contact cleaner.

### Main relay

**8** The main relay controls power from the ignition switch to the fuses (except the main fuse), thereby controlling all lighting, signalling and instrumentation functions. When the ignition is switched ON the relay should click. If the relay is suspected of being faulty, the easiest way to tell is to substitute it with another one, if available. To access the relay, on 2001 to 2004 SH models open the glove box; on 2005 to 2008 SH models and PS models open the glove box then displace its inner panel **(see illustration)**; on later SH, Dylan and @ models remove the upper front panel (see Chapter 9); on Pantheon and S-wing models remove the storage compartment (see Chapter 9). Displace the relay from its mount and disconnect the wiring connector **(see illustrations)**.

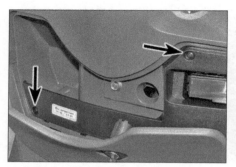

5.8a On SH and PS models undo the screws (arrowed) and remove the panel

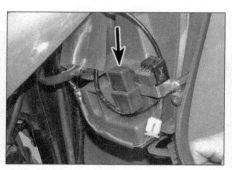

5.8b Main relay (arrowed) – Dylan models

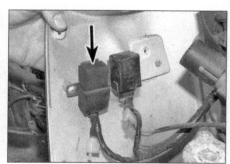

5.8c Main relay (arrowed) – @ models

**5.8d Main relay (arrowed) – Pantheon and S-wing models**

**9** If a substitute is not available, remove the suspect one and test it as follows: set a multimeter to the ohms x 1 scale and connect it across the relay's red and red/yellow wire terminals. There should be no continuity (infinite resistance). Using a fully-charged 12 volt battery and two insulated jumper wires, connect the positive (+) terminal of the battery to the red/black wire terminal on the relay, and the negative (–) terminal to the green wire terminal. At this point the relay should be heard to click and the meter read 0 ohms (continuity). If this is the case the relay is good. If the relay does not click when battery voltage is applied and indicates no continuity (infinite resistance) across its terminals, it is faulty and must be replaced with a new one.

**10** If the relay is good, check for battery voltage at the red wire terminal in the connector with the ignition OFF, and at the red/black wire terminal with the ignition ON. Also check for continuity to earth in the green wire, and for continuity to the fusebox in the red/yellow wire, referring to the wiring diagrams at the end of the Chapter. Also make sure that all the terminals in the connectors are clean and secure. Repair or renew the wiring or connectors as necessary.

## 6  Lighting system check

**1** The battery provides power for operation of the lights. If a light fails first check the bulb (see relevant Section), and the bulb terminals in the holder. If none of the lights work, always check battery voltage before proceeding. Low battery voltage indicates either a faulty battery or a defective charging system. Refer to Section 3 for battery checks and Section 27 for charging system tests. Also, check the fuses and main relay (section 5) – if there is more than one problem at the same time, it is likely to be a fault relating to a multi-function component, such as one of the fuses governing more than one circuit, or the main relay or the ignition switch. When checking for a blown filament in a bulb, it is advisable to back up a visual check with a continuity test of the filament as it is not always apparent

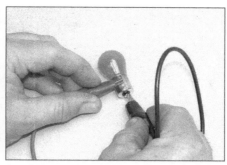

**6.1 Checking a bulb filament for continuity**

that a bulb has blown **(see illustration)**. When testing for continuity, remember that on single terminal bulbs it is the metal body of the bulb that is the earth (ground).

### Headlight

**2** All models have either one or two twin filament bulbs. If one headlight beam fails to work, first check the bulb (see Section 7). If both headlight beams fail to work, first check the fuse (see Section 5), and then the bulb(s) (see Section 7). If they are good, the problem lies in the wiring or connectors, the light switch (where fitted), or the dimmer switch. Refer to Section 20 for the switch testing procedures, and also to electrical system fault finding (Section 2) and the wiring diagrams at the end of this Chapter.

**3** If the bulb is good, check for battery voltage at the blue or white wire terminal (according to beam) on the headlight wiring connector with the ignition ON. If voltage is present, check for continuity to earth (ground) in the green wire from the wiring connector. If no voltage is indicated, check the wiring and connectors in the circuit, referring to electrical system fault finding (Section 2) and the wiring diagrams at the end of this Chapter.

### Tail light/sidelight(s)

**4** If the tail light fails to work, first check the bulb (Section 9 or 7), then the fuse (Section 5). If they are good, disconnect the tail light or sidelight wiring connector, and check for battery voltage at the brown or black/brown wire terminal (according to model) on the loom side of the connector with the ignition switch ON. If voltage is present, check for continuity to earth (ground) in the green wire from the wiring connector. If no voltage is indicated, check the wiring and connectors in the circuit, referring to electrical system fault finding (Section 2) and the wiring diagrams at the end of this Chapter.

### Brake light

**5** If the brake light fails to work, first check the bulb (Section 9), then the fuse (Section 5). If they are good disconnect the tail light wiring connector, and check for battery voltage at the green/yellow wire terminal on the loom side of the connector, first with the front brake

lever pulled in, then with the rear brake lever pulled in. If voltage is present with one brake on but not the other, then the switch or its wiring is faulty. If voltage is present in both cases, check for continuity to earth (ground) in the green wire from the wiring connector. If no voltage is indicated, check the wiring and connectors between the brake light and the brake switches, the fuse, and the ignition switch, then check the switches themselves. Refer to Section 14 for the switch testing procedures, to electrical system fault finding (Section 2) and to the wiring diagrams at the end of this Chapter.

### Licence plate light (SH, Pantheon and S-wing models)

**6** If the licence plate light bulb fails to work, first check the bulb (Section 9), then the fuse (Section 5). If they are good disconnect the licence plate light wiring connector and check for battery voltage at the brown or black/brown wire terminal (according to model) on the loom side of the wiring connector with the ignition switch ON. If voltage is present, check for continuity to earth (ground) in the green wire from the wiring connector. If no voltage is indicated, check the wiring and connectors in the license plate light circuit, referring to the wiring diagrams at the end of this Chapter.

### Turn signals

**7** See Section 11.

## 7  Headlight and sidelight bulbs

**Note:** *The headlight bulbs are of the quartz-halogen type. Do not touch the bulb glass as skin acids will shorten the bulb's service life. If the bulb is accidentally touched, it should be wiped carefully when cold with a rag soaked in methylated spirit and dried before fitting.*

⚠ *Warning: Allow the bulb time to cool before removing it if the headlight has just been on.*

### Headlight

**1** On SH and PS models remove the front handlebar cover (see Chapter 9). Remove the rubber dust cover **(see illustration)**.

**7.1a Remove the dust cover . . .**

7.1b ... disconnect the wiring connector ...

7.1c ... release the retainer (shown) or clip ...

7.1d ... and remove the bulb

Disconnect the wiring connector **(see illustration)**. Either turn the bulb retainer anti-clockwise, or release the bulb retaining clip, noting how it fits, according to type **(see**

illustration). Withdraw the bulb, noting how it locates **(see illustration)**.
**2** On Dylan, @, and Pantheon models remove the upper front panel (see Chapter 9). On

@ models unscrew the headlight mounting bolts and displace the headlight **(see illustration)**. Remove the rubber dust cover **(see illustrations)**. Disconnect the wiring connector. Either turn the bulb retainer anti-clockwise, or release the bulb retaining clip, noting how it fits, according to type **(see illustration 7.1c)**. Withdraw the bulb, noting how it locates **(see illustration 7.1d)**.
**3** On S-wing models undo the three screws securing the trim panel to the inner front panel **(see illustration)**. Carefully ease the five snap-fit clips free using a taped-up screwdriver, inserting it at the top-right-hand corner and working it down the side and along the bottom to free the three clips there, then starting again top-right and working along the top to release the two clips **(see illustration)**. If after removing the panel you find that access to the bulbs via the apertures is too

7.2a On @ models unscrew the bolt (arrowed) on each side and tilt the headlight forwards

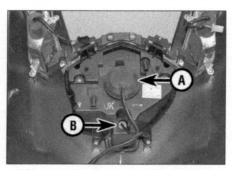

7.2b Headlight bulb cover (A), sidelight bulb (B) – Dylan models

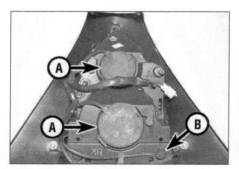

7.2c Headlight bulb covers (A), sidelight bulb (B) – Pantheon models

7.2d Remove the cover to access the wiring connector(s) and bulb

7.3a Undo the screws (arrowed) ...

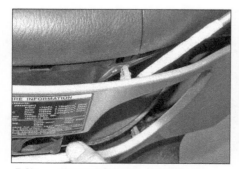

7.3b ... then release the snap-fit clips as described and remove the panel ...

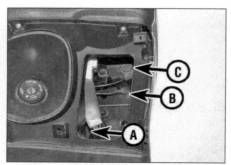

7.3c ... then access the headlight (A), sidelight (B) and turn signal (C) bulbs

7.3d Remove the dust cover ...

**7.3e . . . disconnect the wiring connector . . .**

**7.3f . . . release the clip . . .**

**7.3g . . . and remove the bulb**

restricted for you, remove the upper front panels (see Chapter 9). Remove the rubber dust cover **(see illustrations)**. Disconnect the wiring connector **(see illustration)**. Release the bulb retaining clip, noting how it fits **(see illustration)**. Withdraw the bulb, noting how it locates **(see illustration)**.

**4** Fit the new bulb in reverse order.

**HAYNES HiNT**  *Always use a paper towel or dry cloth when handling new bulbs to prevent injury if the bulb should break and to increase bulb life.*

**5** Check the operation of the headlight.

### Sidelight

**6** On 2001 to 2004 SH and all PS models remove the front handlebar cover (see Chapter 9). Carefully pull the bulb holder out of the headlight, then pull the bulb out of the holder **(see illustrations)**.

**7** On 2005-on SH models remove the upper front panel (see Chapter 9). Carefully pull the bulb holder out of the turn signal/sidelight unit, then pull the bulb out of the holder **(see illustrations)**.

**8** On Dylan and Pantheon models remove the upper front panel (see Chapter 9). Carefully pull the bulb holder out of the headlight, then pull the bulb out of the holder **(see illustration 7.2b or c)**.

**9** On @ models access the sidelight from the underside of the headlight. Carefully pull the bulb holder out of the headlight, then pull the bulb out of the holder.

**7.6a Withdraw the bulb holder . . .**

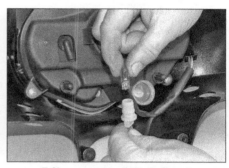

**7.6b . . . and pull the bulb out**

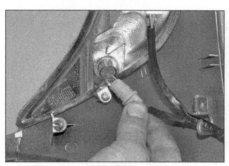

**7.7a Withdraw the bulb holder . . .**

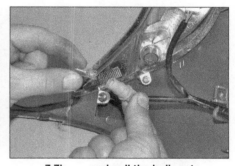

**7.7b . . . and pull the bulb out**

**10** On S-wing models undo the three screws securing the trim panel to the inner front panel **(see illustration 7.3a)**. Carefully ease the five snap-fit clips free using a taped-up screwdriver, inserting it at the top-right-hand corner and working it down the side and along the bottom to free the three clips there, then starting again top-right and working along the

top to release the two clips **(see illustration 7.3b)**. Carefully pull the bulb holder out of the headlight, then pull the bulb out of the holder **(see illustration 7.3c)**.

**11** Fit the new bulb in reverse order.

**12** Check the operation of the sidelight.

 **8  Headlight**

### Removal

**1** On SH and PS models remove the front handlebar cover (see Chapter 9). Undo the screws securing the headlight and lift it out **(see illustration)**.

**2** On Dylan models remove the lower front panel (see Chapter 9). Undo the screws securing the headlight and lift it out **(see illustration)**.

**3** On @ models remove the upper front panel (see Chapter 9). Disconnect the headlight

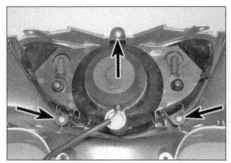

**8.1  Headlight screws (arrowed) – SH models**

**8.2  Headlight screws (arrowed) – Dylan models**

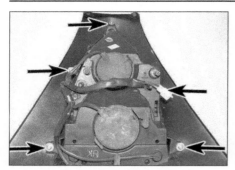

**8.4 Headlight screws (arrowed) –
Pantheon models**

**8.5a Disconnect the wiring connector**

**8.5b Undo the screws (arrowed) on each
side**

wiring connector. Unscrew the headlight mounting bolts and remove the headlight **(see illustration 7.2a)**.

4 On Pantheon models remove the upper front panel (see Chapter 9). Undo the screws securing the headlight and lift it out **(see**

illustration).

5 On S-wing models remove the upper front panels and the inner front panel (see Chapter 9). Disconnect the headlight wiring connector **(see illustration)**. Undo the three screws along each rear side **(see illustration)**. Unscrew the

centre bolt in the front and lift the headlight assembly out, noting how the pegs locate in the grommets **(see illustrations)**.

6 If required remove the headlight bulb(s) and the sidelight bulbholder(s) (see Section 7), and free the wiring from any ties, noting its routing. On S-wing models separate the headlight units if required **(see illustration)**.

### Installation

7 Installation is the reverse of removal. Make sure all the wiring is correctly routed, connected and secured. Check the operation of the headlight(s) and sidelight(s). Check the headlight aim.

### Headlight aim

**Note:** *An improperly adjusted headlight may cause problems for oncoming traffic or provide poor, unsafe illumination of the road ahead. Before adjusting the headlight aim, be sure to consult with local traffic laws.*

8 The headlight beams can adjusted vertically. Before making any adjustment, check that the tyre pressures are correct and the suspension is adjusted as required. Make any adjustments to the headlight aim with the machine on level ground, with the fuel tank half full and with an assistant sitting on the seat. If the bike is usually ridden with a passenger on the back, have a second assistant to do this.

9 On SH and PS models adjustment is made by turning the adjuster screw on the underside of the headlight **(see illustrations)**.

10 On Dylan and @ models open the glove compartment – adjustment is made by turning the adjuster screw inside **(see illustration)**.

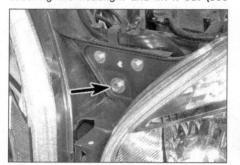

**8.5c Unscrew the bolt (arrowed) . . .**

**8.5d . . . and remove the headlight
assembly . . .**

**8.5e . . . noting how it locates**

**8.6 Unscrew the bolts and separate each
unit if required**

**8.9a Headlight adjuster (arrowed) –
SH models**

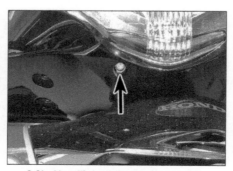

**8.9b Headlight adjuster (arrowed) –
PS models**

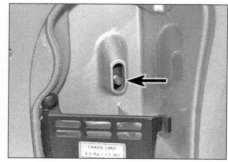

**8.10 Headlight adjuster (arrowed) –
@ models**

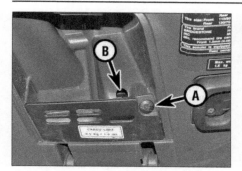

**8.11 Release the trim clip (A) and remove the guard to access the adjuster (B)**

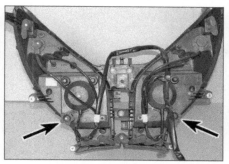

**8.12 Headlight adjusters (arrowed)**

**9.1a Undo the screws (arrowed – PS models) . . .**

**11** On Pantheon models open the glove compartment, then release the trim clip and remove the guard – adjustment is made by turning the adjuster screw inside (**see illustration**).

**12** On S-wing models adjustment of each headlight unit is made by turning the adjuster knob on the back of each unit, which are accessed by reaching up from below the headlight (**see illustration**).

| 9 | Brake/tail light bulb and licence plate bulb |
|---|---|

**Note:** *It is a good idea to use a paper towel or dry cloth when handling the new bulb to prevent injury if it breaks, and to increase bulb life.*

### Brake/tail light bulbs

**1** On SH, Dylan, @ and PS models undo

**9.1b . . . and remove the lens**

the screws and remove the lens (**see illustrations**). Carefully push the bulb in and turn it anti-clockwise to release it (**see illustration**).

**2** On Pantheon and S-wing models unlock and raise the seat (**see illustration**). Undo

**9.1c Release and remove the bulb**

the tail light bulb access panel screws and displace the panel (**see illustration**) – if required disconnect the power socket and storage compartment light wiring connectors (**see illustration**). Turn the bulbholder anti-clockwise to release it. Carefully push the bulb

**9.2a Unlock and raise the seat**

**9.2b Undo the screws (arrowed) and displace the panel . . .**

**9.2c . . . and disconnect the wiring connectors if required**

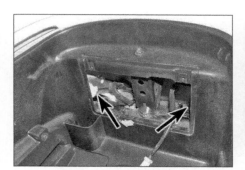

**9.2d Reach inside to access the bulb holders . . .**

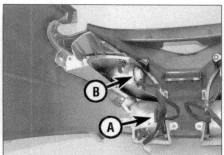

**9.2e . . . for the brake and tail light (A) and the turn signal (B) – S-wing models**

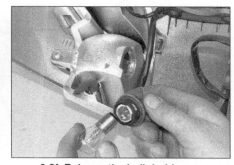

**9.2f Release the bulb holder . . .**

9.2g  . . . then release the bulb from it

9.4  Undo the screw (arrowed) and detach the housing

in and turn it anti-clockwise to release it **(see illustrations)**.
3 Fit the new bulb in reverse order. On SH, Dylan, @ and PS models do not over-tighten the screws as it is easy to strip the threads or crack the lens.

### Licence plate light bulb (SH, Pantheon and S-wing models)

4 Undo the screw and remove the light housing **(see illustration)**.
5 Carefully pull the bulbholder out, then pull the bulb out of its socket **(see illustrations)**.
6 Fit the new bulb in reverse order.

9.5a  Pull the bulb holder out . . .

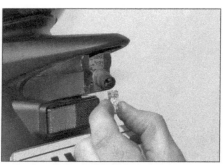

9.5b  . . . then pull the bulb out of the holder

## 10  Tail light

1 Remove the body cover (see Chapter 9).
2 On @ models disconnect the tail light wiring connector, then unscrew the bolt on each side and remove the tail light **(see illustrations)**.
3 On all other models undo the screws securing the tail light unit(s) and remove them from the body cover **(see illustrations)**.
4 Installation is the reverse of removal. Check the operation of the tail and brake lights.

10.2a  Disconnect the relevant wiring connector in the boot (arrowed) . . .

10.2b  . . . then unscrew the bolt (arrowed) on each side

## 11  Turn signal circuit check

1 Most turn signal problems are the result of a burned out bulb or corroded socket. This is especially true when the turn signals function on one side (although possibly too quickly), but fail to work on the other side. If this is the case, first check the bulbs, the sockets and the wiring connectors. If all the turn signals fail to work, first check the fuse (see Section 5), and then the relay (see below). If they are good, the problem lies in the wiring or connectors, or

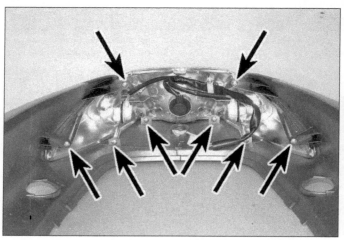

10.3a  Tail light unit screws (arrowed) – SH models

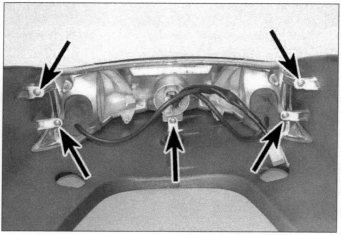

10.3b  Tail light unit screws (arrowed) – Dylan models

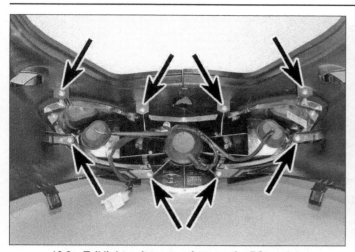

10.3c Tail light unit screws (arrowed) – PS models

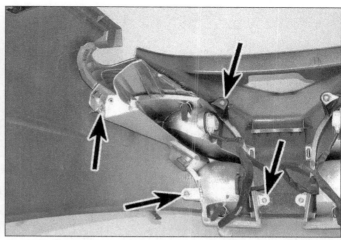

10.3d Tail light unit screws (arrowed) – S-wing models (Pantheon similar)

the switch. Refer to Section 20 for the switch testing procedures, and also to the wiring diagrams at the end of this Chapter.

**2** To access the relay, on 2001 to 2004 SH models open the glove box; on 2005 to 2008 SH models and PS models open the glove box then displace its inner panel **(see illustration 5.8a)**; on later SH, Dylan and @ models remove the upper front panel (see Chapter 9); on Pantheon models remove the inner front handlebar cover (see Chapter 9); on S-wing models remove the upper front panels (see Chapter 9). Displace the relay from its mount

and disconnect the wiring connector **(see illustrations)**.

**3** Check for battery voltage at the black/brown wire terminal on the loom side of the connector with the ignition ON. If no voltage is present, check the wiring from the relay to the ignition (main) switch (via the fuse) for continuity.

**4** If voltage was present, short between the black/brown and grey wire terminals on the connector using a jumper wire. Turn the ignition ON and operate the turn signal switch. If the turn signals come on, the relay is confirmed faulty.

**5** If the turn signals do not come on, check the grey wire for continuity to the left-hand switch housing, and the green wire for continuity to earth. Repair or replace the wiring or connectors as required.

**6** If all is good so far, or if the turn signals work on one side but not the other, check the wiring between the left-hand switch housing and the turn signals themselves. Repair or renew the wiring or connectors as necessary.

## 12 Turn signal bulbs

**Note:** *It is a good idea to use a paper towel or dry cloth when handling the new bulb to prevent injury if the bulb should break and to increase bulb life.*

### Front

**1** On 2001 to 2004 SH and all Dylan, @ and PS models undo the screw securing the lens and detach the lens from the housing, noting how it fits **(see illustration)**. Push the bulb into the holder and twist it anti-clockwise to remove it **(see illustration)**.

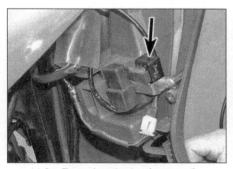

11.2a Turn signal relay (arrowed) – Dylan models

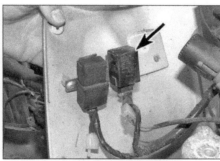

11.2b Turn signal relay (arrowed) – @ models

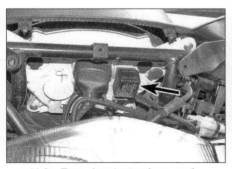

11.2c Turn signal relay (arrowed) – Pantheon and S-wing models

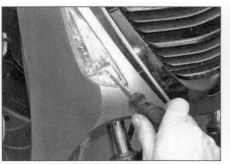

12.1a Undo the screw and remove the lens

12.1b Release the bulb and replace it with a new one

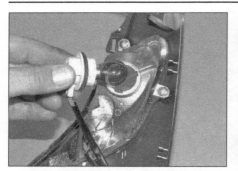

12.2a Release the bulb holder . . .

12.2b . . . then release the bulb from it

12.3 Turn signal bulb holder (arrowed)

12.6a Undo the screw and remove the lens

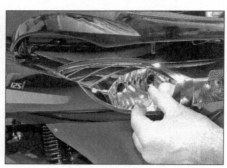

12.6b Release the bulb and replace it with a new one

2 On 2005-on SH models remove the upper front panel (see Chapter 9). Turn the bulbholder anti-clockwise to release it **(see illustration)**. Carefully push the bulb in and turn it anti-clockwise to release it **(see illustration)**.

3 On Pantheon models remove the upper front panel (see Chapter 9). Turn the bulbholder

anti-clockwise to release it **(see illustration)**. Push the bulb into the holder and twist it anti-clockwise to remove it.

4 On S-wing models undo the three screws securing the trim panel to the inner front panel **(see illustration 7.3a)**. Carefully ease the five snap-fit clips free using a taped-up screwdriver,

inserting it at the top-right-hand corner and working it down the side and along the bottom to free the three clips there, then starting again top-right and working along the top to release the two clips **(see illustration 7.3b)**. Turn the bulbholder anti-clockwise to release it. Push the bulb into the holder and twist it anti-clockwise to remove it **(see illustration 7.3c)**.

5 Fit the new bulb in reverse order. On 2001 to 2004 SH and all Dylan, @ and PS models do not over-tighten the screw as it is easy to strip the threads or crack the lens.

### Rear

6 On SH, Dylan, @ and PS models undo the screw and remove the lens **(see illustration)**. Carefully push the bulb in and turn it anti-clockwise to release it **(see illustration)**.

7 On Pantheon and S-wing models unlock and raise the seat **(see illustration 9.2a)**. Undo the tail light bulb access panel screws and displace the panel **(see illustration 9.2b)** – if required disconnect the power socket and storage compartment light wiring connectors **(see illustration 9.2c)**. Turn the bulbholder anti-clockwise to release it **(see illustrations 9.2d and e)**. Carefully push the bulb in and turn it anti-clockwise to release it.

8 Fit the new bulb in reverse order. On SH, Dylan, @ and PS models do not over-tighten the screw as it is easy to strip the threads or crack the lens.

### 13 Turn signal assemblies

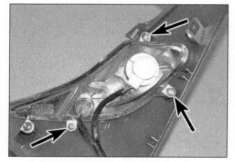

13.3a Turn signal screws (arrowed) – 2005-on SH models

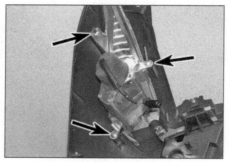

13.3b Turn signal screws (arrowed) – Dylan models

13.3c Turn signal screws (arrowed) – @ models

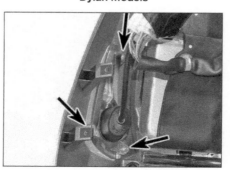

13.3d Turn signal screws (arrowed) – PS models

### Front turn signals

1 On 2001 to 2004 SH and @ models remove the upper front panel (see Chapter 9). On later SH models remove the lower front panel (see Chapter 9). On Dylan and PS models remove the inner front panel (see Chapter 9). On Pantheon models remove the upper front panel, and if required for improved access the inner front panel (see Chapter 9). On S-wing models the front turn signals are part of the headlight assembly (see Section 8).

2 Where necessary (i.e. the turn signal is not mounted in a panel that has been removed) disconnect the turn signal wiring connector.

3 Undo the turn signal screws and remove it from the panel **(see illustrations)**.

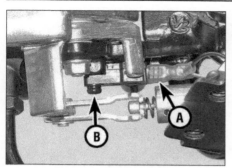

**14.2a Front brake switch wiring connectors (A) and mounting screw (B)**

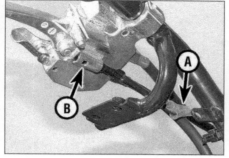

**14.2b Rear brake switch connectors (A) and retaining clip (B) – drum brake models**

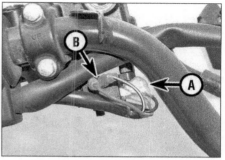

**14.2c Rear brake switch wiring connectors (A), inhibitor switch connectors (B) . . .**

4 Installation is the reverse of removal. Check the operation of the turn signals.

### Rear turn signals

5 The turn signals are part of the tail light unit (see Section 10).

## 14 Brake light switches

### Circuit check

1 Before checking the switches, and if not already done, check the brake light circuit (see Section 6).
2 The switch is mounted on the underside of the brake master cylinder or drum brake equalizer mechanism – remove the handlebar cover(s) as required according to model for access (see Chapter 9). Disconnect the switch wiring connectors **(see illustrations)** – on Pantheon and S-wing models and 2009-on SH models with a rear disc brake, where the rear brake light switch is integral with the starter inhibitor switch, the brake light switch connectors are the ones on the side of the switch, not at the back **(see illustrations)**.
3 Using a continuity tester, connect the probes to the terminals of the switch, or to the terminals in the switch side connectors.

With the brake lever at rest, there should be no continuity. With the brake lever applied, there should be continuity. If the switch does not behave as described, replace it with a new one.
4 If the switches are good, check for voltage at the black wire terminal on the loom side with the ignition switch ON – there should be battery voltage. If there's no voltage present, check the wiring between the connector and the ignition switch via the fusebox (see the wiring diagrams at the end of this Chapter). If voltage is present, check the green/yellow (rear) wire for continuity to the brake light wiring connector, referring to the relevant wiring diagram. Repair or replace the wiring or connectors as necessary.

### Switch replacement

5 The switch is mounted on the underside of the brake master cylinder or drum brake equalizer mechanism – remove the front cover(s) as required according to model for access (see Chapter 9). Disconnect the switch wiring connectors **(see illustrations 14.2a, b and c)** – on Pantheon and S-wing models and 2009-on SH models with rear disc brake also disconnect the starter inhibitor switch wiring.
6 Either undo the screw(s) securing the switch and remove it, or press in the retaining clip and pull the switch out of its housing, according to model **(see illustrations 14.2a, b, c and d)**.

7 Installation is the reverse of removal. Make sure the switch is correctly located before tightening the screw. The switch isn't adjustable.

## 15 Instrument cluster

### Removal

1 On 2001 to 2004 SH models remove the handlebar covers (see Chapter 9). Disconnect the wiring connectors for the handlebar switches in the rear cover, noting where they fit. **Note:** *When disconnecting the wiring, it is advisable to mark or tag the connectors as a reminder of where they connect.* Undo the instrument cluster screws and lift it out of the rear cover.
2 On 2005-on SH models remove the handlebar covers (see Chapter 9). Disconnect the brake light switch wiring connectors **(see illustrations 14.2a and b)**. Disconnect the instrument cluster/handlebar switch loom wiring connectors. Remove the in-fill panel at the front of the inner front panel by sliding it forwards **(see illustration)**. Release the instrument cluster/handlebar switch loom from any ties. Disconnect the speedometer cable **(see illustration)**.
3 On Dylan models remove the handlebar covers (see Chapter 9). Undo the instrument

**14.2d . . . and switch mounting screws (arrowed) – Pantheon and S-wing models**

**15.2a Release and remove the panel**

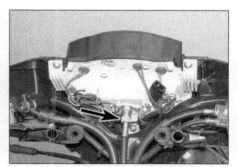

**15.2b Unscrew the ring (arrowed) and detach the cable**

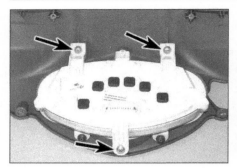

15.3 Instrument cluster screws (arrowed)

15.4a Unscrew the ring (arrowed) and detach the cable – @ models

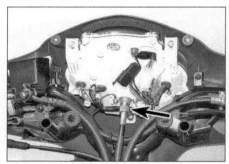

15.4b Unscrew the ring (arrowed) and detach the cable – PS models

cluster screws and lift it out of the rear cover **(see illustration)**.

4 On @ and PS models remove the handlebar covers (see Chapter 9). Disconnect the brake light switch wiring connectors **(see illustrations 14.2a and b)**. Disconnect the instrument cluster/handlebar switch loom wiring connectors. Release the instrument cluster/handlebar switch loom from any ties. Disconnect the speedometer cable **(see illustrations)**. Lift the instrument cluster out along with the sub-loom, noting its routing as you draw it out.

5 On Pantheon and S-wing models remove the instrument cover (see Chapter 9). Undo the instrument cluster screws and lift it out of the cover **(see illustration)**.

### Installation

6 Installation is the reverse of removal. Make sure all wiring is correctly routed and all connectors are secure.

## 16 Instruments check

1 Where necessary refer to Section 15 for access to the instrument cluster wiring connector for your model.

### Power circuit check

2 If none of the instruments or displays are working, first check the fuse (see Section 5).
3 Next check for battery voltage at the black/brown wire terminal in the loom side

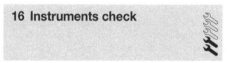

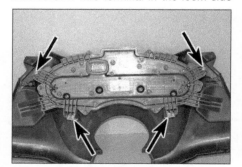

15.5 Instrument cluster screws (arrowed) – S-wing models

of the relevant (where there is more than one connector) wiring connector with the ignition ON. There should be battery voltage. If there is no voltage, refer to the wiring diagrams and check the wire between the connector and the fuse for loose or broken connections or a damaged wire. Where the connector does not go directly into the back of the instrument cluster next check for continuity between the black/brown wire terminal in the instrument side of the wiring connector and each relevant terminal on the back of the instrument cluster.

4 Check for continuity to earth in the green and green/black wires in the loom side of the relevant connector.

### Instrument checks

5 On SH, @ and PS models, if the speedometer does not work, first check the cable (section 18), then remove the front wheel and check the drive gear and plate (see Chapter 8).
6 On Dylan models, if the speedometer does not work, first check the speed sensor wire and connectors between the front wheel and the instruments, then remove the front wheel and check the sensor and rotor (see Chapter 8).
7 On Pantheon and S-wing models, if the speedometer does not work, first check the voltage between the pink wire (+) in the instrument wiring connector, with it still connected, and ground, with the ignition ON, the scooter on the centrestand and turning the rear wheel by hand – a pulsing voltage of 0 to 5 volts should be present. If that is found, the sensor and the wiring are good, but the

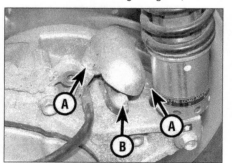

16.7 Speed sensor cover bolts (A) and sensor mounting bolt (B)

instrument board is faulty. If there is no voltage check the pink and yellow/red wires between the connector and the speed sensor connector for continuity – unscrew the sensor cover bolts on the back of the transmission casing to access the connector **(see illustration)**. If that is good check there is 5 volts present at the yellow/red wire terminal in the loom side of the sensor wiring connector. If there isn't, but the wire showed continuity, the instrument board is faulty. If there is, check for continuity to earth in the green/black wire. If all is good, the sensor could be faulty – unscrew the bolt and remove the sensor, and make sure the head is clean and check for damage. If all is good unscrew the bolt and replace the senor with a new one.

8 On S-wing models, if the tachometer does not work, first check that when the ignition is switched on the needle moves around the meter and back along with the other instrument needles. If none do, check the power circuit. If all except the tacho needle move replace the instrument board with a new one. If the tacho needle moves, but does not register engine speed when the engine is running, it must be tested as follows using the specified equipment and with the connector still connected, or by a Honda dealer. Honda specify their own Imrie diagnostic tester (model 625), or the peak voltage adapter (Pt. No. 07HGJ-0020100) with an aftermarket digital multimeter having an impedance of 10 M-ohm/DCV minimum, for a complete test. If this equipment is available, connect the positive (+) lead of the voltmeter and peak voltage adapter arrangement to the blue/yellow wire terminal in the wiring connector, and the negative (–) lead to earth. Start the engine and note the peak voltage reading on the meter – there should be a minimum of 10.5 volts. If the peak voltage reading is normal the instrument board is faulty. If there is a reading but it is below 10.5 volts the ECU could be faulty. If there is no reading check the wire between the connector and the ECU for continuity. If that is good the ECU could be faulty. For information on the ECU see Chapter 6.

9 The temperature gauge and sensor are covered in Chapter 4.
10 The fuel gauge and level sensor are covered in Chapter 5A.

**11** Referring to Electrical system fault finding in Section 2 and to the wiring diagram at the end of this Chapter for your model, check the wiring and connectors between the relevant instrument or bulb and its source for continuity and security.

### Instrument replacement

**12** Remove the instrument cluster (Section 15). Individual instruments are not available, but the instrument board is available separately from the front cover and housing.
**13** Where applicable (according to model) undo the individual wiring connector screws and detach the wires, tagging them if necessary (their colour code may or may not be marked next to their terminal) according to their location. Also pull each bulbholder out. Release any wiring guides.
**14** Undo the front cover and housing screws and separate them.
**15** Carefully lift the instrument board out.
**16** Installation is the reverse of removal.

---

## 17 Instrument and warning light bulbs

**1** On SH, @ and PS models remove the front handlebar cover (see Chapter 9). Carefully pull the relevant bulb holder out of the back of the instrument cluster, then pull the bulb out of the holder and replace it with a new one (**see illustration 15.2b, 15.4a or 15.4b**).
**2** On Dylan models remove the front handlebar cover (see Chapter 9). Remove the relevant bulb holder rubber cap (**see illustration**). Twist the bulbholder anti-clockwise to release it, then pull the bulb out of the holder and replace it with a new one (**see illustrations**).
**3** On Pantheon models remove the inner front handlebar cover. Remove the relevant bulb holder rubber cap (**see illustration**). Twist the bulbholder anti-clockwise to release it, then pull the bulb out of the holder and replace it with a new one.
**4** On S-wing models all instrument and warning bulbs are LEDs. If one fails, and the cause is not due to the source that supplies its

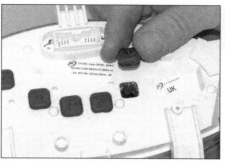
17.2a  Remove the cap

17.2c  ... then remove the bulb

signal, and all wiring and connectors between the source and the instrument cluster are good, a new instrument board may have to be fitted – individual LEDs are not available.

---

## 18 Speedometer cable or speed sensor

### Speedometer cable – SH, @ and PS models

**1** Remove the front handlebar cover (see Chapter 9).
**2** Undo the screw securing the speedometer cable in the drive housing on the right-hand side of the front wheel and draw the cable out (**see illustrations**).

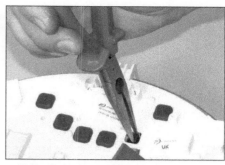
17.2b  Carefully release and pull out the bulb holder ...

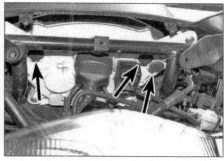
17.3  Instrument light caps (arrowed)

**3** Unscrew the knurled ring and detach the cable from the instrument cluster (**see illustration 15.2b, 15.4a or 15.4b**).
**4** Withdraw the cable, noting its routing.
**5** Installation is the reverse of removal. Make sure the O-ring on the end of the speedometer cable is fitted and smear it with grease (**see illustration**). Push the cable into the drive housing, making sure the slot in the cable locates correctly over the drive tab.

### Speed sensor – Dylan models

**6** Remove the upper front panel, and if required for better access the inner front panel (see Chapter 9).
**7** Trace the wiring from the sensor in the drive housing on the right-hand side of the front wheel and disconnect it at the connector. Release the wiring from any ties and feed it down to the sensor, noting its routing.

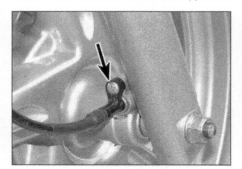
18.2a  Undo the screw (arrowed) ...

18.2b  ... and detach the cable

18.5  Make sure the O-ring (arrowed) is fitted

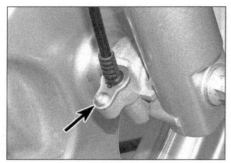

**18.8 Undo the screw (arrowed) and detach the sensor**

8 Undo the screw securing the sensor and draw it out **(see illustration)**.
9 Installation is the reverse of removal. Make sure the O-ring on the end of the speedometer cable is fitted and smear it with grease. Push the cable into the drive housing, making sure the inner cable locates in the shaft, setting the retaining tab in the cut-out.

### Speed sensor – Pantheon and S-wing models

10 Unscrew the bolts and remove the sensor cover **(see illustration 16.7)**.
11 Disconnect the wiring connector.
12 Unscrew the bolt and remove the sensor.
13 Installation is the reverse of removal. Use a new O-ring and smear it with oil.

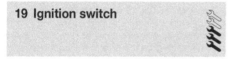

## 19 Ignition switch

 *Warning: To prevent the risk of short circuits, disconnect the battery negative (–) lead before making any ignition switch checks.*

### Check

1 Remove the upper front panel (see Chapter 9). Disconnect the ignition switch wiring connector.
2 Using an ohmmeter or a continuity tester, check there is continuity between the red and red/black wire terminals in the switch side of the connector with the ignition switch ON, and there is no continuity with it OFF. On Pantheon

**19.6 Release and remove the cover**

models, repeat the check between the red and red/blue wire terminals.
3 If the switch fails the test, replace it with a new one. If it is good, check for battery voltage at the red wire terminal on the loom side of the connector. If there is none, check for continuity in the wire to the starter relay (Section 24), and check the main fuse (Section 5). If there is voltage, check the red/black wire between the connector and the fusebox and main relay for continuity, then check the relay itself (Section 5).

### Removal and installation

4 Remove the upper front panel (see Chapter 9).
5 On SH and PS models displace the radiator, or if required for greater clearance remove it (see Chapter 4). Release the wiring from the air guide plate and remove the plate.
6 On all except @ models release the ignition switch cover by turning it anti-clockwise and draw it off the switch, noting how it locates **(see illustration)** – it may need to be eased off the tabs on the switch using a screwdriver.
7 As required according to model detach the seat lock cable, and on Pantheon and S-wing models the fuel filler cover lock cable **(see illustration 19.9a)**.
8 Disconnect the ignition switch connector. Feed the wiring back to the switch, freeing it from any clips and ties and noting its routing.
9 Unscrew the switch bolts and remove the switch **(see illustrations)** – where shear-head or one way bolts are used carefully drift them round until loose using a suitable chisel or punch, and use new bolts on installation.
10 Installation is the reverse of removal. Make sure the wiring connector is correctly routed and securely connected.

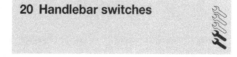

## 20 Handlebar switches

### Check

1 Generally speaking, the switches are reliable and trouble-free. Most troubles, when they do occur, are caused by dirty or corroded contacts, but wear and breakage of internal parts is a possibility that should not be

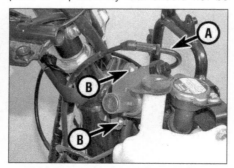

**19.9a Seat lock cable (A) and ignition switch shear-head bolts (B) – Dylan models**

overlooked. If breakage does occur, the entire switch and related wiring harness will have to be replaced with a new one, as individual parts are not available.
2 The switches can be checked for continuity using an ohmmeter or a continuity test light. Always disconnect the battery negative (–) cable, which will prevent the possibility of a short circuit, before making the checks.
3 On all except S-wing models remove the handlebar covers (see Chapter 9). Check for continuity between the terminals of the switch with the switch in the various positions (i.e. switch off – no continuity, switch on – continuity) **(see illustration 20.7)** – see the wiring diagrams at the end of this Chapter. Continuity should exist between the terminals connected by a solid line on the diagram when the switch is in the indicated position.
4 On S-wing models undo the three screws securing the trim panel on the inner front panel **(see illustration 7.3a)**. Carefully ease the five snap-fit clips free using a taped-up screwdriver, inserting it at the top-right-hand corner and working it down the side and along the bottom to free the three clips there, then starting again top-right and working along the top to release the two clips **(see illustration 7.3b)**. Disconnect the relevant switch wiring connector(s) **(see illustration 7.3c)**. Check for continuity between the terminals of the switch connector with the switch in the various positions (i.e. switch off – no continuity, switch on – continuity) – see the wiring diagrams at the end of this Chapter. Continuity should exist between the terminals connected by a solid line on the diagram when the switch is in the indicated position.
5 If the continuity check indicates a problem exists, on S-wing models displace the switch housing (see below). On all models spray the switch contacts with electrical contact cleaner (there is no need to remove the switch completely). If they are accessible, the contacts can be scraped clean with a knife or polished with crocus cloth. If switch components are damaged or broken, it will be obvious.

### Removal

6 Remove the handlebar covers (see Chapter 9).

**19.9b Ignition switch shear-head bolts (arrowed) – @ models**

**20.7 Handlebar switches are retained in the cover by tabs**

**20.8 Left-hand switch housing screws (arrowed)**

**21.2 Sidestand switch (arrowed)**

**7** On all except S-wing models release the switch tabs and withdraw it from the cover **(see illustration)**.

**8** On S-wing models undo the three screws securing the trim panel on the inner front panel **(see illustration 7.3a)**. Carefully ease the five snap-fit clips free using a taped-up screwdriver, inserting it at the top-right-hand corner and working it down the side and along the bottom to free the three clips there, then starting again top-right and working along the top to release the two clips **(see illustration 7.3b)**. Disconnect the relevant switch wiring connector(s) **(see illustration 7.3c)**. Feed the wiring back to the switch, freeing it from any clips and ties and noting its routing. If removing the right-hand switch disconnect the wires from the brake light switch **(see illustration 14.2a)**. If removing the left-hand switch disconnect the wires from the brake light/inhibitor switch **(see illustration 14.2c)**. To remove the right-hand switch, refer to Chapter 5A for disconnection of the throttle cable, which involves detaching the switch housing from the handlebars. Free the throttle cable from the twistgrip and remove it from the housing. To remove the left-hand switch, unscrew the two handlebar switch screws and free the switch from the handlebar by separating the halves **(see illustration)**.

## Installation

**9** Installation is the reverse of removal.

**10** On all except S-wing models make sure the switch tabs locate correctly in the cover **(see illustration 20.7)**.

**11** On S-wing models make sure the locating pin in the switch housing locates in the hole in the handlebar. Refer to Chapter 5A for installation of the throttle cable and right-hand switch housing.

**12** Check the operation of the switches before riding the scooter.

## 21 Sidestand switch

**1** A sidestand switch is fitted as standard to @, Pantheon and S-wing models, and may be fitted as an option on Dylan models. The switch prevents the engine starting if the sidestand is down, and will stop the engine if the stand is extended while running.

### Check

**2** The sidestand switch is mounted on the stand pivot **(see illustration)**. On Dylan and @ models remove the belly panel (see Chapter 9). On Pantheon models remove the maintenance panel for access to the right-hand side of the engine (see Chapter 9). On S-wing models remove the centre cover (see Chapter 9). Disconnect the green 2-pin wiring connector.

**3** Check the operation of the switch using an ohmmeter or continuity test light. Connect the meter between the terminals on the switch side of the connector. With the sidestand up there should be continuity (zero resistance) between the terminals, and with the stand down there should be no continuity (infinite resistance).

**4** Check for voltage at the green/white wire terminal on the loom side of the connector with the ignition ON – there should be battery voltage.

**5** If the switch does not perform as expected, it is faulty and must be replaced with a new one. If the switch is good, check the other components and their wiring and connectors in the starter circuit as described in the relevant sections of this Chapter. If all components are good, check the wiring between the various components (see the wiring diagrams at the end of this Chapter). Repair or replace the wiring as required.

### Replacement

**6** The sidestand switch is mounted on the stand pivot **(see illustration 21.2)**. On Dylan and @ models remove the belly panel (see Chapter 9). On Pantheon models remove the maintenance panel for access to the right-hand side of the engine (see Chapter 9). On S-wing models remove the centre cover (see Chapter 9). Disconnect the green 2-pin wiring connector. Feed the wiring back to the switch, freeing it from any clips and ties and noting its routing, and removing any other body panels as required according to model.

**7** Unscrew the bolt and remove the switch, noting how it locates.

**8** Fit the new switch onto the sidestand, making sure the pin locates in the hole, and the lug on the stand bracket locates into the cut-out in the switch body. Secure the switch with the bolt **(see illustration 21.2)**.

**9** Feed the wiring back to its connector, making sure it is correctly routed and secured by any clips and ties.

**10** Reconnect the wiring connector and check the operation of the sidestand switch.

**11** Install the body panels (see Chapter 9).

## 22 Starter inhibitor switch

**1** The switch prevents the engine from starting unless the rear brake lever is pulled in. On models with a rear disc brake the switch is integral with the rear brake light switch, but has its own connectors. On all other models the function is incorporated into the brake light switch circuit (see the wiring diagrams at the end of the Chapter).

### Circuit check

**2** The switch is mounted on the underside of the brake master cylinder or drum brake equalizer mechanism – remove the handlebar cover(s) as required according to model for access (see Chapter 9). Disconnect the switch wiring connectors – where the rear brake light switch is combined with the starter inhibitor switch, the brake light switch connectors are the ones on the side of the switch, not at the back **(see illustrations 14.2a, b, c and d)**.

**3** Using a continuity tester, connect the probes to the terminals of the switch, or to the terminals in the switch side connectors. With the brake lever at rest, there should be no continuity. With the brake lever applied, there should be continuity. If the switch does not behave as described, replace it with a new one.

**4** If the switch is good, check for voltage at the black/white or black wire terminal (according to model) on the loom side with the ignition switch ON – there should be battery voltage. If there's no voltage present, check the wiring between the connector and the ignition switch via the fusebox (see the wiring diagrams at the end of this Chapter).

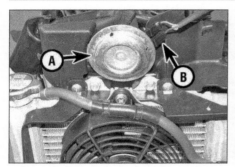

**23.2a Horn (A) and its wiring connectors (B) – SH and PS models**

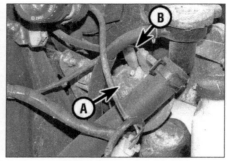

**23.2b Horn (A) and its wiring connectors (B) – Dylan and @ models**

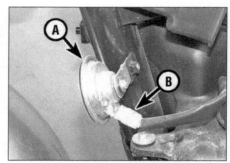

**23.2c Horn (A) and its wiring connectors (B) – Pantheon and S-wing models**

If voltage is present, check the green/yellow, green/red or pink wire (according to model) for continuity to the starter button, referring to the relevant wiring diagram. Repair or replace the wiring or connectors as necessary.

### Switch replacement

5 See Section 14.

## 23 Horn

### Check

1 On SH and PS models remove the upper front panel (see Chapter 9). On Dylan, @, Pantheon and S-wing models remove the inner front panel (see Chapter 9).
2 Disconnect the wiring connectors from the horn **(see illustrations)**. Check them for loose wires. Using two jumper wires, apply voltage from a fully-charged 12V battery directly to the terminals on the horn. If the horn doesn't sound, replace it with a new one.
3 If the horn works check the fuse (Section 5), then check for voltage at the light green wire connector with the ignition ON and the horn button pressed. If voltage is present, check the green wire for continuity to earth.
4 If no voltage was present, check the light green wire for continuity between the horn and the switch, and the black/brown wire from the switch to the fuse (see the wiring diagrams at the end of this Chapter). With the ignition switch ON, check that there is voltage at the black/brown wire to the horn button in the

left-hand switch gear. If there is, the problem lies between the switch and the horn. If there isn't, the problem lies between the ignition switch and the horn switch via the fuse.
5 If all the wiring and connectors are good, check the horn button contacts in the switch (see Section 20).

### Replacement

6 On SH and PS models remove the upper front panel (see Chapter 9). On Dylan, @, Pantheon and S-wing models remove the inner front panel (see Chapter 9).
7 Disconnect the wiring connectors from the horn **(see illustration 23.2a, b or c)**. Unscrew the bolt securing the horn.
8 Install the horn and connect the wiring. Check that it works.

## 24 Starter relay

### Check

1 If the starter circuit is faulty, first check the fuses (see Section 5).
2 The starter relay is located next to the battery **(see illustration 5.3a, c or d)** – remove the maintenance access panel to the battery/ fusebox/starter relay (see Chapter 9).
3 Lift the main terminal cover and unscrew the bolt securing the starter motor lead **(see illustration)**; position the lead away from the relay terminal. With the ignition switch ON, the sidestand up where fitted, and the rear brake

lever pulled in, press the starter switch. The relay should be heard to click.
4 If the relay doesn't click, switch off the ignition, remove the relay as described below, and test it as follows.
5 Set a multimeter to the ohms x 1 scale and connect it across the relay's starter motor and battery lead terminals **(see illustration 24.3)**. There should be no continuity. Using a fully-charged 12 volt battery and two insulated jumper wires, connect the positive (+) terminal of the battery to the yellow/red wire terminal of the relay, and the negative (–) terminal to the green or green/white (according to model) wire terminal of the relay. At this point the relay should be heard to click and the multimeter read 0 ohms (continuity). If this is the case the relay is proved good. If the relay does not click when battery voltage is applied and indicates no continuity (infinite resistance) across its terminals, it is faulty and must be replaced with a new one.
6 If the relay is good, check for continuity in the main lead from the battery to the relay. Also check that the terminals and connectors at each end of the lead are tight and corrosion-free.
7 Next check for battery voltage at the yellow/ red wire terminal on the relay wiring connector with the ignition ON, the sidestand up where fitted, the rear brake lever pulled in, and the starter button pressed. If there is no voltage, check the wiring and connectors between the relay wiring connector and the starter button, and then from the starter button back to the fusebox via the brake light switches or inhibitor switch, according to model. Next check the switches themselves.
8 If voltage is present, check that there is continuity to earth in the green or green white wire, on models with a sidestand making sure it is retracted. If not check the wiring and connectors, and where fitted the sidestand switch.

### Replacement

9 The starter relay is located next to the battery **(see illustration 5.3a, c or d)** – remove the maintenance access panel to the battery/ fusebox/starter relay (see Chapter 9).
10 Disconnect the battery, remembering to disconnect the negative (–) terminal first (see Section 3).
11 Disconnect the relay wiring connector **(see illustration)**. Lift the main terminal cover and

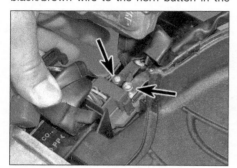

**24.3 Starter motor lead and battery lead (arrowed)**

**24.11 Disconnect the relay wiring connector**

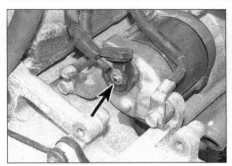

**25.3 Pull back the terminal cover then unscrew the nut (arrowed) and detach the lead**

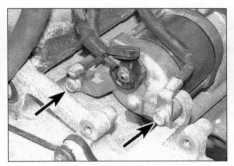

**25.4a Unscrew the two bolts (arrowed), noting the earth lead(s) . . .**

**25.4b . . . and remove the starter motor**

unscrew the bolts securing the starter motor and battery leads to the relay and detach the leads **(see illustration 24.3)**. Remove the relay from its rubber sleeve. If the relay is being replaced with a new one, remove the main fuse from the relay.

**12** Installation is the reverse of removal. Make sure the terminal bolts are securely tightened. Do not forget to fit the main fuse into the relay, if removed. Connect the negative (–) lead last when reconnecting the battery.

## 25 Starter motor removal and installation

### Removal

**1** Disconnect the battery negative (–) lead (see Section 3). The starter motor is mounted on the top of the crankcase.

**2** Remove the air filter housing (see Chapter 5A or B). For best access also remove the storage compartment (see Chapter 9).

**3** Peel back the rubber terminal cover on the starter motor **(see illustration)**. Unscrew the nut securing the starter lead to the motor and detach the lead – if the terminal is corroded spray it with some penetrating fluid and leave it for a while before attempting to undo it.

**4** Unscrew the two bolts securing the starter motor to the crankcase, where fitted noting the earth lead(s) **(see illustration)**. Slide the starter motor out and remove it **(see illustration)**.

**5** Remove the O-ring on the end of the starter motor and discard it as a new one must be used.

### Installation

**6** Fit a new O-ring onto the end of the starter motor, making sure it is seated in its groove **(see illustration)**. Apply a smear of engine oil to the O-ring.

**7** Manoeuvre the motor into position and slide it into the crankcase **(see illustration 25.4b)**. Ensure that the starter motor teeth mesh correctly with those of the starter idle/reduction gear. Install the mounting bolts, not forgetting to secure the earth lead(s) where fitted, and tighten them **(see illustration 25.4a)**.

**8** Connect the starter lead to the motor and secure it with the nut **(see illustration 25.3)**. Fit the rubber cover over the terminal.

**9** Install the air filter housing (see Chapter 5A or B).

**10** Connect the battery negative (–) lead (see Section 3). Install any removed body panels (see Chapter 9).

## 26 Starter motor overhaul

### Check

**1** Remove the starter motor (see Sec-

tion 25). Cover the body in some rag and clamp the motor in a soft-jawed vice – do not over-tighten it.

**2** Using a fully-charged 12 volt battery and two insulated jumper wires, connect the positive (+) terminal of the battery to the protruding terminal on the starter motor, and the negative (–) terminal to one of the motor's mounting lugs. At this point the starter motor should spin. If this is the case the motor is proved good, though it is worth overhauling it if you suspect it of not working properly under load. If the motor does not spin, disassemble it for inspection.

### 2001 to 2008 SH, Dylan, @, PS and Pantheon models

#### Disassembly

**3** Remove the starter motor (see Section 25).

**4** Note any alignment marks between the main housing and the front and rear covers, or make your own if they aren't clear **(see illustration 26.26)**.

**5** Unscrew the two long bolts, noting the O-rings, then remove the front cover **(see illustrations)**. Remove the tabbed washer from the cover and slide the insulating washer and shim(s) from the front end of the armature (though they could be stuck to the tabbed washer), noting the number of shims and their correct fitted order.

**6** Hold the rear cover and armature and draw

**25.6 Fit a new O-ring (arrowed) and lubricate it**

**26.5a Unscrew and remove the two bolts . . .**

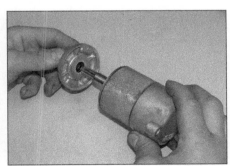

**26.5b . . . then remove the front cover**

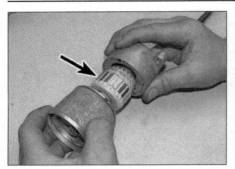

**26.6 Remove the housing, then draw the armature (arrowed) out of the rear cover**

**26.9a Unscrew the nut and remove the plain washer and the large and small insulating washers . . .**

**26.9b . . . then remove the brush plate**

the main housing off **(see illustration)** – it will be held in by the attraction of the magnets. Note the sealing ring on each end of the housing.

**7** Withdraw the armature from the rear cover **(see illustration 26.6)**. Remove the shim(s) from the rear end of the armature or from in the rear cover noting how many and their correct fitted positions.

**8** At this stage check for continuity between the terminal bolt and its brush – there should be continuity (zero resistance). Check for continuity between the terminal bolt and the cover – there should be no continuity (infinite resistance). Also check for continuity between the other brush and the rear cover – there should be continuity (zero resistance). If there is no continuity when there should be or *vice versa*, identify the faulty component and replace it with a new one.

**9** Noting the correct fitted location of each component, unscrew the nut from the terminal bolt and remove the plain washer, the one large and two small insulating washers **(see illustration)**. Lift the brush plate out of the rear cover, noting how it locates, and withdraw the terminal bolt from the cover **(see illustration)**. Remove the O-ring from the bolt and the insulator piece from the cover.

### Inspection

**10** The parts of the starter motor that are most likely to require attention are the brushes. Slide each brush out of its housing. Measure the length of each brush and compare the results to the length listed in this Chapter's

Specifications **(see illustration 26.33)**. If either of the brushes are worn beyond the service limit, fit a new set. If the brushes are not worn excessively, nor cracked, chipped, or otherwise damaged, they may be reused. Check the brush springs for distortion and fatigue. Check the brushplate and insulators for damage.

**11** Inspect the commutator bars on the armature for scoring, scratches and discoloration. The commutator can be cleaned and polished with crocus cloth, but do not use sandpaper or emery paper. After cleaning, wipe away any residue with a cloth soaked in electrical system cleaner or denatured alcohol.

**12** Using an ohmmeter or a continuity test light, check for continuity between the commutator bars **(see illustration)**. Continuity should exist between each bar and all of the others. Also, check for continuity between the commutator bars and the armature shaft **(see illustration)**. There should be no continuity (infinite resistance) between the commutator and the shaft. If the checks indicate otherwise, the armature is defective and a new starter motor bust be obtained – the armature is not available separately.

**13** Check the front end of the armature shaft for worn, cracked, chipped and broken teeth. If the shaft is damaged or worn, a new starter motor must be obtained – the armature is not available separately.

**14** Inspect the front and rear covers for signs of cracks or wear. Check the oil seal and the

needle bearing in the front cover and the bush in the rear cover for wear and damage – the seal, bearing, bush and covers are not listed as being available separately so if necessary a new starter motor must be fitted **(see illustrations 26.37a and b)**.

**15** Inspect the magnets in the main housing and the housing itself for cracks.

**16** Inspect the insulating washers, O-rings, and sealing rings for signs of damage, deformation and deterioration and replace them with new ones if necessary. Honda specify to use new O-rings and sealing rings whatever the condition of the old ones.

### Reassembly

**17** Make sure each brush is correctly located in its housing. Fit the insulator piece onto the terminal bolt. Insert the terminal bolt through its hole and seat the brush plate in the rear cover, locating the tab in the groove. Fit the O-ring down over the bolt and press it into place between the bolt and the cover. Slide the small insulating washers onto the terminal bolt, followed by the large insulating washer and the plain washer. Fit the nut onto the terminal bolt and tighten it.

**18** At this stage check for continuity between the terminal bolt and the cover – there should be no continuity (infinite resistance). Also check for continuity between the negative brush and the rear cover – there should be continuity (zero resistance). If there is no continuity when there should be or *vice versa*, identify the faulty component and replace it with a new one.

**19** Fit the shim(s) onto the rear of the armature shaft. Apply a smear of grease to the end of the shaft. Fit the armature into the rear cover, locating the brushes against the commutator bars, then pushing them back into their housings to align the shaft end with its bush, and push the armature in.

**20** Fit the sealing ring onto the rear of the main housing, which has a cut-out in its rim. Grasp both the armature and the rear cover in one hand and hold them together – this will prevent the armature being drawn out by the magnets in the housing. Note however that you should take care not to let the housing be drawn forcibly onto the armature by the

**26.12a There should be continuity between the bars . . .**

**26.12b . . . and no continuity between the bars and the shaft**

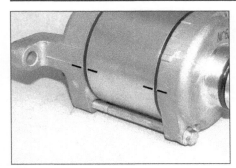

26.26 Note the alignment marks between the housing and the covers

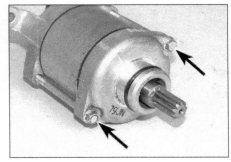

26.27a Unscrew and remove the two bolts (arrowed) . . .

26.27b . . . then remove the front cover

magnets. Carefully allow the housing to be drawn onto the armature, making sure the end with the cut-out faces the rear cover, that the cut-out locates over the tab on the insulator piece, and the marks between the cover and housing align (Step 4) **(see illustration 26.6)**.

**21** Apply a smear of grease to the front cover oil seal lip. Fit the tabbed washer into the cover so that its teeth are correctly located with the cover ribs.

**22** Fit the sealing ring onto the front of the housing. Slide the shim(s) onto the front end of the armature shaft then fit the insulating washer. Slide the front cover into position, aligning the marks **(see illustration 26.5b)**.

**23** Check the marks made on removal are correctly aligned then fit the long bolts, not forgetting the O-rings, and tighten them **(see illustration 26.5a)**.

**24** Install the starter motor (see Section 25).

### 2009-on SH and all S-wing models

#### Disassembly

**25** Remove the starter motor (see Section 25).

**26** Note any alignment marks between the main housing and the front and rear covers, or make your own if they aren't clear **(see illustration)**.

**27** Unscrew the two long bolts, then remove the front cover from the motor **(see illustrations)**.

**28** Hold the rear cover and armature and draw the main housing off **(see illustration)** – it will be held in by the attraction of the magnets. Note the sealing ring on each end of the housing.

**29** Withdraw the armature from the rear cover **(see illustration)**.

**30** At this stage check for continuity between the terminal bolt and the positive brush **(see illustrations 26.32 and 26.31b)** – there should be continuity (zero resistance). Check for continuity between the terminal bolt and the cover – there should be no continuity (infinite resistance). Also check for continuity between the negative brush and the rear cover – there should be continuity (zero resistance). If there is no continuity when there should be or *vice versa*, identify the faulty component and replace it with a new one.

**31** Slide the brushes out of their housings and remove the springs **(see illustration)**. Undo the screw securing the negative brush and remove the brush **(see illustration)**.

**32** Unscrew the nut from the terminal bolt and remove the washer, the insulator, the terminal housing and the O-ring **(see illustration)**. Remove the terminal bolt and positive brush from the cover, then remove the brush holder **(see illustration 26.31b)**.

### Inspection

**33** The parts of the starter motor that are most likely to require attention are the brushes. Measure the length of each brush and compare the results to the length listed in this Chapter's Specifications **(see illus-**

26.28 Draw the housing off

26.29 Draw the armature out of the rear cover

26.31a Slide the brushes out and remove the springs (arrowed)

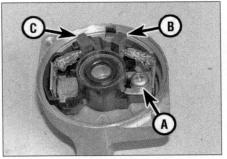

26.31b Negative brush screw (A), negative brush (B), positive brush (C)

26.32 Terminal bolt (arrowed)

**26.33 Measure the length of each brush**

**26.37a Check the bearing and seal in the front cover . . .**

**26.37b . . . and the bush (arrowed) in the rear cover**

tration). If either of the brushes are worn beyond the service limit, fit a new set. If the brushes are not worn excessively, nor cracked, chipped, or otherwise damaged, they may be reused. Check the brush springs for distortion and fatigue. Check the brushplate and insulators for damage.

**34** Inspect the commutator bars on the armature for scoring, scratches and discoloration. The commutator can be cleaned and polished with crocus cloth, but do not use sandpaper or emery paper. After cleaning, wipe away any residue with a cloth soaked in electrical system cleaner or denatured alcohol.

**35** Using an ohmmeter or a continuity test light, check for continuity between the commutator bars. Continuity should exist between each bar and all of the others. Also, check for continuity between the commutator bars and the armature shaft. There should be no continuity (infinite resistance) between the commutator and the shaft. If the checks indicate otherwise, the armature is defective and a new starter motor bust be obtained – the armature is not available separately.

**36** Check the front end of the armature shaft for worn, cracked, chipped and broken teeth. If the shaft is damaged or worn, a new starter motor bust be obtained – the armature is not available separately.

**37** Inspect the front and rear covers for signs of cracks or wear. Check the oil seal and the bearing in the front cover and the bush in the rear cover for wear and damage – the seal, bearing, bush and covers are not listed

as being available separately so if necessary a new starter motor must be fitted **(see illustrations)**.

**38** Inspect the magnets in the main housing and the housing itself for cracks.

**39** Inspect the insulator, O-rings, and sealing rings for signs of damage, deformation and deterioration and replace them with new ones if necessary. Honda specify to use new O-rings and sealing rings whatever the condition of the old ones.

### Reassembly

**40** Fit the brush holder into the rear cover **(see illustration 26.31b)**. Locate the positive brush on the holder and insert the terminal bolt through its hole. Fit the O-ring down over the bolt and press it into place between the bolt and the cover. Fit the terminal housing, the insulator and the washer **(see illustration 26.32)**. Fit the nut onto the terminal bolt and tighten it.

**41** Fit the negative brush and secure it with the screw **(see illustration 26.31b)**. Fit the brush springs into the brush housings, then fit the brushes onto the springs **(see illustration 26.31a)**.

**42** At this stage check for continuity between the terminal bolt and the cover – there should be no continuity (infinite resistance). Also check for continuity between the negative brush and the rear cover – there should be continuity (zero resistance). If there is no continuity when there should be or *vice versa*, identify the faulty component and replace it with a new one.

**43** Apply a smear of grease to the end of the

armature shaft. Fit the armature onto the rear cover so that the shaft end locates in its bush **(see illustration 26.29)**.

**44** Fit the sealing ring onto the rear of the main housing, which has a cut-out in its rim. Grasp both the armature and the rear cover in one hand and hold them together – this will prevent the armature being drawn out by the magnets in the housing. Note however that you should take care not to let the housing be drawn forcibly onto the armature by the magnets. Carefully allow the housing to be drawn onto the armature **(see illustration 26.28)**, making sure the end with the cut-out faces the rear cover, that the cut-out locates over the tab, and the marks between the cover and housing align (Step 26) **(see illustration)**.

**45** Fit the sealing ring onto the front of the housing. Apply a smear of grease to the front cover oil seal lip. Slide the front cover into position, aligning the marks **(see illustration 26.27b)**.

**46** Check the marks made on removal are correctly aligned **(see illustration 26.26)** then fit the long bolts and tighten them **(see illustration)**.

**47** Install the starter motor (see Section 25).

## 27 Charging system testing

**1** If the performance of the charging system is suspect, the system as a whole should be checked first, followed by testing of the individual components. **Note:** *Before beginning the checks, make sure the battery is fully charged and that all system connections are clean and tight.*

**2** Checking the output of the charging system and the performance of the various components within the charging system requires the use of a multimeter (with voltage, current, resistance checking facilities). If a multimeter is not available, the job of checking the charging system should be left to a Honda dealer.

**3** When making the checks, follow the procedures carefully to prevent incorrect connections or short circuits resulting in irreparable damage to electrical system components.

**26.44 Fit the housing onto the armature locating the cut-out over the tab**

**26.46 Fit the long bolts and tighten them**

## Leakage test

**Caution: Always connect an ammeter in series, never in parallel with the battery, otherwise it will be damaged. Do not turn the ignition ON or operate the starter motor when the ammeter is connected – a sudden surge in current will blow the meter's fuse.**

**4** Ensure the ignition is OFF, then disconnect the battery negative (-) lead (see Section 3).

**5** Set the multimeter to the Amps function and connect its negative (-) probe to the battery negative (-) terminal, and positive (+) probe to the disconnected negative (-) lead **(see illustration)**. Always set the meter to a high amps range initially and then bring it down to the mA (milli Amps) range; if there is a high current flow in the circuit it may blow the meter's fuse.

**6** Battery current leakage should not exceed the maximum limit (see Specifications). If a higher leakage rate is shown there is a short circuit in the wiring, although if an after-market immobiliser or alarm is fitted, its current draw should be taken into account. Disconnect the meter and reconnect the battery negative (-) lead.

**7** If leakage is indicated, refer to *Wiring Diagrams* at the end of this Chapter to systematically disconnect individual electrical components and repeat the test until the source is identified.

## Regulated output test

**8** Start the engine and warm it up. Remove the maintenance access panel to the battery/fusebox/starter relay (see Chapter 9).

**9** To check the regulated (DC) voltage output, allow the engine to idle with the headlight main beam (HI) turned ON. Connect a multimeter set to the 0-20 volts DC scale across the terminals of the battery with the positive (+) meter probe to battery positive (+) terminal and the negative (-) meter probe to battery negative (-) terminal (see Section 3) **(see illustration)**.

**10** Slowly increase the engine speed to 5000 rpm and note the reading obtained. Compare the result with the Specification at

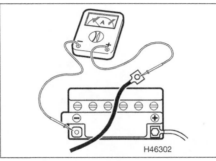

**27.5 Checking the charging system leakage rate – connect the meter as shown**

the beginning of this Chapter. If the regulated voltage output is outside the specification, check the alternator and the regulator (see Sections 28 and 29).

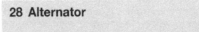

*Clues to a faulty regulator are constantly blowing bulbs, with brightness varying considerably with engine speed, and battery overheating.*

## 28 Alternator

### Check

**1** Remove the storage compartment (see Chapter 9). Trace the alternator wiring from the cover on the right-hand side of the engine and disconnect it at the white wiring connector with the three yellow wires – if necessary, on 2001 to 2004 SH, Dylan and @ models also remove the body cover for better access (see Chapter 9).

**2** Check the connector terminals for corrosion and security.

**3** Using a multimeter set to the ohms x 1 (ohmmeter) scale measure the resistance between each of the yellow wires on the alternator side of the connector, taking a total

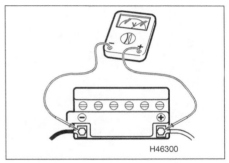

**27.9 Checking regulated voltage output – connect the meter as shown**

of three readings, then check for continuity between each terminal and ground (earth). If the stator coil windings are in good condition the three readings should be within the range shown in the Specifications at the start of this Chapter, and there should be no continuity (infinite resistance) between any of the terminals and ground (earth). If not, the alternator stator coil assembly is at fault and should be replaced with a new one. **Note:** *Before condemning the stator coils, check the fault is not due to damaged wiring between the connector and the coils.*

### Removal

**4** Remove the storage compartment and the body cover (see Chapter 9).

**5** Drain the engine oil (see Chapter 1). Drain the coolant (see Chapter 4). Remove the exhaust system (see Chapter 5A or B).

**6** Release the clamps and detach the coolant hoses from the water pump **(see illustration)**.

**7** On SH models lower the right-hand passenger footrest and undo the screw behind it. Unscrew the footrest bracket bolts and remove the footrest, pulling the floor panel away as required for clearance.

**8** Check the hooking point of the right-hand spring for the centrestand on your model – where it hooks onto a post on the alternator cover, retract the stand and support the scooter, then unhook the spring **(see illustration)**. Place

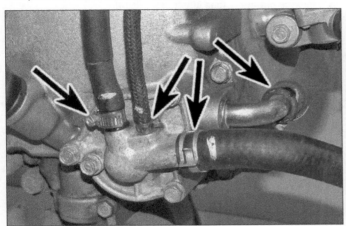

**28.6 Release the clamps (arrowed) and detach the hoses**

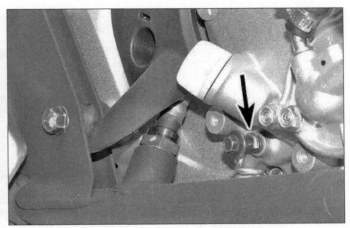

**28.8 Unhook the spring from its post (arrowed) on the cover**

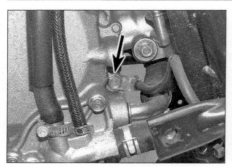

**28.11 Note the earth lead (arrowed) secured by one of the cover bolts on some models**

**28.13 Withdraw the shaft (arrowed) and remove the gear**

**28.16 Stator bolts (arrowed)**

the scooter back on the stand – the left-hand spring is sufficient to hold it.

**9** On 2001 to 2004 SH models, all Dylan and @ models displace or remove the ignition coil (see Chapter 6).

**10** Trace the alternator and pulse generator coil wiring from the cover and disconnect it at the connectors. Free all necessary wiring from any guides and ties around the alternator cover. Check around the cover and make sure everything is clear for the bolts to be undone and the cover to be removed – remove or displace anything in the way.

**11** Working in a criss-cross pattern, evenly slacken the alternator cover bolts, noting the position of the engine earth lead where fitted **(see illustration)**.

**12** Draw the cover off the engine, noting that it will be restrained by the force of the rotor magnets, and be prepared to catch any residual oil. Remove and discard the gasket **(see illustration 28.24a)**. Remove the dowels from either the cover or the crankcase if loose.

**13** Withdraw the idle/reduction gear shaft and remove the gear **(see illustration)**.

**14** To remove the rotor nut it is necessary to stop the rotor from turning using a commercially available rotor strap **(see illustration 28.22)**. With the rotor held, unscrew the nut and remove the washer.

**15** To remove the rotor from the shaft it is necessary to use a rotor puller (Honda part No.07KMC-HE00100, or its commercially available equivalent). Thread the rotor puller

onto the centre of the rotor, then counter-hold it using a spanner on the flats and tighten the bolt in its centre until the rotor is displaced from the shaft **(see illustration 28.21)**. Remove the Woodruff key from its slot in the crankcase if it is loose. If required detach the starter clutch from the rotor (see Chapter 2).

**16** To remove the stator from the cover, first remove the pulse generator coil (see Chapter 6), then unscrew the stator bolts and lift the stator out, noting how the rubber wiring grommet fits **(see illustration)**.

**17** Note that there is an oil seal in the alternator cover that is crucial for the oil supply to the crankshaft, and it is best to fit a new one whenever the alternator cover is removed. Remove the circlip securing the seal, then lever the seal out using a screwdriver or seal hook, or use a puller if necessary **(see illustration)**.

### Installation

**18** Fit a new oil seal into the cover with its marked side facing out of the cover. Smear the seal lips with oil. Fit the circlip **(see illustration 28.17)**.

**19** Fit the stator into the cover, aligning the rubber wiring grommet with the groove **(see illustration 28.16)**. Tighten the bolts to the torque setting specified at the beginning of the Chapter. Apply a suitable sealant to the wiring grommet, then press it into the cut-out in the cover. Install the pulse generator coil (see Chapter 6).

**20** Clean the tapered end of the crankshaft and the corresponding mating surface on the inside of the rotor with a suitable solvent. Fit the Woodruff key into its slot in the crankshaft if removed **(see illustration 28.21)**. Lubricate the flat section of the crankshaft that the starter driven gear turns on with molybdenum oil (a 50/50 mix of engine oil and molybdenum grease).

**21** If removed fit the starter clutch onto the rotor (see Chapter 2). Make sure that no metal objects have attached themselves to the magnet on the inside of the rotor. Slide the rotor onto the shaft, making sure the groove on the inside of the rotor is aligned with and fits over the Woodruff key **(see illustration)**. Make sure the Woodruff key does not become dislodged when installing the rotor.

**22** Apply some clean oil to the rotor nut threads and the underside of the head. Fit the nut with its washer and tighten it to the torque setting specified at the beginning of the Chapter, using the method employed on removal to prevent the rotor from turning **(see illustration)**.

**23** Lubricate the idle/reduction gear shaft with clean engine oil, then locate the gear, meshing the small inner gear teeth with those on the driven gear and the larger outer gear teeth with those of the starter motor shaft, and insert the shaft into its bore in the crankcase **(see illustration 28.13)**.

**24** Fit the dowels into the crankcase if removed, then locate a new gasket onto the

**28.17 Release the circlip (arrowed) then remove the seal**

**28.21 Slide the rotor onto the shaft, aligning the cut-out with the Woodruff key (arrowed)**

**28.22 Hold the rotor and tighten the nut to the specified torque**

28.24a  Make sure the dowels (arrowed) are in place, then fit the new gasket

28.24b  Smear sealant onto the grommet (arrowed)

dowels **(see illustration)**. Smear a suitable sealant onto the wiring grommet **(see illustration)**. Install the alternator cover, noting that the rotor magnets will forcibly draw the cover/stator on, making sure it locates onto the dowels. Tighten the cover bolts evenly in a criss-cross sequence, not forgetting the earth lead where detached **(see illustration 28.11)**.

**25**  Reconnect the wiring at the connector.

**26**  Install all remaining components as required according to model in a reverse of the removal procedure (Steps 11 back to 4), referring to the relevant Chapters where directed. Make sure all wiring and hoses are securely connected and correctly routed.

## 29  Regulator/rectifier

### Check

**1**  On 2001 to 2004 SH, all Dylan and @ models remove the body cover (see Chapter 9). On later SH and all PS models remove the storage compartment (see Chapter 9). On Pantheon models remove the upper front panel (see Chapter 9). On S-wing models remove the instrument cover (see Chapter 9).

**2**  Disconnect the regulator/rectifier wiring connector(s) **(see illustrations)**. Check the connector terminals for corrosion and security.

**3**  Set the multimeter to the 0-20 DC volts setting. Connect the meter positive (+) probe to the red/white wire terminal on the loom side of the connector and the negative (–) probe to a suitable ground (earth) and check for voltage. Full battery voltage should be present at all times. On models with two connectors, also check for battery voltage at the black wire terminal with the ignition ON.

**4**  Switch the multimeter to the resistance (ohms) scale. Check for continuity between the green wire terminal on the loom side of the connector and ground (earth). There should be continuity.

**5**  Set the multimeter to the ohms x 1 (ohmmeter) scale and measure the resistance between each of the yellow wires on the loom side of the connector, taking a total of three readings, then check for continuity between each terminal and ground (earth). The three readings should be within the range shown in the Specifications for the alternator stator coil at the start of this Chapter, and there should be no continuity (infinite resistance) between any of the terminals and ground (earth).

**6**  If the above checks do not provide the expected results check the wiring and connectors between the battery, regulator/rectifier and alternator, and where fitted the black wire to the fusebox, for shorts, breaks, and loose or corroded terminals (see the wiring diagrams at the end of this chapter).

**7**  If the wiring checks out, the regulator/rectifier unit is probably faulty. Honda provide no test data for the unit itself. Take it to a Honda dealer for confirmation of its condition before replacing it with a new one.

> **HAYNES HINT**  *Clues to a faulty regulator are constantly blowing bulbs, with brightness varying considerably with engine speed, and battery overheating.*

### Removal and installation

**8**  On SH, Dylan @ and PS models remove the body cover (see Chapter 9). On Pantheon models remove the upper front panel and the centre cover (see Chapter 9). On S-wing models remove the instrument cover and the inner front panel (see Chapter 9).

**9**  Disconnect the regulator/rectifier wiring connector(s) **(see illustration 29.2a, b or c)**.

**10**  Unscrew the two bolts securing the regulator/rectifier, noting the earth wire on 2001 to 2004 SH, Dylan and @ models **(see illustration 29.2a)**.

**11**  Fit the new unit and tighten its bolts, not forgetting the earth wire on 2001 to 2004 SH, Dylan and @ models. Connect the wiring connector(s).

**12**  Install the body panels as required (see Chapter 9).

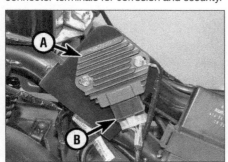

29.2a  Regulator/rectifier (A) and its wiring connector (B) – 2001 to 2004 SH, and all Dylan and @ models

29.2b  Regulator/rectifier (A) and its wiring connectors (B) – 2005-on SH and all PS models

29.2c  Regulator/rectifier (A) and its wiring connectors (B) – S-wing models (Pantheon similar)

**Notes**

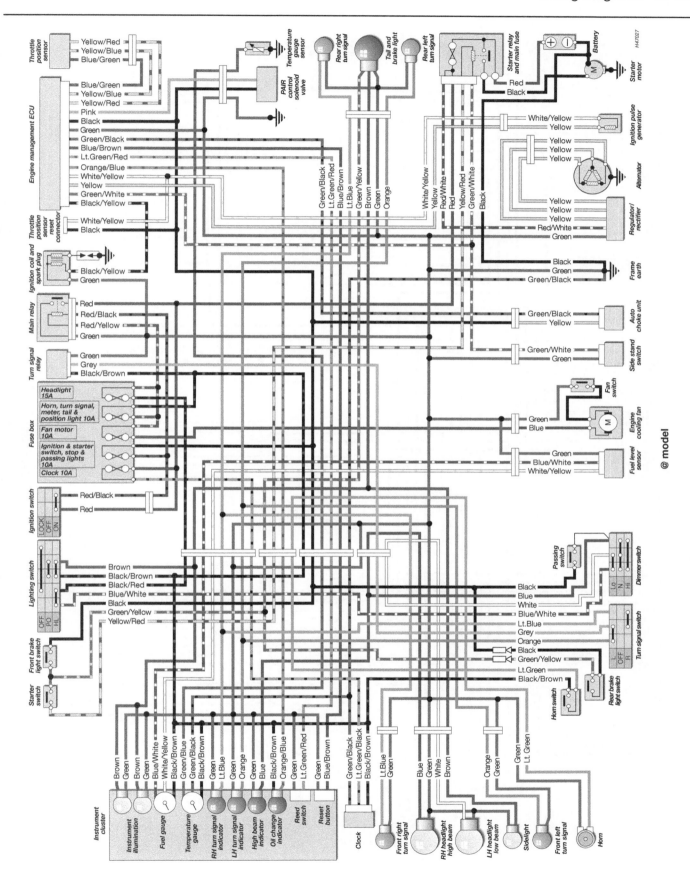

H47027

@ model

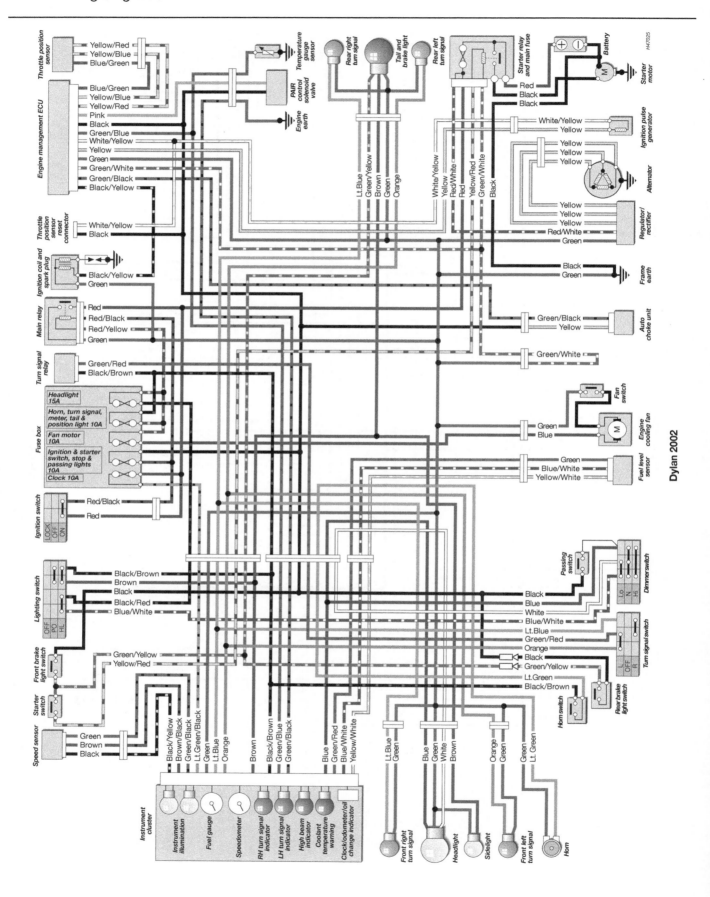

Dylan 2002

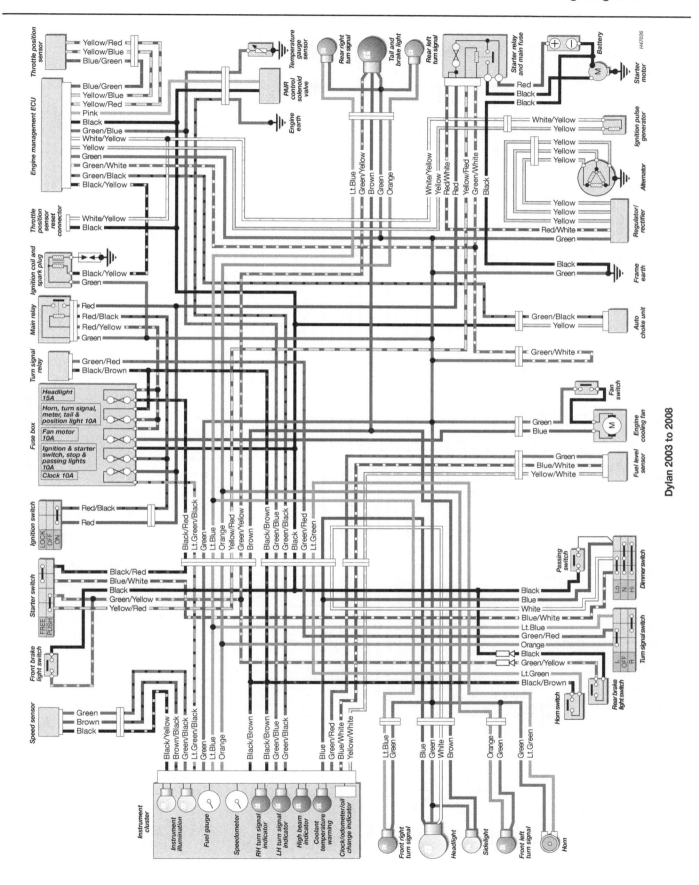

Dylan 2003 to 2008

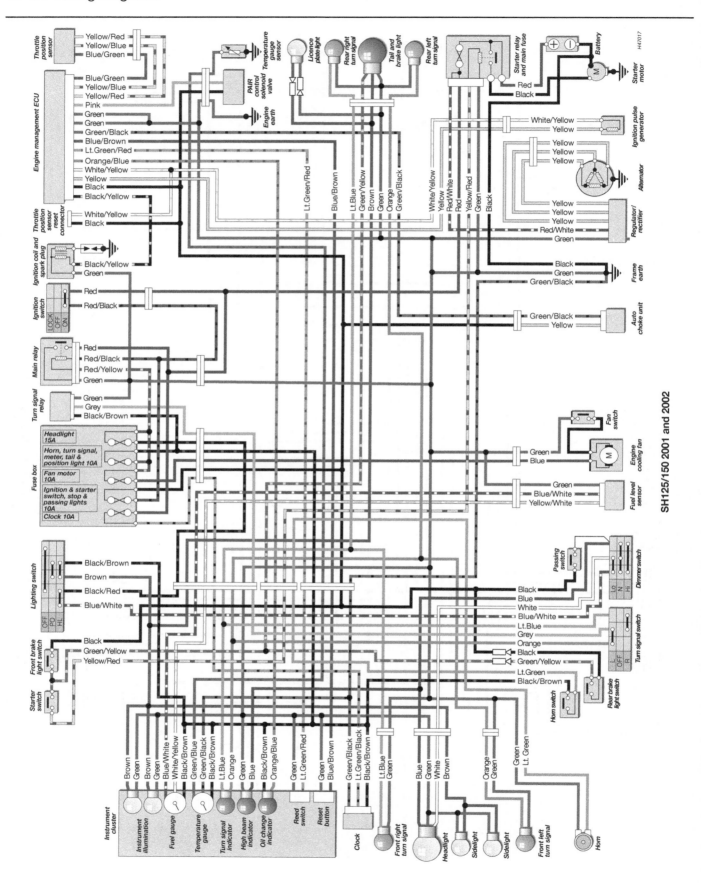

SH125/150 2001 and 2002

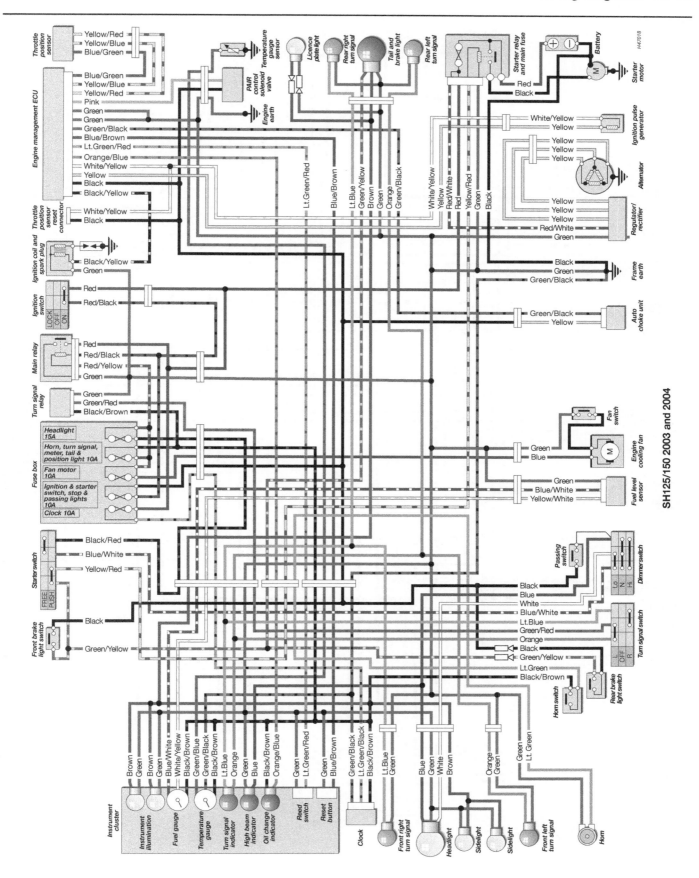

SH125/150 2003 and 2004

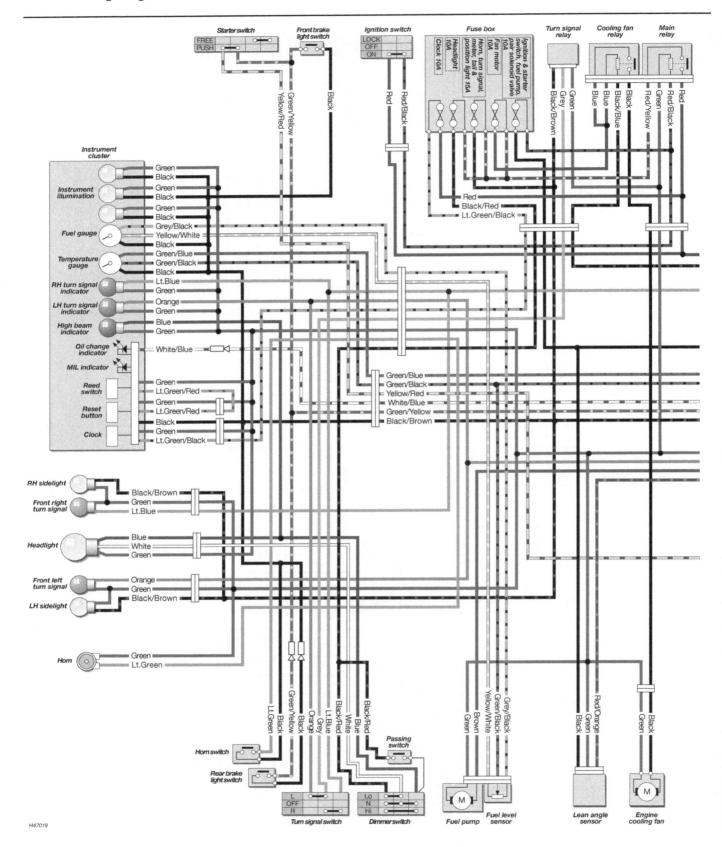

SH125/150 2005 to 2008

H47019

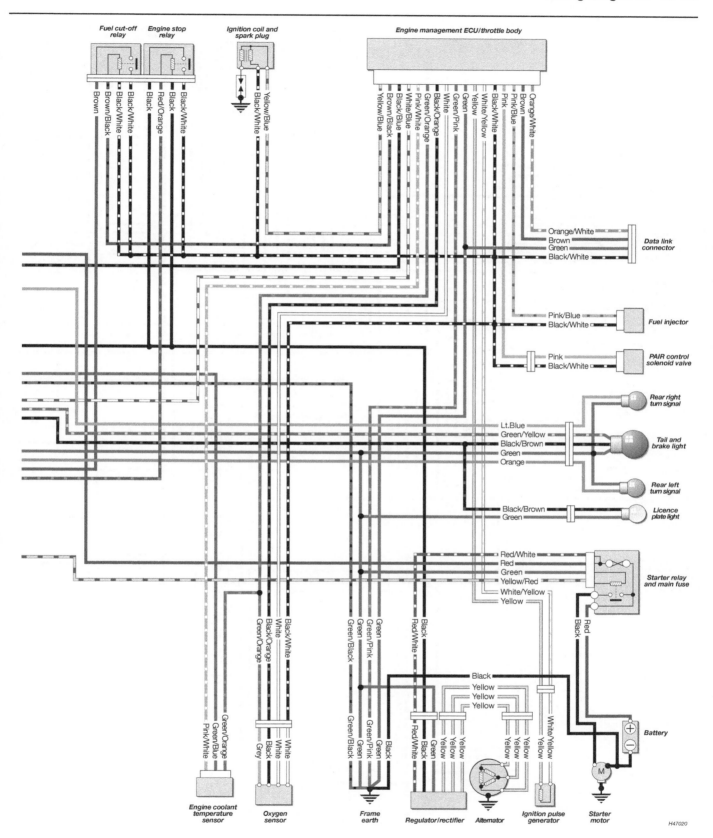

SH125/150 2005 to 2008

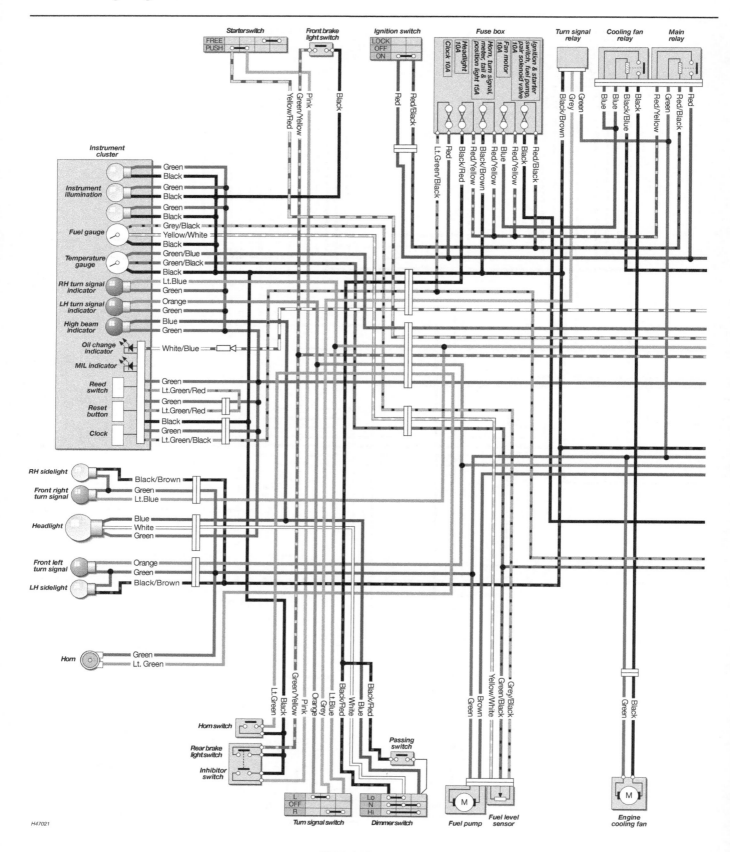

**SH125/150 2009-on**

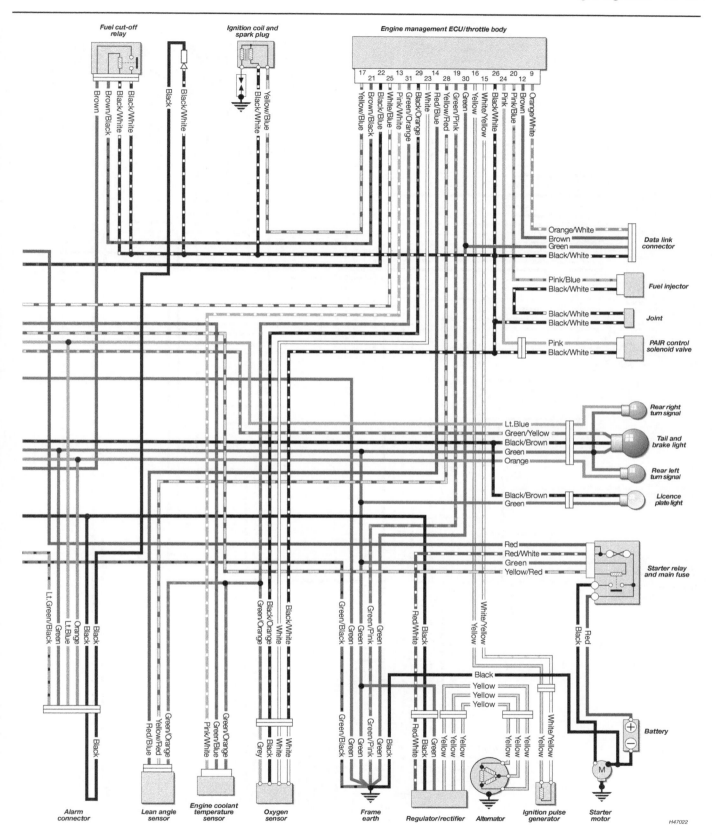

**SH125/150 2009-on**

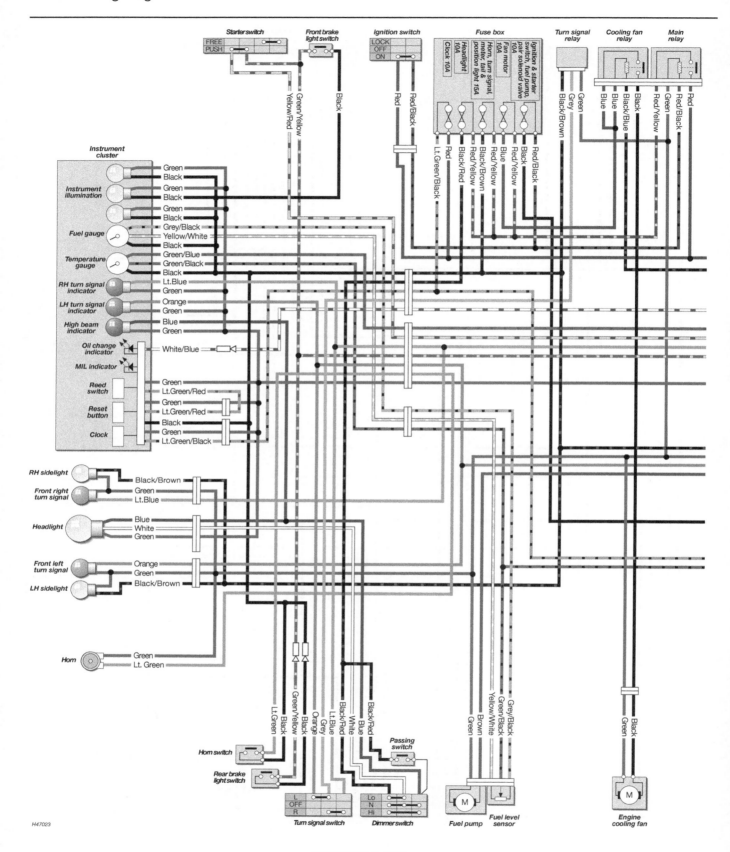

**SH125/150-D 2009-on**

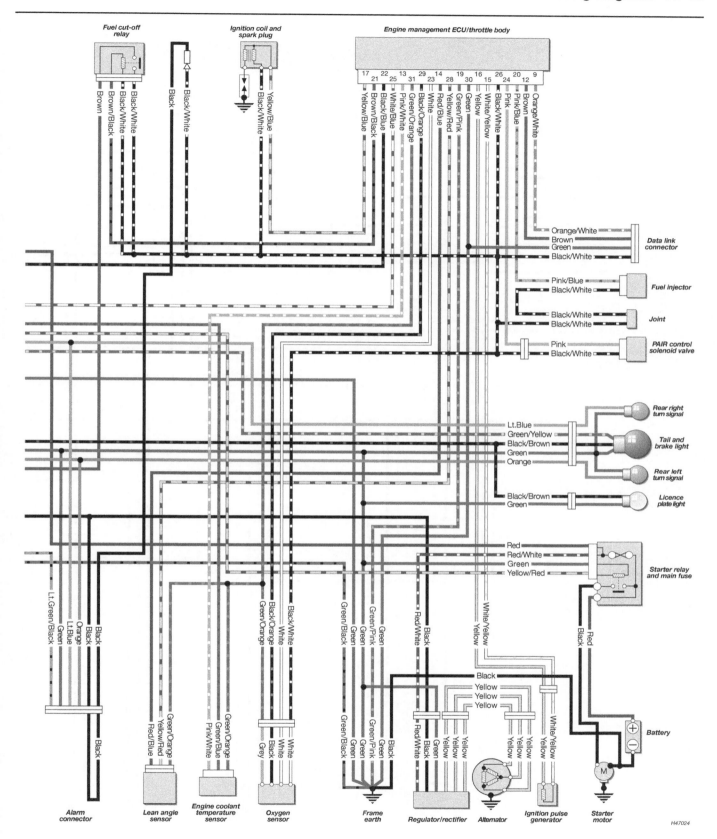

**SH125/150-D 2009-on**

H47024

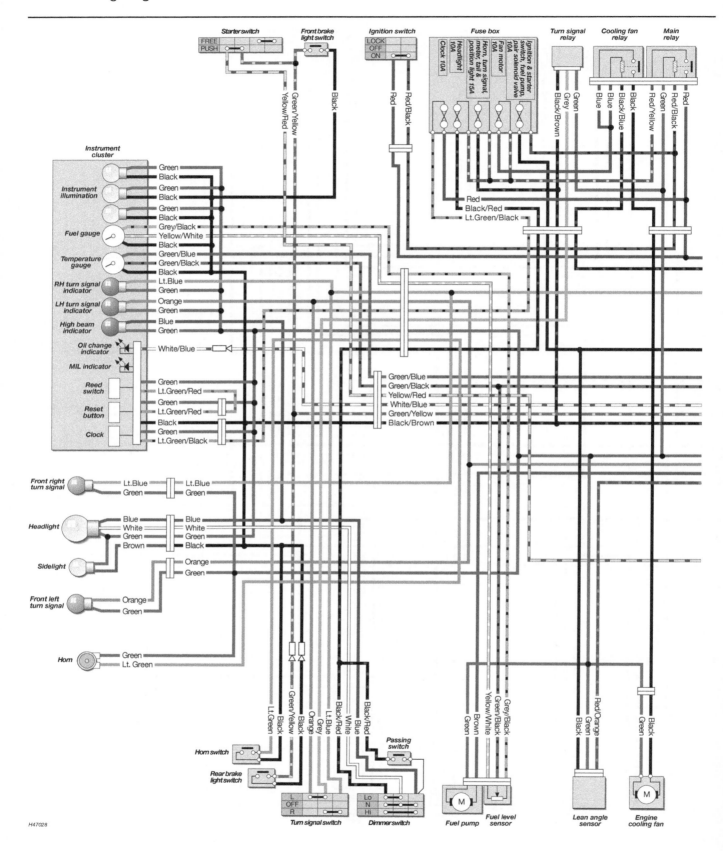

**PS125/150**

H47028

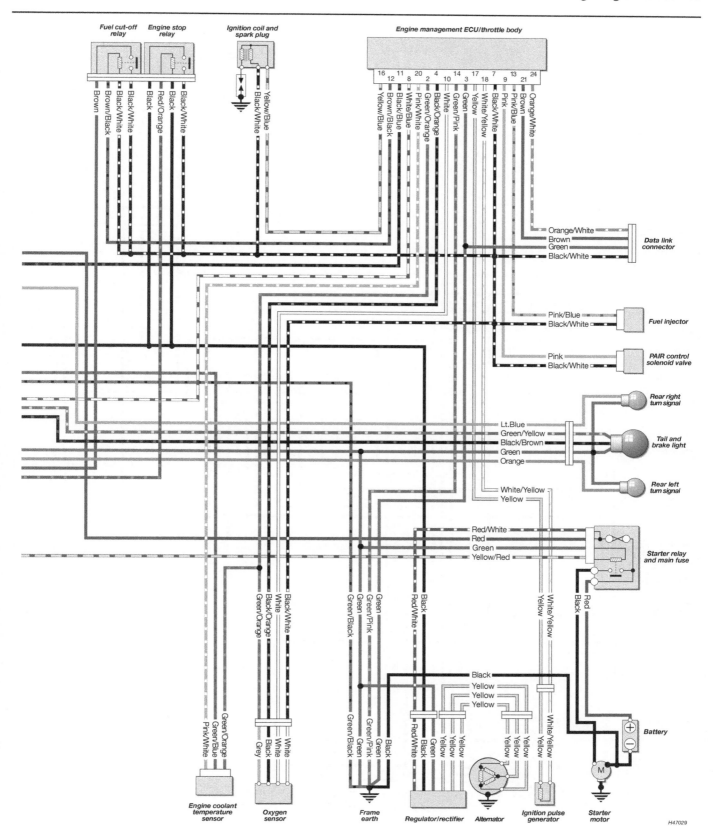

**Fuel cut-off relay** — Brown, Brown/Black, Black/White, Black

**Engine stop relay** — Red/Orange, Black, Black/White

**Ignition coil and spark plug** — Yellow/Blue, Black/White

**Engine management ECU/throttle body**

| 16 | 11 | 20 | 4 | 14 | 17 | 7 | 13 | 24 |
| 12 | 8 | 2 | 10 | 3 | 18 | 9 | 21 | |

Yellow/Blue, Brown/Black, Black/Blue, White/Blue, Pink/White, Green/Orange, Black/Orange, White, Green/Pink, Green, Yellow, White/Yellow, Black/White, Pink, Brown, Orange/White

Orange/White
Brown
Green
Black/White — **Data link connector**

Pink/Blue
Black/White — **Fuel injector**

Pink
Black/White — **PAIR control solenoid valve**

**Rear right turn signal**

Lt.Blue
Green/Yellow
Black/Brown
Green
Orange — **Tail and brake light**

White/Yellow
Yellow — **Rear left turn signal**

Red/White
Red
Green
Yellow/Red — **Starter relay and main fuse**

White/Yellow
Yellow
Red
Black — **Battery**

Black
Yellow
Yellow
Yellow

Green/Orange, Black/Orange, White, Black/White — 
Pink/White, Green/Blue, Green/Orange — **Engine coolant temperature sensor**

Grey, Black, White — **Oxygen sensor**

Green/Black, Green, Green/Pink — **Frame earth**

Black, Red/White, Green, Black — **Regulator/rectifier**

Yellow, Yellow, Yellow — **Alternator**

White/Yellow, Yellow — **Ignition pulse generator**

Red, Black — **Starter motor**

H47029

**PS125/150**

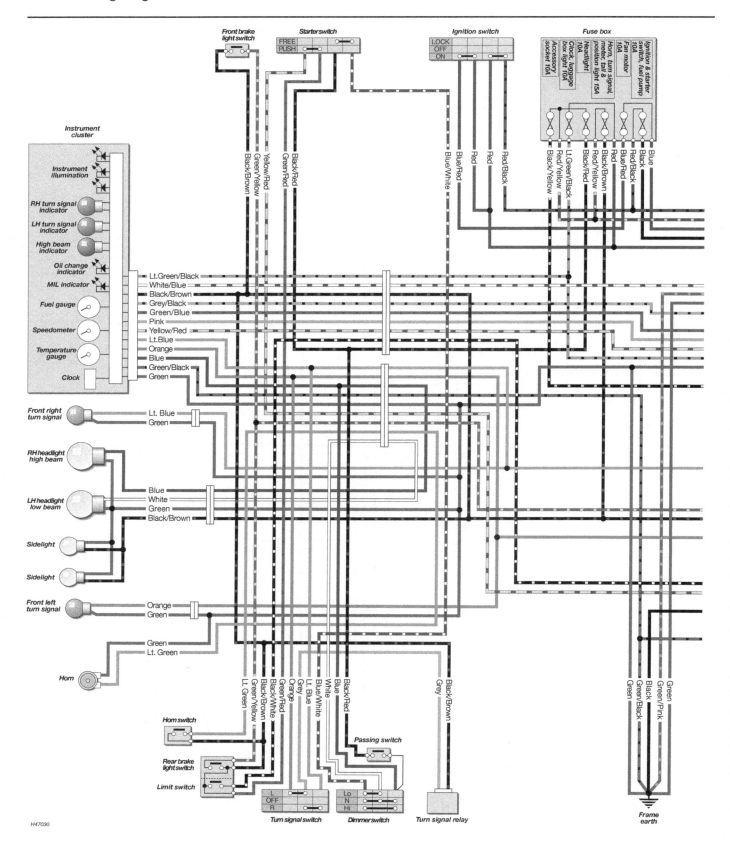

**Pantheon 125/150**

H47030

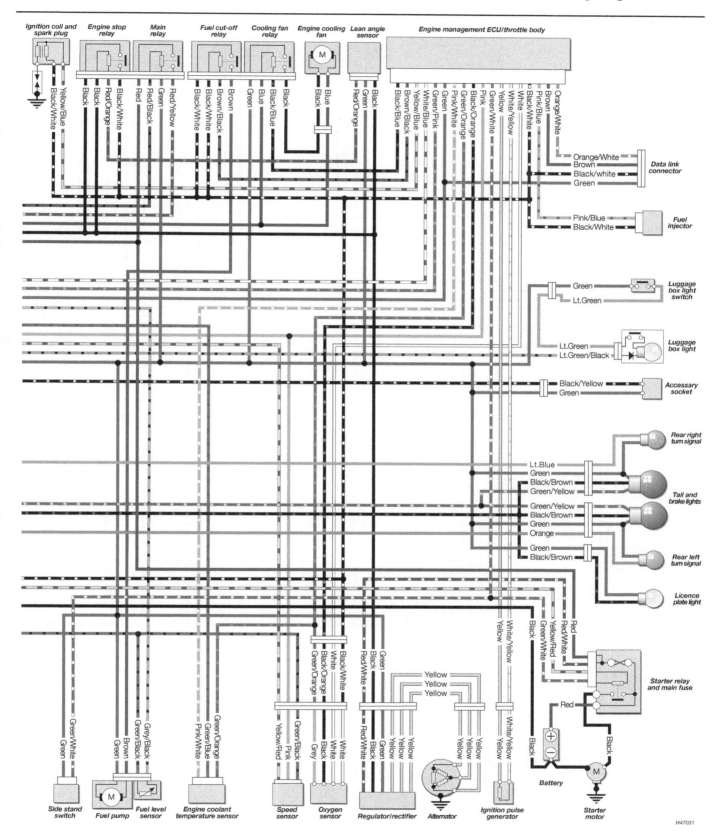

**Pantheon 125/150**

H47031

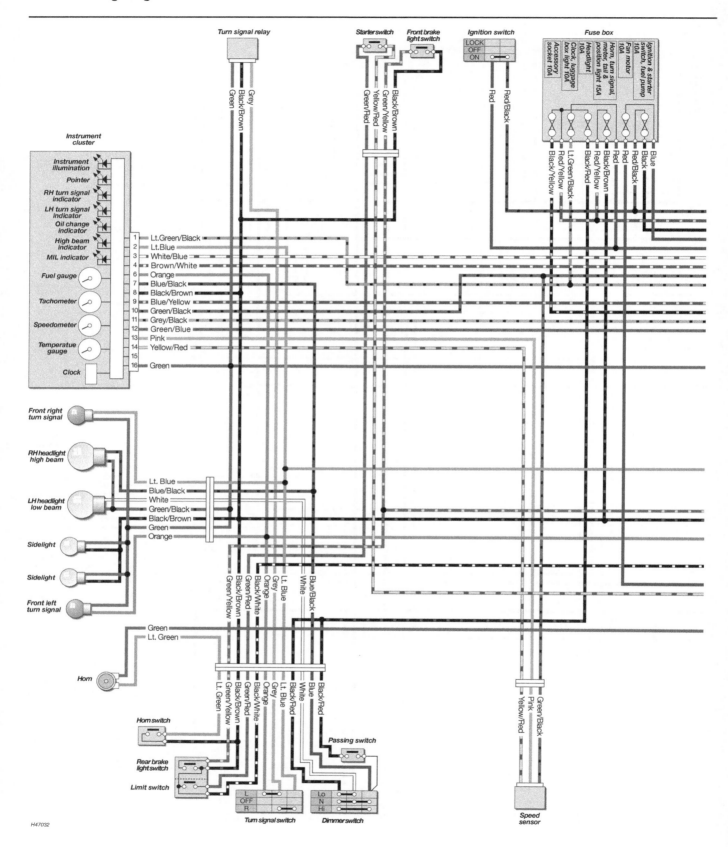

**S-wing 125/150**

H47032

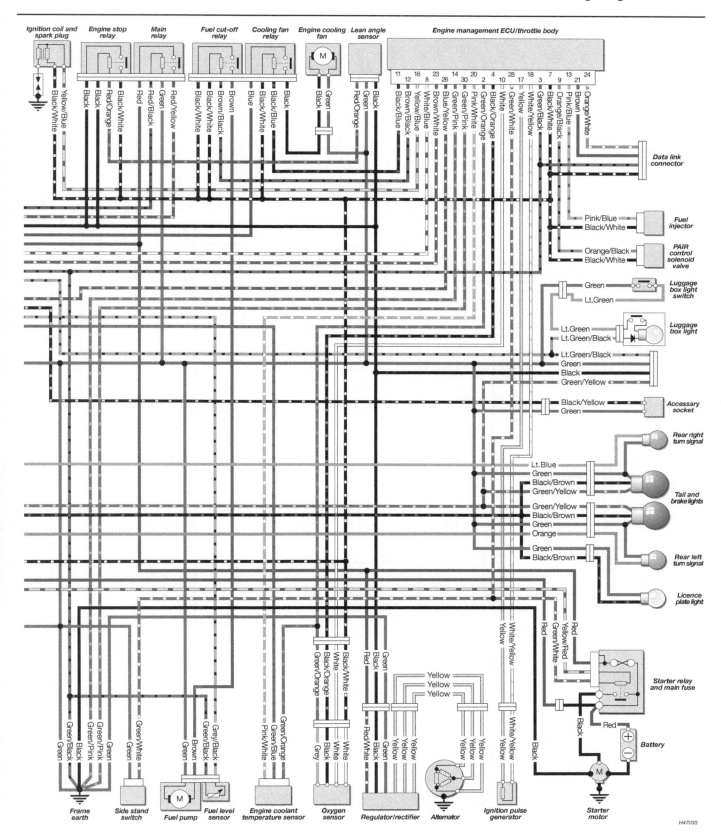

**S-wing 125/150**

H47033

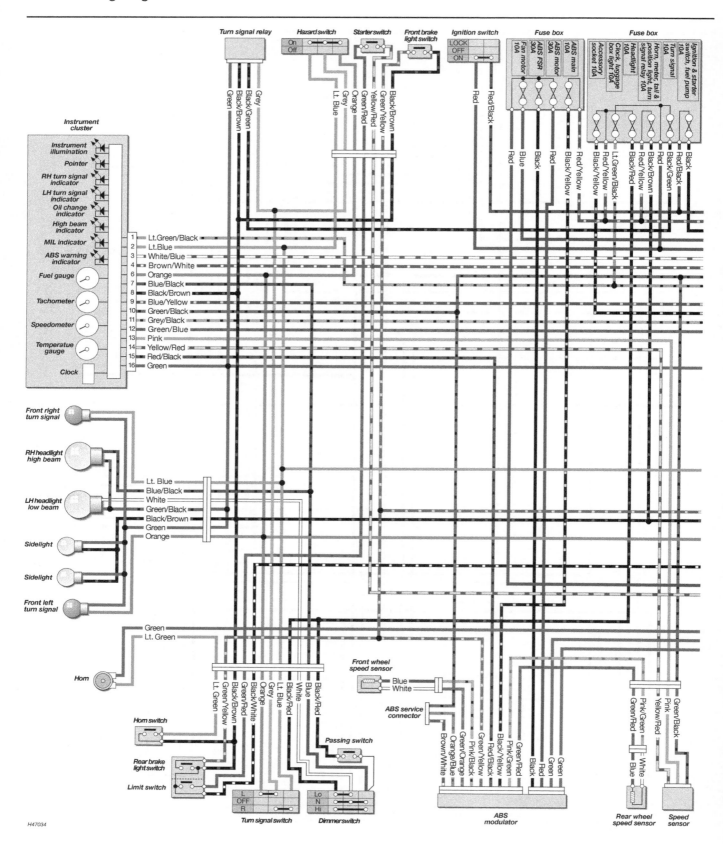

**S-wing 125/150 with ABS**

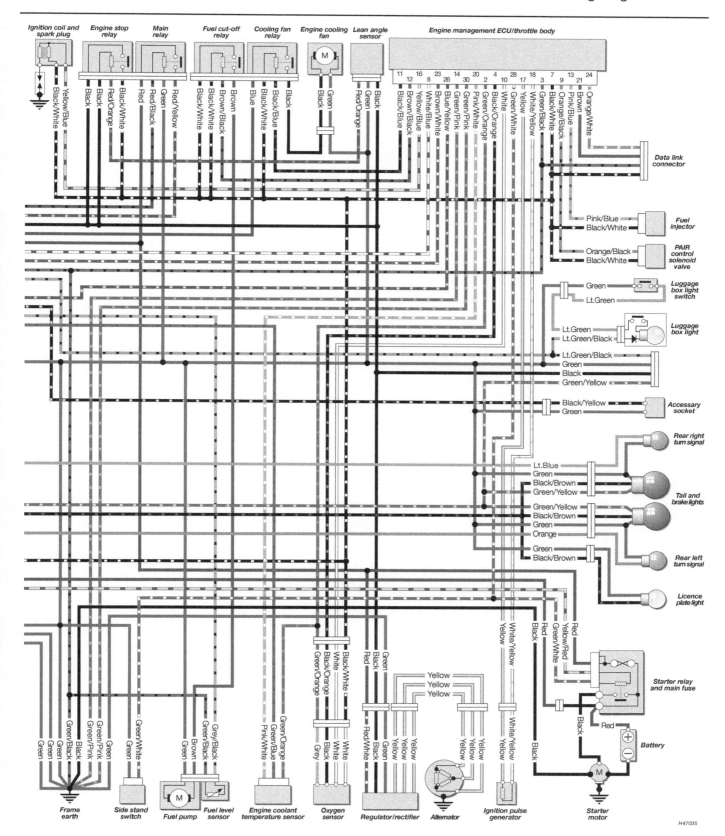

**S-wing 125/150 with ABS**

H47035

**Notes**

# Reference

# Tools and Workshop Tips

## Buying tools

A toolkit is a fundamental requirement for servicing and repairing a scooter. Although there will be an initial expense in building up enough tools for servicing, this will soon be offset by the savings made by doing the job yourself. As experience and confidence grow, additional tools can be added to enable the repair and overhaul of the scooter. Many of the specialist tools are expensive and not often used so it may be preferable to hire them, or for a group of friends or scooter club to join in the purchase.

As a rule, it is better to buy more expensive, good quality tools. Cheaper tools are likely to wear out faster and need to be renewed more often, nullifying the original saving.

 **Warning: To avoid the risk of a poor quality tool breaking in use, causing injury or damage to the component being worked on, always aim to purchase tools which meet the relevant national safety standards.**

The following lists of tools do not represent the manufacturer's service tools, but serve as a guide to help the owner decide which tools are needed for this level of work. In addition, items such as an electric drill, hacksaw, files, soldering iron and a workbench equipped with a vice, may be needed. Although not classed as tools, a selection of bolts, screws, nuts, washers and pieces of tubing always come in useful.

For more information about tools, refer to the Haynes *Motorcycle Workshop Practice Techbook* (Bk. No. 3470).

## Manufacturer's service tools

Inevitably certain tasks require the use of a service tool. Where possible an alternative tool or method of approach is recommended, but sometimes there is no option if personal injury or damage to the component is to be avoided. Where required, service tools are referred to in the relevant procedure.

Service tools can usually only be purchased from a scooter dealer and are identified by a part number. Some of the commonly-used tools, such as rotor pullers, are available in aftermarket form from mail-order motorcycle tool and accessory suppliers.

## Maintenance and minor repair tools

☐ Set of flat-bladed screwdrivers
☐ Set of Phillips head screwdrivers
☐ Combination open-end and ring spanners
☐ Socket set (3/8 inch or 1/2 inch drive)
☐ Set of Allen keys or bits
☐ Set of Torx keys or bits
☐ Pliers, cutters and self-locking grips (Mole grips)
☐ Adjustable spanners
☐ C-spanners
☐ Tread depth gauge and tyre pressure gauge
☐ Cable oiler clamp
☐ Feeler gauges
☐ Spark plug gap measuring tool
☐ Spark plug spanner or deep plug sockets
☐ Wire brush and emery paper
☐ Calibrated syringe, measuring vessel and funnel

☐ Oil filter adapters (4-stroke engines)
☐ Oil drainer can or tray
☐ Pump type oil can
☐ Grease gun
☐ Straight-edge and steel rule
☐ Continuity tester
☐ Battery charger
☐ Hydrometer (for battery specific gravity check)
☐ Anti-freeze tester (for liquid-cooled engines)

## Repair and overhaul tools

☐ Torque wrench (small and mid-ranges)
☐ Conventional, plastic or soft-faced hammers
☐ Impact driver set
☐ Vernier gauge
☐ Circlip pliers (internal and external, or combination)
☐ Set of cold chisels and punches
☐ Selection of pullers
☐ Breaker bars
☐ One-man brake bleeder kit
☐ Wire stripper and crimper tool
☐ Multimeter (measures amps, volts and ohms)
☐ Stroboscope (for dynamic timing checks)
☐ Hose clamp
☐ Clutch holding tool

## Specialist tools

☐ Micrometers (external type)
☐ Telescoping gauges
☐ Dial gauge
☐ Stud extractor
☐ Screw extractor set
☐ Bearing driver set
☐ Valve spring compressor (4-stroke engines)
☐ Piston pin drawbolt tool
☐ Piston ring clamp

**1.1 Hydraulic motorcycle ramp**

**1.2 Use an approved can only for storing petrol (gasoline)**

**1.3 A fire extinguisher, goggles, mask and protective gloves should be at hand in the workshop**

## 1 Workshop equipment and facilities

### The workbench

● Work is made much easier by raising the scooter up on a ramp – components are much more accessible if raised to waist level. The hydraulic or pneumatic types seen in the dealer's workshop are a sound investment if you undertake a lot of repairs or overhauls **(see illustration 1.1)**.

● If raised off ground level, the scooter must be supported on the ramp to avoid it falling. Most ramps incorporate a front wheel locating clamp which can be adjusted to suit different diameter wheels. When tightening the clamp, take care not to mark the wheel rim or damage the tyre – use wood blocks on each side to prevent this.

### Fumes and fire

● Refer to the Safety first! page at the beginning of the manual for full details. Make sure your workshop is equipped with a fire extinguisher suitable for fuel-related fires (Class B fire – flammable liquids) – it is not sufficient to have a water-filled extinguisher.

● Always ensure adequate ventilation is available. Unless an exhaust gas extraction system is available for use, ensure that the engine is run outside of the workshop.

● If working on the fuel system, make sure the workshop is ventilated to avoid a build-up of fumes. This applies equally to fume build-up when charging a battery. Do not smoke or allow anyone else to smoke in the workshop.

### Fluids

● If you need to drain fuel from the tank, store it in an approved container marked as suitable for the storage of petrol (gasoline) **(see illustration 1.2)**. Do not store fuel in glass jars or bottles.

● Use proprietary engine degreasers or solvents which have a high flash-point, such as paraffin (kerosene), for cleaning off oil, grease and dirt – never use petrol (gasoline) for cleaning. Wear rubber gloves when handling solvent and engine degreaser. The fumes from certain solvents can be dangerous – always work in a well-ventilated area.

### Dust, eye and hand protection

● Protect your lungs from inhalation of dust particles by wearing a filtering mask over the nose and mouth. Many frictional materials still contain asbestos which is dangerous to your health. Protect your eyes from spouts of liquid and sprung components by wearing a pair of protective goggles **(see illustration 1.3)**.

● Protect your hands from contact with solvents, fuel and oils by wearing rubber gloves. Alternatively apply a barrier cream to your hands before starting work. If handling hot components or fluids, wear suitable gloves to protect your hands from scalding and burns.

### What to do with old fluids

● Old cleaning solvent, fuel, coolant and oils should not be poured down domestic drains or onto the ground. Package the fluid up in old oil containers, label it accordingly, and take it to a garage or disposal facility. Contact your local authority for location of such sites.

## 2 Fasteners – screws, bolts and nuts

### Fastener types and applications

#### Bolts and screws

● Fastener head types are either of hexagonal, Torx or splined design, with internal and external versions of each type **(see illustrations 2.1 and 2.2)**; splined head fasteners are not in common use on scooters. The conventional slotted or Phillips head design is used for certain screws. Bolt or screw length is always measured from the underside of the head to the end of the item **(see illustration 2.11)**.

● Certain fasteners on the scooter have a tensile marking on their heads, the higher the marking the stronger the fastener. High tensile fasteners generally carry a 10 or higher marking. Never replace a high tensile fastener with one of a lower tensile strength.

#### Washers (see illustration 2.3)

● Plain washers are used between a fastener

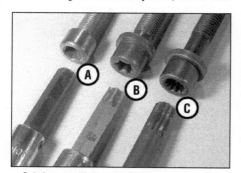

**2.1 Internal hexagon/Allen (A), Torx (B) and splined (C) fasteners, with corresponding bits**

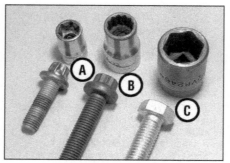

**2.2 External Torx (A), splined (B) and hexagon (C) fasteners, with corresponding sockets**

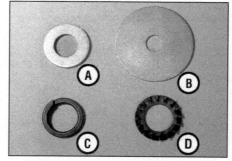

**2.3 Plain washer (A), penny washer (B), spring washer (C) and serrated washer (D)**

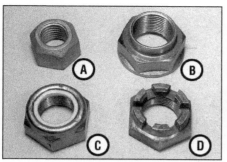

**2.4 Plain nut (A), shouldered locknut (B), nylon insert nut (C) and castellated nut (D)**

**2.5 Bend split pin (cotter pin) arms as shown (arrows) to secure a castellated nut**

**2.6 Bend split pin (cotter pin) arms as shown to secure a plain nut**

head and a component to prevent damage to the component or to spread the load when torque is applied. Plain washers can also be used as spacers or shims in certain assemblies. Copper or aluminium plain washers are often used as sealing washers on drain plugs.

● The split-ring spring washer works by applying axial tension between the fastener head and component. If flattened, it is fatigued and must be renewed. If a plain (flat) washer is used on the fastener, position the spring washer between the fastener and the plain washer.

● Serrated star type washers dig into the fastener and component faces, preventing loosening. They are often used on electrical earth (ground) connections to the frame.

● Cone type washers (sometimes called Belleville) are conical and when tightened apply axial tension between the fastener head and component. They must be installed with the dished side against the component and often carry an OUTSIDE marking on their outer face. If flattened, they are fatigued and must be renewed.

● Tab washers are used to lock plain nuts or bolts on a shaft. A portion of the tab washer is bent up hard against one flat of the nut or bolt to prevent it loosening. Due to the tab washer being deformed in use, a new tab washer should be used every time it is disturbed.

● Wave washers are used to take up endfloat on a shaft. They provide light springing and prevent excessive side-to-side play of a component. Can be found on rocker arm shafts.

## Nuts and split pins

● Conventional plain nuts are usually six-sided (**see illustration 2.4**). They are sized by thread diameter and pitch. High tensile nuts carry a number on one end to denote their tensile strength.

● Self-locking nuts either have a nylon insert, or two spring metal tabs, or a shoulder which is staked into a groove in the shaft – their advantage over conventional plain nuts is a resistance to loosening due to vibration. The nylon insert type can be used a number of times, but must be renewed when the friction of the nylon insert is reduced, ie when the nut spins freely on the shaft. The spring tab type

**2.7 Correct fitting of R-pin. Arrow indicates forward direction**

can be reused unless the tabs are damaged. The shouldered type must be renewed every time it is disturbed.

● Split pins (cotter pins) are used to lock a castellated nut to a shaft or to prevent slackening of a plain nut. Common applications are wheel axles and brake torque arms. Because the split pin arms are deformed to lock around the nut a new split pin must always be used on installation – always fit the correct size split pin which will fit snugly in the shaft hole. Make sure the split pin arms are correctly located around the nut (**see illustrations 2.5 and 2.6**).

● R-pins (shaped like the letter R), or slip pins as they are sometimes called, are sprung and can be reused if they are otherwise in good condition. Always install R-pins with their closed end facing forwards (**see illustration 2.7**).

*Caution: If the castellated nut slots do not align with the shaft hole after tightening to the torque setting, tighten the nut until the*

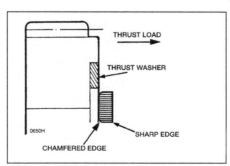

**2.9 Correct fitting of a stamped circlip**

*next slot aligns with the hole – never slacken the nut to align its slot.*

## Circlips (see illustration 2.8)

● Circlips (sometimes called snap-rings) are used to retain components on a shaft or in a housing and have corresponding external or internal ears to permit removal. Parallel-sided (machined) circlips can be installed either way round in their groove, whereas stamped circlips (which have a chamfered edge on one face) must be installed with the chamfer facing away from the direction of thrust load (**see illustration 2.9**).

● Always use circlip pliers to remove and install circlips; expand or compress them just enough to remove them. After installation, rotate the circlip in its groove to ensure it is securely seated. If installing a circlip on a splined shaft, always align its opening with a shaft channel to ensure the circlip ends are well supported and unlikely to catch (**see illustration 2.10**).

● Circlips can wear due to the thrust of components and become loose in their

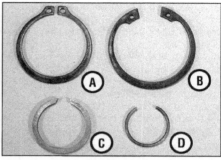

**2.8 External stamped circlip (A), internal stamped circlip (B), machined circlip (C) and wire circlip (D)**

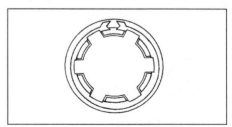

**2.10 Align circlip opening with shaft channel**

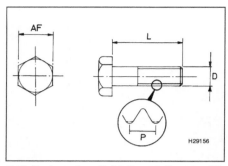

**2.11 Fastener length (L), thread diameter (D), thread pitch (P) and head size (AF)**

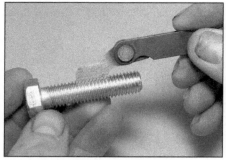

**2.12 Using a thread gauge to measure pitch**

**2.13 A sharp tap on the head of a fastener will often break free a corroded thread**

grooves, with the subsequent danger of becoming dislodged in operation. For this reason, renewal is advised every time a circlip is disturbed.

● Wire circlips are commonly used as piston pin retaining clips. If a removal tang is provided, long-nosed pliers can be used to dislodge them, otherwise careful use of a small flat-bladed screwdriver is necessary. Wire circlips should be renewed every time they are disturbed.

### Thread diameter and pitch

● Diameter of a male thread (screw, bolt or stud) is the outside diameter of the threaded portion (see illustration 2.11). Most scooter manufacturers use the ISO (International Standards Organisation) metric system expressed in millimetres, eg M6 refers to a 6 mm diameter thread. Sizing is the same for nuts, except that the thread diameter is measured across the valleys of the nut.

● Pitch is the distance between the peaks of the thread (see illustration 2.11). It is expressed in millimetres, thus a common bolt size may be expressed as 6.0 x 1.0 mm (6 mm thread diameter and 1 mm pitch). Generally pitch increases in proportion to thread diameter, although there are always exceptions.

● Thread diameter and pitch are related for conventional fastener applications and the accompanying table can be used as a guide. Additionally, the AF (Across Flats), spanner or socket size dimension of the bolt or nut (see illustration 2.11) is linked to thread and pitch specification. Thread pitch can be measured with a thread gauge (see illustration 2.12).

● The threads of most fasteners are of the right-hand type, ie they are turned clockwise to tighten and anti-clockwise to loosen. The reverse situation applies to left-hand thread fasteners, which are turned anti-clockwise to tighten and clockwise to loosen. Left-hand threads are used where rotation of a component might loosen a conventional right-hand thread fastener.

| AF size | Thread diameter x pitch (mm) |
|---------|------------------------------|
| 8 mm    | M5 x 0.8                     |
| 8 mm    | M6 x 1.0                     |
| 10 mm   | M6 x 1.0                     |
| 12 mm   | M8 x 1.25                    |
| 14 mm   | M10 x 1.25                   |
| 17 mm   | M12 x 1.25                   |

### Seized fasteners

● Corrosion of external fasteners due to water or reaction between two dissimilar metals can occur over a period of time. It will build up sooner in wet conditions or in countries where salt is used on the roads during the winter. If a fastener is severely corroded it is likely that normal methods of removal will fail and result in its head being ruined. When you attempt removal, the fastener thread should be heard to crack free and unscrew easily – if it doesn't, stop there before damaging something.

● A smart tap on the head of the fastener will often succeed in breaking free corrosion which has occurred in the threads (see illustration 2.13).

● An aerosol penetrating fluid (such as WD-40) applied the night beforehand may work its way down into the thread and ease removal.

Depending on the location, you may be able to make up a Plasticine well around the fastener head and fill it with penetrating fluid.

● If you are working on an engine internal component, corrosion will most likely not be a problem due to the well lubricated environment. However, components can be very tight and an impact driver is a useful tool in freeing them (see illustration 2.14).

● Where corrosion has occurred between dissimilar metals (eg steel and aluminium alloy), the application of heat to the fastener head will create a disproportionate expansion rate between the two metals and break the seizure caused by the corrosion. Whether heat can be applied depends on the location of the fastener – any surrounding components likely to be damaged must first be removed (see illustration 2.15). Heat can be applied using a paint stripper heat gun or clothes iron, or by immersing the component in boiling water – wear protective gloves to prevent scalding or burns to the hands.

● As a last resort, it is possible to use a hammer and cold chisel to work the fastener head unscrewed (see illustration 2.16). This will damage the fastener, but more importantly extreme care must be taken not to damage the surrounding component.

*Caution: Remember that the component being secured is generally of more value than the bolt, nut or screw – when the fastener is freed, do not unscrew it with force, instead work the fastener back and forth when resistance is felt to prevent thread damage.*

**2.14 Using an impact driver to free a fastener**

**2.15 Using heat to free a seized fastener**

**2.16 Using a hammer and chisel to free a seized fastener**

**2.17 Using a stud extractor tool to remove a broken crankcase stud**

**2.18 Two nuts can be locked together to unscrew a stud from a component**

**2.19 When using a screw extractor, first drill a hole in the fastener . . .**

## Broken fasteners and damaged heads

● If the shank of a broken bolt or screw is accessible you can grip it with self-locking grips. The knurled wheel type stud extractor tool or self-gripping stud puller tool is particularly useful for removing the long studs which screw into the cylinder mouth surface of the crankcase or bolts and screws from which the head has broken off **(see illustration 2.17)**. Studs can also be removed by locking two nuts together on the threaded end of the stud and using a spanner on the lower nut **(see illustration 2.18)**.

● A bolt or screw which has broken off below or level with the casing must be extracted using a screw extractor set. Centre punch the fastener to centralise the drill bit, then drill a hole in the fastener **(see illustration 2.19)**. Select a drill bit which is approximately half to three-quarters the diameter of the fastener and drill to a depth which will accommodate the extractor. Use the largest size extractor

possible, but avoid leaving too small a wall thickness otherwise the extractor will merely force the fastener walls outwards wedging it in the casing thread.

● If a spiral type extractor is used, thread it anti-clockwise into the fastener. As it is screwed in, it will grip the fastener and unscrew it from the casing **(see illustration 2.20)**.

 **Warning: Stud extractors are very hard and may break off in the fastener if care is not taken – ask an engineer about spark erosion if this happens.**

● If a taper type extractor is used, tap it into the fastener so that it is firmly wedged in place. Unscrew the extractor (anti-clockwise) to draw the fastener out.

● Alternatively, the broken bolt/screw can be drilled out and the hole retapped for an oversize bolt/screw or a diamond-section thread insert. It is essential that the drilling is carried out squarely and to the correct depth, otherwise the casing may be ruined – if in

doubt, entrust the work to an engineer.

● Bolts and nuts with rounded corners cause the correct size spanner or socket to slip when force is applied. Of the types of spanner/socket available always use a six-point type rather than an eight or twelve-point type – better grip is obtained. Surface drive spanners grip the middle of the hex flats, rather than the corners, and are thus good in cases of damaged heads **(see illustration 2.21)**.

● Slotted-head or Phillips-head screws are often damaged by the use of the wrong size screwdriver. Allen-head and Torx-head screws are much less likely to sustain damage. If enough of the screw head is exposed you can use a hacksaw to cut a slot in its head and then use a conventional flat-bladed screwdriver to remove it. Alternatively use a hammer and cold chisel to tap the head of the fastener around to slacken it. Always replace damaged fasteners with new ones, preferably Torx or Allen-head type.

**2.20 . . . then thread the extractor anti-clockwise into the fastener**

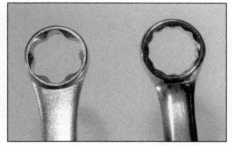

**2.21 Comparison of surface drive ring spanner (left) with 12-point type (right)**

**HAYNES HiNT**

*A dab of valve grinding compound between the screw head and screw-driver tip will often give a good grip.*

## Thread repair

● Threads (particularly those in aluminium alloy components) can be damaged by overtightening, being assembled with dirt in the threads, or from a component working loose and vibrating. Eventually the thread will fail completely, and it will be impossible to tighten the fastener.

● If a thread is damaged or clogged with old locking compound it can be renovated with a thread repair tool (thread chaser) **(see illustrations 2.22 and 2.23)**; special thread

**2.22 A thread repair tool being used to correct an internal thread**

**2.23 A thread repair tool being used to correct an external thread**

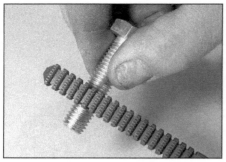

**2.24 Using a thread restorer file**

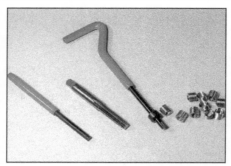

**2.25 Obtain a thread insert kit to suit the thread diameter and pitch required**

**2.26 To install a thread insert, first drill out the original thread . . .**

chasers are available for spark plug hole threads. The tool will not cut a new thread, but clean and true the original thread. Make sure that you use the correct diameter and pitch tool. Similarly, external threads can be cleaned up with a die or a thread restorer file **(see illustration 2.24)**.

● It is possible to drill out the old thread and retap the component to the next thread size. This will work where there is enough surrounding material and a new bolt or screw can be obtained. Sometimes, however, this is not possible – such as where the bolt/screw passes through another component which must also be suitably modified, also in cases where a spark plug or oil drain plug cannot be obtained in a larger diameter thread size.

● The diamond-section thread insert (often known by its popular trade name of Heli-Coil)

is a simple and effective method of renewing the thread and retaining the original size. A kit can be purchased which contains the tap, insert and installing tool **(see illustration 2.25)**. Drill out the damaged thread with the size drill specified **(see illustration 2.26)**. Carefully retap the thread **(see illustration 2.27)**. Install the insert on the installing tool and thread it slowly into place using a light downward pressure **(see illustrations 2.28 and 2.29)**. When positioned between a 1/4 and 1/2 turn below the surface withdraw the installing tool and use the break-off tool to press down on the tang, breaking it off **(see illustration 2.30)**.

● There are epoxy thread repair kits on the market which can rebuild stripped internal threads, although this repair should not be used on high load-bearing components.

### Thread locking and sealing compounds

● Locking compounds are used in locations where the fastener is prone to loosening due to vibration or on important safety-related items which might cause loss of control of the scooter if they fail. It is also used where important fasteners cannot be secured by other means such as lockwashers or split pins.

● Before applying locking compound, make sure that the threads (internal and external) are clean and dry with all old compound removed. Select a compound to suit the component being secured – a non-permanent general locking and sealing type is suitable for most applications, but a high strength type is needed for permanent fixing of studs in castings. Apply a drop or two of the compound to the first few threads of the fastener, then thread it into place and tighten to the specified torque. Do not apply excessive thread locking compound otherwise the thread may be damaged on subsequent removal.

● Certain fasteners are impregnated with a dry film type coating of locking compound on their threads. Always renew this type of fastener if disturbed.

● Anti-seize compounds, such as copper-based greases, can be applied to protect threads from seizure due to extreme heat and corrosion. A common instance is spark plug threads and exhaust system fasteners.

**2.27 . . . tap a new thread . . .**

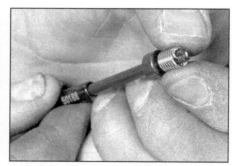

**2.28 . . . fit insert on the installing tool . . .**

### 3 Measuring tools and gauges

### Feeler gauges

● Feeler gauges (or blades) are used for measuring small gaps and clearances **(see illustration 3.1)**. They can also be used to measure endfloat (sideplay) of a component on a shaft where access is not possible with a dial gauge.

● Feeler gauge sets should be treated with care and not bent or damaged. They are etched with their size on one face. Keep them

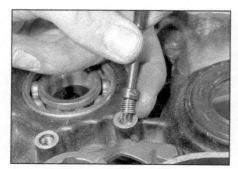

**2.29 . . . and thread into the component . . .**

**2.30 . . . break off the tang when complete**

**3.1 Feeler gauges are used for measuring small gaps and clearances – thickness is marked on one face of gauge**

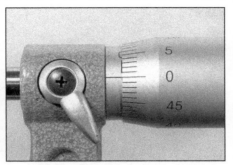

**3.2 Check micrometer calibration before use**

clean and very lightly oiled to prevent corrosion build-up.

● When measuring a clearance, select a gauge which is a light sliding fit between the two components. You may need to use two gauges together to measure the clearance accurately.

## Micrometers

● A micrometer is a precision tool capable of measuring to 0.01 or 0.001 of a millimetre. It should always be stored in its case and not in the general toolbox. It must be kept clean and never dropped, otherwise its frame or measuring anvils could be distorted resulting in inaccurate readings.

● External micrometers are used for measuring outside diameters of components and have many more applications than internal micrometers. Micrometers are available in different size ranges, eg 0 to 25 mm, 25 to 50 mm, and upwards in 25 mm steps; some large micrometers have interchangeable anvils to allow a range of measurements to be taken. Generally the largest precision measurement you are likely to take on a scooter is the piston diameter.

● Internal micrometers (or bore micrometers) are used for measuring inside diameters, such as valve guides and cylinder bores. Telescoping gauges and small hole gauges are used in conjunction with an external micrometer, whereas the more expensive internal micrometers have their own measuring device.

### External micrometer

**Note:** *The conventional analogue type instrument is described. Although much easier to read, digital micrometers are considerably more expensive.*

● Always check the calibration of the micrometer before use. With the anvils closed (0 to 25 mm type) or set over a test gauge (for the larger types) the scale should read zero **(see illustration 3.2)**; make sure that the anvils (and test piece) are clean first. Any discrepancy can be adjusted by referring to the instructions supplied with the tool. Remember that the micrometer is a precision measuring tool – don't force the anvils closed, use the ratchet (4) on the end of the micrometer to close it. In this way, a measured force is always applied.

● To use, first make sure that the item being measured is clean. Place the anvil of the micrometer (1) against the item and use the thimble (2) to bring the spindle (3) lightly into contact with the other side of the item **(see illustration 3.3)**. Don't tighten the thimble down because this will damage the micrometer – instead use the ratchet (4) on the end of the micrometer. The ratchet mechanism applies a measured force preventing damage to the instrument.

● The micrometer is read by referring to the linear scale on the sleeve and the annular scale on the thimble. Read off the sleeve first to obtain the base measurement, then add the fine measurement from the thimble to obtain the overall reading. The linear scale on the sleeve represents the measuring range of the micrometer (eg 0 to 25 mm). The annular scale on the thimble will be in graduations of 0.01 mm (or as marked on the frame) – one full revolution of the thimble will move 0.5 mm on the linear scale. Take the reading where the datum line on the sleeve intersects the thimble's scale. Always position the eye directly above the scale otherwise an inaccurate reading will result.

In the example shown the item measures 2.95 mm **(see illustration 3.4)**:

| | |
|---|---|
| Linear scale | 2.00 mm |
| Linear scale | 0.50 mm |
| Annular scale | 0.45 mm |
| **Total figure** | **2.95 mm** |

Most micrometers have a locking lever (6) on the frame to hold the setting in place, allowing the item to be removed from the micrometer.

● Some micrometers have a vernier scale on their sleeve, providing an even finer measurement to be taken, in 0.001 increments of a millimetre. Take the sleeve and thimble measurement as described above, then check which graduation on the vernier scale aligns with that of the annular scale on the thimble **Note:** *The eye must be perpendicular to the scale when taking the vernier reading – if necessary rotate the body of the micrometer to ensure this.* Multiply the vernier scale figure by 0.001 and add it to the base and fine measurement figures.

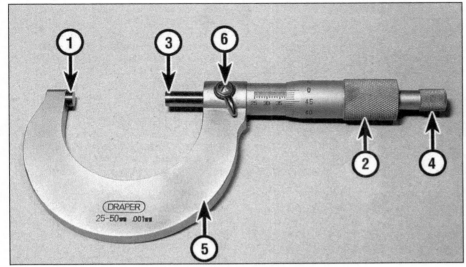

**3.3 Micrometer component parts**

| | | | | | |
|---|---|---|---|---|---|
| 1 | Anvil | 3 | Spindle | 5 | Frame |
| 2 | Thimble | 4 | Ratchet | 6 | Locking lever |

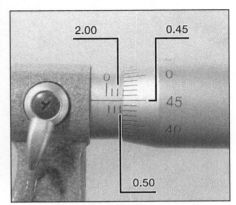

**3.4 Micrometer reading of 2.95 mm**

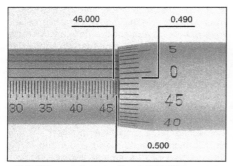

**3.5 Micrometer reading of 46.99 mm on linear and annular scales . . .**

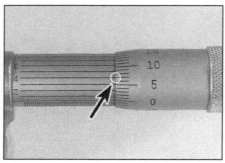

**3.6 . . . and 0.004 mm on vernier scale**

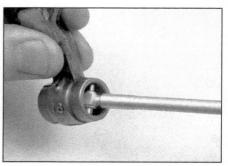

**3.7 Expand the telescoping gauge in the bore, lock its position . . .**

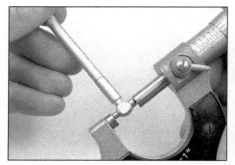

**3.8 . . . then measure the gauge with a micrometer**

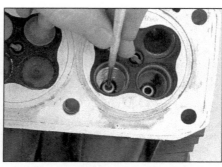

**3.9 Expand the small hole gauge in the bore, lock its position . . .**

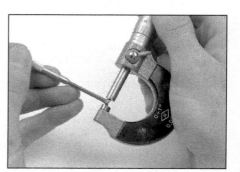

**3.10 . . . then measure the gauge with a micrometer**

In the example shown the item measures 46.994 mm **(see illustrations 3.5 and 3.6):**

| | |
|---|---|
| Linear scale (base) | 46.000 mm |
| Linear scale (base) | 00.500 mm |
| Annular scale (fine) | 00.490 mm |
| Vernier scale | 00.004 mm |
| Total figure | **46.994 mm** |

### Internal micrometer

● Internal micrometers are available for measuring bore diameters, but are expensive and unlikely to be available for home use. It is suggested that a set of telescoping gauges and small hole gauges, both of which must be used with an external micrometer, will suffice for taking internal measurements on a scooter.
● Telescoping gauges can be used to measure internal diameters of components. Select a gauge with the correct size range, make sure its ends are clean and insert it into the bore. Expand the gauge, then lock its position and withdraw it from the bore **(see illustration 3.7)**. Measure across the gauge ends with a micrometer **(see illustration 3.8)**.
● Very small diameter bores (such as valve guides) are measured with a small hole gauge. Once adjusted to a slip-fit inside the component, its position is locked and the gauge withdrawn for measurement with a micrometer **(see illustrations 3.9 and 3.10)**.

### Vernier caliper

**Note:** *The conventional linear and dial gauge type instruments are described. Digital types are easier to read, but are far more expensive.*
● The vernier caliper does not provide the precision of a micrometer, but is versatile in being able to measure internal and external diameters. Some types also incorporate a depth gauge. It is ideal for measuring clutch plate friction material and spring free lengths.
● To use the conventional linear scale vernier, slacken off the vernier clamp screws (1) and set its jaws over (2), or inside (3), the item to be measured **(see illustration 3.11)**. Slide the jaw into contact, using the thumb-wheel (4) for fine movement of the sliding scale (5) then tighten the clamp screws (1). Read off the main scale (6) where the zero on the sliding scale (5) intersects it, taking the whole number to the left of the zero; this provides the base measurement. View along the sliding scale and select the division which lines up exactly with any of the divisions on the main scale, noting that the divisions usually represents 0.02 of a millimetre. Add this fine measurement to the base measurement to obtain the total reading.

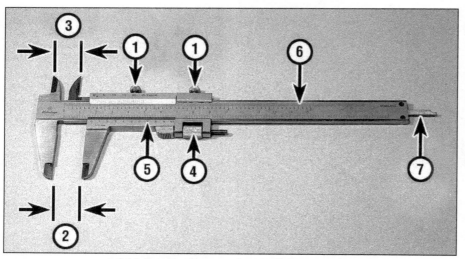

**3.11 Vernier component parts (linear gauge)**

| | | | | | | | |
|---|---|---|---|---|---|---|---|
| 1 | Clamp screws | 3 | Internal jaws | 5 | Sliding scale | 7 | Depth gauge |
| 2 | External jaws | 4 | Thumbwheel | 6 | Main scale | | |

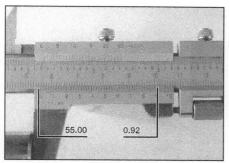

**3.12  Vernier gauge reading of 55.92 mm**

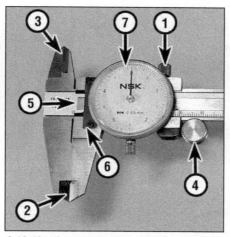

**3.13  Vernier component parts (dial gauge)**

1  Clamp screw
2  External jaws
3  Internal jaws
4  Thumbwheel
5  Main scale
6  Sliding scale
7  Dial gauge

**3.14  Vernier gauge reading of 55.95 mm**

In the example shown the item measures 55.92 mm (see illustration 3.12):

| | |
|---|---|
| Base measurement | 55.00 mm |
| Fine measurement | 00.92 mm |
| Total figure | **55.92 mm** |

● Some vernier calipers are equipped with a dial gauge for fine measurement. Before use, check that the jaws are clean, then close them fully and check that the dial gauge reads zero. If necessary adjust the gauge ring accordingly. Slacken the vernier clamp screw (1) and set its jaws over (2), or inside (3), the item to be measured (see illustration 3.13). Slide the jaws into contact, using the thumbwheel (4) for fine movement. Read off the main scale (5) where the edge of the sliding scale (6) intersects it, taking the whole number to the left of the zero; this provides the base measurement. Read off the needle position on the dial gauge (7) scale to provide the fine measurement; each division represents 0.05 of a millimetre. Add this fine measurement to the base measurement to obtain the total reading.

In the example shown the item measures 55.95 mm (see illustration 3.14):

| | |
|---|---|
| Base measurement | 55.00 mm |
| Fine measurement | 00.95 mm |
| Total figure | **55.95 mm** |

## Dial gauge or DTI (Dial Test Indicator)

● A dial gauge can be used to accurately measure small amounts of movement. Typical uses are measuring shaft runout or shaft endfloat (sideplay) and setting piston position for ignition timing on two-strokes. A dial gauge

set usually comes with a range of different probes and adapters and mounting equipment.
● The gauge needle must point to zero when at rest. Rotate the ring around its periphery to zero the gauge.
● Check that the gauge is capable of reading the extent of movement in the work. Most gauges have a small dial set in the face which records whole millimetres of movement as well as the fine scale around the face periphery which is calibrated in 0.01 mm divisions. Read off the small dial first to obtain the base measurement, then add the measurement from the fine scale to obtain the total reading.

In the example shown the gauge reads 1.48 mm (see illustration 3.15):

| | |
|---|---|
| Base measurement | 1.00 mm |
| Fine measurement | 0.48 mm |
| Total figure | **1.48 mm** |

● If measuring shaft runout, the shaft must be supported in vee-blocks and the gauge mounted on a stand perpendicular to the shaft. Rest the tip of the gauge against the centre of the shaft and rotate the shaft slowly whilst watching the gauge reading (see illustration 3.16). Take several measurements along the length of the shaft and record the maximum

gauge reading as the amount of runout in the shaft. **Note:** *The reading obtained will be total runout at that point – some manufacturers specify that the runout figure is halved to compare with their specified runout limit.*
● Endfloat (sideplay) measurement requires that the gauge is mounted securely to the surrounding component with its probe touching the end of the shaft. Using hand pressure, push and pull on the shaft noting the maximum endfloat recorded on the gauge (see illustration 3.17).
● A dial gauge with suitable adapters can be used to determine piston position BTDC on two-stroke engines for the purposes of ignition timing. The gauge, adapter and suitable length probe are installed in the place of the spark plug and the gauge zeroed at TDC. If the piston position is specified as 1.14 mm BTDC, rotate the engine back to 2.00 mm BTDC, then slowly forwards to 1.14 mm BTDC.

## 4  Torque and leverage

### What is torque?

● Torque describes the twisting force about a shaft. The amount of torque applied is determined by the distance from the centre of the shaft to the end of the lever and the amount of force being applied to the end of the lever; distance multiplied by force equals torque.
● The manufacturer applies a measured

**3.15  Dial gauge reading of 1.48 mm**

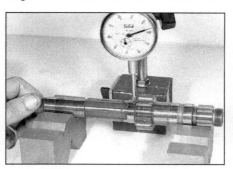

**3.16  Using a dial gauge to measure shaft runout**

**3.17  Using a dial gauge to measure shaft endfloat**

**4.1 Set the torque wrench index mark to the setting required, in this case 12 Nm**

**4.2 Angle tightening can be accomplished with a torque-angle gauge . . .**

**4.3 . . . or by marking the angle on the surrounding component**

torque to a bolt or nut to ensure that it will not slacken in use and to hold two components securely together without movement in the joint. The actual torque setting depends on the thread size, bolt or nut material and the composition of the components being held.
● Too little torque may cause the fastener to loosen due to vibration, whereas too much torque will distort the joint faces of the component or cause the fastener to shear off. Always stick to the specified torque setting.

### Using a torque wrench

● Check the calibration of the torque wrench and make sure it has a suitable range for the job. Torque wrenches are available in Nm (Newton-metres), kgf m (kilograms-force metre), lbf ft (pounds-feet), lbf in (inch-pounds). Do not confuse lbf ft with lbf in.
● Adjust the tool to the desired torque on the scale **(see illustration 4.1)**. If your torque wrench is not calibrated in the units specified, carefully convert the figure (see *Conversion Factors*). A manufacturer sometimes gives a torque setting as a range (8 to 10 Nm) rather than a single figure – in this case set the tool midway between the two settings. The same torque may be expressed as 9 Nm ± 1 Nm. Some torque wrenches have a method of locking the setting so that it isn't inadvertently altered during use.
● Install the bolts/nuts in their correct location and secure them lightly. Their threads must be clean and free of any old locking compound. Unless specified the threads and flange should be dry – oiled threads are necessary in certain

circumstances and the manufacturer will take this into account in the specified torque figure. Similarly, the manufacturer may also specify the application of thread-locking compound.
● Tighten the fasteners in the specified sequence until the torque wrench clicks, indicating that the torque setting has been reached. Apply the torque again to double-check the setting. Where different thread diameter fasteners secure the component, as a rule tighten the larger diameter ones first.
● When the torque wrench has been finished with, release the lock (where applicable) and fully back off its setting to zero – do not leave the torque wrench tensioned. Also, do not use a torque wrench for slackening a fastener.

### Angle-tightening

● Manufacturers often specify a figure in degrees for final tightening of a fastener. This usually follows tightening to a specific torque setting.
● A degree disc can be set and attached to the socket **(see illustration 4.2)** or a protractor can be used to mark the angle of movement on the bolt/nut head and the surrounding casting **(see illustration 4.3)**.

### Loosening sequences

● Where more than one bolt/nut secures a component, loosen each fastener evenly a little at a time. In this way, not all the stress of the joint is held by one fastener and the components are not likely to distort.
● If a tightening sequence is provided, work

in the REVERSE of this, but if not, work from the outside in, in a criss-cross sequence **(see illustration 4.4)**.

### Tightening sequences

● If a component is held by more than one fastener it is important that the retaining bolts/nuts are tightened evenly to prevent uneven stress build-up and distortion of sealing faces. This is especially important on high-compression joints such as the cylinder head.
● A sequence is usually provided by the manufacturer, either in a diagram or actually marked in the casting. If not, always start in the centre and work outwards in a criss-cross pattern **(see illustration 4.5)**. Start off by securing all bolts/nuts finger-tight, then set the torque wrench and tighten each fastener by a small amount in sequence until the final torque is reached. By following this practice, the joint will be held evenly and will not be distorted. Important joints, such as the cylinder head and big-end fasteners often have two- or three-stage torque settings.

### Applying leverage

● Use tools at the correct angle. Position a socket wrench or spanner on the bolt/nut so that you pull it towards you when loosening. If this can't be done, push the spanner without curling your fingers around it **(see illustration 4.6)** – the spanner may slip or the fastener loosen suddenly, resulting in your fingers being crushed against a component.
● Additional leverage is gained by extending the length of the lever. The best way to do this is to use a breaker bar instead of the regular length tool, or to slip a length of tubing over the end of the spanner or socket wrench.
● If additional leverage will not work, the fastener head is either damaged or firmly corroded in place (see *Fasteners*).

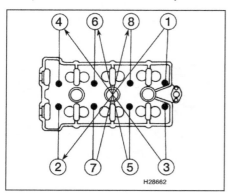

**4.4 When slackening, work from the outside inwards**

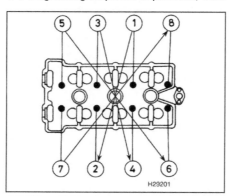

**4.5 When tightening, work from the inside outwards**

**4.6 If you can't pull on the spanner to loosen a fastener, push with your hand open**

**5.1 Using a bearing driver against the bearing's outer race**

**5.2 Using a large socket against the bearing's outer race**

**5.3 This bearing puller clamps behind the bearing and pressure is applied to the shaft end to draw the bearing off**

## 5 Bearings

### Bearing removal and installation

#### Drivers and sockets

● Before removing a bearing, always inspect the casing to see which way it must be driven out – some casings will have retaining plates or a cast step. Also check for any identifying markings on the bearing and if installed to a certain depth, measure this at this stage. Some roller bearings are sealed on one side – take note of the original fitted position.

● Bearings can be driven out of a casing using a bearing driver tool (with the correct size head) or a socket of the correct diameter. Select the driver head or socket so that it contacts the outer race of the bearing, not the balls/rollers or inner race. Always support the casing around the bearing housing with wood blocks, otherwise there is a risk of fracture. The bearing is driven out with a few blows on the driver or socket from a heavy mallet. Unless access is severely restricted (as with wheel bearings), a pin-punch is not recommended unless it is moved around the bearing to keep it square in its housing.

● The same equipment can be used to install bearings. Make sure the bearing housing is supported on wood blocks and line up the bearing in its housing. Fit the bearing as noted on removal – generally they are installed with their marked side facing outwards. Tap the bearing squarely into its housing using a driver or socket which bears only on the bearing's outer race – contact with the bearing balls/rollers or inner race will destroy it **(see illustrations 5.1 and 5.2)**.

● Check that the bearing inner race and balls/rollers rotate freely.

#### Pullers and slide-hammers

● Where a bearing is pressed on a shaft a puller will be required to extract it **(see illustration 5.3)**. Make sure that the puller clamp or legs fit securely behind the bearing and are unlikely to slip out. If pulling a bearing off a gear shaft for example, you may have to

locate the puller behind a gear pinion if there is no access to the race and draw the gear pinion off the shaft as well **(see illustration 5.4)**.
*Caution: Ensure that the puller's centre bolt locates securely against the end of the shaft and will not slip when pressure is applied. Also ensure that puller does not damage the shaft end.*

● Operate the puller so that its centre bolt exerts pressure on the shaft end and draws the bearing off the shaft.

● When installing the bearing on the shaft, tap only on the bearing's inner race – contact with the balls/rollers or outer race will destroy the bearing. Use a socket or length of tubing as a drift which fits over the shaft end **(see illustration 5.5)**.

**5.4 Where no access is available to the rear of the bearing, it is sometimes possible to draw off the adjacent component**

**5.5 When installing a bearing on a shaft use a piece of tubing which bears only on the bearing's inner race**

● Where a bearing locates in a blind hole in a casing, it cannot be driven or pulled out as described above. A slide-hammer with knife-edged bearing puller attachment will be required. The puller attachment passes through the bearing and when tightened expands to fit firmly behind the bearing **(see illustration 5.6)**. By operating the slide-hammer part of the tool the bearing is jarred out of its housing **(see illustration 5.7)**.

● It is possible, if the bearing is of reasonable weight, for it to drop out of its housing if the casing is heated as described opposite. If this method is attempted, first prepare a work surface which will enable the casing to be tapped face down to help dislodge the bearing – a wood surface is ideal since it will not damage the casing's gasket surface.

**5.6 Expand the bearing puller so that it locks behind the bearing . . .**

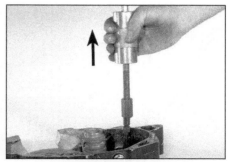

**5.7 . . . attach the slide hammer to the bearing puller**

**5.8 Tapping a casing face down on wood blocks can often dislodge a bearing**

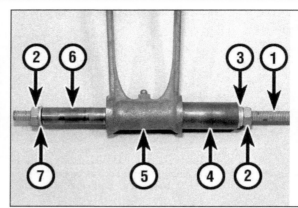

1 Bolt or length of threaded bar
2 Nuts
3 Washer (external diameter greater than tubing internal diameter)
4 Tubing (internal diameter sufficient to accommodate bearing)
5 Suspension arm with bearing
6 Tubing (external diameter slightly smaller than bearing)
7 Washer (external diameter slightly smaller than bearing)

**5.9 Drawbolt component parts assembled on a suspension arm**

Wearing protective gloves, tap the heated casing several times against the work surface to dislodge the bearing under its own weight **(see illustration 5.8)**.

● Bearings can be installed in blind holes using the driver or socket method described above.

## Drawbolts

● Where a bearing or bush is set in the eye of a component, such as a suspension linkage arm or connecting rod small-end, removal by drift may damage the component. Furthermore, a rubber bushing in a shock absorber eye cannot successfully be driven out of position. If access is available to a engineering press, the task is straightforward. If not, a drawbolt can be fabricated to extract the bearing or bush.

● To extract the bearing/bush you will need a long bolt with nut (or piece of threaded bar with two nuts), a piece of tubing which has an

internal diameter larger than the bearing/bush, another piece of tubing which has an external diameter slightly smaller than the bearing/bush, and a selection of washers **(see illustrations 5.9 and 5.10)**. Note that the pieces of tubing must be of the same length, or longer, than the bearing/bush.

● The same kit (without the pieces of tubing) can be used to draw the new bearing/bush back into place **(see illustration 5.11)**.

## Temperature change

● If the bearing's outer race is a tight fit in the casing, the aluminium casing can be heated to release its grip on the bearing. Aluminium will expand at a greater rate than the steel bearing outer race. There are several ways to do this, but avoid any localised extreme heat

(such as a blow torch) – aluminium alloy has a low melting point.

● Approved methods of heating a casing are using a domestic oven (heated to 100°C) or immersing the casing in boiling water **(see illustration 5.12)**. Low temperature range localised heat sources such as a paint stripper heat gun or clothes iron can also be used **(see illustration 5.13)**. Alternatively, soak a rag in boiling water, wring it out and wrap it around the bearing housing.

> ⚠️ **Warning: All of these methods require care in use to prevent scalding and burns to the hands. Wear protective gloves when handling hot components.**

● If heating the whole casing note that plastic components, such as the oil pressure switch, may suffer – remove them beforehand.

● After heating, remove the bearing as described above. You may find that the expansion is sufficient for the bearing to fall out of the casing under its own weight or with a light tap on the driver or socket.

● If necessary, the casing can be heated to aid bearing installation, and this is sometimes the recommended procedure if the scooter manufacturer has designed the housing and bearing fit with this intention.

● Installation of bearings can be eased by placing them in a freezer the night before installation. The steel bearing will contract slightly, allowing easy insertion in its housing. This is often useful when installing steering head outer races in the frame.

## Bearing types and markings

● Plain bearings, ball bearings, needle roller bearings and tapered roller bearings will all be found on scooters **(see illustrations 5.14 and 5.15)**. The ball and roller types are usually caged between an inner and outer race, but uncaged variations may be found.

● Plain bearings are sometimes found at the crankshaft main and connecting rod big-end where they are good at coping with high loads. They are made of a phosphor-bronze material and are impregnated with self-lubricating properties.

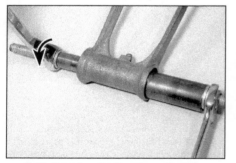

**5.10 Drawing the bearing out of the suspension arm**

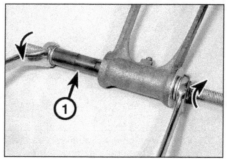

**5.11 Installing a new bearing (1) in the suspension arm**

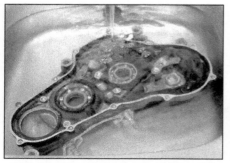

**5.12 A casing can be immersed in a sink of boiling water to aid bearing removal**

**5.13 Using a localised heat source to aid bearing removal**

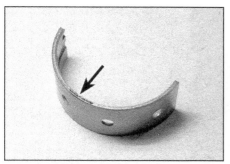

**5.14 Bearings are either plain or grooved. They are usually identified by colour code (arrow)**

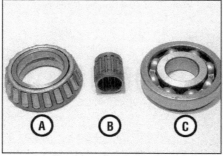

**5.15 Tapered roller bearing (A), needle roller bearing (B) and ball journal bearing (C)**

**5.16 Typical bearing marking**

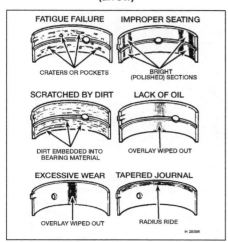

**5.17 Typical bearing failures**

**5.18 Example of ball journal bearing with damaged balls and cages**

**5.19 Hold outer race and listen to inner race when spun**

● Ball bearings and needle roller bearings consist of a steel inner and outer race with the balls or rollers between the races. They require constant lubrication by oil or grease and are good at coping with axial loads. Tapered roller bearings consist of rollers set in a tapered cage set on the inner race; the outer race is separate. They are good at coping with axial loads and prevent movement along the shaft – a typical application is in the steering head.

● Bearing manufacturers produce bearings to ISO size standards and stamp one face of the bearing to indicate its internal and external diameter, load capacity and type **(see illustration 5.16)**.

● Metal bushes are usually of phosphor-bronze material. Rubber bushes are used in suspension mounting eyes. Fibre bushes have also been used in suspension pivots.

### Bearing fault finding

● If a bearing outer race has spun in its housing, the housing material will be damaged. You can use a bearing locking compound to bond the outer race in place if damage is not too severe.

● Plain bearings will fail due to damage of their working surface, as a result of lack of lubrication, corrosion or abrasive particles in the oil **(see illustration 5.17)**. Small particles

of dirt in the oil may embed in the bearing material whereas larger particles will score the bearing and shaft journal. If a number of short journeys are made, insufficient heat will be generated to drive off condensation which has built up on the bearings.

● Ball and roller bearings will fail due to lack of lubrication or damage to the balls or rollers. Tapered roller bearings can be damaged by overloading them. Unless the bearing is sealed on both sides, wash it in paraffin (kerosene) to remove all old grease then allow it to dry. Make a visual inspection looking to dented balls or rollers, damaged cages and worn or pitted races **(see illustration 5.18)**.

● A ball bearing can be checked for wear by listening to it when spun. Apply a film of light oil to the bearing and hold it close to the ear – hold the outer race with one hand and spin the inner race with the other hand **(see illustration 5.19)**. The bearing should be almost silent when spun; if it grates or rattles it is worn.

## 6 Oil seals

### Oil seal removal and installation

● Oil seals should be renewed every time a component is dismantled. This is because the seal lips will become set to the sealing surface and will not necessarily reseal.

● Oil seals can be prised out of position using a large flat-bladed screwdriver **(see**

**illustration 6.1)**. In the case of crankcase seals, check first that the seal is not lipped on the inside, preventing its removal with the crankcases joined.

● New seals are usually installed with their marked face (containing the seal reference code) outwards and the spring side towards the fluid being retained. In certain cases, such as a two-stroke engine crankshaft seal, a double lipped seal may be used due to there being fluid or gas on each side of the joint.

● Use a bearing driver or socket which bears only on the outer hard edge of the seal to install it in the casing – tapping on the inner edge will damage the sealing lip.

### Oil seal types and markings

● Oil seals are usually of the single-lipped type. Double-lipped seals are found where a liquid or gas is on both sides of the joint.

**6.1 Prise out oil seals with a large flat-bladed screwdriver**

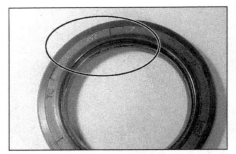

**6.2 These oil seal markings indicate inside diameter, outside diameter and seal thickness**

● Oil seals can harden and lose their sealing ability if the scooter has been in storage for a long period – renewal is the only solution.
● Oil seal manufacturers also conform to the ISO markings for seal size – these are moulded into the outer face of the seal (see illustration 6.2).

## 7  Gaskets and sealants

### Types of gasket and sealant

● Gaskets are used to seal the mating surfaces between components and keep lubricants, fluids, vacuum or pressure contained within the assembly. Aluminium gaskets are sometimes found at the cylinder joints, but most gaskets are paper-based. If the mating surfaces of the components being joined are undamaged the gasket can be installed dry, although a dab of sealant or grease will be useful to hold it in place during assembly.
● RTV (Room Temperature Vulcanising) silicone rubber sealants cure when exposed to moisture in the atmosphere. These sealants are good at filling pits or irregular gasket faces, but will tend to be forced out of the joint under very high torque. They can be used to replace a paper gasket, but first make sure that the width of the paper gasket is not essential to the shimming of internal components. RTV sealants should not be used on components containing petrol (gasoline).
● Non-hardening, semi-hardening and hard

setting liquid gasket compounds can be used with a gasket or between a metal-to-metal joint. Select the sealant to suit the application: universal non-hardening sealant can be used on virtually all joints; semi-hardening on joint faces which are rough or damaged; hard setting sealant on joints which require a permanent bond and are subjected to high temperature and pressure. **Note:** *Check first if the paper gasket has a bead of sealant impregnated in its surface before applying additional sealant.*
● When choosing a sealant, make sure it is suitable for the application, particularly if being applied in a high-temperature area or in the vicinity of fuel. Certain manufacturers produce sealants in either clear, silver or black colours to match the finish of the engine.
● Do not over-apply sealant. That which is squeezed out on the outside of the joint can be wiped off, whereas an excess of sealant on the inside can break off and clog oilways.

### Breaking a sealed joint

● Age, heat, pressure and the use of hard setting sealant can cause two components to stick together so tightly that they are difficult to separate using finger pressure alone. Do not resort to using levers unless there is a pry point provided for this purpose (see illustration 7.1) or else the gasket surfaces will be damaged.
● Use a soft-faced hammer (see illustration 7.2) or a wood block and conventional hammer to strike the component near the mating surface. Avoid hammering against cast extremities since they may break off. If this method fails, try using a wood wedge between the two components.

**7.1 If a pry point is provided, apply gently pressure with a flat-bladed screwdriver**

**7.2 Tap around the joint with a soft-faced mallet if necessary – don't strike cooling fins**

*Most components have one or two hollow locating dowels between the two gasket faces. If a dowel cannot be removed, do not resort to gripping it with pliers – it will almost certainly be distorted. Install a close-fitting socket or Phillips screwdriver into the dowel and then grip the outer edge of the dowel to free it.*

Caution: *If the joint will not separate, double-check that you have removed all the fasteners.*

### Removal of old gasket and sealant

● Paper gaskets will most likely come away complete, leaving only a few traces stuck on the sealing faces of the components. It is imperative that all traces are removed to ensure correct sealing of the new gasket.
● Very carefully scrape all traces of gasket away making sure that the sealing surfaces are not gouged or scored by the scraper (see illustrations 7.3, 7.4 and 7.5). Stubborn

**7.3 Paper gaskets can be scraped off with a gasket scraper tool . . .**

**7.4 . . . a knife blade . . .**

**7.5 . . . or a household scraper**

**7.6 Fine abrasive paper is wrapped around a flat file to clean up the gasket face**

**7.7 A kitchen scourer can be used on stubborn deposits**

deposits can be removed by spraying with an aerosol gasket remover. Final preparation of the gasket surface can be made with very fine abrasive paper or a plastic kitchen scourer **(see illustrations 7.6 and 7.7)**.

● Old sealant can be scraped or peeled off components, depending on the type originally used. Note that gasket removal compounds are available to avoid scraping the components clean; make sure the gasket remover suits the type of sealant used.

## 8 Hoses

### Clamping to prevent flow

● Small-bore flexible hoses can be clamped to prevent fluid flow whilst a component is worked on. Whichever method is used, ensure that the hose material is not permanently distorted or damaged by the clamp.

a) A brake hose clamp available from auto accessory shops **(see illustration 8.1)**.
b) A wingnut type hose clamp **(see illustration 8.2)**.

c) Two sockets placed each side of the hose and held with straight-jawed self-locking grips **(see illustration 8.3)**.
d) Thick card each side of the hose held between straight-jawed self-locking grips **(see illustration 8.4)**.

### Freeing and fitting hoses

● Always make sure the hose clamp is moved well clear of the hose end. Grip the hose with your hand and rotate it whilst pulling it off the union. If the hose has hardened due to age and will not move, slit it with a sharp knife and peel its ends off the union **(see illustration 8.5)**.

● Resist the temptation to use grease or soap on the unions to aid installation; although it helps the hose slip over the union it will equally aid the escape of fluid from the joint. It is preferable to soften the hose ends in hot water and wet the inside surface of the hose with water or a fluid which will evaporate.

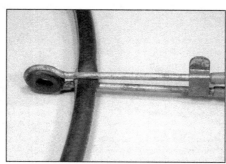

**8.1 Hoses can be clamped with an automotive brake hose clamp . . .**

**8.2 . . . a wingnut type hose clamp . . .**

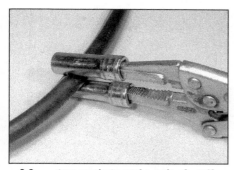

**8.3 . . . two sockets and a pair of self-locking grips . . .**

**8.4 . . . or thick card and self-locking grips**

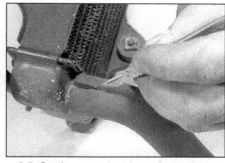

**8.5 Cutting a coolant hose free with a sharp knife**

# Conversion Factors

## Length (distance)

| | | | | |
|---|---|---|---|---|
| Inches (in) | x 25.4 | = Millimetres (mm) | x 0.0394 | = Inches (in) |
| Feet (ft) | x 0.305 | = Metres (m) | x 3.281 | = Feet (ft) |
| Miles | x 1.609 | = Kilometres (km) | x 0.621 | = Miles |

## Volume (capacity)

| | | | | |
|---|---|---|---|---|
| Cubic inches (cu in; in³) | x 16.387 | = Cubic centimetres (cc; cm³) | x 0.061 | = Cubic inches (cu in; in³) |
| Imperial pints (Imp pt) | x 0.568 | = Litres (l) | x 1.76 | = Imperial pints (Imp pt) |
| Imperial quarts (Imp qt) | x 1.137 | = Litres (l) | x 0.88 | = Imperial quarts (Imp qt) |
| Imperial quarts (Imp qt) | x 1.201 | = US quarts (US qt) | x 0.833 | = Imperial quarts (Imp qt) |
| US quarts (US qt) | x 0.946 | = Litres (l) | x 1.057 | = US quarts (US qt) |
| Imperial gallons (Imp gal) | x 4.546 | = Litres (l) | x 0.22 | = Imperial gallons (Imp gal) |
| Imperial gallons (Imp gal) | x 1.201 | = US gallons (US gal) | x 0.833 | = Imperial gallons (Imp gal) |
| US gallons (US gal) | x 3.785 | = Litres (l) | x 0.264 | = US gallons (US gal) |

## Mass (weight)

| | | | | |
|---|---|---|---|---|
| Ounces (oz) | x 28.35 | = Grams (g) | x 0.035 | = Ounces (oz) |
| Pounds (lb) | x 0.454 | = Kilograms (kg) | x 2.205 | = Pounds (lb) |

## Force

| | | | | |
|---|---|---|---|---|
| Ounces-force (ozf; oz) | x 0.278 | = Newtons (N) | x 3.6 | = Ounces-force (ozf; oz) |
| Pounds-force (lbf; lb) | x 4.448 | = Newtons (N) | x 0.225 | = Pounds-force (lbf; lb) |
| Newtons (N) | x 0.1 | = Kilograms-force (kgf; kg) | x 9.81 | = Newtons (N) |

## Pressure

| | | | | |
|---|---|---|---|---|
| Pounds-force per square inch (psi; lbf/in²; lb/in²) | x 0.070 | = Kilograms-force per square centimetre (kgf/cm²; kg/cm²) | x 14.223 | = Pounds-force per square inch (psi; lbf/in²; lb/in²) |
| Pounds-force per square inch (psi; lbf/in²; lb/in²) | x 0.068 | = Atmospheres (atm) | x 14.696 | = Pounds-force per square inch (psi; lbf/in²; lb/in²) |
| Pounds-force per square inch (psi; lbf/in²; lb/in²) | x 0.069 | = Bars | x 14.5 | = Pounds-force per square inch (psi; lbf/in²; lb/in²) |
| Pounds-force per square inch (psi; lbf/in²; lb/in²) | x 6.895 | = Kilopascals (kPa) | x 0.145 | = Pounds-force per square inch (psi; lbf/in²; lb/in²) |
| Kilopascals (kPa) | x 0.01 | = Kilograms-force per square centimetre (kgf/cm²; kg/cm²) | x 98.1 | = Kilopascals (kPa) |
| Millibar (mbar) | x 100 | = Pascals (Pa) | x 0.01 | = Millibar (mbar) |
| Millibar (mbar) | x 0.0145 | = Pounds-force per square inch (psi; lbf/in²; lb/in²) | x 68.947 | = Millibar (mbar) |
| Millibar (mbar) | x 0.75 | = Millimetres of mercury (mmHg) | x 1.333 | = Millibar (mbar) |
| Millibar (mbar) | x 0.401 | = Inches of water (inH$_2$O) | x 2.491 | = Millibar (mbar) |
| Millimetres of mercury (mmHg) | x 0.535 | = Inches of water (inH$_2$O) | x 1.868 | = Millimetres of mercury (mmHg) |
| Inches of water (inH$_2$O) | x 0.036 | = Pounds-force per square inch (psi; lbf/in²; lb/in²) | x 27.68 | = Inches of water (inH$_2$O) |

## Torque (moment of force)

| | | | | |
|---|---|---|---|---|
| Pounds-force inches (lbf in; lb in) | x 1.152 | = Kilograms-force centimetre (kgf cm; kg cm) | x 0.868 | = Pounds-force inches (lbf in; lb in) |
| Pounds-force inches (lbf in; lb in) | x 0.113 | = Newton metres (Nm) | x 8.85 | = Pounds-force inches (lbf in; lb in) |
| Pounds-force inches (lbf in; lb in) | x 0.083 | = Pounds-force feet (lbf ft; lb ft) | x 12 | = Pounds-force inches (lbf in; lb in) |
| Pounds-force feet (lbf ft; lb ft) | x 0.138 | = Kilograms-force metres (kgf m; kg m) | x 7.233 | = Pounds-force feet (lbf ft; lb ft) |
| Pounds-force feet (lbf ft; lb ft) | x 1.356 | = Newton metres (Nm) | x 0.738 | = Pounds-force feet (lbf ft; lb ft) |
| Newton metres (Nm) | x 0.102 | = Kilograms-force metres (kgf m; kg m) | x 9.804 | = Newton metres (Nm) |

## Power

| | | | | |
|---|---|---|---|---|
| Horsepower (hp) | x 745.7 | = Watts (W) | x 0.0013 | = Horsepower (hp) |

## Velocity (speed)

| | | | | |
|---|---|---|---|---|
| Miles per hour (miles/hr; mph) | x 1.609 | = Kilometres per hour (km/hr; kph) | x 0.621 | = Miles per hour (miles/hr; mph) |

## Fuel consumption*

| | | | | |
|---|---|---|---|---|
| Miles per gallon (mpg) | x 0.354 | = Kilometres per litre (km/l) | x 2.825 | = Miles per gallon (mpg) |

## Temperature

Degrees Fahrenheit = (°C x 1.8) + 32          Degrees Celsius (Degrees Centigrade; °C) = (°F - 32) x 0.56

*It is common practice to convert from miles per gallon (mpg) to litres/100 kilometres (l/100km), where mpg x l/100 km = 282*

This Section provides an easy reference-guide to the more common faults that are likely to afflict your machine. Obviously, the opportunities are almost limitless for faults to occur as a result of obscure failures, and to try and cover all eventualities would require a book. Indeed, a number have been written on the subject.

Successful troubleshooting is not a mysterious 'black art' but the application of a bit of knowledge combined with a systematic and logical approach to the problem. Approach any troubleshooting by first accurately identifying the symptom and then checking through the list of possible causes, starting with the simplest or most obvious and progressing in stages to the most complex.

Take nothing for granted, but above all apply liberal quantities of common sense.

The main symptom of a fault is given in the text as a major heading below which are listed the various systems or areas which may contain the fault. Details of each possible cause for a fault and the remedial action to be taken are given, in brief, in the paragraphs below each heading. Further information should be sought in the relevant Chapter.

## 1 Engine doesn't start or is difficult to start

- ☐ Starter motor doesn't rotate
- ☐ Starter motor rotates but engine does not turn over
- ☐ Starter works but engine won't turn over (seized)
- ☐ No fuel flow
- ☐ Engine flooded
- ☐ No spark or weak spark
- ☐ Compression low
- ☐ Stalls after starting
- ☐ Rough idle

## 2 Poor running at low speed

- ☐ Spark weak
- ☐ Fuel/air mixture incorrect
- ☐ Compression low
- ☐ Poor acceleration

## 3 Poor running or no power at high speed

- ☐ Firing incorrect
- ☐ Fuel/air mixture incorrect
- ☐ Compression low
- ☐ Knocking or pinking
- ☐ Miscellaneous causes

## 4 Overheating

- ☐ Engine overheats
- ☐ Firing incorrect
- ☐ Fuel/air mixture incorrect
- ☐ Compression too high
- ☐ Engine load excessive
- ☐ Lubrication inadequate
- ☐ Miscellaneous causes

## 5 Transmission problems

- ☐ No drive to rear wheel
- ☐ Vibration
- ☐ Poor performance
- ☐ Clutch not disengaging completely

## 6 Abnormal engine noise

- ☐ Knocking or pinking
- ☐ Piston slap or rattling
- ☐ Valve noise
- ☐ Other noise

## 7 Abnormal frame and suspension noise

- ☐ Front end noise
- ☐ Shock absorber noise
- ☐ Brake noise

## 8 Excessive exhaust smoke

- ☐ White smoke
- ☐ Black smoke
- ☐ Brown smoke

## 9 Poor handling or stability

- ☐ Handlebar hard to turn
- ☐ Handlebar shakes or vibrates excessively
- ☐ Handlebar pulls to one side
- ☐ Poor shock absorbing qualities

## 10 Braking problems – disc brakes

- ☐ Brakes are ineffective
- ☐ Brake lever pulsates
- ☐ Brakes drag

## 11 Braking problems – drum brakes

- ☐ Brakes are ineffective
- ☐ Brake lever pulsates
- ☐ Brakes drag

## 12 Electrical problems

- ☐ Battery dead or weak
- ☐ Battery overcharged

# 1 Engine doesn't start or is difficult to start

### Starter motor doesn't rotate

☐ Fuse blown. Check fuse and starter circuit (Chapter 10).
☐ Battery voltage low. Check and recharge battery (Chapter 10).
☐ Starter motor defective. Make sure the wiring to the starter is secure. Make sure the starter relay clicks when the start button is pushed. If the relay clicks, then the fault is in the wiring or motor.
☐ Starter relay faulty. Check it (Chapter 10).
☐ Starter button on handlebar not contacting. The contacts could be wet, corroded or dirty. Disassemble and clean the switch (Chapter 10).
☐ Wiring open or shorted. Check all wiring connections and harnesses to make sure that they are dry, tight and not corroded. Also check for broken or frayed wires that can cause a short to earth.
☐ Ignition switch defective. Check the switch according to the procedure in Chapter 10. Renew the switch if it is defective.
☐ Starter safety circuit fault. Check brake light switches and/or inhibitor switch (according to model) and wiring (Chapter 10).

### Starter motor rotates but engine does not turn over

☐ Starter clutch defective. Inspect and repair or renew (Chapter 2).
☐ Damaged starter gears. Inspect and renew the damaged parts (Chapter 2).

### Starter works but engine won't turn over (seized)

☐ Seized engine caused by one or more internally damaged components. Failure due to wear, abuse or lack of lubrication. Damage can include piston, cylinder, connecting rod, crankshaft and bearings (Chapter 2).

### No fuel flow – carburettor models

☐ No fuel in tank.
☐ Fuel hose pinched – check the hose and its routing.
☐ Fuel hose clogged. Remove the fuel hose and carefully blow through it.
☐ Fuel tank vent in filler cap blocked. Clean and blow through or replace with a new one.
☐ Fuel filter clogged. Remove the tap and clean the filter.
☐ Fuel valve vacuum hose split or detached. Check the hose.
☐ Fuel valve diaphragm split. Renew the valve (Chapter 5A).
☐ Float needle valve or carburettor jets clogged. The carburettor should be removed and overhauled if draining the float chamber doesn't solve the problem.

### No fuel flow – fuel injection models

☐ No fuel in tank.
☐ Fuel tank vent in filler cap blocked. Clean and blow through or replace with a new one.
☐ Fuel hose pinched – check the hose and its routing.
☐ Fuel hose clogged. Remove the fuel hose and carefully blow through it.
☐ Fuel pump circuit fault – check all components in the circuit (Chapter 5B).
☐ Fuel pump defective – problems could include a faulty pump motor, faulty pressure regulator or blocked filter. In all cases replace the pump with a new one (Chapter 5B).
☐ Fuel injection system fault. See Chapter 5B.

### Engine flooded

☐ On carburettor models the float needle valve could be worn or stuck open. A piece of dirt, rust or other debris can cause the valve to seat improperly, causing excess fuel to be admitted to the float chamber. In this case, the float chamber should be cleaned and the needle valve and seat inspected. If the needle and seat

are worn, then the leaking will persist and the parts should be renewed (Chapter 5).
☐ On fuel injection models the injector could be stuck open, or there could be too much pressure in the system. Check the injector first, then check fuel pressure (Chapter 5B).
☐ Starting technique incorrect. Under normal circumstances the machine should start with no throttle, whatever the temperature.

### No spark or weak spark

☐ Battery voltage low. Check and recharge the battery as necessary (Chapter 10).
☐ Spark plug dirty, defective or worn out. Locate reason for fouled plug using spark plug condition chart at the end of this manual and follow the plug maintenance procedures (Chapter 1).
☐ Spark plug cap or lead faulty. Check condition (Chapter 6).
☐ Spark plug cap not making good contact. Make sure that the plug cap fits snugly over the plug end.
☐ Electronic control unit (ECU) defective. Check the unit, referring to Chapter 6 for details.
☐ Pulse generator coil defective. Check it, referring to Chapter 6 for details.
☐ Ignition coil defective. Check the coil, referring to Chapter 6.
☐ Wiring shorted or broken. Make sure that all wiring connections are clean, dry and tight. Look for chafed and broken wires (Chapters 6 and 10).

### Compression low

☐ Spark plug loose (Chapter 1).
☐ Cylinder head not sufficiently tightened down. If the cylinder head is suspected of being loose, then there's a chance that the gasket or head is damaged if the problem has persisted for any length of time. The camshaft holder nuts should be tightened to the proper torque in a criss-cross sequence (Chapter 2).
☐ Cylinder and/or piston worn. Excessive wear will cause compression pressure to leak past the rings. This is usually accompanied by worn rings as well. A top-end overhaul is necessary (Chapter 2).
☐ Piston rings worn, weak, broken, or sticking. Broken or sticking piston rings usually indicate a lubrication or fuelling problem that causes excess carbon deposits to form on the pistons and rings. Top-end overhaul is necessary (Chapter 2).
☐ Piston ring-to-groove clearance excessive. This is caused by excessive wear of the piston ring lands. Piston renewal is necessary (Chapter 2).
☐ Cylinder head gasket damaged. If the head is allowed to become loose, or if excessive carbon build-up on the piston crown and combustion chamber causes extremely high compression, the head gasket may leak. Retorquing the head is not always sufficient to restore the seal, so gasket renewal is necessary (Chapter 2).
☐ Cylinder head warped. This is caused by overheating or improperly tightened camshaft holder nuts. Machine shop resurfacing or head renewal is necessary (Chapter 2).
☐ Incorrect valve clearance. If a valve is not closing completely then engine pressure will leak past the valve. Check and adjust the valve clearances (Chapter 1).
☐ Valve not seating properly. This is caused by a bent valve (from over-revving or improper valve adjustment), burned valve or seat (improper combustion) or an accumulation of carbon deposits on the seat (from combustion or lubrication problems). The valves must be cleaned and/or renewed and the seats serviced if possible (Chapter 2).
☐ Valve spring broken or weak. Caused by component failure or wear; the springs must be renewed (Chapter 2).

# 1 Engine doesn't start or is difficult to start (continued)

## Stalls after starting – carburettor models

☐ Faulty automatic choke unit (Chapter 5A).
☐ Faulty idle air control valve (Chapter 5A).
☐ Carburettor fault (Chapter 5).
☐ Ignition system fault (Chapter 6).
☐ Fuel contaminated. The fuel can be contaminated with either dirt or water, or can change chemically if the machine is allowed to sit for several months or more. Drain the tank and carburettor (Chapter 5A).
☐ Intake air leak. Check for loose carburettor-to-intake manifold connection, loose carburettor top (Chapter 5A).

## Stalls after starting – fuel injection models

☐ Faulty idle air control valve – the valve is part of the throttle body (Chapter 5B).
☐ Ignition malfunction (Chapter 6).
☐ Fuel injection system fault (Chapter 5B).

☐ Fuel contaminated. The fuel can be contaminated with either dirt or water, or can change chemically if the machine is allowed to sit for several months or more. Drain the tank (Chapter 5B).
☐ Intake air leak. Check for loose throttle body-to-intake manifold connection (Chapter 5B).

## Rough idle

☐ Ignition malfunction (Chapter 5).
☐ Idle speed incorrect (Chapter 1).
☐ Carburettor or fuel injection system fault (Chapter 5A or 5B).
☐ Fuel contaminated. The fuel can be contaminated with either dirt or water, or can change chemically if the machine is allowed to sit for several months or more. Drain the tank and fuel system components (Chapter 5).
☐ Intake air leak. Check for loose intake manifold connection (Chapter 5A or 5B).
☐ Air filter clogged. Clean or renew the air filter element (Chapter 1).

# 2 Poor running at low speeds

## Spark weak

☐ Battery voltage low. Check and recharge battery (Chapter 10).
☐ Spark plug fouled, defective or worn out. Refer to Chapter 1 for spark plug maintenance.
☐ Spark plug cap or HT wiring defective. Refer to Chapter 6 for details on the ignition system.
☐ Spark plug cap not making contact.
☐ Incorrect spark plug. Wrong type, heat range or cap configuration. Check and install correct plug listed in Chapter 1.
☐ Electronic control unit (ECU) defective (Chapter 6).
☐ Pulse generator coil defective (Chapter 6).
☐ Ignition coil defective (Chapter 6).

## Fuel/air mixture incorrect – carburettor models

☐ Faulty automatic choke unit (Chapter 5A).
☐ Faulty idle air control valve (Chapter 5A).
☐ Pilot screw out of adjustment (Chapter 5A).
☐ Pilot jet or air passage clogged. Remove and clean the carburettor (Chapter 5A).
☐ Air hole clogged. Remove carburettor and blow out all passages (Chapter 5A).
☐ Air filter clogged, poorly sealed or missing (Chapter 1).
☐ Air filter housing poorly sealed. Look for cracks, holes or loose screws and renew or repair defective parts.
☐ Carburettor intake duct loose. Check for cracks, breaks, tears or loose fixings.
☐ Fuel tank vent in filler cap blocked. Clean and blow through or replace with a new one.

## Fuel/air mixture incorrect – fuel injection models

☐ Fuel injector clogged or fuel injection system fault (see Chapter 5B).
☐ Air filter clogged, poorly sealed or missing (Chapter 1).
☐ Air filter housing poorly sealed. Look for cracks, holes or loose clamps and renew or repair defective parts.
☐ Intake air leak. Check for loose throttle body-to-intake manifold connections or a leaking gasket (Chapter 5B).
☐ Faulty idle air control valve (Chapter 5B).
☐ Fuel tank vent in filler cap blocked. Clean and blow through or replace with a new one.

## Compression low

☐ Spark plug loose (Chapter 1).
☐ Cylinder head not sufficiently tightened down. If the cylinder head is suspected of being loose, then there's a chance that the gasket

or head is damaged if the problem has persisted for any length of time. The camshaft holder nuts should be tightened to the proper torque in the correct sequence (Chapter 2).
☐ Cylinder and/or piston worn. Excessive wear will cause compression pressure to leak past the rings. This is usually accompanied by worn rings as well. A top-end overhaul is necessary (Chapter 2).
☐ Piston rings worn, weak, broken, or sticking. Broken or sticking piston rings usually indicate a lubrication or fuelling problem that causes excess carbon deposits to form on the pistons and rings. Top-end overhaul is necessary (Chapter 2).
☐ Piston ring-to-groove clearance excessive. This is caused by excessive wear of the piston ring lands. Piston renewal is necessary (Chapter 2).
☐ Cylinder head gasket damaged. If the head is allowed to become loose, or if excessive carbon build-up on the piston crown and combustion chamber causes extremely high compression, the head gasket may leak. Retorquing the head is not always sufficient to restore the seal, so gasket renewal is necessary (Chapter 2).
☐ Cylinder head warped. This is caused by overheating or improperly tightened camshaft holder nuts. Machine shop resurfacing or head renewal is necessary (Chapter 2).
☐ Incorrect valve clearance. If a valve is not closing completely then engine pressure will leak past the valve. Check and adjust the valve clearances (Chapter 1).
☐ Valve not seating properly. This is caused by a bent valve (from over-revving or improper valve adjustment), burned valve or seat (improper combustion) or an accumulation of carbon deposits on the seat (from combustion or lubrication problems). The valves must be cleaned and/or renewed and the seats serviced if possible (Chapter 2).
☐ Valve spring broken or weak. Caused by component failure or wear; the springs must be renewed (Chapter 2).

## Poor acceleration

☐ Carburettor leaking or dirty. Overhaul the carburettor (Chapter 5A).
☐ Faulty automatic choke unit or idle air control valve (Chapter 5A or 5B).
☐ Fuel injection system fault (Chapter 5B).
☐ Timing not advancing. The pulse generator coil or the electronic control unit (ECU) may be defective (Chapter 6).
☐ Brakes dragging. On disc brakes, usually caused by debris which has entered the brake piston seals, or from a warped disc or bent axle, or cable out of adjustment where appropriate. On drum brakes, cable out of adjustment, shoe return spring broken. Repair as necessary (Chapter 8).
☐ Clutch slipping, drive belt worn, or variator faulty (Chapter 3).

# 3 Poor running or no power at high speed

## *Firing incorrect*

☐ Air filter clogged. Clean or renew filter (Chapter 1).
☐ Spark plug fouled, defective or worn out (Chapter 1).
☐ Spark plug cap or HT lead defective. See Chapter 6 for details of the ignition system.
☐ Spark plug cap not in good contact (Chapter 6).
☐ Incorrect spark plug. Wrong type, heat range or cap configuration. Check and install correct plug listed in Chapter 1.
☐ Electronic control unit (ECU) or ignition coil defective (Chapter 6).

## *Fuel/air mixture incorrect – carburettor models*

☐ Faulty automatic choke unit (Chapter 5A).
☐ Faulty idle air control valve (Chapter 5A).
☐ Pilot screw out of adjustment (Chapter 5A).
☐ Pilot jet or air passage clogged. Remove and clean the carburettor (Chapter 5A).
☐ Air hole clogged. Remove carburettor and blow out all passages (Chapter 5A).
☐ Air filter clogged, poorly sealed or missing (Chapter 1).
☐ Air filter housing poorly sealed. Look for cracks, holes or loose screws and renew or repair defective parts.
☐ Carburettor intake duct loose. Check for cracks, breaks, tears or loose fixings.
☐ Fuel tank vent in filler cap blocked. Clean and blow through or replace with a new one.

## *Fuel/air mixture incorrect – fuel injection models*

☐ Fuel injector clogged or fuel injection system fault (see Chapter 5B).
☐ Air filter clogged, poorly sealed or missing (Chapter 1).
☐ Air filter housing poorly sealed. Look for cracks, holes or loose clamps and renew or repair defective parts.
☐ Intake air leak. Check for loose throttle body-to-intake manifold connections or a leaking gasket (Chapter 5B).
☐ Faulty idle air control valve (Chapter 5B).
☐ Fuel tank vent in filler cap blocked. Clean and blow through or replace with a new one.

## *Compression low*

☐ Spark plug loose (Chapter 1).
☐ Cylinder head not sufficiently tightened down. If the cylinder head is suspected of being loose, then there's a chance that the gasket or head is damaged if the problem has persisted for any length of time. The camshaft holder nuts should be tightened to the proper torque in the correct sequence (Chapter 2).
☐ Cylinder and/or piston worn. Excessive wear will cause compression pressure to leak past the rings. This is usually accompanied by worn rings as well. A top-end overhaul is necessary (Chapter 2).
☐ Piston rings worn, weak, broken, or sticking. Broken or sticking piston rings usually indicate a lubrication or fuelling problem that causes excess carbon deposits to form on the pistons and rings. Top-end overhaul is necessary (Chapter 2).

☐ Piston ring-to-groove clearance excessive. This is caused by excessive wear of the piston ring lands. Piston renewal is necessary (Chapter 2).
☐ Cylinder head gasket damaged. If the head is allowed to become loose, or if excessive carbon build-up on the piston crown and combustion chamber causes extremely high compression, the head gasket may leak. Retorquing the head is not always sufficient to restore the seal, so gasket renewal is necessary (Chapter 2).
☐ Cylinder head warped. This is caused by overheating or improperly tightened camshaft holder nuts. Machine shop resurfacing or head renewal is necessary (Chapter 2).
☐ Incorrect valve clearance. If a valve is not closing completely then engine pressure will leak past the valve. Check and adjust the valve clearances (Chapter 1).
☐ Valve not seating properly. This is caused by a bent valve (from over-revving or improper valve adjustment), burned valve or seat (improper combustion) or an accumulation of carbon deposits on the seat (from combustion or lubrication problems). The valves must be cleaned and/or renewed and the seats serviced if possible (Chapter 2).
☐ Valve spring broken or weak. Caused by component failure or wear; the springs must be renewed (Chapter 2).

## *Knocking or pinking*

☐ Carbon build-up in combustion chamber. Use of a fuel additive that will dissolve the adhesive bonding the carbon particles to the crown and chamber is the easiest way to remove the build-up. Otherwise, the cylinder head will have to be removed and decarbonised (Chapter 2).
☐ Incorrect or poor quality fuel. Old or improper grades of fuel can cause detonation. This causes the piston to rattle, thus the knocking or pinking sound. Drain old fuel and always use the recommended fuel grade.
☐ Spark plug heat range incorrect. Uncontrolled detonation indicates the plug heat range is too hot. The plug in effect becomes a glow plug, raising cylinder temperatures. Install the proper heat range plug (Chapter 1).
☐ Improper air/fuel mixture. This will cause the cylinder to run hot, which leads to detonation. Clogged carburettor jets, a fuel injection system fault or an air leak can cause this imbalance (Chapter 5A or 5B).

## *Miscellaneous causes*

☐ Throttle valve doesn't open fully. Check the action of the twistgrip, and check the cable for kinks and incorrect routing. Adjust the throttle twistgrip freeplay (Chapter 1).
☐ Clutch slipping, drive belt worn, or variator faulty (Chapter 3).
☐ Timing not advancing (Chapter 6).
☐ Brakes dragging. On disc brakes, usually caused by debris which has entered the brake piston seals, or from a warped disc or bent axle. On drum brakes, cable out of adjustment, shoe return spring broken. Repair as necessary (Chapter 8).

# 4 Overheating

## Cooling system fault

- ☐ Coolant level low. Check and add coolant (*Pre-ride checks*).
- ☐ Leak in cooling system. Check cooling system hoses and radiator for leaks and other damage. Repair or renew parts as necessary (Chapter 4).
- ☐ Thermostat sticking open or closed (Chapter 4).
- ☐ Coolant passages clogged. Drain and flush the entire system, then refill with fresh coolant (Chapter 4).
- ☐ Air lock in system – usually follows draining and refilling of the system. If less than the specified amount of coolant could be added when filling, drain the system again, then refill adding the coolant slowly, and tip the scooter from side to side to dislodge any trapped air (Chapter 4).
- ☐ Water pump defective. Remove the pump and check the components (Chapter 4).
- ☐ Clogged radiator fins. Clean them by blowing compressed air through the fins from the back of the radiator.

## Firing incorrect

- ☐ Air filter clogged. Clean or renew filter (Chapter 1).
- ☐ Spark plug fouled, defective or worn out (Chapter 1).
- ☐ Spark plug cap or HT lead defective. See Chapter 6 for details of the ignition system.
- ☐ Spark plug cap not in good contact (Chapter 6).
- ☐ Incorrect spark plug. Wrong type, heat range or cap configuration. Check and install correct plug listed in Chapter 1.
- ☐ Electronic control unit (ECU) or ignition coil defective (Chapter 6).

## Fuel/air mixture incorrect – carburettor models

- ☐ Faulty automatic choke unit (Chapter 5A).
- ☐ Faulty idle air control valve (Chapter 5A).
- ☐ Pilot screw out of adjustment (Chapter 5A).
- ☐ Pilot jet or air passage clogged. Remove and clean the carburettor (Chapter 5A).
- ☐ Air hole clogged. Remove carburettor and blow out all passages (Chapter 5A).
- ☐ Air filter clogged, poorly sealed or missing (Chapter 1).
- ☐ Air filter housing poorly sealed. Look for cracks, holes or loose screws and renew or repair defective parts.
- ☐ Carburettor intake duct loose. Check for cracks, breaks, tears or loose fixings.
- ☐ Fuel tank vent in filler cap blocked. Clean and blow through or replace with a new one.

## Fuel/air mixture incorrect – fuel injection models

- ☐ Fuel injector clogged or fuel injection system fault (see Chapter 5B).
- ☐ Air filter clogged, poorly sealed or missing (Chapter 1).
- ☐ Air filter housing poorly sealed. Look for cracks, holes or loose clamps and renew or repair defective parts.
- ☐ Intake air leak. Check for loose throttle body-to-intake manifold connections or a leaking gasket (Chapter 5B).
- ☐ Faulty idle air control valve (Chapter 5B).
- ☐ Fuel tank vent in filler cap blocked. Clean and blow through or replace with a new one.

## Compression too high

- ☐ Carbon build-up in combustion chamber. Use of a fuel additive that will dissolve the adhesive bonding the carbon particles to the piston crown and chamber is the easiest way to remove the build-up. Otherwise, the cylinder head will have to be removed and cleaned (Chapter 2).

## Engine load excessive

- ☐ Clutch slipping, drive belt worn, or variator faulty (Chapter 3).
- ☐ Brakes dragging. On disc brakes, usually caused by debris which has entered the brake piston seals, or from a warped disc or bent axle. On drum brakes, cable out of adjustment, shoe return spring broken. Repair as necessary (Chapter 8).

## Lubrication inadequate

- ☐ Engine oil level too low. Friction caused by intermittent lack of lubrication or from oil that is overworked can cause overheating. The oil provides a definite cooling function in the engine. Check the oil level (*Pre-ride checks*).
- ☐ Poor quality engine oil or incorrect viscosity or type. Oil is rated not only according to viscosity but also according to type. Some oils are not rated high enough for use in this engine. Check the Specifications section and change to the correct oil (Chapter 1).

## Miscellaneous causes

- ☐ Modification to exhaust system. Most aftermarket exhaust systems cause the engine to run leaner, which make them run hotter. When installing an accessory exhaust system, always obtain advice on rejetting the carburettor.

# 5 Transmission problems

## No drive to rear wheel

- ☐ Drive belt broken (Chapter 3).
- ☐ Clutch not engaging (Chapter 3).
- ☐ Clutch or drum excessively worn (Chapter 3).

## Transmission noise or vibration

- ☐ Bearings worn. Also includes the possibility that the shafts are worn. Overhaul the gearbox (Chapter 3).
- ☐ Gears worn or chipped (Chapter 3).
- ☐ Clutch drum worn unevenly (Chapter 3).
- ☐ Worn bearings or bent shaft (Chapter 3).
- ☐ Loose clutch nut or drum nut (Chapter 3).

## Poor performance

- ☐ Variator worn or damaged (Chapter 3).
- ☐ Weak or broken clutch pulley spring (Chapter 3).
- ☐ Clutch shoes or drum excessively worn (Chapter 3).
- ☐ Grease on clutch friction material (Chapter 3).
- ☐ Drive belt excessively worn (Chapter 3).

## Clutch not disengaging completely

- ☐ Weak or broken clutch shoe springs (Chapter 3).
- ☐ Engine idle speed too high (Chapter 1).

# 6 Abnormal engine noise

### Knocking or pinking

☐ Carbon build-up in combustion chamber. Use of a fuel additive that will dissolve the adhesive bonding the carbon particles to the piston crown and chamber is the easiest way to remove the build-up. Otherwise, the cylinder head will have to be removed and decarbonised (Chapter 2).

☐ Incorrect or poor quality fuel. Old or improper fuel can cause detonation. This causes the piston to rattle, thus the knocking or pinking sound. Drain the old fuel and always use the recommended grade fuel (Chapter 5A or 5B).

☐ Spark plug type incorrect. Uncontrolled detonation indicates that the plug heat range is too hot. The plug in effect becomes a glow plug, raising cylinder temperatures. Install the proper plug (Chapter 1).

☐ Improper air/fuel mixture. This will cause the cylinder to run hot and lead to detonation. Clogged carburettor jets, a fuel injection system fault or an air leak can cause this imbalance (Chapter 5A or 5B).

### Piston slap or rattling

☐ Cylinder-to-piston clearance excessive. Caused by improper assembly. Inspect and overhaul top-end parts (Chapter 2).

☐ Connecting rod bent. Caused by over-revving, trying to start a badly flooded engine or from ingesting a foreign object into the combustion chamber. Renew the damaged parts (Chapter 2).

☐ Piston pin or piston pin bore worn or seized from wear or lack of lubrication. Renew damaged parts (Chapter 2).

☐ Piston ring(s) worn, broken or sticking. Overhaul the top-end (Chapter 2).

☐ Piston seizure damage. Usually from lack of lubrication or overheating. First find and cure the cause of the problem (Chapters 2 and 4), then rebore the cylinder and fit an oversize piston and rings (Chapter 2).

☐ Connecting rod small- or big-end clearance excessive. Caused by excessive wear or lack of lubrication. Renew worn parts (Chapter 2).

### Other noise

☐ Exhaust pipe leaking at cylinder head connection. Caused by improper fit of pipe or damaged gasket. All exhaust fasteners should be tightened evenly and carefully (Chapter 5A or 5B).

☐ Crankshaft runout excessive. Caused by a bent crankshaft (from over-revving) or damage from an upper cylinder component failure (Chapter 2).

☐ Engine mounting bolts loose. Tighten all engine mounting bolts (Chapter 2).

☐ Crankshaft bearings worn (Chapter 2).

# 7 Abnormal frame and suspension noise

### Front end noise

☐ Steering head bearings loose or damaged. Clicks when braking. Check and adjust or replace as necessary (Chapters 1 and 7).

☐ Bolts loose. Make sure all bolts are tightened to the specified torque (Chapter 7).

☐ Fork tube bent. Good possibility if machine has been in a collision. Renew the tube or the fork assembly (Chapter 7).

☐ Front axle nut loose. Tighten to the specified torque (Chapter 8).

☐ Loose or worn wheel bearings. Check and renew as needed (Chapter 8).

### Shock absorber noise

☐ Fluid level low due to leakage from defective seal. Shock will be covered with oil. Renew the shock (Chapter 7).

☐ Defective shock absorber with internal damage. Renew the shock (Chapter 7).

☐ Bent or damaged shock body. Renew the shock (Chapter 7).

☐ Loose or worn rear suspension swingarm components. Check and renew as necessary (Chapter 7).

### Brake noise

☐ Squeal caused by dust on brake pads or shoes. Usually found in combination with glazed pads or shoes. Renew the pads/shoes (Chapter 8).

☐ Contamination of brake pads or shoes. Oil or brake fluid causing brake to chatter or squeal. Renew pads or shoes (Chapter 8).

☐ Pads or shoes glazed. Caused by excessive heat from prolonged use or from contamination. Do not use sandpaper, emery cloth, carborundum cloth or any other abrasive to roughen the pad surfaces as abrasives will stay in the pad material and damage the disc or drum. A very fine flat file can be used, but pad or shoe renewal is advised (Chapter 8).

☐ Disc or drum warped. Can cause a chattering, clicking or intermittent squeal. Usually accompanied by a pulsating lever and uneven braking. Check the disc runout and the drum ovality (Chapter 8).

☐ Loose or worn wheel (front) or transmission (rear) bearings. Check and renew as needed (Chapter 8).

# 8 Excessive exhaust smoke

## White smoke

☐ Piston oil ring worn. The ring may be broken or damaged, causing oil from the crankcase to be pulled past the piston into the combustion chamber. Replace the rings with new ones (Chapter 2).

☐ Cylinder worn, cracked, or scored. Caused by overheating or oil starvation. First find and cure the cause of the problem (Chapters 2 and 4), then rebore the cylinder and fit an oversize piston and rings (Chapter 2).

☐ Valve stem seal damaged or worn. Remove valves and replace seals with new ones (Chapter 2).

☐ Valve guide worn. Perform a complete valve job (Chapter 2).

☐ Engine oil level too high, which causes the oil to be forced past the rings. Drain oil to the proper level (*Pre-ride checks*).

☐ Head gasket broken between oil return and cylinder. Causes oil to be pulled into the combustion chamber. Renew the head gasket and check the head for warpage (Chapter 2).

☐ Abnormal crankcase pressurisation, which forces oil past the rings. Clogged breather is usually the cause.

## Black smoke (rich mixture) – carburettor models

☐ Air filter clogged. Clean or renew the element (Chapter 1).

☐ Main jet too large or loose. Compare the jet size to the Specifications (Chapter 5A).

☐ Automatic choke unit or idle air control valve faulty (Chapter 5A).

☐ Float needle valve held off needle seat. Clean the float chamber and fuel line and renew the needle if necessary (Chapter 5A).

## Black smoke (rich mixture) – fuel injection models

☐ Air filter clogged. Clean or renew the element (Chapter 1).

☐ Fuel injection system or idle air control valve malfunction (Chapter 5B).

☐ Fuel pressure too high. Check the fuel pressure (Chapter 5B).

## Brown smoke (lean mixture) – carburettor models

☐ Main jet too small or clogged. Lean condition caused by wrong size main jet or by a restricted orifice. Clean float chamber and jets and compare jet size to specifications (Chapter 5A).

☐ Fuel flow insufficient. Float needle valve stuck closed due to chemical reaction with old fuel. Restricted fuel hose. Clean hose and float chamber (Chapter 5A).

☐ Carburettor clamp or intake duct bolts loose (Chapter 5A).

☐ Air filter poorly sealed or not installed (Chapter 1).

☐ Ignition timing incorrect (Chapter 6).

## Brown smoke (lean mixture) – fuel injection models

☐ Fuel pump faulty or pressure regulator stuck open (Chapter 5B).

☐ Throttle body clamp or intake duct bolts loose (Chapter 5B).

☐ Air filter poorly sealed or not installed (Chapter 1).

☐ Fuel injection system malfunction (Chapter 5B).

# 9 Poor handling or stability

## Handlebar hard to turn

☐ Steering head bearing adjuster nut too tight. Check adjustment as described in Chapter 1.

☐ Bearings damaged. Roughness can be felt as the bars are turned from side-to-side. Replace bearings and races (Chapter 7).

☐ Races dented or worn. Denting results from wear in only one position (e.g. straight ahead), from a collision or hitting a pothole or from dropping the machine. Renew races and bearings (Chapter 7).

☐ Steering stem lubrication inadequate. Causes are grease getting hard from age or being washed out by high pressure car washes. Disassemble steering head and repack bearings (Chapter 7).

☐ Steering stem bent. Caused by a collision, hitting a pothole or by dropping the machine. Renew damaged part. Don't try to straighten the steering stem (Chapter 7).

☐ Front tyre air pressure too low (*Pre-ride checks*).

## Handlebar shakes or vibrates excessively

☐ Tyres worn (*Pre-ride checks*).

☐ Suspension worn. Renew worn components (Chapter 7).

☐ Wheel rim(s) warped or damaged. Inspect wheels for runout (Chapter 8).

☐ Wheel bearings worn. Worn wheel bearings (front) or transmission bearings (rear) can cause poor tracking. Worn front bearings will cause wobble (Chapter 8).

☐ Handlebar mounting loose (Chapter 7).

☐ Front suspension bolts loose. Tighten them to the specified torque (Chapter 7).

☐ Engine mounting bolts loose. Will cause excessive vibration with increased engine rpm (Chapter 2).

## Handlebar pulls to one side

☐ Frame bent. Definitely suspect this if the machine has been in a collision. May or may not be accompanied by cracking near the bend. Renew the frame (Chapter 7).

☐ Wheels out of alignment. Caused by improper location of axle spacers or from bent steering stem or frame (Chapter 8).

☐ Steering stem bent. Caused by impact damage or by dropping the machine. Renew the steering stem (Chapter 7).

☐ Fork tube bent. Disassemble the forks and renew the damaged parts (Chapter 7).

## Poor shock absorbing qualities

**Too hard:**
a) *Fork oil quantity excessive (Chapter 7).*
b) *Fork oil viscosity too high (Chapter 7).*
c) *Suspension bent. Causes a harsh, sticking feeling (Chapter 7).*
d) *Fork internal damage (Chapter 7).*
e) *Rear shock internal damage (Chapter 7).*
f) *Tyre pressure too high (Pre-ride checks).*

**Too soft:**
a) *Fork oil viscosity too light (Chapter 7).*
b) *Fork or shock spring(s) weak or broken (Chapter 7).*
c) *Fork or shock internal damage or leakage (Chapter 7).*

## 10 Braking problems – disc brakes

### Brake is ineffective

☐ Air in brake hose. Caused by inattention to master cylinder fluid level (*Pre-ride checks*) or by leakage. Locate problem and bleed brake (Chapter 8).
☐ Pads or disc worn (Chapters 1 and 8).
☐ Brake fluid leak. Locate problem and rectify (Chapter 8).
☐ Contaminated pads. Caused by contamination with oil, grease, brake fluid, etc. Renew pads. Clean disc thoroughly with brake cleaner (Chapter 8).
☐ Brake fluid deteriorated. Fluid is old or contaminated. Drain system, replenish with new fluid and bleed the system (Chapter 8).
☐ Master cylinder internal parts worn or damaged causing fluid to bypass (Chapter 8).
☐ Master cylinder bore scratched by foreign material or broken spring. Repair or renew master cylinder (Chapter 8).
☐ Disc warped. Renew disc (Chapter 8).

### Brake lever pulsates

☐ Disc warped. Renew disc (Chapter 8).
☐ Axle bent. Renew axle (Chapter 8).
☐ Brake caliper bolts loose (Chapter 8).
☐ Wheel warped or otherwise damaged (Chapter 8).
☐ Wheel or hub bearings damaged or worn (Chapter 8).

### Brake drags

☐ Master cylinder piston seized. Caused by wear or damage to piston or cylinder bore (Chapter 7).
☐ Lever balky or stuck. Check pivot and lubricate (Chapter 7).
☐ Brake caliper piston seized in bore. Caused by wear or ingestion of dirt past deteriorated seal (Chapter 7).
☐ Brake pads damaged. Pad material separated from backing plate. Usually caused by faulty manufacturing process or from contact with chemicals. Renew pads (Chapter 7).
☐ Caliper slider pins sticking (sliding caliper). Clean the slider pins and apply a smear of silicone grease (Chapter 7).
☐ Pads improperly installed (Chapter 7).

## 11 Braking problems – rear drum brake

### Brake is ineffective

☐ Cable incorrectly adjusted. Check cable (Chapter 1).
☐ Shoes or drum worn (Chapter 8).
☐ Contaminated shoes. Caused by contamination with oil, grease etc. Renew shoes. Clean drum thoroughly with brake cleaner (Chapter 8).
☐ Brake arm incorrectly positioned, or cam excessively worn (Chapter 8).

### Brake lever pulsates

☐ Drum warped. Renew drum (Chapter 8).
☐ Axle bent. Renew axle (Chapter 8).
☐ Wheel warped or otherwise damaged (Chapter 8).
☐ Wheel/hub bearings (front) or transmission bearings (rear) damaged or worn (Chapter 8).

### Brake drags

☐ Cable incorrectly adjusted or requires lubrication. Check cable (Chapter 8).
☐ Shoe return springs broken (Chapter 8).
☐ Lever balky or stuck. Check pivot and lubricate (Chapter 7).
☐ Brake arm or cam binds. Caused by inadequate lubrication or damage (Chapter 8).
☐ Brake shoe damaged. Friction material separated from shoe. Usually caused by faulty manufacturing process or from contact with chemicals. Renew shoes (Chapter 8).
☐ Shoes improperly installed (Chapter 8).

## 12 Electrical problems

### Battery dead or weak

☐ Battery faulty. Caused by sulphated plates which are shorted through sedimentation. Also, broken battery terminal making only occasional contact (Chapter 10).
☐ Battery leads making poor electrical contact (Chapter 10).
☐ Load excessive. Caused by addition of high wattage lights or other electrical accessories.
☐ Ignition switch defective. Switch either earths internally or fails to shut off system. Renew the switch (Chapter 10).
☐ Regulator/rectifier defective (Chapter 10).

☐ Alternator stator coil open or shorted (Chapter 10).
☐ Wiring faulty. Wiring either shorted to earth or connections loose in ignition, charging or lighting circuits (Chapter 10).

### Battery overcharged

☐ Regulator/rectifier defective. Overcharging is noticed when battery gets excessively warm (Chapter 10).
☐ Battery defective. Renew battery (Chapter 10).
☐ Battery amperage too low, wrong type or size. Install manufacturer's specified amp-hour battery to handle charging load (Chapter 10).

**Note:** *References throughout this index are in the form* **"Chapter number"** • **"Page number"**. *So, for example, 2•10 refers to page 10 of Chapter 2.*

**Note:** *References throughout this index are in the form* "**Chapter number**" • "**Page number**". *So, for example, 2•10 refers to page 10 of Chapter 2.*

Note: *References throughout this index are in the form "**Chapter number**" • "**Page number**". So, for example, 2•10 refers to page 10 of Chapter 2.*

# Preserving Our Motoring Heritage

<
*The Model J Duesenberg Derham Tourster. Only eight of these magnificent cars were ever built – this is the only example to be found outside the United States of America*

Almost every car you've ever loved, loathed or desired is gathered under one roof at the Haynes Motor Museum. Over 300 immaculately presented cars and motorbikes represent every aspect of our motoring heritage, from elegant reminders of bygone days, such as the superb Model J Duesenberg to curiosities like the bug-eyed BMW Isetta. There are also many old friends and flames. Perhaps you remember the 1959 Ford Popular that you did your courting in? The magnificent 'Red Collection' is a spectacle of classic sports cars including AC, Alfa Romeo, Austin Healey, Ferrari, Lamborghini, Maserati, MG, Riley, Porsche and Triumph.

## A Perfect Day Out

Each and every vehicle at the Haynes Motor Museum has played its part in the history and culture of Motoring. Today, they make a wonderful spectacle and a great day out for all the family. Bring the kids, bring Mum and Dad, but above all bring your camera to capture those golden memories for ever. You will also find an impressive array of motoring memorabilia, a comfortable 70 seat video cinema and one of the most extensive transport book shops in Britain. The Pit Stop Cafe serves everything from a cup of tea to wholesome, home-made meals or, if you prefer, you can enjoy the large picnic area nestled in the beautiful rural surroundings of Somerset.

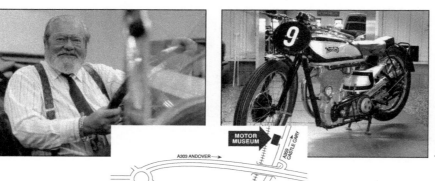

>
*John Haynes O.B.E., Founder and Chairman of the museum at the wheel of a Haynes Light 12.*

<
*The 1936 490cc sohc-engined International Norton – well known for its racing success*

The Museum is situated on the A359 Yeovil to Frome road at Sparkford, just off the A303 in Somerset. It is about 40 miles south of Bristol, and 25 minutes drive from the M5 intersection at Taunton.
Open 9.30am - 5.30pm (10.00am - 4.00pm Winter) 7 days a week, *except Christmas Day, Boxing Day and New Years Day*
Special rates available for schools, coach parties and outings  Charitable Trust No. 292048